THE HUMANITY OF CITIES

AN INTRODUCTION TO URBAN SOCIETIES

John Gulick

BERGIN & GARVEY
Westport, Connecticut • London

Library of Congress Cataloging-in-Publication Data

Gulick, John, 1924—
    The humanity of cities: an introduction to urban societies / John
Gulick.
        p. cm.
    Bibliography: p.
    Includes index.
    ISBN 0-89789-158-9 (alk. paper)
    ISBN 0-89789-159-7 (pbk.: alk. paper)
    1. Sociology, Urban. 2. Cities and towns. 3. Metropolitan
areas. 4. Urbanization. I. Title.
HT151.G798   1989
307.7′6—dc19   88-19283

Library of Congress Catalog Card Number: 88-19283
ISBN: 0-89789-158-9
        0-89789-159-7 (pbk.)

First published in 1989

Bergin & Garvey, One Madison Avenue, New York, NY 10010
An imprint of Greenwood Publishing Group, Inc.

Printed in the United States of America

∞™

The paper used in this book complies with the
Permanent Paper Standard issued by the National
Information Standards Organization (Z39.48-1984).

10 9 8 7 6 5 4

Cover: World Bank Photo/Ray Witlin

Contents

THE HUMANITY
OF CITIES

Planned Parenthood/World Population

Acknowledgments

I began teaching a course on urban anthropology at the University of North Carolina at Chapel Hill in the early 1960s. I continued to teach it regularly for almost a quarter of a century, until my retirement in 1986. During that time, I learned a great deal about cities from many different sources, only some of which were anthropological. Apart from a rather small coterie of kindred urban spirits, anthropology has been only one of many sources of inspiration and insight, for the orientation of mainstream anthropology seems to be as nonurban now as it always has been.

However, in addition to those kindred spirits, who include Jack Rollwagen, Leonard Plotnicov, and Estellie Smith, I am happy to acknowledge my gratitude to a number of individuals who have given me different, but specific, kinds of assistance, and so made it possible for me to write this book.

James L. Peacock, III, Donald L. Brockington, and George R. Holcomb—as successive chairmen of the Department of Anthropology of the University of North Carolina at Chapel Hill—facilitated my endeavors in many ways.

I also wish to express my thanks and appreciation to Carolyn A. Merritt and Suphronia M. Cheek of the administrative and secretarial staff of the Department of Anthropology for their helpfulness and patience over many years. Shirley F. Weiss, of the university's Department of City and Regional Planning, gave me valuable information and encouragement.

I began work on an earlier version of this book around 1977 when a publisher suggested that I write it. At that time, my late wife Margaret and I had well-advanced plans for three years of research on teenaged girls and their life-course alternatives to early marriage and high fertility in Shiraz, Iran. In accordance with an agreement with our Iranian counterparts, we went to Shiraz in September 1978, hoping to get the project started, but we had to leave in November because of the intensification of the Islamic Revolution.

Our fall-back plan was to spend the remainder of my year's leave of absence in London, and there we went in November 1978. Professors Adrian C. Mayer and John F. Middleton arranged our professional home-away-from-home in the Department of Anthropology, School of Oriental and Asian Studies, University of London. I heartily thank them and their colleagues for their many courtesies and kindnesses.

Having initiated negotiations for transferring the Shiraz project to Cairo, I turned my attention entirely to urban studies for the sake of this book. In the library of the London School of Economics, I found and read many books and monographs about which I had not known and about which I probably never would have known had it not been for the London experience. We took several intelligently guided walking tours in various parts of the city and observed Bethnal Green, Dagenham, the Inter-Action facility in Kentish Town, Stockwell, and Tolmers Square at first hand. We also interviewed Ed Berman, Peter Willmott, John F. C. Turner, and Nick Wates, and I want particularly to thank them for their patience and courtesy. Talking with them and visiting the London locations with which they were associated did much to reinforce my conviction that the humanity of cities is real.

On 12 February 1979, Margaret received a diagnosis of terminal illness, and we returned home. Despite its abrupt and tragic ending, the sojourn in London contributed greatly to this book.

In March 1979, I was provided with an office at the Carolina Population Center, and I have had one there ever since. For this, and for many other kinds of support, I wish to thank Dr. J. Richard Udry, director of the center. Almost all of this book, the earlier and final versions, was written on the premises of the center. A humanistic, qualitative anthropologist, I have felt welcome and at home in this bastion of computers and quantitative research. While many other people have played a part in this relationship, I name only the following who have particularly helped me, in many ways, in writing this book: Catheryn Brandon, Freda Cameron, Ruth Crabtree, John Cromartie, Chanya Harris, Annette Hedaya, Lynn Igoe, Judy Kovenock, Karen Kromer, Karen Kurczewski, Nancy Kuzil, Alexandra Leach, James Lewis, Amanda Lyerly, Priscilla Newby, and Nancy Dole Runkle. While I could say something special about each of them, I single out Nancy Dole Runkle, who taught me how to use a personal computer, and Lynn Igoe, who edited the manuscript through several phases and did other indispensable chores.

I wish to express my appreciation to Dr. Fred D. Hall who carefully read the almost final version of the manuscript in preparation for his writing the instructor's manual that accompanies the book. He saw the text with a fresh eye, which resulted in a number of important improvements.

In November 1985, my present wife, Betty E. Cogswell, and I traveled in the People's Republic of China with a study group sponsored by the State Family Planning Commission of China and The Population Institute of Washington, D.C. This largely urban experience was uniquely important for me, and I wish to express my appreciation to Werner H. Fornos, Shirley Anderson, and Moyne Gross of The Population Institute and Madame Wang Xiangying and her associates of the State Family Planning Commission.

The photographs that illustrate this book were made available to me by the following persons from photograph collections in the possession of their respective institutions: Hal Burdett, The Population Institute, Washington, D.C.; Yosef Hadar, The World Bank, Washington, D.C.; and Mary Sebold, The Middle East Institute, Washington, D.C. In addition, Charles M. Weiss of Chapel Hill, N.C., contributed one of his own photographs. I thank all of these people for their helpfulness and generosity.

To Margaret E. Gulick, in memory, and to Betty E. Cogswell, I say love and thanks.

John Gulick
Professor Emeritus of Anthropology,
University of North Carolina at Chapel Hill,
and Fellow, Carolina Population Center

Introduction

T he *humanity* of cities? The very idea may seem preposterous at best, cruelly insensitive at worst.

Consider these incidents which received great attention in the mass media. In a New York subway train, a man shoots four allegedly threatening youths with a pistol he has concealed on his person; this act receives wide public acclaim. In Beirut and Belfast, a seemingly endless series of car bombings kill and maim thousands of defenseless people who are not actively involved in the political issues at stake. In Brussels, soccer fans from Liverpool cause a riot in which 38 people are killed. In Philadelphia ("the city of brotherly love"), the police, seeking to dislodge a troublesome group from a house, cause an explosion that starts a fire that destroys a viable neighborhood. On the congested freeways of Los Angeles, and some other American cities, enraged motorists shoot to kill other motorists.

These are not isolated incidents. Each was part of one or another social problem that had festered for years. All of these problems continue to fester.

There can be no argument that these were acts of gross inhumanity *in* cities.

But can they be taken as evidence of an intrinsic inhumanity *of* cities? On this question there can be, has been, and is much argument.

That argument is the subject of this book, and the book takes one side of it, namely that the concept of "inhumanity *of* cities" (as contrasted with other forms of human settlement) is empirically and intellectually unsound and that it is also a deterrent to peoples' constructive thought and action in urban everyday life.

The distinction between "in cities" and "of cities" is not trivial or hairsplitting. Using these simple phrases at the beginning is merely a convenient way of introducing a highly complex subject that will unfold as the book proceeds.

If "intrinsic inhumanity of cities" is an unsound concept, is "humanity of cities" necessarily a sound one? The issues are far too complicated to warrant such an either/or choice. This book's position is that humanity of cities is a realistic and constructive base concept, while inhumanity of cities as a base concept is the product and generator of destructive illusions. The reasons for taking this position will develop as we proceed.

In setting forth the humanity of cities, this book does not gloss over the inhumanities committed in them. Nor are cities presented in utopian terms. On the contrary, the prevailing method of presentation is empirical; this book consists of facts based on observations and studies of cities as they actually are—or at least as observers perceived them to be. The choice of topics has largely been based on availability of source material. So, for example, although coverage is intended to be worldwide, descriptive details come almost entirely from Western industrial and Third World cities and only to a small extent from the revolutionary industrial cities of the People's Republic of China and the Soviet Union. Such material as is available from those cities is included, but very few empirical studies of the sort that are relatively abundant from other parts of the world have been done in the Soviet Union and China.

While this book expresses definite points of view on cities, it is not a polemical tract but a text. It describes various aspects of life in cities as found in a great variety of studies. It also presents, as facts, contradictory and controversial theories and interpretations of urban life. The intention is that when you finish the book, you will be more widely and deeply informed than you were before and that you will have become familiar with the many ramifications of a positive perspective on cities, but that you will not feel unduly constrained by that point of view.

Just as the contents are based on empirical findings, so are the arrangement of chapters and their internal organization. Each chapter title signals a set of issues of major concern and interest to urban scholars in general. There are several important kinds of these scholars—urban historians, urban economists, urban geographers, urban sociologists, urban political scientists, urban planners and designers, and urban anthropologists.

Chapter 1. The Study of Cities

The first important point is that the proper focus is on cities in the plural, not on "the city" in a monolithic singular. As we shall see in detail, cities are highly varied in terms of comparisons between cities of different cultural areas and the internal diversity of individual cities. In contrast, phrases like "the city," "the urban family," "the urban economy," "urban*ism* as *a* way of life," and so on, invite the stereotyping of cities, which is one of the major contributors to the notion of urban inhumanity. For example, Louis Wirth's often republished, often quoted 1938 article, "Urbanism as a Way of Life," depicts the subject in what are generally felt to be negative terms, and it has usually been accepted as epitomizing "the city." In fact, the article does nothing of the kind. At best, it is a generalized depiction of a presumed subculture in a particular kind of city, namely, early twentieth-century American industrial.

Wirth's article is part of a long intellectual tradition out of which urban anthropology evolved, in part perpetuating the tradition and in part breaking free of it. The concepts involved in this tradition are encapsulated in what the author calls the Bipolar Moralistic Model which is discussed at length.

Urban anthropology, in its various facets, is placed in the context of other disciplines devoted to the study of cities. The tendency of urban anthropologists to concentrate their studies on small groups of individual persons in a wide variety of cultures is contrasted with the tendency of other disciplines to concentrate on aggregate statistics and large, impersonal sample surveys primarily in Western industrial cities. The humanity of cities cannot be adequately comprehended except by means of a vision that integrates the small-scale immediacies of everyday life with the massive, large-scale realities that impinge on city dwellers' daily lives. One hopes that not only urban anthropologists but also the other types of urban scholar may receive this vital message.

Chapter 2. Scales

Human scale, as applied to buildings, communities, and institutions, implies degrees of size and complexity that feel manageable to people involved. It is likely further to imply smallness and goodness. *Dehumanized scale*, on the contrary, implies unmanageable size and complexity in which the ordinary individual feels helpless, meaningless, and alienated. Dehumanized scale is a wretched condition, and, in the major tradition of urban studies introduced in chapter 1, it has typically been assumed to be the essential condition of cities in general. This assumption denies the reality of the humanity of cities. Chapter 2 examines a number of empirical applications of the scale concept critically and refines them into two paradigms that admit the reality of the humanity of cities without denying the reality of inhumanity in them. In this discussion, the contexts of scale in which city dwellers actually live are differentiated from the scale contexts of urban life as selectively perceived by those who study and write on urban life. This differentiation is essential because much confusion and misunderstanding has been caused by observers' assuming that their own scale perceptions are identical with city dwellers' everyday life experiences of scale. One of the most damaging consequences of this confusion is the well-established stereotype that "city life" is large scale by nature and therefore dehumanized. That cities *are* big has reinforced this stereotype. On close scrutiny, the large size of cities turns out to be a problematic subject.

Chapter 3. Magnitudes

The exposition of scale concepts begun in chapter 2 extends and expands into a critical examination of large size as an essential criterion of "cityness." From this discussion, we proceed to consider ways in which city dwellers reduce the magnitude of large cities to smaller-scale living units. As in previous chapters, we question stereotypes reinforcing the notion of the inhumanity of cities and develop further the important fact that cities are highly varied.

Density is one dimension of reality which varies greatly in cities, compared to one another and internally. The widespread idea that the "high density" of cities is a primary cause of their inhumanity is subjected to critical examination.

Emerging from this discussion is the approximately three-thousand-year age range of the world's present-day cities. While cities cannot be categorized meaningfully in terms of age types, their characteristics today are products of evolution through time and of the histories of the areas of the world where they are.

Chapter 4. Evolution

Cities definitely existed in the Middle East at least six thousand years ago. Presumably, they originated there at an earlier time, but exactly when, and under what circumstances, are debatable. One theory assumes that the existence of cities depends on prior existence of agricultural hinterlands and surpluses. Another theory assumes that a city is essentially a nexus of trade and the processing of traded commodities.

These theories, applied to various archaeological sites in the Middle East, would postulate the origin of cities at between six and ten thousand years ago. The chronological uncertainties are less important for the thesis of this book than are the various ideas about what characteristics make a given locality a city. Having dealt with these matters first, we then review the development of cities in all parts of the world from their beginnings to the present.

A very general, but useful, categorization of cities derives from this discussion: primordial, preindustrial, Third World, Western industrial, and revolutionary industrial. In addition, many examples are adduced of the "vicissitudes"—the waxings and wanings—through which cities have gone. City vicissitudes are obvious and well known from the historical perspective. Rome, for example, grew tremendously to become the capital of the republic and the early empire; it then deteriorated drastically as the Western Roman Empire disintegrated; it was subsequently redeveloped and has had numerous ups and downs until reaching its present state as a major world city—but a very different major city from what it was two thousand years ago. Also well recognized are the political and economic concomitants of Rome's vicissitudes. Many other examples include cities that once flourished but are now in ruins or greatly diminished in size and prosperity.

All of this is familiar history. Put very simply, it would seem that while individual cities may come and go, city life, in various locations, has continuously existed since its beginning. What does not seem well recognized is that vicissitudes are operating *now*, that the evolution of cities continues today and will, presumably, go on in the future.

The concept of evolutionary vicissitudes is important because it offers an alternative to a prevalent mind-set that can be called "disasterism." Spokespeople for disasterism say, in effect, that changes for the worse in cities are symptoms of disaster. They imply that such changes are disastrous because they are irreversible, owing to the intrinsic inhumanity of cities. The widespread abandonment of buildings in older parts of Western industrial cities and increased public, criminal violence in the same cities are their evidence. Putting such trends into the perspective of vicissitudes requires us to seek multiple and macrocauses (and solutions) rather than to surrender to the hopelessness of negative models.

Several sections of chapter 4 are concerned with two of the most important phenomena of twentieth-century urban evolution: the squatter settlements of Third World cities and suburbs of Western industrial cities. Deeply involved in these phenomena are the processes of internal migration of people within cities and external migration to and from them.

Numerous studies reveal that by far the most important reasons for people's uprooting themselves have to do with work and survival, the subject of chapter 5.

Chapter 5. Livelihoods

As with all other aspects of life in cities, stereotypes and overgeneralizations cloud the subject of work and livelihoods. The prevailing notion is that urban work is alienating and dehumanizing, especially in contrast to rural work. Failure to consider the enormous variety of jobs in cities is an important contributor to this intellectual problem. Two other contributors are (1) the difficulty, if not impossibility, of studying people while they are on the job and (2) the Western ethnocentrism of the stereotypes. For example, many occupations that Western industrial city dwellers typically avoid because they consider them to be "dead-end jobs" are eagerly sought by Third World migrants from rural areas to cities.

Closely connected with the alienation stereotype is the notion that city dwellers' work is so compartmentalized that it and the rest of their lives are mutually meaningless. This view is often contrasted with farmers' work which supposedly forms an integral whole with the rest of their lives, as well as with nature. On closer scrutiny, compartmentalization turns out to be a slippery and multidimensional idea. The focus of the discussion of these issues is predominantly macrocosmic.

The focus then changes to microcosmic, illustrated by a series of ethnographic cases that demonstrate ways in which many kinds of urban work *are* more or less integrated with other aspects of workers' lives. In some instances, indeed, the degree of integration is such that we may think in terms of "occupational communities."

At this point, we renew our discussion of how city dwellers characteristically find ways to reduce the great size of their cities to manageable, small-scale social entities, which leads to the consideration of small-scale support systems in chapter 6.

Chapter 6. Connections

The very idea that city dwellers can and do form connections with one another—connections that can meaningfully be called networks, institutions, and even communities—is denied by the stereotype that urban life is categorically anonymous and impersonal. And so we come to the nub of the argument on the primacy of the humanity over the inhumanity of cities.

"Community," a greatly overworked word, is nevertheless useful if it is used with clear references in mind. Discussing the concept of community introduces some necessary modifications of it. Especially important is the argument that readiness—if not willingness—to adapt to change is a necessary component of urban community behavior. This idea is one of the microdimensions of the macroconcept of vicissitudes introduced in chapter 4. Moreover, it is the degree of community resilience in the face of change that enables city dwellers to live in the midst of vicissitudes without always or necessarily being overwhelmed by disaster. Here, the approach to community and adaptability is contrary to traditional antiurban theories that set rural unchanging community against urban changing *non*community.

We also consider circumstances under which connectedness *is* deficient. These circumstances do result in anomie and anonymity, those dire conditions that traditional theory says typify city life. Though they certainly exist, they are exceptional, and most of chapter 6 documents the richness of human connections in cities. Quarters, neighborhoods, various nonterritorial networks, and households are prominent among the types of social unit considered in detail.

The importance of such connections in the lives of most city dwellers is the foundation on which the humanity of cities rests. However, these units, typically small in scale, operate within frameworks of large-scale connections.

Chapter 7. Subcultures

The subcultures that provide large-scale connections in city life are also the essence of the heterogeneity of cities. Universal subcultures are those to which virtually everyone belongs: ethnic (sometimes also racial), social class, gender, and life-cycle. The discussion of these subcultures, which crosscut and overlap one another, also leads to several important and controversial issues. One is the melting pot metaphor, according to which the various immigrant ethnic groups in United States cities are gradually homogenized into a common American culture. This process is found not to be entirely true, as the subculture concept itself clearly implies, but the degrees of ethnic subcultural differentiation vary. Hence the melting pot metaphor is not an all-or-nothing idea.

The concept of underclass subculture, otherwise known as the "culture of poverty," has generated much heat among social scientists. At issue is disagreement on the reasons why a substantial proportion of the urban population remains very poor, beset by social problems while also contributing to them. One explanation is that the underclass has a self-perpetuating subculture, and the other is that the underclass is socially oppressed. Both explanations are true.

Among the life-cycle subcultures, those of adolescents and elderly people receive particular attention. Teenage boys' gangs constitute a recognized urban problem, as do living arrangements of the increasing number of old people in American society.

Collective life-styles are subcultures in which not everyone participates but which have important impacts on the texture of urban life. We discuss homosexual subcultures, subcultures founded on various pastimes, and the subculture of violence at some length.

Finally, we look at bureaucratic subcultures and problems of scale. It is in the bureaucratic context that most city dwellers' microscale, everyday lives are confronted by macroscale realities.

While subcultures contribute much to the variety and excitement of city life, they also pose the major challenge to the humanity of cities. Supportive behavior within subcultures is common and predictable, but relations among different subcultures tend to be very limited and sometimes extremely hostile.

In chapter 8, we examine ways in which these negative concomitants of subcultural heterogeneity can be mitigated.

Chapter 8. Agenda for the Humanity of Cities

The agenda for concerned and involved people is to identify all the ways in which the humanity of cities is actually experienced, so that city dwellers may heighten their awareness of how to enhance the humanity of cities. Static utopia is not the goal, but rather, well-informed constant mobilization for improvement.

The boundaries between different subcultures can be bridged or dissolved under various circumstances. We examine the costs and benefits of the residential juxtaposition of different subcultures. One of the benefits is that the actors may learn that they share subcultural interests (such as those of social class) and that this realization counteracts differences such as ethnic ones. A related benefit is the recognition that members of other subcultures are varied, that they do not all fit a negative stereotype.

Bureaucratic subcultures, so frequently appearing to ordinary people to be antagonistic and inhumane, are examined with a view to penetrating their monolithic facades, and a major section of the chapter focuses on grass-roots movements in which ordinary people mobilize themselves against bureaucratic and other powerful urban structures.

Another major section of the chapter is concerned with distemic space, space that all city dwellers must share but which belongs to no individual or group. We consider the widespread misbehavior in distemic space, along with practicable remedies for it.

Greed for money and power and fear of others' greed are panhuman feelings that seriously affect city life but are not city-specific. The same is true of attitudes such as racism, frequently imbedded in national cultures and national political systems. While the roots of these evils lie beyond ordinary people's reach, their effects and agents can be directly fought, as in grass-roots movements. Meanwhile, there are worldwide problems posing threats not only to cities but to humanity itself. They include overpopulation, environmental degradation, and excessive expenditures for military armaments. All are caused by human beings, and all can be counteracted by human beings, but meeting all these challenges is beyond the scope of any one city, or region, or nation.

In asserting that the humanity of cities is real, we do not claim that cities ever were, are now, or ever will be, utopias. What we do claim is that the humanity of cities requires the constant striving for the best by and for all city dwellers, rich and poor, and that this striving, to be successful, must be informed by knowledge and awareness of all the options life in the cities of the world offers.

1
The Study of Cities

W hat is a city? How may "city" best be defined so that the subject of this book is clearly understood?

No acceptable definition of *a* city or *the* city exists. The reason, which needs to be understood from the outset, is that all generalizations about the city *in the singular* are inevitably flawed and therefore confusing and unclear. To start off on the right track, we must learn to think of cities *in the plural*. In the first part of this chapter, we consider why this is the case.

Here is perhaps the most famous, most quoted definition of city in the singular: "[A] city may be defined as a relatively large, dense and permanent settlement of socially heterogeneous individuals" (Wirth 1938:8). With all due respect to Louis Wirth, this definition is virtually useless. Part of the problem is the word "relatively." Relative to what? Wirth does not say. Distinctive city criteria *can* be identified relative to peasant villages, in which much of humankind lives, but this comparison does not seem to be Wirth's concern. What does "large" mean? According to common usage, cities are settlements with populations of anywhere from 20 thousand (or fewer) to approximately 15 million. What does "dense" mean? Residential density in present-day cities ranges from about 45 hundred people per square mile in United States cities with mostly single-family dwellings and plenty of open space to about 250 thousand people per square mile in certain parts of cities like Cairo. With such wide ranges in crucially important dimensions of city living, "relatively large [and] dense" is meaningless as a general descriptive definition. Even "heterogeneous" presents difficulties: while urban heterogeneity can certainly be demonstrated empirically, there are suggestions that it is ambiguous, that its intensity varies from one place to another, and that many people's reactions to it tend to minimize it as a factor in their urban life. In other words, cities are highly diverse, and most simple generalizations about them are bound to be too simple to yield understanding of the subject.

Wirth's statement comes from "Urbanism as a Way of Life," a title further reinforcing the image of life in cities as being uniform, with only one essential nature:

> The contacts of the city may indeed be face to face, but they are nevertheless impersonal, superficial, transitory, and segmental. The reserve, the indifference, and the blasé outlook which urbanites manifest in their relationships may thus be regarded as devices for immunizing themselves against the personal claims and expectations of others (1938:12).

If this characterization of urban life is accepted as being complete—as it has been very widely accepted—life in cities must be seen as essentially inhumane. In opposition to such a view, this book consists of a series of demonstrations that Wirth's characterization and others like it are, at best, only a fragmentary and incomplete depiction of the lives of people in the world's cities. At less than best, it is a highly inaccurate and misleading caricature.

Behavior fitting Wirth's picture is frequently experienced in cities, especially in encounters with strangers and dealings with bureaucrats employed by large public and private organizations. But this type of experience is only one dimension of most people's lives in cities. Other dimensions include, for most people, intense relationships with relatives, friends, and neighbors.

Are there any individuals whose entire life-style fits Wirth's depiction? In the absence of definitive empirical studies, it is hard to say, but one can guess that young adults just beginning their professional careers—who know that they must repeatedly move from one city to another in search of success— might come close. A sample of unmarried, recent college graduates living in apartments in Chicago seems to fit the picture as far as group and neighborhood participation is concerned. However, the point of the study done of them is that they were involved in building friendships in their workplaces (Starr and Carns 1973:96–97).

Young professionals—upwardly mobile, they hope—are not numerically typical, let alone representative, of American city dwellers, to say nothing of city dwellers elsewhere in the world. However, they were prominent in the academic setting in which Wirth and his colleagues lived, and pervasive in that same setting was a view of the world that .was (and still is) fundamentally antiurban. Since urban anthropology evolved in part out of this intellectual matrix, it is discussed in greater detail later in this chapter.

The empirical evidence is overwhelming that the significant social relationships of most city dwellers everywhere are not impersonal, superficial, transitory, or segmental.

DIVERSITY

We have already mentioned the great diversity of cities in terms of population density and size. These features have concomitants which further enrich the diversity. However, cities are different and varied in many other ways.

First, for example, some general categories of cities are transnational and transcultural in world distribution. Three of these categories are Western industrial, revolutionary industrial, and Third World (discussed with others in chapter 4). Second, national cultures and even regional subcultures to which they belong affect cities (for example, Sun Belt and Frost Belt cities in the United States). Third, cities are often felt to have individually distinctive features, as with the long-lasting reputations attached to Boston, New York, Chicago, Houston, and Los Angeles (Suttles 1984:291–92).

Individual cities are internally diverse. What is a typical Bostonian? There is none except in terms of subjective stereotypes. Residents of Beacon Hill, the North End, and the South End are all Bostonians, but very different from one another (Firey 1968), representing different subcultures (see chapter 7), as do Cairo's "modern urban" and "traditional urban" (*baladi*) residents (Abu-Lughod 1971).

Yet another example is different types of city dwellers' feelings occurring in the same city. David Hummon's study of Californians compares feelings of residents of San Francisco, of two of its suburbs, and of a nearby small town. Interviews reveal three types of San Franciscans. "Cosmopolitan urbanists" like the city because of its diversity of activities and people, liberal mindedness, and opportunities for personal freedom. "Local urbanists" like San Francisco because of the local communities and neighborhoods in which they live. In contrast to these enthusiasts are "reluctant urbanites" who have become disenchanted with life in San Francisco because of various changes in it or because they feel themselves to be temporary residents (Hummon 1986:16–24). Wholly different from all the city dwellers are the small towners whose feelings are antiurban, in terms closely parallel to the bipolar moralistic model, discussed later. Hummon's study has implications that go beyond the immediate results of his research, particularly in regard to people's different perceptions of the scale dimensions in which they live. One could go on almost indefinitely, but these are three well-documented examples.

From the perspective of individuals' everyday life, a city is not a single large-scale social unit comparable to a single small-scale unit. Neither Cairo nor London is comparable, analytically, to a small city like Newburyport, Mass. (site of a famous, pioneering urban study), let alone small towns of a few thousand people. Large cities are complexes of less inclusive social units which, in turn, vary in scale from small to relatively large. City dwellers participate in small-scale units as well as in large-scale ones. Lewis Mumford, with his emphasis on the importance of family and neighborhood combined with his great knowledge of cities as wholes, was fully aware of this phenomenon, but a startlingly large number of city specialists have chosen to minimize or disregard it. The importance of small- and medium-range scale in city life is a major theme in this book, dealt with in much more detail in later chapters.

Let us dramatize this internal diversity by considering the impact certain parts of two world-famous Western industrial cities have had on two observers. The first is depressing. Do you feel that it epitomizes the city?

[It is] a street of dreadful formica snackeries and chicken-and-chips take-aways. Its pubs have bloodstains on the lavatory walls; its pavements swirl with waste paper, and on Sunday mornings are streaked with thin, bilious vomit. Down narrow basements and tucked into alleys, there are dubious clubs where prostitutes lean in the hallways and boys with faces of corrupted cherubs smile winningly at fussy men of middle age who look like blackmail victims.

The quarter is temporarily coloured by a variety of tribal groups. . . . In the evenings it belongs to the 'gays'; one of the few places in the city where men can fondle each other on the street . . . in the small hours, it drifts into the hands of pimps, sharks and drunks, unsavoury men who watch from doorways or cruise slowly in squashy American cars (Raban 1975:196–97).

The second scene is altogether different. Can it possibly be located in a city at all?

The sky was black, yet sharply bright with stars when we began. When the sun came up, it became more beautiful. The hills and houses rise on that route in such a way as to hide the east, so that you cannot see the dawning color if there is any. That day the color was transported in pink clouds almost directly above us. The lightening sky was an unusual baby blue. A gull flying at a great height was caught in the sun's rays, incandescent, rosy, and haloed from sunlight still hidden from us. The gull announced the dawn when the sun had not yet reached the little canyons of the . . . streets. The work was transformed by the beauty of the morning (S. E. Perry 1978:65).

Jonathan Raban describes London's Earl's Court Road section. Its atmosphere makes it a very different London from the elegance of Kensington, the quaintness of Hampstead, the serenity of Hyde Park, the bustle of the West End, or the pomp and circumstance of Buckingham Palace, Westminster, and St. Paul's. However different they be, they are all London, and London is all of them, and more.

Stewart Perry was a garbage collector; his location was San Francisco's Haight-Ashbury section, then a dilapidated residential area frequented by hippies. The view that so impressed Perry was not one of the magnificent panoramas for which the city is famous, nor did the location have any of the glamour of Ghirardelli Square, the exoticism of Chinatown, or the sophisticated affluence of the downtown business district. But San Francisco is all of these places, and more.

Given the diverse realities that constitute London and San Francisco, it should be clear why no unidimensional characterization of them is adequate. Yet the acceptance of unidimensional characterizations underlies oversimplified notions like *the* city.

Since the diversities are rather obvious, it is remarkable that those oversimplified notions have been so popular, persistent, and influential in the study of cities. Why? The answer lies in the accumulation over time of a set of largely negative characteristics attributed to cities that were and are inspired by anticity bias.

ANTIURBANISM

A major contributor to studies on modern life in cities writes:

[T]here has traditionally been an anti-urban bias among intellectuals and indeed among serious students of the city. Men have been attracted to its study because of the lurid fascination of evils which demanded explanation. It is ironic that one of the most pronounced phenomena of our time, the overwhelming concentration of the cities, is accompanied by an ethos that glorifies rural virtues (Michelson 1976:148).

In the passage from which this quotation comes, William Michelson cites Lucia and Morton White's *The Intellectual Versus the City: From Thomas Jefferson to Frank Lloyd Wright* (1962). This book is a splendid review of the subject and takes notice of the social scientists and others who have inveighed against cities. It would be a serious error to think that the antiurban bias dates only from the eighteenth century. There is clear evidence for it among classical writers as well as some medieval and Renaissance authors (Caro Baroja 1963:27ff). Julio Caro Baroja refers to these people as moralists, and his basic explanation is that they saw in city life certain threats to traditional ways of doing things and also a general threat to social order in the restive proletarians in city populations (p. 35). The same fear of an unstable proletariat is still expressed today with respect to inhabitants of squatter settlements in Third World cities, a fear greatly exaggerated (Nelson 1969:6ff). That modern cities are where the action is—action involving innovations in social patterns—is generally agreed, but whether this notion is seen as threatening or beneficial depends on many things, including the various biases we are considering.

The variety of these biases is made evident in Park Goist's study (1977) of the concept of community in American literature from about 1890 to 1940. Some early twentieth-century authors idealized the small town in America and celebrated it as a specific place where geographic community flourished. Community "means enjoying a sense of solidarity among one's own kind . . . realizing one's potential among these people, having a social role to play" which they recognize as valuable (Goist 1977:17). Such authors saw the city as the antithesis of community. Others, however, though disliking what they saw as the anticommunity effects of the machine age, did not idealize the small town.

Faced with opposing views of life in small settlements, as well as of life in cities, we must make ourselves as sensitive as possible to the effects of observers' biases of all kinds. One fundamental bias involves the projection of emotions, such as nostalgia or despair over certain conditions of present-day life, onto specific geographical places. This projection often makes those places seem to epitomize certain conditions or behavior patterns. The result is to stereotype those places and so make perceiving their realities difficult, if not impossible.

One of the best informed and most balanced students of cities is Lewis Mumford. His *The Culture of Cities* (1938) and *The City in History* (1961), among other books, are classics of the field. Goist succinctly captures some of Mumford's basic attitudes:

> Mumford has never suggested that small towns have a monopoly on the possibilities of community. . . . [He] does not attribute the plight of contemporary civilization to an inability to recapture a sense of small town community within cities. On the contrary, [he] connects the growing disorder, violence, and alienation in modern society to a habit of mind that reveres the value of money, power, and machine technology. . . . [He] has advocated a community life based on the family and the neighborhood unit as a countervailing force to our growing obsession with technological abundance, power and money. He sees the city, in contrast to the village and suburb, as a place of diversity and variety, of healthy antagonisms and disorder . . . "the city . . . must emphasize—and reconcile—varieties, differences, even antagonisms." His emphasis on the neighborhood . . . in the city is not . . . based on the hope of returning to a "cozier, warmer form of human association." Mumford has never held that things were cozier or warmer or better in the past . . . [but] certain historic forms . . . satisfied [specific social needs] that still exist and must be provided for within modern equivalents of those past forms (Goist 1977:155–56).

Goist's quotation sets a tone that this work sustains. Cities are places of variety, tension, and opportunity. They embody neither utopia nor antiutopia. The reasons for conspicuous conditions in them, good or bad, should be sought first in the cultures and regions of which they are only parts; those conditions should not be assumed to be immutable forms intrinsic to, or determined by, cityness. Samuel Kaplan's study of American suburbia (Port Washington, N.Y.) provides one example. Many middle-class whites moved to suburbia because they did not want to live near the poor blacks moving into the inner cities. Now that blacks themselves are moving to the suburbs, the same forms of discrimination are affecting them, and deteriorating conditions, supposedly intrinsic to inner cities, are becoming evident in some suburbs, resulting in "slurbs" (1977:94–97). The primary problem is not the specific locations in themselves, but the attitudes, values, and behaviors brought to them. Of course, once deteriorating conditions become established in a location, the location itself *appears to be* the primary problem, but it is not. We must look beyond it.

Where? Michael Lewis, for one, looks at what he believes to be core values in middle-class, mainstream American culture. He thinks individualistic striving for limitless success commits many middle-class people to perpetual threat to their own self-worth because they can but fail to achieve limitless success—no achievement is enough. They have found a way out of this bind—not by changing their values—but by ensuring that there will be in American society those who are conspicuously and unequivocally greater failures than they are. Consequently, none of the programs to alleviate poverty and its behavioral components ever works because those in charge of the programs do not want them to work.

> But to the extent that those who need to discredit the poor . . . to buttress their own threatened self-worth can view the poor as having, of their own volition or incompetence, failed in this society of chances, the existence of poverty becomes a virtual necessity in American society. All the anti-poverty rhetoric notwithstanding, and irrespective of the many skirmishes entered into by poverty warriors past and present, the culturally mandated need for visible failure in American society carries with it a need to maintain poverty (1979:51).

If Lewis is correct, then an important source of anticity bias is rooted in the human condition itself. Let us carry this idea further.

Theodore Roszak, spokesman for the counterculture movement and "a city dweller born and bred," provides some possible clues:

> I cannot ever say that I love the city or hate it. . . . By what right, then, do I presume to know that rural or primitive ways are "better?". . . . I don't . . . I would not choose [the rural] world for myself or romanticize its virtues . . . [but] what I do contend is that there have always been different ways of life other than city ways. . . . The legend of Cain can teach us more about the nature of the city. . . . Cain, the first urbanite, had so estranged himself from God and nature that . . . he could no longer provide for his own needs. . . . The city comes into existence by withdrawing people from the primary production of their life needs—fuel, food, raw materials.
>
> The city has a peculiar way of corrupting the appetites of people. . . . [T]his is intimately connected with some of the most precious qualities of urban culture . . . to open people to the variety of human possibilities. The city . . . encourages people to want things—out of curiosity or envy (pp. 244–45, 251).

Laying the curse of Cain on the city is another gambit appealing to city haters. Notice that Roszak, like many other writers, always refers to "the city" as if it were a single entity. This tactic enables him to assume, evidently, that "city ways" are of a particular sort, and apparently even the "most precious qualities" of cities are corrupting.

Poor Roszak! He tells his readers he has not lived very much outside of metropolitan areas, and, not being ready to do so, he is caught in an environment he perceives negatively. No wonder he seeks a counterculture. However, the book from which the quotation comes is not primarily about cities but about the threats to, if not loss of, "personhood" in the modern world. Like many such books, it is a cry of outrage against the human condition in general as the author feels it to be.

This outcry is true of much of the urban literature, as well. Consider four books published in the 1960s. Two are autobiographies; two are highly suggestive of this genre. All are set in New York City, all are horrifying, and all are written by spokesmen for Michael Lewis's discredited poor: *Manchild in the Promised Land* by Claude Brown; *Down These Mean Streets* by Piri Thomas; *Last Exit to Brooklyn* by Hubert Selby, Jr.; and *Call It Sleep* by Henry Roth. Brown and Thomas write about their own lives as a black and a Puerto Rican, respectively. Their books emphasize the brutality and deprivation their own ethnic groups experienced in the city. Selby's work is a phantasmagoria of sadism and sex in Brooklyn's bars, back alleys, and empty lots. Roth's book, originally published in 1934, is less shocking than the other three, but has its own horrors. Its protagonist is a boy, son of the loveless marriage of Jewish immigrants. A masterful technique of Roth's is the eloquence of the boy's mother when talking with him, in contrast to her crude, bumbling expressions when confronting the police. To her son, she is speaking Yiddish, her native language (translated by Roth into English); to the police, she speaks her broken, immigrant English, and seems to be less human as a result.

All four books dramatize various negative aspects of inner-city ghetto life. The unwary reader, or one inclined to assume the worst about cities, cannot be blamed for assuming that these books, and many others like them, represent and typify urban life. Such readers must, however, realize that the migration of ethnic and racial groups to New York and other cities was motivated in large part by their *oppression in rural areas*. We must address the question: Are the destructive patterns of life depicted by such authors as Brown, Thomas, Selby, and Roth, peculiarly, essentially, or exclusively urban, or are they reflections in a city setting of ailments of the human condition generally? The question must at least be argued both ways.

THE BIPOLAR MORALISTIC MODEL

With this brief review of the intellectual and emotional roots of the study of cities, we are ready to narrow the subject and focus it more precisely.

Louis Wirth did not originate the ideas he expressed in "Urbanism as a Way of Life." Rather, he articulates the ideas and feelings of a group of colleagues, mostly sociologists, at the University of Chicago—a group widely known as the Chicago school of urban sociology, but including Robert Redfield, an important anthropologist. These scholars were very much influenced by the general antiurban world view of their time, which we have just discussed, and they were also academic successors to Ferdinand Tönnies, Emile Durkheim, Georg Simmel, and others, who were prominent European observers of the cities of their day. What they saw was very rapid growth and industrialization spurred by profit-seeking private enterprise and largely unguided by altruistic social concerns. This major social upheaval involved much dislocation of traditional cultural patterns and much hardship among large masses of people.

One reaction was formulation of the Marxian alternative to capitalism. Another reaction was formulation by the Chicago school, its European predecessors, and others of a model of urban society called the "bipolar moralistic model" (Gulick 1974b:984).

This model is better known by other names, most notably Robert Redfield's "folk-urban dichotomy." In the latter part of his career, Redfield modified the term to "folk-urban continuum," but this change does not alter how "folk" (or rural) and "urban" were conceived as being not just different, but polar opposites.

Redfield's predecessors had initiated the pattern of thinking about their subject in terms of binary oppositions. Tönnies contrasts *gemeinschaft* (community) with *gesellschaft* (society). By community he means essentially the same things as those Goist mentions above. By society he means a social organization lacking the qualities of community. Durkheim contrasts "sacred" versus "profane" and "integration" versus "anomie" (absence of guiding values in life). *Gesellschaft*, profane, and anomie (or normlessness) are all identified as negative qualities of cities, in contrast to their opposites, assumed to be among the positive qualities of tribal, village, folk, or rural settlements. Various writers propose other bipolar opposites, and, in a 1974 publication, this author assembled 15 of these pairs of terms. Of these, the following generally are used negatively in association with urban and positively in association with rural:

"Rural"	*"Urban"*
Community	Noncommunity
Natural	Spurious
Tribal society	Mass society
Moral	Corrupt
Human in scale	Dehumanized
Personal	Anonymous
Integrated	Anomic
Sacred	Secular

Redfield emphasizes the last three pairs in *The Folk Culture of Yucatan* (1941), perhaps the fullest and most purely anthropological book on the subject. He uses Yucatan villages and towns and the city of Mérida for source material.

These further pairs of terms are used ambiguously as far as moralistic judgments are concerned, but they are not neutral:

"Rural"	*"Urban"*
Primitive	Civilized
Simple	Sophisticated
Inherently stable	Inherently changing
Homogeneous	Heterogeneous

The urban terms refer to cities as undifferentiated wholes and, when convenient, to societies as wholes, even though no societies consist primarily of cities, apart from a handful of city-states. These terms are essentially stereotyping and express bias and feeling far more than they do empirical findings.

The issue *is not* that the terms represent imaginary human conditions. Verifiable examples of all of them can be found. Conditions generally perceived as "dehumanized," among other things, are the subject of later chapters. Heterogeneity, a condition most observers concede to be true of most cities as wholes, is discussed in the positive and negative contexts that various realities of everyday city life appear to require.

The issue is, rather, the uncritical, unempirical manner in which these terms have too often been applied. They represent moralistic biases and emotions that seem essentially to be feelings about the human condition generally, not about cities in particular. One need only consider the intellectual games that can be played with these terms to become hesitant to use them analytically. For example, a correlate of city anonymity is freedom from personal surveillance as opposed to the social constraints of small-town or rural life; a correlate of city anomie is lack of pressures to conform—the rural opposite is conformity. Many observers would associate social constraints and conformity with rural, nonurban life. However, to assume this association would be to indulge in stereotyping. As we shall see in chapter 2, this phenomenon may not be rural/ urban but rather a matter of scale.

EMPIRICAL STUDIES OF CITIES

Members of the Chicago school pioneered in urban research, using Chicago as their primary subject. Among other accomplishments, they established precedents for research on topics that urban sociologists, economists, political scientists, city planners, and others continue to study today. Emphasis is on the spatial distribution of population characteristics available from census records and to some extent from survey questionnaire responses. Urban ecology, focusing on spatial distribution of incomes and land values, including changes in their distribution through time, has a prominent place in these studies. Among the important results are the large amounts of data now available on the increasing concentration of blacks and Hispanics in United States central cities and the continued, concomitant flight of whites to suburbs (see, for example, Tschirhart and Kaull 1986).

These data are important, but they have limitations, too. Urban anthropologists specializing in thorough microstudies of small groups of people with whom they become personally acquainted need the macrostudies. Urban or suburban neighborhood life, however intimately studied, must be seen in macrocontext as well. Otherwise, it will not be understood fully. On the other hand, macrocensus analyses and surveys abstracted from actual behavior of people generally (if unintentionally) reinforce the impersonal, anonymous stereotype and are not instructive on social networks and related subjects.

URBAN ANTHROPOLOGY

It should now be clear that this book draws its insights from many different fields of study. However, the author's synthesis of these insights is rooted in his perceptions as an urban anthropologist. Consequently, in the remainder of this chapter, and at various points in subsequent chapters, discussion focuses on the special strengths, as well as the limitations, of urban anthropology as the author sees them.

There is no general agreement as to what urban anthropology is—certainly no orthodox ideology. Urban anthropologists are still experimenting, still feeling their way. It is not an evasion to say that urban anthropology is what its practitioners are doing and thinking (see Ellovich and Stack 1985).

The bipolar moralistic model has already been introduced, along with its European architects whose perspectives were philosophically deep but ethnographically shallow, being limited to industrializing nineteenth-century Europe. They found a ready audience in the United States where sociologists responded enthusiastically, as we have seen. American anthropologists, on the other hand, were, during the first half of the twentieth century, hardly concerned with cities at all, but rather with tribal peoples in various parts of the world. Four of the greatest pacesetters in American anthropology—Franz

Boas, Alfred Kroeber, Margaret Mead, and Clyde Kluckhohn (all sophisticated, big-city people)—paid virtually no attention to cities, as such, in their professional work.

Such attention as cities or urban cultures received was negative. Edward Sapir's widely cited notion of "spurious culture" (1949) may well have epitomized most anthropologists' feelings about cities before World War II, and probably to a considerable extent today. Pioneers in the anthropological study of American cities, such as Lloyd Warner (Newburyport, Mass., 1941 to 1963) and Robert and Helen Lynd (Muncie, Ind., 1929 to 1956) did not study large metropolitan cities, and their work was absorbed into the American sociological concentration on social stratification. Robert Redfield did broaden the urban perspective to Latin America, but his work largely reinforced already entrenched anticity biases. Archeological research on origins of Middle Eastern and Latin American cities was an established field of study in anthropology, but not considered relevant to present-day urban research.

Like Warner's and the Lynds' work, William Foote Whyte's *Street Corner Society* (1943), a study of an Italian-American gang in Boston, failed to catch the anthropological imagination. Instead, it found its rightfully famous way into the sociological and psychological literature, though it was a study done by participant observation on a small, human scale in a "natural" environment.

Among the earliest publications in a subsequently continuous stream of work in urban anthropology are two studies on Africa, one on Latin America. The two African studies make the same important point in different ways. Horace Miner's book on Timbuctoo (1953) very neatly shows that this small and remote—yet surprisingly cosmopolitan—town, in what is now Mali, exhibited both rural and urban characteristics as set forth in the bipolar moralistic model. Thus, Miner described Timbuctoo in less absolutistic urban terms than Redfield had described Mérida almost a decade earlier. William Schwab (1954) discusses his experiments with culturally sensitive survey and longitudinal research methods (as substitutes for classical participant observation in a large-scale population) in the Nigerian city of Oshogbo. In 1965 he presented Oshogbo's culture as being rural and urban, depending on what aspects of it were being considered; but by that time, empirical revisions of the bipolar concept by several others were underway.

Meanwhile, in 1952, Oscar Lewis published a short paper, "Urbanization without Breakdown," refuting the bipolar moralistic assumption that migrants from a peasant village (Tepoztlán, Mexico) would inevitably be demoralized by life in Mexico City. He emphasizes their maintenance of kinship and religious support systems in the urban environment. While similar findings have subsequently been reported from cities in all parts of the world, Lewis himself later eclipsed his own 1952 article with his famous publications on the "culture of poverty" (considered further in chapter 7). Lewis attributed his version of the culture of poverty more to oppressive industrial social stratification than to urban conditions as such, yet many anthropologists since then seem to associate it specifically with cities.

In 1957, British sociologists Michael Young and Peter Willmott published a classic of urban anthropology, *Family and Kinship in East London*. This book establishes the importance, among working-class Londoners, of close but extensive kinship ties and local hangouts and the destructive effects of urban renewal. Abner Cohen (1974:27) is astonished that Young and Willmott's book should have caused such a stir among social scientists, but, in view of the influence of the bipolar stereotype, it really is not surprising. Cohen points out the importance of nonkinship networks and support systems in cities (see also chapter 6). Young and Willmott's study had a direct influence on Herbert Gans in his research on the West End of Boston, a working-class quarter then doomed to obliteration by urban renewal. Gans (1962) established the concept "urban village" and the reality of closely knit, small-scale, localized support systems in large industrial cities. In doing this, Gans ran directly counter to the assumptions of the bipolar moralistic model. Since then urban villages have been found everywhere.

While the urban village concept is contrary to the bipolar definition of industrial city, it fits closely with the realities of preindustrial cities, a hypothetical type of city sociologist Gideon Sjoberg set forth in full in 1960.

Sjoberg attacks the bipolar model and the uncritical assumption that it fits any settlement labelled "urban." He does not, however, discuss whether the model fits industrial cities. Rather, he postulates another type of city, the preindustrial, and shows that the bipolar model does not fit it. Sjoberg draws his material from a wide variety of mostly historical works on cities in medieval Europe, early nineteenth-century Egypt, early twentieth-century China and India, and some others. These cities belonged to cultures widely known as feudal or agrarian, the majority of whose members were peasant villagers. Very clearly, preindustrial cities are conceived as parts of larger social or national wholes, as integral parts of "complex culture," as many anthropologists use the term in contrast to "primitive culture." Sjoberg perceived a number of common features among his sample cities, despite their diversity in time and place: a rigid two-class social hierarchy, the importance of quarters (urban villages) as subsystems, diversified family structures (no single type of urban family), and the importance of religious symbolic systems in communal life. As scholars of present-day cities observe the field, they can discern all of Sjoberg's preindustrial urban phenomena, not only in the Third World cities that are the most direct descendants of Sjoberg's cases, but also in cities of industrial cultures.

However, Sjoberg's formulation leaves open the question of whether the preindustrial city may not simply evolve into the industrial city as stereotyped by the bipolar moralistic model. And so, though Sjoberg's work should force critical questioning of Wirth's association of the bipolar model with anything urban—of relatively high density, large size, and heterogeneity—it only displaces some of the important misconceptions of urban. It does not, unfortunately, eliminate them.

From the anthropological point of view, a second fault of Sjoberg's effort is his exclusion of data from sub-Saharan African cities in his formulation. His focus is on cultures with literary traditions (command of literacy being one factor in the dominance and subordination of social classes), and sub-Saharan cultures do not have literary traditions of the sort common to those cultures Sjoberg draws on for data. Yet "relatively large, dense, and heterogeneous" settlements have been present in sub-Saharan Africa since before nineteenth-century European imperialism added new dimensions to African urban life.

Another early development of present-day urban anthropology was the research of British social anthropologists in Africa including that of the former Rhodes-Livingstone Institute established in 1937. The early emphasis was on detribalization and disequilibrium (concepts strongly reminiscent of the bipolar model), especially among rural migrants to new industrial cities.

A convenient way to learn about urban anthropology is to review the relatively recent comprehensive books about it. The earliest, by British urban Africanist Peter Gutkind (1974), is based heavily, though not exclusively, on findings from sub-Saharan Africa. Like Sjoberg, Gutkind devotes considerable space to showing the inapplicability of the bipolar model to the African scene despite the attention given to detribalization there. Gutkind is alert to the new syntheses of social meaning and organization that are evolving in Africa. At the same time, he warns urban anthropologists not to allow themselves to be pressed into generalizing before they are ready to do so. He advises them to move cautiously, developing models carefully on a thoroughly comparative basis and looking beyond traditional anthropological concerns (pp. 222–23).

In accord with his skepticism concerning existing models of urbanism, Gutkind poses the following "fundamental" questions:

What kind of urbanism are we studying, and how should we go about our research? Are cities and towns of the Third World going to take on the same characteristics as those of the Western World? Can we look forward to megalopolises—those vast mechanized entities which, despite concentration of populations, stretch for endless miles over the landscape? Or will the urbanism of Africa, Asia and Latin America turn into itself and hence produce an urbanism of a quite different variety? Apocalyptic predictions are hazardous (1974:214–15).

Gutkind says that urban anthropologists should set their "research on Third World urbanism in the context of development theory which is designed to analyze total system change. Only then can we be sure we have considered urbanization and urbanism in relation to economic and political transformation" (p. 215). In other words, urban anthropology must expand the scale of its perceptions, as well as free itself from those premature generalizations about the nature of urban cultures to which urban anthropology was, itself, a reaction.

J. Douglas Uzzell and Ronald Provencher's short introduction to the field (1976) makes a vitally important point in addition to Gutkind's. Anthropology encompasses *all* cultures. Therefore, urban anthropology comprehends not only Third World cities but also industrial cities of the West. At the same time, they argue that "if we were to skip lightly over other examples of urbanism in a rush to focus on contemporary urbanism in our own culture, we would lose the special perspective of anthropology that derives from careful comparison. . . . Without that perspective, urban problems cannot be identified properly, much less solved" (1976:7).

In 1972 in the first volume of the journal *Urban Anthropology*, Richard Fox makes a strong statement in favor of studying cities as wholes. In 1975, *Urban Anthropology* devoted a whole issue to "The City-as-Context," and, in 1977, Fox carried the theme forward in the third comprehensive book on urban anthropology being reviewed. In this expansion of his 1972 article, Fox links the worldwide domain of urban anthropology—as realized by Gutkind and

Uzzell and Provencher—and anthropology's holistic view. In this instance, the holistic view is triple: (1) microsystems, such as family, kinship, neighborhoods, and local associations, seen as parts of the city as a whole; (2) cities seen as parts of urban regional systems; and (3) regional urban systems seen as parts of national—and even international—systems. While urban anthropology emphasizes the personal, small-scale dimensions of life, its holism, which originated in the comprehension of small-scale communal systems, must extend its vision and grasp as much as is necessary to make possible full explication of city life as it is lived on the human scale. Fox's contribution is to propose a typology of cities which reflects a wider temporal and spatial culture and, at the same time, directly influences the lives of its inhabitants. Fox's types of city are "regal-ritual" (sub-Saharan Africa, Imperial India, Carolingian Europe); "administrative" (Mamluk Egypt, Tokugawa Japan, seventeenth-century France); "mercantile" cities and "city-states" (medieval Mediterranean, fourteenth- to sixteenth-century Japan, fourteenth- to fifteenth-century Java); "colonial" cities (Dutch and British colonialism in Java and India); and "industrial" cities (a black ghetto in Washington, D.C.; Skid Road alcoholics in Seattle; Newport, R.I.; and Charleston, S.C.).

Without apparently intending to do so, Fox delineates four types of cities that, taken together, could be seen as refinements of Sjoberg's single preindustrial type. Like Sjoberg, he uses perspectives from times past to illustrate these types, thus raising the question of whether they may no longer exist, having either been obliterated or transformed into industrial cities. Unlike Sjoberg, Fox tries to delineate industrial cities, and he does so in ways that should give us pause about single-type taxonomies. The two microstudies (both by anthropologists) show special groups which have been formed, in part, by demonstrable influences from the larger systems of which they are parts. But are Washington and Seattle representative industrial cities in their own right? Surely Washington qualifies as an administrative city; or perhaps Fox's point is that both are cities belonging to an industrial culture. As for Newport and Charleston, one could argue even more strenuously about their industrial status. Fox's purpose in drawing on data from these cities, however, is to show the multistage analysis proper for urban anthropology: whole society to city seen as a whole, city as a whole to subsystems (microsystems) of that city. Herein lies the great value of Fox's work.

Anthropology of the City: An Introduction to Urban Anthropology, also published in 1977, takes an approach quite different from Fox's. Edwin Eames and Judith Goode first anchor the book in the context of anthropology generally. Some anthropologists have followed peasants (an important component of traditional anthropology's constituency) as they migrate to cities. Such studies often emphasize the persistence of traditional customs among these migrants living in cities, an emphasis Eames and Goode suggest may mask flexibility and change (p. 21). Second, they focus on problems in cities, among which poverty and oppression of ethnic minorities and deviant subcultures are prominent. Studies of such people may have too narrow and unrealistic a focus, since they ignore the lives and problems of mainstream or dominant groups of city dwellers. Also, many of the problems in question are not city specific (pp. 22–23). The third general approach of urban anthropology, according to these authors, is studying traditional topics such as kinship systems and spatially bound groups in cities. These studies frequently suffer from lack of the holistic, city-as-context perspective Fox and others advocate. They are too micro in focus.

Having defined urban anthropology in terms of what, in the main, urban anthropologists have done, Eames and Goode then generalize to two generic approaches: anthropology *in* the city and anthropology *of* the city (p. 31). Anthropology in the city consists primarily of traditional anthropological research topics pursued in city settings. The city environment is treated as a backdrop, and the question of its relationship to the topic(s) being studied frequently is not addressed at all. In other words, the specific urbanness of the anthropological observations in the city can, at best, only be guessed at. Of necessity, this book draws on many studies of this type, for, as Eames and Goode say, they constitute much of urban anthropology today. Anthropology of the city is basically the same thing as the study of city-as-context. Eames and Goode see "this area of research activity as central to urban anthropology and the development of new research strategies" (p. 33). They want to know the nature of cities themselves:

> What is unique about the city in contrast to other settlements? In what ways does the city as an institution influence behavior and beliefs? How does the relationship between groups and quasigroups in the city influence the urban center? To what extent can we develop a typology of cities . . . to determine those characteristics that account for differentiation? (p. 33).

These remain open questions. Neither the bipolar moralistic model nor Fox's typology supplies satisfactory answers.

What is needed is an empirically verifiable typology of cities within each culture and a valid system of comparing those typologies cross-culturally, so that unique types and general types can be identified and, in turn, related to the cultures of which they are parts. Unfortunately, we are very far from having such typologies or comparative models with which to work.

Nevertheless, we cannot ignore the effects of general cultures—such as American, Egyptian, Brazilian, or Japanese—on their respective urban subcultures. Some anthropologists insist that the proper anthropological study of cities is not of cities themselves but of the complex cultures of which cities are parts. So much needs to be discovered and learned about cities themselves that it would be premature to bypass them in the manner that seems to be implied. Eames and Goode (1977:32) warn against the tendency of many anthropologists to confuse urban anthropology with the anthropology of complex societies. We must develop the skills and techniques necessary to analyze microsystems (such as perceptions of crowding in one-room apartments), to analyze a specific city as a whole (such as Hong Kong with its high-rise public housing projects), and to analyze the culture of which the city is a part (such as Chinese culture which, in its city and rural sections, has whole sets of patterns of interpersonal relations and space use that directly affect perceptions of crowding). E. N. Anderson captures all of these analytic dimensions in a short article, "Some Chinese Methods that Deal with Crowding" (1972).

The relationship of cities to complex societies is very important. Richard Basham's 1978 book, yet another called *Urban Anthropology*, has this relationship as a major theme. Basham covers many of the same topics as do Eames and Goode, but he emphasizes the transformation in the urban environment of traditional, small-scale "primordial" social structures into new social structures adapted to cities, reflecting the complex cultures to which the cities belong. For example, with reference to sub-Saharan Africa, he writes:

Persistence of tribalism in the city is not the same as rural tribalism. Tribesmen in urban areas quickly learn that strict tribal power and the power of chiefs is [*sic*] restricted to their homeland. In the city they encounter new sources of power and prestige, based upon education and the acquisition of special skills, to which many willingly transfer their loyalty [even though] common tribal or ethnic bonds may still keep members together (p. 216).

Basham gives the bipolar moralistic model its due but rejects it as a guide to reality. He recognizes the difficulties people encounter in city living but emphasizes the capability many have shown in adapting to urban conditions by forming appropriate kinds of microsystems of bonds and support groups. He also accepts the reality of impulses to maintain social distance (a double-edged strategy that can result in alienation as well as social solidarity), and he illustrates this in particular detail in his chapter on class, caste, and ethnicity.

Finally, there is Ulf Hannerz's *Exploring the City* (1980). Hannerz is a Swedish anthropologist whose study of a black neighborhood in Washington, D.C., is discussed in chapter 7. To a considerable extent, Hannerz's book is a history of urban anthropological ideas, but as in this book, he considers the work of some nonanthropologists to be part of urban anthropology. Most of his text is devoted to critical reviews of the Chicago school of urban sociology, to African research emanating from the Rhodes-Livingstone Institute, to network analysis, and to the dramaturgical view of social relations Erving Goffman made famous (see, for example, his *Relations in Public*, 1972). Hannerz extends each review further to develop his own ideas of what the core concepts of urban anthropology should be. He sees them as centering on the "relational analysis" of roles whose inventory can be divided into five domains: household and kinship, provisioning, recreation, neighboring, and traffic (p. 102). Provisioning refers to how city dwellers receive and redistribute their resources; traffic refers to relationships involving minimal interaction, essentially those involved with strangers. Hannerz thinks the provisioning and traffic domains of role and relationship "seem especially significant in making any city what it is" (p. 105). Hannerz's hope seems to be that by detailed research in terms of these domains the rigidities of various conceptual taxonomies—such as rural/urban, micro/macro, and city types—can be overcome. Yet, though he recognizes the whole-city, macrodimension of urban life, Hannerz's predominant impact is at the microlevel of individuals and their relationships. Near the end of his book, he tentatively identifies four "modes of urban existence" (enscapsulation, segregativity, integrativity, and solitude) all of which refer primarily to the orientations of individuals (p. 255).

Several years before Gutkind's book, some anthologies of urban anthropology articles appeared in print, and more followed (Eddy 1968; Foster and Kemper 1974; Friedl and Chrisman 1975; Gmelch and Zenner 1980; Mangin 1970; Press and Smith 1980; Southall 1975; and Weaver and White 1972). Discussions of methodological and perceptual issues are scattered throughout these volumes, but most of their contents are basically descriptive. George

Foster and Robert Kemper's volume is devoted entirely to anthropologists discussing their research experiences in cities, but one learns as much about what they found out as about how they did it. From the very beginning (Eddy 1968), serious concerns are expressed regarding such matters as the more and less appropriate contexts (micro/macro) to which urban anthropologists should relate their research and whether urban anthropology should be "relevant" to the acknowledged societal problems of the United States today. Opinions on the latter subject range from lack of interest in those problems (because of concentration on other cultures) to identifying urban anthropology with anthropology of the social problems of the United States.

Among the major subject categories featured in the anthologies are urban networks and kinship, migrants' adaptations to cities, ethnicity and social class, poverty (including critical treatments of Oscar Lewis's culture of poverty concept), and inconclusive efforts to define urbanism (in the course of which Wirth's "Urbanism as a Way of Life" is included in three of the eight books).

The richness and variety of urban anthropology and other characteristics of the field at its best are well illustrated in two of the many volumes of the published proceedings of the 1973 International Congress of Anthropological and Ethnological Sciences. Throughout *Processes of Urbanism* (1978), edited by Joyce Aschenbrenner and Lloyd Collins, the authors stress the importance of anthropologists' bringing multidisciplinary and macroscale perspectives to bear on their customary microscale fields of observation. *Migration and Urbanization* (1975), edited by Brian Du Toit and Helen Safa, reveals the many subtleties of migrants' adaptations to city life.

This book is built on the ideas and descriptive materials in many of these previously published works, but it is different from all of them in its organization and pursuit of a single, but multifaceted theme: the humanity of cities. The following quotation defines urban anthropology in terms that fit the approach of this book very well:

> No other social or humanistic science exhibits the special combination of historical, contemporary, ecological, and comparative concerns that characterizes anthropology. This broad perspective ensures that each urban anthropologist . . . brings to the study of the city a fundamental grounding in the variety of human experience and cultural manifestations, an eclecticism born of awareness of alternative solutions in other times and places, a built-in skepticism of so-called universals or natural behavior, and a penchant for witholding judgment. . . . These understandings complement and build upon the contributions of sociology, psychology, economics, political science, and history—disciplines . . . traditionally focused upon Western, industrial cities and urban processes.
> Cities are not easy to understand or study. They are the most complex of human communities, often seeming to concentrate the cumulative social and cultural creations of the species. Small wonder, therefore, that no single discipline can have a lock on urban studies (Press and Smith 1980:14).

CONCLUSION

This chapter began with an oversimplified definition of an oversimplified concept—the city—and a negative stereotype of it. It closes with a much more complicated definition of cities, combined with a positive point of view.

Based on the eclecticism Irwin Press and M. Estellie Smith associate with urban anthropology, it is possible to propose tentative definitions of city and urban and to propose the hypothesis that they can fit all cases. The definitions are not simple because the subjects are not simple. If they should prove unacceptable as definitions, they can, at least, serve as a checklist of characteristics widely observed to be present in settlements considered to be cities or urban places, rather than noncities or nonurban places.

One characteristic is the combination in one place and time of large size and high density. This much seems clear, although we have little understanding of the impact of this combination on the lives of city dwellers. One reason for this lack of understanding is the wide range of sizes and densities. Another characteristic is the presence of institutions, services, and opportunities not present in settlements perceived as not being cities or urban. A third characteristic is a set of phenomena elsewhere called "urban essentials" (Gulick 1974b:993–95). These essentials are factors in interpersonal relations whose presence in a settlement makes it urban or citified regardless of its size:

(1) Local residents and institutions serve as brokers between the larger society of which the settlement is a part and the immediate region that it dominates by reason of the brokerage functions located in it.

(2) In connection with the brokerage functions, strangers and outsiders are regularly and normally present in the settlement.

(3) A distinct system of social classes exists among the inhabitants. Members of different classes tend to behave toward each other in terms of categorical or stereotypic roles.

(4) Members of the uppermost class have various personal and business associations in other, larger cities and in wider regions. These connections impart prestige and betoken power. Also, they usually exhibit life-styles that are, in the context of the particular culture, seen as sophisticated, cosmopolitan, cultivated, universalistic, and urbane. However, other inhabitants of the settlement who are not seen in these terms are not any the less urban or citified.

(5) The presence, in many of the above-mentioned activities, of impersonal, rationalistic, or goal-oriented behavior, behavior generally fitting the urban side of the bipolar moralistic model. At the same time, however, the same people are also involved in intensely personal, multiplex relationships with kinsmen, friends, neighbors, and others.

(6) Change is normal in the settlement, the inhabitants tending to recognize the reality of changes that are often beyond their control, being concomitants of changes in the larger society.

(7) Cultural heterogeneity, in various forms and in varying degrees of intensity, is a factor in all of the above characteristics.

The points above are criteria of urbanness or cityness in every part of the world of which we have sufficient knowledge. They serve primarily to differentiate urban places from peasant villages in which a sizable proportion of the world's population still lives. However, they do not quite so clearly differentiate urban places from many rural or small town settlements in the Westernized industrial world. This lack of clear differentiation need not be a serious problem if we do not insist on the rigid, mutually exclusive categories of the bipolar moralistic model.

These criteria were derived inductively from several anthropological studies of small settlements all considered to be urban by the observers. Three more recent studies—two by anthropologists and one by a historian—reveal positive ideas and feelings about what urban is, in contrast to the bipolar moralistic model. These ideas and feelings belong to the inhabitants themselves.

Montecastello is a small hill town in central Italy. With a population of only 345 (plus about 15 hundred more in the agricultural district of which it is the center), it is smaller than many of the nonurban peasant villages in the world. However, its inhabitants emphatically do not regard it as a village:

> The Central Italian town contains a population of mostly non-cultivators . . . clearly distinguished from the *contadini* of the surrounding countryside. The styles of town life bear traces of the sophistication born of a long urban history.
>
> The people of Montecastello are conscious of this quality of town life, indeed they glorify it. The term that most accurately sums it up is *civiltà*. . . . close to "civility," but broader in meaning. It is related to the "civic" and the "urbane," but is not quite either of these. It is more like "civilization, but not quite so broad or so grandiose. In general, it refers to ideas about a civilized way of life. It must be understood in terms of a range of meanings rather than a precise definition, but it always implies an *urban* way of life (Silverman 1975:1–2).

Sydel Silverman's book about Montecastello anchors the abstraction *civiltà* to many factors, including the history of Italy and the agrarian system that links the town and its hinterland, and so we encounter broad cultural phenomena reflected in the life of the settlement.

Salé, near Rabat on the Atlantic coast of Morocco, had a population that grew from about 14 to 26 thousand between 1830 and 1930. By the late 1960s, it had grown to about 100 thousand. Much larger than Montecastello, large enough to be considered a small city by most observers, its people express ideas about themselves and their town remarkably similar to those expressed in Montecastello:

> [A]n indigenous historian . . . portrayed the city as a centre of civilization and commerce. . . . The [people of Salé] maintained a local and national reputation for civilization—that "civilized culture" (*al-hadara*) ascribed to only four cities in Morocco. . . . They had a style of life . . . defined in the Moroccan context as the ideal of sophisticated urbanity. . . . Scholars, merchants and craftsmen held in common their identity as civilized and cultured townsmen. A generation later . . . the population had been greatly increased . . . and become more heterogeneous . . . but the ideology of a socially and culturally cohesive community had not appreciably weakened or altered (K. L. Brown 1976:2).

In concluding his book, Kenneth Brown says that in 1966–67 (when he did his research there), despite all the changes in Salé, its inhabitants' "proud sense of identity with the city" was still very important for them (p. 224).

Silverman and Brown describe ambiences in their respective towns that the inhabitants act out in many contexts in positive ways. To some extent this is also true of Press's analysis of life in present-day Seville. Press is explicit about his fondness for Seville and his consequent lack of complete objectivity, yet he succeeds in portraying various aspects of city life in which positive elements mix with systemic constraints. On the positive side, he presents a picture suggestive of Montecastello and Salé. Seville is far larger—about 600 thousand people—and a beautiful and famous city, as its inhabitants are very much aware. "Hailed in song and poem, it dotes on its image" (Press 1979:23). Many see Seville as epitomizing Spanish culture, and, if one likes Spanish culture, this gives the city a glowing aura indeed. How much of this aura illuminates the intense neighborhood and personalized lives of the Seville people he knew, Press does not say, but he emphasizes how people from all walks of life share the same positive municipal image of themselves.

Montecastello, Salé, and Seville are very different in size and belong to different nations. Each has had a long history full of vicissitudes. Each has a local elite whose members are, in a sense, the most successful survivors of those vicissitudes and guardians of the positive ambience already mentioned. Each has a very clear-cut identity, in part enhanced by important communal festivals, street processions, and the like. It is tempting, in fact, to lump them together as Mediterranean cities, as if this were an empirically established type of city substantially different from the industrial city type. However, the Mediterranean is not an empirically established type of city, and there are industrial cities, also, in the Mediterranean area. These Mediterranean data show that people can and do cut the urban pie in different ways. The bipolar model is only one way, one that seems clearly reflective of a particular period in urban evolution. The Mediterranean data clearly reflect that cities are very different in size and are variously affected by their regional hinterlands and cultures.

That urban life is, in its essence, experienced at different levels of scale now becomes inescapable, and it is the next major topic we investigate.

SUGGESTED ADDITIONAL READING

Agnew, John A., John Mercer, and David E. Sopher, eds. *The City in Cultural Context.* Boston: Allen & Unwin, 1984. The editors' points of view coincide in important ways with John Gulick's, as indicated by this quotation from their preface: "A major problem has been caused by assigning too much explanatory power to such concepts as 'the market,' and 'the mode of production,' while not paying enough attention to human actions and the attitudes, values, and beliefs that relate to these actions" (p. vii). Of the thirteen parts of the book, five are written by authors cited in this volume: Janet Abu-Lughod, James Bater, Peter Hall, Rhoads Murphey, and Amos Rapoport.

City & Society. The editorial policy of the new journal of the Society for Urban Anthropology emphasizes the different levels of urban scale needing to be studied. The first issue (June 1987) includes articles on skyscrapers and gentrification.

Durkheim, Émile. *The Elementary Forms of the Religious Life.* London: Allen & Unwin, 1954. Orig. ed. 1915. See his comments on the sacred and the profane. For an explanation of "anomie," see his *Suicide* (Glencoe, Ill.: The Free Press, 1951), Orig. ed. 1897.

Mullings, Leith, ed. *Cities of the United States: Studies in Urban Anthropology.* New York: Columbia University Press, 1987. According to the editor, this is the first urban anthropology anthology devoted entirely to United States cities. Two important themes of the book are compatible with those of *The Humanity of Cities*: the importance of the macrocosmic dimensions of everyday life and the role of anthropologists as action advocates on behalf of poor people and people who are targets of ethnic discrimination. Gulick cites other publications by some of the contributors (Eleanor Leacock, Helen Safa, Jagda Sharff, and Ida Susser)

Tabb, William K., and Larry Sawers, eds. *Marxism and the Metropolis: New Perspectives in Urban Political Economy*. New York: Oxford University Press, 1978. The Marxist approach is one important way in which to study cities and explain their problems.

2
Scales

The Middle East Institute

M ost people who reside in American cities are accustomed to living simultaneously on several different levels of scale. They (1) live in close,
frequent contact with a rather small number of people whom they know well;
(2) maintain relationships with people whom they know more or less well but
who live beyond the reach of normal everyday contact; and (3) manage relationships with people whom they do not know personally, if at all, who are
likely to be employees of agencies that may be national or international in
scope. More specifically, at the small-scale level, most people are in constant
face-to-face contact with friends, immediate family members, neighbors, and
co-workers or colleagues. At large-scale levels, they routinely shop at supermarkets for foodstuffs transported from all parts of the country, buy clothing
and other products imported from foreign countries, and so forth. All of these
large-scale transactions involve impersonal, superficial—but often regular—
relationships with salespeople and other functionaries, and they involve interdependent relationships with a host of unknown, anonymous middlemen
of many different kinds.

SIMULTANEOUS LARGE AND SMALL SCALES

The bipolar moralistic model says that urban social relationships are, by definition, impersonal, superficial, and anonymous—that all of them are large-scale relationships. The model ignores one key concept in the foregoing passage, namely, the simultaneousness in most urban individuals' lives of small- and large-scale relationships. This point, already made in chapter 1, bears repeating because of its importance. Much of the humanity of life in cities depends on its small-scale dimensions, while at the same time, city dwellers must also steer their way among large-scale trends, influences, and institutions.

This notion is surely an obvious and common-sense perception of reality. Why, then, has it been ignored or distorted by so many urban observers? The answer is that those observers' perceptions have been biased toward looking at urban life primarily or exclusively in large-scale terms.

OBSERVERS' BIASES

Four sources of large-scale bias are especially pertinent to the anthropology of cities. The first is the antiurban moralism of the bipolar thinkers. You will recall that the urban pole of the model discussed in chapter 1 includes such features as dehumanized scale and impersonal, anonymous social contexts which are concomitant with large numbers of people who do not know one another. If one's orientation is antiurban, one will tend to see primarily those features of city life that fit one's feelings, especially if the feelings include a sense of moral commitment.

The second source of bias is the subtle effect of census tract and survey research. Neither data source yields information on the many kinds of personal networks which comprise the small-scale dimensions of city life. Instead, they concentrate on what appear to be impersonal "forces" such as changes in property values. They emphasize individuals as isolates responding to questionnaires the analysis of which treats people as components of large statistical aggregates, not as members of small social groups. The overall effect of large amounts of such data is to hide the reality of the small-scale dimensions of life.

The third source of large-scale bias is the tendency of most observers to assume that their own scale perceptions are the same as those of the people they observe. Thus, the bipolar moralists' perception of urban social life is that it is large scale (with undesirable consequences), and they assume (often implicitly) that city dwellers' perceptions of their social life are also large scale.

The fourth bias is a distortion in the opposite direction: toward an excessively small-scale bias. Such bias, most frequently encountered among anthropologists, has been subjected to harsh and far-reaching criticism. Steven Jones, for example, cites cases of microcosmic studies of blacks in the United States, and argues that their authors' biases are hidden by their small-scale perceptions, concluding:

[D]isciplinary and ideological biases in American anthropology seem to have dictated the avoidance of supralocal structures, especially urban-based structures when these are exploitative of Black populations. For example, such institutions as the law-enforcement agency, the welfare system, and the economic market have not been examined for the effects they have on Black behavior. Even more devastating, institutions of this kind have been omitted in urban anthropological studies of Blacks where the structures clearly affected the behavior of the local population. Urban anthropology at present seems to be capitulating to such trends (1978:38).

In a similar vein, Amelia Mariotti and Bernard Magubane, writing about urban anthropology in Africa, say that present-day urban anthropology's findings tend

to legitimate the current social order by inducing approval or resignation in those who take them seriously. . . . [U]rban anthropologists become consciously or unconsciously ancillary agents of power . . . [and they] pay too little attention . . . to the imperialist context of African problems of urbanization. Precisely by dwelling exclusively on the facts derived from small-scale studies, urban anthropologists blind themselves to the historical processes which underlie the empirical data (1978:65).

It would be unfair and presumptuous to assume that Jones and Mariotti and Magubane favor forsaking small-scale perspectives entirely, but we must note that their macroscale preferences are ideological and that ideological stances can influence anyone's choice of research methods. Mariotti and Magubane leave the door slightly ajar for the integration of micro- and macroperspectives, at least for those inclined to enter:

By its methods and techniques of investigation (participant observation and depth interviews), urban anthropology can give insight into the thinking and the mentality of the subject which can be used by those whose interest it is to manipulate and dominate others if the larger process-shaping individual experiences are not disclosed (1978:65).

Few, if any, urban anthropologists would intentionally use their small- scale perceptions to hide large sources of injustice, but these warnings about the dangers of small-scale misperception of certain aspects of reality must be taken seriously. They are taken seriously in this book, and this is one of the reasons for the insistence on the simultaneity of small-scale and large-scale dimensions of city life, from the actors' points of view and the observers' (Gulick 1986).

Large-scale observer bias is also essentially an anthropological one. Godfrey and Monica Wilson set forth one of the most succinct statements of it in 1945. The Wilsons developed their idea in relation to culture change in sub-Saharan Africa—specifically, colonial urbanization as it affected "tribal" Africans. "The total degree of dependence upon others, i.e., the intensity of relations, is the same in all societies, but . . . it may be more or less spread out. Intensity in the narrower circles of relation necessarily diminishes as intensity in the wider circles increases" (1945:40).

An Englishman, they say, has the "same total degree of interdependence, or intensity of relations," as a Bushman does, but the Englishman's is spread all over the world (for food, for example) whereas the Bushman's is extremely localized. Therefore, they reason, the intensity of the Englishman's close relations is diminished. This conception fits perfectly with the bipolar assumptions that the interpersonal relations of people living in large-scale urban environments are superficial. Both the Wilsons and the bipolar model perceive a zero-sum game at work. Large-scale living can only occur with more diffused intensity of close relationships; increase in scale (such as moving away from a small village or tribal community to a city) necessarily entails diminished intensity of relationships. The individual (regardless of residence) has only finite time, energy, and emotional stamina for personal relationships. But much large-scale dependence (such as the Englishman's for food from all over the world) does not have any direct effect on personal interactions and certainly does not prevent him from having close, intense relationships. In fact, the largeness of the scale in this instance may barely be perceived by the actor himself; it may more likely be evident only to an analytical observer. The actor in a large-scale, urban setting is certainly aware, however, of the many superficial, impersonal relationships that are necessary parts of life, in addition to the intense, highly personal ones. Individuals operate in both large- and small-scale spheres.

Others have expressed the notion of an inverse relationship between the intensity and extensiveness of social relationships since the Wilsons' publication, but it remains an observer's perception of relative scales, not an actor's. Closer to actors' perceptions is the concept of "overload" as applied to extensive interactions. According to it, people who feel overloaded with interactions turn off some of them—as in street behavior—but this does not mean they are incapable of intense, personal relationships (S. Milgram 1970). And so, we must clarify the issue of observers', as opposed to actors', perceptions of scale.

OBSERVERS' AND ACTORS' PERCEPTIONS

All available information on actors' perceptions of scale comes from writings of observers. Therefore, great care must be exercised in deciding if, in a given publication, actors' perceptions are being presented or if observers' perceptions are being presented as those of actors. Theoretical or abstract writings can be a serious problem. The problem becomes less acute when we are dealing with more descriptive and empirical source material, as we do in the following sections.

Observers' perceptions of scale range from small to large, as we have already seen. The next three sections present a series of observations (mostly anthropological) arranged in a progression from small to large perceptions of urban scale, with a discussion of some of the strengths and weaknesses involved in this progression.

Observers' Small-Scale Studies

Some good examples of observers' small-scale research are Elizabeth Bott's *Family and Social Network* (1957), Elliot Liebow's *Tally's Corner* (1967), Oscar Lewis's *Five Families* (1959) and *The Children of Sánchez* (1961), E. E. LeMasters's *Blue-Collar Aristocrats* (1975), Marilyn Salutin's "Stripper Morality" (1973), James Spradley's *You Owe Yourself a Drunk* (1970), James Spradley and Brenda Mann's *The Cocktail Waitress* (1975), and Arlie Hochschild's *The Unexpected Community* (1973).

Bott studied 20 married couples living in London. Her book is a classic in the field of network analysis. Liebow focused on about 25 unskilled black men who congregated in and around a corner carryout store in downtown Washington, D.C., "within walking distance of the White House . . . if anyone cared to walk there, but no one ever does" (1967:17). Lewis's *Five Families*—another classic—is essentially a series of verbal portraits (largely dialogue) of five families in Mexico City. All had emigrated from the village of Tepoztlán (made famous by Redfield as a model of the folk community). In this book, Lewis introduces his concept of the "culture of poverty" which subsequently became highly controversial (see chapter 7). He contributes to the controversy from the outset by including one nouveau riche family among the five. *The Children of Sánchez* is an intensified, elaborated portrait of one of the poor families. The flavor of the dialogues in this, and in Lewis's other books on urban Hispanics, is conveyed by the following incident involving Marta and her brother Manuel, an incident which led to one of the many breakups of the family:

> It was like a man-to-man fight; I kicked and scratched and hit him with whatever I could find; Consuelo was frightened and told us to stop before the neighbors called the police. I got him down on the bed and grabbed his balls and squeezed tight. He couldn't do a thing to me because of the pain. He begged me to let go and told Paula to make me stop, but I wouldn't (p. 296).

The Cocktail Waitress and *Blue-Collar Aristocrats* are studies of behavior in two bars in unidentified midwestern United States cities. *The Cocktail Waitress* emphasizes the sharp division of labor by gender among the employees. The women *serve* the customers (predominantly college students) at tables; the men are bartenders and *manage* the money and business affairs of the bar (Spradley and Mann 1975:31). The picture is of a very traditional pattern of gender roles. LeMasters presents his material from the point of view of a male customer at a bar frequented by well-paid male construction workers, conscious of their high status in their occupation. One theme is male/female relations, including the men's expectations of sexual intercourse in dating—or else their virility would be threatened and the women might gain a dominant role in marriage should dating lead to that. Also emphasized are the men's very hostile and punitive reactions to homosexuality (1975:94–95, 108).

Salutin interviewed women strippers in a Toronto theater. At that time, live burlesque strip shows (which had their heyday in American cities in the 1920s to 1950s) were on the way to near extinction, largely displaced by pornographic movies and videotapes. Nevertheless, the following passage remains pertinent today:

> Burlesque . . . today means the nude dramatization of the sex act, including the orgasm. As such, it is . . . considered an affront to the public definition of morality . . . [and] obscene. . . . [T]he sex act is made a packaged commercial deal, one of a variety . . . offered in a large sex market aimed at exploiting the contingencies in our society that make it hard for some people to get the sex they think they want. . . . [S]ex is made impersonal . . . because it has to be available to large numbers of people at the same time, and it has to offer anonymity to the participants . . . as a salable exchangeable commodity, it confers some semblance of normalcy and stability to the occasion (1973:169–71).

The women strippers bolstered their sense of self-worth by defining their deviant occupation as a useful and harmless service to society (see chapter 5).

Spradley also studies deviants—public drunkards on Skid Road in Seattle. A main theme is that modern, urban United States society is multicultural, but many citizens do not participate in this multicultural society, and so, to create new institutions that make such participation possible, greater understanding and appreciation of the many different subcultures are necessary. To this end, Spradley treats the Seattle Skid Road bums of his sample as such a subculture, one that, like all cultural systems, is perpetuated by constant self-renewal, in this case by the punitive judicial system which, while punishing public drunkenness, also causes it (1970:5). "Skid Row," the more familiar term for an urban area frequented by destitute addicts, is derived from the original Skid Road of Seattle.

Hochschild writes about 43 old people who lived in an apartment house in the San Francisco Bay area. Unexpectedly, she found them neither lonely nor isolated, but rather living with each other in sibling-like relationships that they had established. Like Spradley, Hochschild sees the behavior and status of the people she studied as a result of societywide conditions.

> Removed from the economy, the old have been cast out of the social networks that revolve around work. Lacking work, they are pushed down the social ladder. Being poor, they have fewer social ties. . . . The social life of Merrill Court residents . . . is an exception to the general link between social class and isolation (1973:138).

In every one of these studies, the authors concentrate their attention on a very small domain of social life: a married couple, a nuclear family, a theater, a bar, a corner store, a street (and adjacent jail), an apartment house. In every case, the authors interpret the data as being microcosmic of conditions in wider or larger societies. But as far as urban anthropology is concerned, these are all studies in a city, not of a city. All of the studies are disconnected from the specific urban environments in which the actors live, and only rarely are we able to see any actors' concerns or perceptions that extend beyond the settings the observers chose. This lack does not mean that the actors do not have wider concerns. These are small-scale studies from the observers' perspectives, regardless of the observers' assertions that their data have wider implications.

Observers' Large-Scale Studies

As observers' perspectives become larger in scale, they tend to lose their microintensity. However, the next four examples illustrate that this situation is not always or necessarily the case.

The first is Valdo Pons's 1969 book about Kisangani, Zaire (then Stanleyville, Belgian Congo). Pons uses a multiphased survey to identify various concentrations of the 15 tribal groups living in the city. He finds a general pattern of significant concentrations in small neighborhoods but overall heterogeneity. Absolute majorities of particular groups in any survey area are rare (Pons 1969:67). After a general random survey, Pons focuses his analysis on four so-called neighborhoods (population range: 25 hundred to 48 hundred) and demonstrates highly varied cultural patterns in them (pp. 108–22). He then focuses as a participant observer on the 70 households of "Avenue 21." His analysis is a remarkable presentation of the adaptations of members of a mobile population to each other under circumstances where anonymity and privacy are difficult to maintain. Constant readjustments in relationships combine with stable networks of kin, tribal "brotherhood," and proximity of residence.

Pons succeeds in showing the intense small-scale activities of the people he studies in the wider tribal-aggregate context of the city in which they live. His own perception of scale extends beyond the micro in a way that links his subjects directly to their urban environment.

The second case achieves a similar end but without using surveys. Irwin Press, in *The City as Context: Urbanism and Constraints in Seville* (1979), focuses on a tenement (*corral de vecinos*—corral of neighbors) of 22 apartments—half of them one-room units. Residents of 15 "have kin within easy shouting distance," says Press (p. 63), and he provides meticulously detailed personal characteristics of all the inhabitants—small-scale analysis at its maximum. However, the small-scale perspective is not all there is. Going beyond it, Press says that when he did his study in 1970, there were about two thousand *corrales de vecinos* in Seville, housing about one-quarter of the city's population, and he concludes that the vast majority of Seville's low-salaried blue- and white-collar workers (60–70 percent of its population) were born and raised in *corrales de vecinos*. Moreover, he suggests that the very similar *vecindades* of Mexico City (see Oscar Lewis's *Five Families*) are probably derived, historically, from Spanish prototypes like the present Seville *corrales* (Press 1979:46–47). In other words, he expands the scale of his sample historically and demographically. Press considers other types of housing, as well, and relates the lives of his informants to several large-scale dimensions of the city: neighborhood, sex roles, economics, and government. Seville is presented as a set of contexts for the *corral*, and the city is often placed in the context of Spanish culture generally.

Outside the *corral* (usually a one- or two-story arrangement of rooms around a patio, with one entrance and various shared amenities), the men hang out in one of the many neighborhood bars—each with its special characteristics—where they

> can drink on credit, tell dirty jokes, share gossip, and ogle the girls who pass. Here ... [they] can buy rubbers from latex salesmen (it is embarrassing to ask for them at a pharmacy with women around) and numbers from illegal lottery vendors. For the self-employed laborer or craftsman ... the bar is an office or answering service. Few corrals have phones. Here in the bar is a telephone whose number may be engraved on a personal business card. The bartender will take messages for a loyal customer. Here one's friends can find him when they know of work or need it themselves. The bar is a business office, labor exchange, and social club (Press 1979:87).

This small-scale, intensive, and realistic texture is related in multiple ways to the whole city and the society, and it is anthropology of the city.

The third example is Ronald Dore's *City Life in Japan: A Study of a Tokyo Ward* (1958). The book is about Shitayama-cho, a neighborhood near the division between the Shitamachi and Yamanote sections of old Tokyo. Shitayama-cho escaped the 1923 earthquake fires and the 1945 American fire bombings, so that it has continuities with the past but is certainly not a relic of the past. Dore notes the traditional stereotypes of Shitamachi men (hot-tempered but warm-hearted, sensual, and extravagant—not unlike Cairo's stereotypical *baladi* men) compared with Yamanote men, supposedly more prudent, rational, and inhibited (1958:12). Shitayama-cho is more like Shitamachi than Yamanote and had in 1951 about 310 households sheltering some 12 hundred people. Physically shabby, its streets are very active socially with a "general appearance of neighborly friendliness," and yet the inhabitants are quite heterogeneous in origin, occupation, and education (p. 18). Shitayama-cho seems to be the arena for various support systems without the self-conscious ethnic or social class identities that so often are concomitant with urban support systems. Dore links these and other microobservations with certain types of cultural diversity in Tokyo. He compares household, occupational, and educational statistics for the ward with those for the city as a whole and puts familial and religious patterns into the context of Japanese culture in general.

Ruben Reina's *Paraná: Social Boundaries in an Argentine City* (1973) is the fourth example of a study of a city which combines small- and large-scale perspectives. The book provides a large-scale perspective particularly of the Argentine social-class system plus case studies of neighborhoods and quotations from individuals, sometimes suggestive of Pons, Press, and Dore.

In 1960, Paraná had a population of about 110 thousand. Like many Latin American cities, it is laid out grid-fashion, with a central plaza that is the city's ceremonial and symbolic hub and the upper-class residential area. Residential areas of the other five social classes radiate outward from the plaza in roughly concentric fashion (p. 49). The major theme in Reina's portrait of the city is the dominance of social class and social-class boundaries in Paraná, compounded by the diverse European origins of the people. Reina says there is a strong element of competitiveness and social atomism beyond the immediate family that tends to reduce the potential supportiveness of neighborhoods and clubs (pp. 129–30, 168). Social classes, clearly perceived and symbolized in many ways, provide cohesiveness at some levels but divide people from one another at others.

Paraná's cemetery provides a dramatic, palpable image of its social structure:

When . . . Paraná became a city, the cemetery was for . . . Roman Catholics; it was administered by the Church. The death of the wife of a North American . . . precipitated the issue of non-Catholic burials. The municipal record shows . . . a petition in 1878 by a Protestant group . . . applying for land to establish their own cemetery. This request was denied, but eventually Protestant burials in the main cemetery were allowed. Later one of the Jewish associations purchased a piece of land adjacent to the cemetery over which the Sephardic and the Ashkenazic Jews now share control. The Protestants now use the city cemetery, preferring burial in the ground rather than in niches. In 1891 the public cemetery was reorganized: avenues and streets were constructed according to the gridiron pattern. Along the avenues the wealthy families purchased land and built family mausoleums. Names of the streets and avenues were socially significant, like street names in the city. The title records show a division of the cemetery land into two types: the *primera categoria* for mausoleums, and the *segunda categoria* for popular burials in the ground. . . . Thus each family could purchase a plot according to its social status within this dualistic system. Today, there are three types of burials corresponding roughly to the three classes: in the ground, in *nichos* (niches) the size of a casket, either in the walls of the cemetery or in the mausoleums of ethnic, religious, professional, or labor organizations; and finally, in the private mausoleums (p. 219).

Next in our progression of observers' small- to large-scale perspectives are John Gulick's *Tripoli: A Modern Arab City* (1967b) and Janet Abu-Lughod's

Cairo: 1001 Years of the City Victorious (1971). In both, the authors' macro-perspectives encompass historical, national, and international phenomena, and small-scale factors are relatively minimized.

The main road from Beirut leading into the center of Tripoli passes around the statue of a man who faces south, away from Tripoli and toward Beirut. The reason given the author was that the man's political ambitions drew him away from Tripoli (where he was the political boss for many years) and toward the national culture of Lebanon centralized in the primate city of Beirut. The relative national status of Tripoli is thus epitomized. A provincial capital, its history has always reflected its vulnerability or responsiveness to events of far wider geopolitical scope. Such events included the Crusaders' destruction of the earlier city and subsequent rebuilding; the Egyptian Mamluks' repe-tition of the procedure; the city's deterioration under the Ottoman Turks; and the boom attending the closing of the Iraq Petroleum Company's Haifa ter-minal during the 1948 Arab-Israeli war and its relocation in Tripoli. All such events have drastically affected the everyday lives of Tripolitans, although there is little direct documentation of these effects. This discussion very briefly summarizes an external macroview of this particular city. *Tripoli* extends this view to internal macroviews: the institutions formed by the inhabitants, ethnic identities of residential quarters, diurnal variations in public use of space, and national and local news media perspectives on the city. Nevertheless, one reviewer, an economist, characterized the book as a travelogue because he felt it only described. Another reviewer, an anthropologist, said that it would have been "better anthropology" had it been presented from a smaller-scale point of view. These criticisms illustrate fundamental dilemmas in this type of re-search. The perspective is from the observer's side, but it does not satisfy all observers.

Abu-Lughod's study of Cairo combines census-tract analysis, historical re-construction, and the author's intensive personal knowledge of the city. Her magnum opus is a history of Cairo's morphology, culminating in her division of the present city into 13 "communities," or subcities. In the 1947 Census of Egypt, Cairo was divided into over 200 census tracts, some of which appeared to reflect long-standing community awareness and identity. The census pro-vided information on age/sex distributions, educational attainments, popula-tion densities, and religious identities. Similar information is included in the 1940 Census of Chicago which had been analyzed to reveal the existence of 75 "communities" (Wirth and Bernert 1949). Using the Chicago fact book as a model, Abu-Lughod constructed one for Cairo; from it she derived the 13 subcities. Her book is, for the most part, a chronology of verbal overlays of the various parts of Cairo as they have evolved through the centuries. By the end of the nineteenth century, Cairo consisted of two distinct physical com-munities, separated by barriers far wider than the single street that marked their borders.

To the east lay the native city, still essentially pre-industrial in technology, social structure, and way of life; to the west lay the "colonial" city with its steam-powered techniques, its faster pace and wheeled traffic, and its Eu-ropean identification. To the east lay the labyrinth street pattern of yet unpaved *harat* [lanes] and *durub* [cul-de-sacs], although by then the gates had been dismantled and two new thoroughfares pierced the shade; to the west were broad straight streets of macadam flanked by wide walks and setbacks, militantly crossing one another at rigid right angles or converging here and there in *rondpoint* or *maydan*. . . . Neither parks nor street trees relieved the sand and mud tones of the medieval city; yet the city to the west was elaborately adorned with French formal gardens, strips of decorative flower beds, or artificially shaped trees (Abu-Lughod 1971:98).

Now, almost a century after the time Abu-Lughod describes, there have been many changes, but equivalent contrasts can still be made, even to the border (Port Said Street) whose horrendous traffic is a barrier indeed. However, Cairo was not then, and is not now, simply divided into two parts as far as sociocultural characteristics (seen from a macro, aggregate perspective) are concerned. Abu-Lughod's 13 subcities subdivide Eastern, medieval Cairo and Western, modern Cairo, and, besides, extend beyond them. From these subcities, Abu-Lughod abstracts four life-styles that she says predominate in various sectors of the city. These, and the estimated percentage of the 1960 population of the city entailed in each case, are rural (14 percent), traditional urban (otherwise known as *baladi*—30 percent), mixed traditional and modern urban (40 percent), and modern urban (16 percent) (p. 175).

These images are based on aggregate statistics and immediate observations, but not on small-scale, intensive, or systematic interpersonal fieldwork. In addition to being a large-scale macrostudy, Abu-Lughod's work is also oriented largely in terms of the observer's values, although *baladi* is definitely an Egyptian folk stereotype. Whether hers would be a better study if it included microperspectives is really a moot question. One of its many values is in providing a chronological and spatial context into which small-scale studies can be fitted and seen as segments of the heterogeneous city.

Observers' Ultimate Large-Scale Studies

Social class is an element in city life that typically involves social bridges between a city and its hinterland, between one city and another, between cities and their national cultures, and between cities of different nations. The existence of such bridges is perhaps most obvious among upper-class people— small local elites who have personal ties beyond the immediate locality. If the observer's attention focuses on specific local elites and their extensive linkages, a range of actors' scales can be comprehended by the observer's macroperspective. However, we now move from observers' macroscale studies of cities, in which microscale insights are to some extent accommodated, to observers' macroscale studies of cities in regional contexts. In the examples of the latter which we now review, microscale perspectives are even more attenuated.

Paul English, a geographer, wrote *City and Village in Iran* (1966) on the Iranian city of Kirman and its hinterland. Kirman, like most other Middle Eastern cities, is set in an oasis surrounded by deserts. With a population over 60 thousand in the 1960s, Kirman is the largest settlement in a catchment basin which measures roughly 50 miles from north to south and from west to east. Water from the surrounding mountains (derived from winter rains) flows toward the city from various directions in subterranean aqueducts (*qanats*). Small towns and hamlets, mainly on or near mountain slopes, constitute Kirman's hinterland population.

Kirman city is an administrative and economic center serving its hinterland with schools, clinics, markets, and the like. Hinterland farmers and herders raise food crops and, in particular, very high-quality wool used in weaving Kirmani Persian carpets. Carpet weaving is a major occupation in the Kirman basin, linking the local area with national Iranian and foreign markets.

English's point is that residents of the city dominate the three major realms of the local economy: agriculture, animal husbandry, and weaving:

In each sphere, the upper class of [the] city retains ownership of the production factors. Thus, in agriculture, land and water are principally owned by large landowners (*arbabi*); in animal husbandry the sheep and goats are owned by urban residents; and in weaving the large flocks, dye-houses, and looms are owned by carpet merchants. These elements are rented by members of the elite to lesser individuals—farmers, weavers, and shepherds—who, in return for their labor, receive a subsistence wage (p. 88).

Thus, the Kirman basin, not just Kirman city, is a single socioeconomic system. Anthony Leeds would see the whole basin as a single urban area, its villages and grazing areas being rural only in the sense of being "specialties of an urban society characterized by being inherently . . . 'space-linked' " (1980:7). Leeds thinks all cities must be analyzed in such larger contexts—that the observer's perception must be a large-scale one. He is correct that the study of the humanity of cities must refine its techniques and concepts for this dimension of research, but it would be premature to forsake small-scale perspectives in doing so.

Kirman is smaller than many other Middle Eastern cities with larger, more complicated hinterlands. Nevertheless, the great value of this study is in demonstrating very clearly that certain aspects of city life cannot be understood unless they, and the city itself, are seen in an even larger scale context.

Michael Bonine, Paul English's student, studied Yazd, Iran (population about 100 thousand) from 1969 to 1971. The Yazd hinterland is similar to Kirman's, but carpet weaving is not so important. Bonine arranges the satellite settlements (mostly villages) into four levels, representing a hierarchy of "functions" (social and commercial services) available in each one. The four levels of village supply from 1 to 44 functions; there are also five towns, one of which has 144 functions and four of which have 72 to 93; and Yazd City has 326 (Bonine 1979:144). Bonine interviewed villagers in the Yazd urban region to find out how many and what kinds of goods and services they purchased in their own village, other villages, the towns, Yazd, or outside the region. His major purpose was to apply and test Christaller's Central Place Theory (1966) which postulates that contiguous settlements will be located in a size hierarchy according to strictly rationalistic economic and technical principles—essentially a mechanistic, dehumanized model based on European data. Like Kirman, Yazd is certainly the dominant, primary center of its region, but the reasons include a network of factors that are not purely economic: kinship ties, religious interests, and the villagers' frequent perception of Yazd "as a retailing center with better goods, more honest shopkeepers and superior services while other settlements often were not considered as alternatives" (Bonine 1979:148). The inhabitants of its satellite settlements affect Yazd's nature as a city, and Yazd affects life in them. That villagers often have more trustworthy relationships with merchants in the city than in their own villages, which Bonine documents, contributes to the idea of the humanity of cities.

The last urban region we consider is Cuzco, Peru, and its hinterland (van den Berghe and Primov 1977). Cuzco was the capital of the Inca empire, the largest American Indian political entity to be conquered by the Spaniards or any other European invaders of America. Transportation and long-distance communication in the Inca empire was by means of the human body exclusively. While this situation is no longer true, getting to Cuzco is still an accomplishment. Cuzco is linked to the coast, but not to Lima, by railroad. Air travel is important but dangerous, and (in 1973):

> The shortest automobile road takes the daring driver through a spectacular but tortuous one-thousand-odd kilometers of loose gravel over a half-a-dozen mountain passes of over four thousand meters. Barring mishaps, this can be negotiated in three nerve-jarring days. A somewhat more reliable but much longer road takes one through six hundred kilometers of loose gravel and one thousand kilometers of potholed tar, and a third of intermediate length is often closed during the rainy season (pp. 17–18).

Once arrived, by whatever means, one finds a city that, in 1972, had about 121 thousand people, in a province of 142 thousand, in a department of 713 thousand—all named Cuzco. The department is very large and includes the full range of altitudes in Peru. Pierre van den Berghe and George Primov's analysis is concerned with city and province. In this high, remote Andean setting, a complex system of social inequality operates, a system with roots in the Spanish conquest and its aftermath and in the society of modern Peru. Once again, we have a case of the dominance of a city center over its hinterland. Like Yazd and Kirman, Cuzco is a primate city within its region but a minor city compared to the national capital (Tehran and Lima, respectively). Between 1961 and 1972, Cuzco's population increased over 50 percent, a result of long-term migration of people from other parts of Cuzco Department. In addition, thousands of people constantly move back and forth within the department, an important element in the ethnicity of inequality that is said to characterize the region (p. 22).

Spanish colonial rule in Peru, although devastating, did, in the Cuzco area, preserve portions of the Indian elite who interbred with the Spaniards, resulting in a traditional *mestizo* elite, and it preserved the Quechua language which continues to be spoken today (p. 49). Indians and Quechua speakers are numerically predominant in the villages of Cuzco province, but upper-class *mestizos* are politically dominant in the city and, through the hierarchical network of local oligarchies that ramify throughout the area, in the province as well. Van den Berghe and Primov trace the history of this system and how it works at present—for example, in constantly drawing ambitious people to the city. While describing the formal system, with its ceremonial conspicuousness of the elite on festive occasions, they also emphasize the operation of informal networks. Patron-client relationships, formalized by ritual kinship (*compadrazgo*), are key mechanisms in establishing and maintaining dominant and dependent ties across ethnic and class lines (p. 89). A study of the city of Cuzco alone would show only an arbitrarily selected part of this system at work.

Although the microscale observer's perspective is minimized in the works of English, Bonine, and van den Berghe and Primov, it is not altogether absent from them. All four of these observers lived for extended periods in their respective cities and are, at the very least, sensitive to, and appreciative of, the small-scale realities of their inhabitants.

Here we come to the limit of discernible small-scale concerns in the studies available to us, and now we must attend to some contradictory voices among students of cities. These voices are heard relatively recently. For example, in 1975, the journal *Urban Anthropology* devoted one of its numbers to a symposium, "The City-as-Context." Scarcely five years later, the annual proceedings of the Southern Anthropological Society was entitled *Cities in a Larger Context* (Collins 1980). Papers in the former volume are clearly founded on small-scale insights, but those in the latter do not appear to be. The focus in the 1975 volume is on people living in cities. The focus in the 1980 volume is on cities themselves as units of analysis, and this publication illustrates one of the contradictory voices we must consider. Robert L. Blakely, editor of the monograph series to which it belongs, sets the tone in his preface, saying that urban anthropologists

> are beginning . . . to explore the hierarchical linkages that unite the seemingly disparate components of the city, that bind cities to outlying communities, and, increasingly, to the international arena . . . cities are essential cogs in an evolving, worldwide network [Collins 1980: (vii)].

In the specific case of Memphis, Tenn., Thomas W. Collins says:

> Increasingly, more decisions that dictate local policy are made outside the city and region. . . . [M]uch of the legislation, in addition to the federal programs to eliminate poverty, created a new local bureaucracy . . . financed with federal funds. This bureaucracy has provided new access to white-collar jobs for blacks, thus creating a new and viable black middle class with political power and ways of living . . . whose politics are relatively conservative (1980:3).

The problem here is that Collins, instead of elaborating on microdimensions of the new black middle class, explains how Memphis "had no impact" on the decision of the Radio Corporation of America to move its Memphis plant to Taiwan. He concludes that "the city is part of a wider system, in which it has had very little success in bargaining with multinational corporations, international labor organizations, the federal government, or even its state government" (p. 4). Conceptually, he seems to conceive of the city as if it were a person (which it demonstrably is not). Whatever else this conception may be, it is a rationalization of observers' perceptions of large scale in which small-scale, everyday concerns of the inhabitants have very low priority.

We are now confronted by a point of view some anthropological observers hold in which ignoring or neglecting small-scale perceptions can be easily accomplished and conveniently justified. It is true that an *exclusively* microurban perspective (often derived from the traditional anthropological concentration on small, supposedly isolated, "primitive" cultures) can result in a misleading emphasis on groups of people who are not representative of most city dwellers and in an unrealistic lack of attention to the influence of external controls on those people (Jones 1978:20). On the other hand, detailed microperspectives are absolutely essential to an adequate understanding of the humanity of cities. The point is that they must be placed in wider, large-scale perspectives. The full range of perspectives must be taken into account; the small-scale ones must not now be replaced by something else simply because some anthropologists have in the past accepted them uncritically as representing the only truth that matters. Several of the books already discussed in this chapter demonstrate that taking a wide range of scale perspectives into account is a wholly achievable research goal.

The small-scale observer's perspective is important not only because it is the predominant anthropological perspective that has often yielded insights into the human condition that are beyond the capability of survey research. It is important also because many actors in cities live in awareness of predominantly small-scale perceptions. To be sure, this can make them unwittingly, uncaringly, or resignedly dominated and exploited by large-scale power structures. But the reality of these actors' lives is that they must adapt themselves as best they can to the conditions in which they find themselves, regardless of what ideological, moral, or aesthetic reactions observers may have to those conditions.

ACTORS' SCALES

And so we come to actors' perceptions of scale. Since our knowledge of this subject comes only through observers, it is necessary to differentiate between two modalities of actor's scale. An actor's "active scale" is the extent of his or her interactional networks, the networks in which the individual's actions and characteristics affect everyday life interactions and concerns. An actor's "receptive scale" is the extent of the sociocultural phenomena that affect his or her life, phenomena whose influences the actor *receives from the larger society.* Most of our information indicates that most actors' active scales are small and that few actors perceive their receptive scales at all, or to any great extent. Of course, the observer's recognition of the full range of scales yields awareness of actors' receptive scales, as most of the previous discussion of observers' macroscale perceptions has shown. This discussion has also suggested that many observers, because they are especially interested in actors' receptive, large scales, may be inclined to neglect their active scales. We have seen that these observers' expressions of concern run counter to the anthropological small-scale tradition. Inadvertently, their points of view also coincide with the assumptions of the bipolar model that city dwellers' active scales are all large scale. We need, therefore, to appreciate the importance of the small active scale of many city dwellers, at the same time not ignoring the reality of their larger receptive scales.

William Michelson discusses what he calls the "ego-centered point of view" of many city dwellers:

City planners see cities as entities. Airline pilots are familiar with their shapes. Politicians have to know all areas of cities and how they add up. But most people have no need for such a comprehensive view. . . . [Peter] Orleans . . . demonstrated that residents from different areas of Los Angeles have mutually exclusive images of the city. Only residents of Westwood, where the University of California at Los Angeles is located, have a reasonably comprehensive image of the metropolitan area. . . . An ego-centered point of view does not ignore . . . that people operate in cities as members of groups that have well-defined spatial needs of their own. Nor does it suggest that the macroscopic environment is any less important. All it suggests is that the environment must be conceptualized in terms that are meaningful to the smallest unit that wanders throughout all levels—the individual (1976:44–47).

Elizabeth Colson, using African materials, asserts that as individuals are faced with increasing scale, they limit their active scale by excluding many other individuals with whom they are in contact from any but the most superficial interaction. Colson's idea seems to be identical with Milgram's overload concept and, indeed, she uses the word "overload" in her discussion (1978:155). The idea is that individuals strive to keep their personal active scale small to be able to cope with the increasing number of people who can make demands on them. It is not a matter of callousness or dehumanization but, rather, of necessity. Colson refers to two authors on cities who

> assume a process of reaching out towards others which results in incorporation of the many now available within one's social world. I am arguing rather that people seek to maintain a fundamental status quo of involvement in the face of increasing demands upon their attention which threaten to extinguish their ability to interact in any fashion with sheer exhaustion (p. 151).

If one accepts Colson's view, and there is a large amount of evidence to support it, one realizes that the bipolar moralistic assumptions about the scale of urban life are derived from observers' perspectives, not from actors' perceived experiences.

As discouraging as it may be to politically concerned persons like Jones, Mariotti, and Magubane, poor people in general seem to be "unradicalized." Joan Nelson (1969) cites the extensive literature on squatter settlements in many countries to this effect, and says:

> Realism may not only trim targets but may also shape values. [S. Michael] Miller and [Frank] Reisman find striving for security and stability to be a central element in the basic values and behavior of regularly employed manual workers in the United States. "Getting by rather than getting ahead . . . is likely to be dominant." Those who aspire to middle class status are viewed as deviants. Herbert Gans describes working class Italians in Boston's West End in similar terms. He stresses the *high value placed on sociability, generosity, a helping hand for relatives and neighbors, the comparatively light emphasis on career progress or material accumulation beyond accepted standards of comfort and security* (1969:53; emphasis added).

The emphasized part of this quotation epitomizes small active actors' scales. Again, as in the Colson/Milgram idea of overload, a small active actor's scale is seen *as a necessity* for most people. As such, it must remain a major interest in research on the lives of urban people.

From the previous discussion, it should be clear why an actor or group of actors may live on a small active scale *and* a large receptive scale simultaneously. For example, squatters in Third World cities live on very small active scales, but the conditions that attract them to the cities are frequently attributable to policies of multinational corporations. One of the obvious ambiguities in the concept of scale lies in lack of clarity concerning people's awareness of their receptive scales and, given some awareness, their interest in influencing, or their ability to influence, agents of those scales. Most of the literature depicts people as either unaware of, or passive toward, their receptive scales.

The Range of Actors' Scales

Situations in which both active and receptive scales are extremely small are limited to the cultures of some nonliterate tribal groups, the traditional specialty of some anthropologists. Some of the Australian aboriginal tribes, before European contacts affected them, were cases in point: actors' lives limited to small, isolated, and completely self-sufficient societies. There are no such groups in modern cities. Nevertheless, one can discern a range of actors' scales in cities, keeping in mind the prevailing tendency for active scales to be small.

Seattle's Skid Road tramps, mentioned earlier, live on a small active scale; their receptive scale consists of courts and jails. Comparable to them are people in the Hornsey section of North Islington, London, who are trapped in deteriorated housing; are largely unskilled, unemployed, and unemployable; and are not even able to get onto public housing lists because they cannot pay their arrears (Rowland 1973:41). In a sample of two blocks, Jon Rowland found that a third of the residents had lived in the area for more than 20 years, lacking initiative to leave because of poor work and housing opportunities elsewhere and low rents where they were. A large proportion of them had been born in the area or had moved to it from within a one-mile radius (p. 49). Rowland sees these people as having been alienated by automation and bureaucratization (elements of large receptive scale), but nevertheless extremely constricted in their lives. He characterizes the area as a noncommunity, suggesting that there are not even support systems despite the smallness of active scale. Walter Firey (1968:309–12) describes the rooming-house inhabitants of Boston's South End in the 1940s as having no support systems and being precariously employed in low-skilled, local jobs. Again, here is an example of very restricted active scale owing, Firey hypothesizes, to the inability of the American middle-class family system to accommodate older single and childless members. Consequently, such people become isolates and congregate in certain urban areas such as the South End.

In New York City in the 1960s, about 400 tenements or former hotels had been converted into residences for poor, unattached people—single room occupants (SROs). According to Joan Shapiro (1971:15), about 30 thousand people are (or were) housed in these buildings. Their ties to family are tenuous; there are no voluntary organizations or clubs. Alcoholics, addicts, prostitutes, petty criminals, the mentally ill, chronically ill, and elderly, they are aware of the extremely negative attitudes of other people and institutions toward them, which reinforces their isolation. Yet Shapiro found a "complex and profoundly social community" among them (p. 23). The active scale of these people is apparently limited to the inhabitants of single buildings; their receptive scale comprises the welfare system whose checks establish a mutual dependency between the tenants and the SRO managers (p. 41).

Numerically, the people Spradley, Firey, Rowland, and Shapiro describe are few; many observers would regard them as pathological and certainly not typical city dwellers (ironically, their isolation and alienation *do* fit the bipolar model's urban stereotype!). However, they aptly illustrate maximally restricted active scale under real life conditions.

Now consider small scale among more normal, typical city dwellers. A quotation from Great Britain dramatizes the disparity that can occur between an observer's and an actor's perceptions of the actor's reality:

Norman Dennis [1970] . . . compares two different perceptions of the same Sunderland "slum," first of a professional, and then of a local: Within the first frame of reference, Millfield is a collection of shabby, mean and dreary houses, derelict back lanes, shoddy-fronted shops and broken pavements, the whole unsightly mess mercifully ill-lit. Within the second frame of reference, that, say, of a sixty-year-old woman who lives there, the same area may convey messages of quite another kind. . . . Millfield for her is Bob Smith's, which she thinks (probably correctly) is the best butcher's in town; George McKeith's wet-fish shop and Peary's fried-fish shop . . . Maw's hot pies and peas prepared on the premises; the Willow Pond public house, in which her favorite nephew organizes the darts and dominoes team; the Salvation Army band in a nearby street every Sunday and waking her with carols on Christmas morning; her special claim to attention is the grocer's because her niece worked there for several years; the spacious cottage in which she was born and brought up, which she now owns, has improved and which has not in her memory had defects which have caused her or her neighbors discernible inconvenience (but which has some damp patches which make it classifiable as a "slum dwelling"); the short road to the cemetery where she cares for the graves of her mother, father, and brother; her sister's cottage across the road—she knows that every weekday at 12:30 a hot dinner will be ready for her when she comes from work; the bus route which will take her to the town centre in a few minutes (Taylor 1973:226).

Consistent with this vivid microcosm are William Hampton's findings in Sheffield, England, where 85 percent of those questioned said that they had a named, identifiable "home area" in the city; three-quarters said that their home area consisted of only a few streets surrounding their address; and only 1 percent gave the whole city as their "home area." As many as 70 percent of people living in an area fewer than 5 years identified it as a home area, while 91 percent of those living in an area 10 to 20 years, or born there, identified it as a home area (1970:100–6). These are examples of rooted, active small scales.

So, too, are several other, diverse examples. In Baghdad, Iraq, in the midtwentieth century, the Arabic language was spoken in "three markedly different dialects, each with its own syntactic and lexical peculiarities," by Muslims, Jews, and Christians (Blanc 1964:9). To the extent that members of these sects were residentially segregated, these dialects—persistent over time—were characteristic of different parts of the city. And inhabitants of the West End of Boston, before its destruction in the 1950s, had a highly intense feeling of local identity, familiarity, and comfort. Many of them felt uncomfortable elsewhere, even in other parts of Boston itself, such as the downtown shopping district, easy walking distance from the West End (Fried et al. 1973:102–3). A study of men convicted of household burglaries in Oklahoma City reveals that familiarity with the areas in which their targets were located—in turn related to the areas in which they lived—was an extremely important factor in their decisions as to what houses to burglarize. Black convicts, having been more restricted in their own residential areas than white convicts, were correspondingly more concentrated in their selection of areas to burglarize (Carter and Hill 1979:60).

Most of the teenaged boys Willmott studied in Bethnal Green, East London, spent their working and leisure time primarily in Bethnal Green or the East End, but there were exceptional individuals who illustrate how large-scale awareness and participation can come about. A quarter of the members of the sample had their own motorized transportation, and others had easy access to subway trains and buses. Quite a few of the boys were familiar with the City, Soho, or the West End (the parts of London most familiar to foreign visitors). Some referred to visiting the West End as an exploration; others said they had never been there (1969:25). A minority of the boys worked in nonmanual jobs in the City or Central London, often for large organizations, and their active scale was clearly enlarging in comparison to the majority of their peers working in various manual jobs in Bethnal Green or elsewhere in the East End (p. 109).

Is a small active scale more typical of poor, working-class, and minimally educated city dwellers than it is of better-educated ones with higher status? Better educated people may be inclined to assume some sort of correspondence between smallness of scale and lowliness of status. The evidence is not conclusive. Smallness of scale does occur among some higher status people. Abner Cohen, writing on upper-class people who dominate the financial system in that part of London called "the City," provides a striking example:

> [M]illions of pounds worth of business is conducted daily in the City without the use of written documents, mainly verbally in face-to-face conversations or through the telephone. This is said to be technically necessary if business is to flow. But as the risks involved are formidable, the business is confined to a limited number of people who trust one another. Such a high degree of trust can arise only among men who know one another, whose values are similar, who speak the same language in the same accent, respect the same norms and are involved in a network of primary relationships that are governed by the same values and the same patterns of symbolic behavior (1974:99).

Cohen describes an "old-boy network" rooted in small-scale exclusive schooling and reinforced by friendship and kinship ties.

Possibly many highly educated, high-achievement-oriented people do not live in environments any larger in active scale than working-class ethnics, such as the Italian-Americans whose neighborhood life in New York City is described as extremely parochial (Glazer and Moynihan 1970:186–90). On the other hand, one of the defining characteristics of cities is the presence in them of high-status people who have influence and connections beyond the cities themselves. Such persons' active scales are large. Clearly, there is variation in the size of people's active scales, although for the most part their size is small. It seems clear, also, that actors' receptive scales differ in size as does their awareness of their receptive scales.

SCALES AND SOCIOCULTURAL CHANGE

Godfrey and Monica Wilson postulated that when actors' active social scales expand, they decrease in intensity. We have challenged this postulation in a number of ways, including the citation of Colson's and Milgram's observations that people tend to keep the size and intensity of their active scales constant by minimizing their relationships with the increasing numbers of strangers with whom they have contact. In his book on high-density life in American cities, Mark Baldassare criticizes Milgram's idea that people turn off superficial encounters randomly. Rather, he says, it is a matter of "specialized withdrawal" from contacts less valued than others (1979:165–66).

Several observers, among them Egon Mayer, note another type of reaction to increasing scale because of macrocosmic change. In his study of Boro Park, Brooklyn's Orthodox Jewish community, Mayer says:

[T]he post-modern period has been described by some leading contemporary theorists as one marked by the growing autonomy of major social institutions, placing them not only beyond moral constraints that develop out of a shared value system, but also beyond direct manipulation by individuals (1979:16).

Individuals tend to feel increasingly helpless in the face of their receptive, macrocosmic scales and to react by increasing the privatism of their personal lives and intensifying their active small-group scales, as in the case of Boro Park. Howard Stein and Robert Hill (1977:116–19) note a similar reaction in the "white ethnic" retrenchment movement of the 1960s and 1970s. These reactions involve feelings of alienation from large-scale phenomena, and of anomie; this is, of course, consistent with the bipolar model, but the intensification of small active scales in cities is contrary to the model.

If some city dwellers are inclined to retreat from the realities of their receptive scales, others are not. Manuel Castells has written at length about urban social movements in the past and since the 1950s. Castells studied the latter himself, and the movements involved the *Grands Ensembles* housing projects outside Paris; neighborhood mobilization in San Francisco, with emphasis on gay neighborhood revitalization; squatter settlements in Latin America; and the Citizen Movement in Madrid at the end of the Franco regime. For Castells, the fundamental goal of these movements was "redefinition of urban meaning to emphasize use value and the quality of experience over exchange value and the centralization of management" (1983:309). In our terms, the social movers Castells observed were expanding the scope of their active scales for the precise purpose of "direct manipulation by individuals" (Mayer 1979:16).

CONCLUSION

The evidence does not show unequivocally that, as actors' receptive scales increase (as they have indeed done with increases in rapid communication and transportation), their active scales are made less intense or are diffused or disintegrated. They may indeed be changed, but they are not necessarily diminished in the supportive contexts of life. Two very different examples serve to illustrate this point.

In the 1920s, Ernest Burgess delineated 75 local "community areas" in Chicago. In the 1960s, Albert Hunter used the concept in a restudy to learn the extent to which Chicagoans still perceived their environment in terms of named communities. In the intervening years, single-family dwellings had greatly increased in the suburbs and multiple-family dwellings in the areas of the communities, and racial/ethnic/socioeconomic differentiation had increased in the latter. Hunter characterizes the historical situation as having been one of increasing scale and summarizes what has happened:

[T]he unified conception of community as consisting of residential areas (neighborhoods) surrounding some central focal point (usually shopping) just does not define the varied reality of today's urban areas. The unified, functionally integrated community is lost as some functions increase in their scale—for example, shopping and the labor market—while other functions retain a smaller scale—for example, the neighborhood circle of friends and the local school. . . . [T]he definition of community may be released from its close association with function and people's day-to-day activities and may become a more independent symbolic entity. . . . [I]t is perhaps more accurate to talk about the persistence of "neighborhood" than about the loss of "community." The persistence of symbols used to define community is shown by the fact that 42.3 percent of the entire sample gave the same names used by Burgess. An additional 34.9 percent gave a different name to their areas. . . . This 42.3 percent demonstrates that not only is there persistence in the names of such areas, but these names are part of a shared culture that is fairly widely known (1974:72–77).

Actors in Hunter's sample named areas that varied greatly in size, most areas ranging from 17 to 256 square blocks, but with substantial minorities naming areas smaller than 17 or larger than 256 square blocks. About half the people who named the smallest areas associated them with shopping and worship—these activities increasing in frequency, as would be expected, in the larger areas (p. 107). In addition,

those without children know and define an area very close to home, or a large-scale area encompassing more of the totality of their life space. In contrast, having children or living in areas where families abound tends to pull people out of the home into the surrounding area, but restricts them to a level which encompasses the functions associated with the family and child rearing (p. 109).

Within the context of named community many people live simultaneously at different levels of scale—an example of a general occurrence mentioned at the beginning of this chapter.

The other example is from Agra, India. Agra was, for a while, the capital of the Mughal Empire, and during that time, the Taj Mahal was built on its outskirts. Today its inhabitants include a large group of people called Jatavs who, in 1961, amounted to one-sixth of the city's population (O. M. Lynch 1969:31). Until Indian independence and abolition of the caste system, the Jatavs were one of the lowest, untouchable castes, specializing in the disposal of animal carcasses and leather work. By the end of World War II, the Agra shoe market, dominated by Jatavs, had expanded into all of India and into Iraq, Iran, and Southeast Asia. At the time of Owen Lynch's study, most Jatavs were making shoes in small, familial operations, and some had become wealthy as contractors. With abolition of the caste system, some Jatavs have become prominent politically—"big men" seeking to exert political pressures for better wages, credit, fairer taxes, and so on (p. 61). One result has been that many Jatav neighborhoods now have better public amenities and tend to form voting blocs that have political impact (pp. 118, 127). Ironically, having had a monopoly on shoemaking when they were untouchables, the Jatavs must now compete with others (pp. 210–11), a factor in the large-scale political participation of some of their members. In some respects, the small-scale local community has been affected by these changes, but it is still important.

Lynch describes one neighborhood of about 21 hundred people in great detail. It is divided into ten *thoks*, each with a hereditary headman and a *panchayat* (council of five). Their traditional functions of dispute adjudication and other social controls (inherent in the old caste system) were largely taken out of local control with the system's abolition, and the headman's loss of power has coincided with the increase in power of big men and politicians (pp. 185–86)—all aspects of increased active and receptive scale. At the same time, the *thoks* are still vitally important in local communication and identity maintenance and the administration of revolving loan funds to benefit members (pp. 187–88). The intensity of such small-scale activities appears to remain very high, at the same time that new, large-scale activities are also part of the Jatavs' reality.

Throughout the remainder of this book, we focus on detailed, descriptive studies of life in cities. When necessary, there are reminders about the scale perceptions involved in those studies. In many cases, the major ambiguities in the scale concept are involved (but not necessarily apparent), and one must make allowances for them. These ambiguities lie primarily in confusions between actors' and observers' scales and between actors' active and receptive scales. This chapter points the way toward enabling one to make such allowances, and it does so by making explicit the elements in the ambiguities.

SUGGESTED ADDITIONAL READING

Barth, Fredrik. *Sohar: Culture and Society in an Omani Town.* Baltimore: Johns Hopkins University Press, 1983. This study of a small city in a little-known part of the Middle East is remarkable for its delineation of the city's internal levels of scale and its place in wider levels of scale.

Gulick, John. *The Middle East: An Anthropological Perspective.* Lanham, Md.: University Press of America, 1983; originally published in 1976. Focuses on small-scale everyday life in various large-scale contexts including cities and religious institutions. One chapter is devoted entirely to cities, and urban life is discussed in the other chapters.

Thubron, Colin. *Mirror to Damascus.* London: Heinemann, 1967. This book is an example of a genre that people seriously interested in cities should explore. This description of the city and the authors' personal reaction to it is well-informed but not heavy reading.

Wagenvoord, James. *City Lives.* New York: Holt, Rinehart & Winston, 1976. Includes text and many photographs, by the author, illustrating the varieties of life in New York City, ranging from panoramas to street shots, to close-ups of people.

3
Magnitudes

Charles M. Weiss

Places considered to be cities exhibit enormous differences in population size, from about 20 thousand (or less in many parts of the world) to about 15 million (or more, depending on the most acceptable estimates of the world's largest cities). In this chapter, we examine the largeness of cities as the source of many of the receptive-scale phenomena city dwellers must manage as best they can. Although many of the large-scale phenomena affecting city dwellers originate beyond any particular city (for example, in regional, national, and international arenas), the largeness of cities, in itself, is an inescapable fact of city life. In stronger terms, cities consist of manufactured environments that have impacts on their inhabitants. How successful or unsuccessful are city dwellers in living with those impacts? How and why are they successful or not?

THE PROBLEM OF SIZE

It is difficult to believe that largeness will have the same kinds or intensities of impact in all cities within such a wide range. There is unfortunately no empirical information on the impacts of largeness in cities representing the full range of sizes. Available information is from the very largest cities—the most dramatic cases, undoubtedly—but not necessarily the most typical for city dwellers in general. Even "large size" itself remains a relative concept. For example, Sally Merry (1981:8) refers to Edmonton, Alberta, as a "small city . . . with a population of half a million." Compared to New York, Tokyo, Mexico City, and Calcutta, Edmonton is small. But compared to Greensboro, Durham, or Raleigh, N.C., it is large. If Edmonton is small, are the North Carolina cities therefore not to be considered cities at all? None of their inhabitants or officials, and certainly not the United States Census Bureau, would answer affirmatively. They *are* cities.

What is needed is a typology of cities, based on size and observable impacts of different sizes, from smallest to largest. Creating such a typology would require a complicated program of research projects in which social-class differences, density, and many other cultural variables were taken into account. Such a typology does not now exist.

Typologies like those of Rupert Vance and Nicholas Demerath (1971) and Omer Galle (1963) are based on aggregate, large-scale phenomena, such as distribution of banks, corporations, and their head and branch offices. While connected with small-scale phenomena like individuals' job opportunities, they do not clarify the question of what variables of small, active scale are dependent on maximum magnitudes.

The best we can do is review the impact issue with regard to the largest world cities, bearing in mind that the extent to which we can extrapolate from them to smaller cities is doubtful. A city twice the size of another, for example, cannot be assumed to exert twice the size-related impacts on its inhabitants. Proof of such an assumption would require measurements that do not exist. Think about this matter in connection with some United States cities. With rounded-off populations of their Standard Metropolitan Statistical Areas in 1980, they are:

City	Population
Chicago	6,221,000
Los Angeles	6,039,000
Detroit	3,950,000
Boston	2,688,000
San Francisco	2,649,000
Miami	1,626,000
Atlanta	1,169,000
Kansas City	1,109,000

City	Population
Richmond	632,000
Knoxville	476,000
Fresno	366,000
Madison	323,000

Can we assume that Detroit's largeness impact on its inhabitants is 50 percent greater than the impacts of Boston and San Francisco on theirs; three times greater than Kansas City's; and about ten times Madison's? Can we assume that the largeness impacts of Boston and San Francisco, Atlanta and Kansas City, and Fresno and Madison are, respectively, about the same? Does Chicago have ten times the impact of Richmond? We have no answers, but readers familiar with some of these cities might be able to speculate constructively on what differences size does or does not make in comparing them.

MEGACITIES OF THE WORLD

The six largest metropolitan areas in the world, and their estimated population in millions in the years 1985 and 2000 (United Nations 1985), are:

Metropolitan Area	Population (millions) 1985	2000
Mexico City	18.1	26.3
Tokyo/Yokohama	17.2	17.1
São Paulo	15.9	24.0
New York	15.3	15.5
Calcutta	11.0	16.2
Bombay	10.1	16.0

In the summer of 1986, the author and his wife visited New York, Calcutta, and Bombay within a period of about three weeks; they had in mind the question of the impacts of large size on human beings. Two individuals with little time at their disposal can obviously make only a very limited assessment, but the impressions drawn from their visits illustrates an important issue that no one seems to have evaluated sufficiently.

Midtown Manhattan, east of Broadway, is supposed to be one of the most attractive and elegant inner-city areas in the world. By contrast, Calcutta is notorious as the ultimate sinkhole of urban degradation and decay: over-crowded, poverty-ridden, violent, and filthy. Nevertheless, Fifth Avenue between Central Park and 42nd Street and Jawaharlal Nehru Road (formerly Chowringhee) between the Victoria Memorial and the Raj Bhavan (West Bengal governor's residence) have an important feature in common: on an ordinary working day, the sidewalks are so crowded with pedestrians that it is impossible to walk with the unbroken stride necessary for exercise. In both places, the streets are jammed with traffic, Calcutta's being noisier because of the incessant blaring of horns.

In the southwest corner of Central Park, the broad green expanse of Sheep's Meadow is strewn with sunbathers and picnickers. There are family groups, clusters of friends, couples, and solitary men and women. Bicyclists and skateboarders roll by, and Frisbees whiz through the air. The place is full of people but not overcrowded, and the ambience is benign. Scarcely 20 blocks to the south, at Times Square and 42nd Street, the dirty, broken sidewalks are filled with jostling, hustling, often angry individuals, many of them hawking cheap trinkets or admission to sleazy shows. The ambience is claustrophobic and sinister.

In Calcutta, the huge Maidan, somewhat similar in its expanse and greenery to Central Park, is nearly empty of people except for casual strollers (although sometimes it is the scene of violent political demonstrations). At its north end, the splendor of the governor's residence is surrounded by heavily wooded grounds (fenced with barbed wire) and wide, almost deserted sidewalks. Beyond the Maidan's south end, south of the Victoria Memorial, is the Kalighat, a temple set in a poor, crowded, residential and commercial district. The temple's precincts teem with beggars and worshipers, are cluttered with trash, and, in places, splashed with the blood of sacrificial goats. Here Hindus propitiate the goddess Kali who, among other things, personifies the angry, hateful, and destructive aspects of human nature.

So, in the middle of each of these two great world cities, one can find the overcrowded conditions expected to result from the impact of large size. But one also finds relatively empty spaces. And one encounters environments that may have nothing to do with size at all but are, rather, expressions of human nature filtered through particular cultural screens.

Bombay is built on a peninsula pointing southward (like Manhattan), with the Arabian Sea to the west and a wide bay, separating the city from the mainland of India, to the east. Bombay's docks and shipyards are sheltered in the bay, and Bombay, like New York and Calcutta, is one of the major seaports of the world.

The peninsula was originally an archipelago. The islands were subsequently connected and obliterated by landfills. Like Manhattan's, Bombay's land area has been built on to full capacity, and construction has been extended upward in the form of skyscrapers. They are not so numerous or overwhelming as those of New York, but they occur all over Bombay, differentiating it from Calcutta which has only a few, moderately tall, high-rise buildings.

Structures like skyscrapers which are built beyond human scale, and therefore have a dehumanizing impact on many people, tend to be associated with very large cities, but the association is not consistent. Hong Kong, decidedly smaller than Bombay, has more concentrated and taller high-rises. Shanghai, almost as big as Bombay or Calcutta, has, like Calcutta, few tall buildings. On the other hand, American cities like Atlanta, Denver, and Houston (many times smaller than the world megacities) have impressive clusters of skyscrapers. Many other factors besides city size are involved in this particular aspect of impact.

One phenomenon that does appear to correlate consistently with size is public noise. In New York, Bombay, and Calcutta, alike, a good air-conditioned hotel is a refuge not only from summer heat and humidity, but also from noise. The sealed, double windows shut out the din of traffic, street repairs, and building construction. Noise pollution is undoubtedly one of the negative, unlivable characteristics of large cities, made worse in proportion to size.

A culturally particular kind of noise pollution was troubling many people in Bombay in 1986. A news item in *The Times of India* for 14 August 1986 reported on a drive by voluntary organizations, civic-minded people, and the police for "noise-free festivals." A cosmopolitan city like Bombay, in which festivals are celebrated every few weeks, has a real need for regulating them. Particularly irksome were loudspeakers in public places and unauthorized shrines on pavements, blocking free passage in the streets. One citizen was quoted as saying, "Festivals, religious or otherwise, have become a nightmarish experience."

This reference to Bombay's cosmopolitanism alerts us to another concomitant of large city size: the diversity of cultures and subcultures characterizing all cities, the variety tending to increase as city size increases. Bombay and Calcutta have attracted people from all parts of India and beyond. New York has attracted people from all over the United States and, indeed, the world. The ways in which city dwellers cope with this diversity in their personal, everyday lives are the subject of chapter 7. Here we mention diversity as one impact of largeness. On the crowded streets of midtown Manhattan in August 1986, foreign languages are spoken at least as often as English. In Calcutta and Bombay, Indians frequently speak English to each other; they do so because English is the lingua franca they must use to overcome the barriers separating their many mutually unintelligible languages.

The Bombay news item also reminds us of the religious diversity that typically accompanies very large size. In Bombay are Hindus, Muslims, Jains, Sikhs, and Parsees, each with their own festival cycles. Although the news item did not mention the well-known antagonisms among these religions (a very sensitive subject in India), they presumably were involved in the complaints about public rituals as nuisances.

Finally, in New York, Bombay, and Calcutta—as in all very large cities—the extremes of wealth and poverty are very striking. In all three cities, destitute people sleep in doorways and on sidewalks. As in most Third World cities, clusters of squatters' homes—makeshift structures of used boards and bricks roofed over with matting, burlap, and plastic sheets secured by rocks and old tires—fill otherwise empty lots in Bombay and Calcutta as near to the squatters' workplaces as possible. In Bombay and Manhattan, the very rich live in high-rise apartments, although in Bombay, as used to be the case in Manhattan, some of them still live in great mansions secluded within large grounds and high walls. In Calcutta, as in New York, mansions of the very rich are in the suburbs (Moorhouse 1983:133).

SOME THEMES OF MEGACITY IMPACT

Let us now consider the impacts of maximum city size on the inhabitants from points of view expressed in a number of recent publications. Recurrent themes are (1) positive feelings about city living in spite of impact problems such as overcrowding and various kinds of environmental pollution; (2) people's preference for living in the city despite being poor as a result of being exploited, as some writers assert vehemently; (3) the growing threat of irreversible environmental damage resulting from the growth of cities to magnitudes unprecedented in world history; and (4) the steady and rapid increase in size and number of megacities as an aspect of the continuing world population problem projected well into the twenty-first century.

A squatter in Mexico City, contemplating the earthquake ruins of his tailor shop and responding to an architect who thought the ruins should be replaced by a park to slow down the city's growth, asked, "How many people does a park hire? I came to this city to work. I would have stayed in Veracruz if I wanted trees and grass" (Kandell 1985:1). One thousand rural people a day, like this man, move into Mexico City because they are more likely to find reasonably well-paying jobs. A successful resident of many years in Mexico City, commenting on recent migrants and squatters, says, "I can't say I would blame anyone who refused to move to places like Zacatecas or Sonora. I have young children. What sort of education, culture, friends could they expect out there? I'm not prepared to make these sorts of sacrifices" (Kandell 1985:11). And the squatter from Veracruz comments, "For the first time in my life, I'm living with running water and a toilet that flushes." These statements were made in the context of a city whose population grew from 1.5 million in 1940 to 18 million in 1985, its industrial growth deliberately fostered by the Mexican government. The environmental impact features 11 thousand tons of pollutants poured into the air every day by 130 thousand factories and three million vehicles—the equivalent of each person's smoking two packs of cigarettes a day. Increasingly scarce water is another impact (Morgan 1986:A–9).

Tokyo, recently displaced by Mexico City as the world's largest city, has, in addition to noise and air pollution, a land shortage that is causing an inflation in land values of as much as 50 percent a year.

Stoics though they are, Tokyo residents are getting increasingly angry at the thought of a city that large—rubbish alone could fill Tokyo Bay if reclamation continues at the present rate. Nevertheless, residents—some of whom commute two to three hours—say they love the city, among the safest in the world. Only 23 residents per 1,000 are crime victims, compared with 73 per 1,000 in Munich, Germany, and 60 per 1,000 in Chicago (Goodall 1986:A–9).

Tokyo "is really a vast conglomeration of villages and towns. The first impression one receives is not so much of a city as of some huge, shapeless industrial suburb, extremely ugly and noisy, but alive and radiant with the presence of one of the world's most charming and attractive peoples" (Kirkup 1966:1). Later on, we see how Tokyoites manage to maintain their small active and receptive scales, thus buffering the impacts of the city's sheer size. They cannot, however, overcome the environmental impacts.

A study of São Paulo, Brazil, sponsored by its Roman Catholic Archdiocese, concludes that the city's large-scale social impacts on its millions of poor people are so exploitative and repressive that the only social support systems they have are at the personal and informal network level (São Paulo Justice and Peace Commission 1978:126). Their active scales are exclusively small, which is true for most people, but the theme of the study is that these people are *prevented* from participating in larger active scales, such as labor unions, by government oppression and exploitation by the rich. The result is that "economic growth of the city has involved the perpetuation of existing inequalities," including racial discrimination (p. 84). The study presents data showing that financial and health conditions of the poor have been deteriorating at the same time that the city and its industries have been growing.

As long as the social and political initiative of the working classes continues to be blocked, it is difficult to imagine São Paulo as a truly human city. It is capital—and not labour—which is destroying life in the city. For capitalists, this city is a source of profit. For workers it is a way of life (pp. 54–55).

Unlike many studies of squatter settlements, this one presents those of São Paulo in bleak terms. Rising land values, as the city grows, have continually pushed the poor to the peripheries where they are far from their work. Bad as traffic problems are for car owners, they are worse for those dependent on public transportation:

Queues, overcrowding, delays, losing a day's work, and, at times, the anger that explodes into the stoning of trains and buses, cannot be dismissed as simple "traffic problems." The long hours spent waiting or travelling when one could be resting, whether before or after a long and arduous day's work, add daily to the exhaustion of those who have to use buses and trains to get to their jobs (p. 36).

Calcutta's poor are not at present so politically repressed as are those of São Paulo, although the city's recent (seventeenth century) origin and most of its subsequent history were generated by British imperialists who extracted local wealth and exploited workers by maintaining poor wages, inadequate or nonexistent health services, and social segregation that reinforced the indigenous caste system.

Even now, after the end of imperialism, Calcutta's extremely wealthy families have been described as economic exploiters, indifferent to the problems of the millions of poor workers surrounding them (Moorhouse 1983: chapter 4). Geoffrey Moorhouse and Dominique Lapierre (1985) present Calcutta in contrasting terms, each in his own way. They emphasize the massive poverty of most of the inhabitants—exacerbated by inmigration of millions of refugees from what is now Bangladesh—but they also repeatedly mention vitality and life force in the midst of death and misery. Moorhouse's historical essay emphasizes recent history and conditions. Lapierre's personal memoir is based on two years' residence in a slum of 75 thousand residents (200 thousand per square mile) called "The City of Joy" by the man who originally set aside the land. Like Oscar Lewis, Lapierre concentrates on the dialogue of a small number of individuals. Through them, the reader is immersed, in detail, in such realities as Mother Teresa's home for dying destitutes (next door to the Kalighat), the disastrous effects on slum dwellers of a latrine cleaners' and cattle manure collectors' strike, the daily lives of lepers, the normality of filth, overcrowding, wasting disease, slow starvation, and more. The City of Joy is a slum, not a squatter settlement. (Note the distinction between slum and squatter settlement, clarified by research in Latin America, in chapter 4). What The City of Joy lacks, as a slum, is social support systems. Although Lapierre describes many acts of kindness, compassion, and noble generosity, they are all individual acts, often surprising and unpredictable. "Nothing was ever totally rotten in this inhuman city," he says (p. 211). With one dubious exception, The City of Joy has no social organization of its own. One character participated in a ricksha-pullers' strike, but it was organized on a citywide basis by a union affiliated with the Communist Party, dominant in West Bengal. The only local organization of any kind is a mafia, complete with goons who beat up or burn out uncooperative people; it runs a protection racket that abuses lepers, as well as carrying on the local drug traffic, prostitution, and fencing operations (pp. 274–75).

Ironically, the "godfather" of this predatory organization, being the only authority figure in the slum, is frequently sought to arbitrate disputes. "In the course of years he had thus become a redresser of wrongs, a kind of Robin Hood" (Lapierre 1985:275).

Simple disputes sometimes explode into savage, pitched battles; one of Lapierre's interlocutors explains the motivation:

> You bow your head, you shut up, you put up with everything indefinitely. You bottle up your grievances against the owner of your hovel who is exploiting you, the usurer who is bleeding you dry, the speculators who push up the price of rice, the factory bosses who don't give you a job, the neighbor's children who won't let you sleep for coughing their lungs out all night, the political parties who suck the life out of you and don't give a damn, the Brahmins who take ten rupees [about $1.25] from you for a mere *mantra* [a Hindu incantation]. You take all the mud, the shit, the stink, the heat, the insects, the rats, until one day, wham! you're presented with an opportunity to shout, ransack, kill. You don't know why, but it's stronger than you are, and you just pile on in there (p. 282).

We are considering the impacts of size on inhabitants of megacities of the world. In São Paulo and Calcutta those impacts include such rapid growth that the infrastructures have not been able to cope with the consequences nor mitigate the mass-scale social and economic exploitation by groups responsible, in part, for the growth. It is not easy to document the humanity of cities like São Paulo and Calcutta. It is there, but, according to the information available, it is overwhelmed by inhumanity. The questions arise, therefore: Are these megacities too large? Are all megacities too large? Some observers would unhesitatingly answer "Yes," and some would add that *any* city is too large! This last answer would certainly be an overreaction; the others are arguable.

A poll conducted by the *Wall Street Journal* and NBC News in March 1986 provides a more balanced picture than that of extreme poverty in São Paulo and Calcutta. Telephone interviews with 1,679 adults who had lived in New York City ten years or more were supplemented by a small discussion panel (Blundell 1986). Serious complaints concerned public safety (42 percent), government corruption (20 percent), public education (18 percent) (a public school is described as a "grimy fortress in which the grossly underpaid do battle with the wildly undisciplined"), and public transportation (12 percent). Yet, the bottom line is that the percentages of people answering the question, "How much do you like living in New York City?" were "a lot" (59 percent), "some" (27 percent), "not very much" (9 percent), "not at all" (4 percent), and "not sure" (1 percent)—only 13 percent express any negative feeling.

All of the interviewees' positive reactions are results of the impact of the city's very large size on its inhabitants.

> For most, the pulse and pace and convenient, go-all-night action of the city, its rich ethnic and cultural stew, still outweigh its horrors. Mr. Mandell loves to mix with the human swarm on Wall Street at noon and gets excited just entering the lobby of a Broadway theater at night. Out of the city, many panelists feel restless, lost. When Manhattanite Linda Freccia, a merchandise coordinator for a retail chain, visits her sister in Ohio she sees

nothing but "blond, blue-eyed people who can talk about nothing of particular interest." She adds, "There's more going on in one block in Manhattan than in the whole state of Ohio." Albert Terry, a 36-year-old mailroom clerk for Marvel Comics, insists he isn't emotionally wedded to the city and would leave tomorrow—but when he visited Harrisburg, Pa., last year, he found it too cold, too bland, and, worst of all, lacking an all-night deli on the corner (Blundell 1986:20).

Granted, these New Yorkers were not slum dwellers or squatters, but many of the latter also prefer living where they are. "I don't want to go back to the village," says Urmila. "If I am forced to [by family pressures to marry], I will. But I won't like it." Urmila, a 14-year-old resident of a squatter settlement in Delhi, India, has in five years come to like the city's entertainment and better food. Her health is better. She has a domestic job with an upper-class family; she is now a wage earner in her own right, is more assertive toward her family, and her aspirations have gone beyond the village life from which she came and to which she might be forced to return (Singh 1986).

MEGACITIES AND WORLD POPULATION

Most, if not all, of the megacity phenomena we are considering are aspects of the world population problem. Overpopulation, and consequent underemployment in rural areas, are major reasons for the migration of millions of people to cities. The growth of cities like the ones we are discussing is not only because of inmigration from rural areas but also continued high birth rates, especially in the Third World. (See, for example, data from Isfahan, Iran [Gulick and Gulick 1975], and Guayaquil, Ecuador [Scrimshaw 1975].)

In 1987 the world population reached the five-billion mark. In the year 2000, it is expected to be six billion or more, and at least half of those people will be living in cities. Let us think about three billion city dwellers in the year 2000. Included are cities of all sizes, the smallest being around 20 thousand. To the six largest megacities, let us add the runners-up, each of which is expected to have a population of ten million or more by the year 2000. They are, with their estimated populations:

City	Estimated Population in 2000 A. D. (millions)
Seoul	13.5
Shanghai	13.5
Rio de Janeiro	13.3
New Delhi	13.3
Buenos Aires	13.2
Cairo	13.2
Jakarta	12.8
Baghdad	12.8
Tehran	12.7
Karachi	12.2
Istanbul	11.9

City	Estimated Population in 2000 A. D. (millions)
Los Angeles	11.2
Dacca	11.2
Manila	11.1
Beijing	10.8
Moscow	10.1

These and the six largest total 22 cities—a third of the 66 that will have an estimated total population of 600 million in 2000 (Population Institute 1986a). Subtracting 600 million from 3 billion, we have 2.4 billion *other, smaller city* dwellers in the year 2000. In other words, enormous though the megacity phenomenon is, most city dwellers will be, in the near future as they are now, residents of smaller cities than the ones whose problems are causing such concern. This situation is no reason for complacency, but it does offer encouragement, provided that a significant check on world population growth can be achieved.

Environmental pollution is one impact of large city size, and its volume is correlated directly with size. While some pollution problems appear to be local, others pose regional threats. For example, Boston produces a nitrogen oxide atmospheric plume which, fortunately, blows eastward over the Atlantic (Spicer 1982:1095). In other cities this phenomenon, and others like it, affect terrestrial environments supporting plants, animals, and people. In Cairo, long-neglected pollution problems are beginning to frighten people as well as endanger their health. "Every person in Cairo breathes air that is roughly equivalent to smoking at least 40 cigarettes daily, in addition to inhaling a big dose of the 200 tons of cement dust escaping each day from the Helwan cement factory" (Ahmed 1986:1). The cement dust has killed trees and orchards in the Helwan area (upstream from Cairo) and contributes to the high rate of respiratory illness there, as well as in Cairo. In addition, four billion cubic meters of industrial wastewater from factories and power plants is discharged every year into the Nile and the irrigation system associated with it. The 500 percent increase in the number of vehicles in Cairo since 1970 has "far surpassed the geographical expansion in Cairo, resulting in the city's epic traffic jams and blue-grey haze of polluted air that hangs over everywhere" (Ahmed 1986:20).

Some years ago, acute air pollution problems in London and Pittsburgh, Pa., were solved by stringent measures controlling the burning of soft coal. There is the possibility and hope that today's massive urban environmental pollution problems can be similarly solved. The solutions are not only technological, however; they also require the cooperation of inhabitants whose shortsighted, profit-oriented ambitions have often stymied the achievement of long-range goals.

A Nigerian anthropologist provides valuable insights on this issue, using the city of Onitsha, Nigeria (population 310 thousand), as an example. Azuka Dike (1985) says the pollution problem in Onitsha and other Third World cities "is still at the stage where it can be curbed," but that the involved governments must be prodded and guided to more effective developmental policies. "It might be assumed that the public would revolt against the environmental pollution created by industry. Not so. In the Third World, where food, shelter, and other immediate necessities are the primary concern of the populace, employment for most people is the major need" (p. 504).

One problem can only get worse with increasingly large concentrations of people: permanent water shortages, including the lowering of water tables. Desert-oasis cities like those of southern California survive and grow by taking water from much of the United States southwest, to the detriment of other settlements in the area. This situation cannot continue indefinitely, for the water supply will eventually be exhausted. The problem is worldwide. Karachi, Pakistan, "is running an astonishing 47 million gallons per day behind the needs of its population. . . . [A] new water supply scheme should bring the city an additional 50 million gallons per day later this year. However, if current trends continue, the city will have grown by another 200 thousand people. And the water deficit will still be critical" (The Population Institute 1986b:3). Karachi in 1986 had a population of 7.5 million and an annual growth rate of 6 percent (3 percent from natural increase, 3 percent from inmigration). By the year 2000 it will have 12.2 million people.

Even if solutions are found to the worldwide problem of "lost water" through leaks and illegal connections (World Bank 1986), the world is headed for a water shortage which, if nothing else, may force humankind to decrease its urban and rural population by humane means or to see many human beings die of thirst.

In 1986, the Israeli cabinet made a drastic decision that received very little media attention: it would reduce the national water supply 10 percent in 1986 and maintain that reduced rate for ten years to replenish Israel's water resources, drained by excessive pumping and polluted by chemicals. City dwellers are to reduce their water consumption by 25 percent (*Jerusalem Post International* 21 June 1986). The consequences of this decision are bound to be extensive; as yet, only a reduction in agricultural production is definitely predictable. This Israeli decision may well be a harbinger of what must be undertaken elsewhere on a much larger scale.

MAGNITUDES AND INTERNAL DIVERSITY

Meanwhile, most of the urban population of the world lives in smaller cities than the ones discussed so far in this chapter. The same problems occur in smaller cities, presumably on reduced scales, but we do not know by what factors they are reduced.

We *do* know, thanks to empirical studies, if not our own experiences, that the great magnitude of a city is not an undifferentiated mass with an undifferentiated impact on the inhabitants. Even in the largest megacities, there are very different microenvironments. This subject is vitally important because it is the internal diversity of a city that provides buffers between the big totality and the small, vulnerable world of individual inhabitants, their families, friends, neighbors, and associates. Internal diversity mediates between gross magnitude and small-scale life as most people live it—one of the realities that formulators of the bipolar moralistic model ignored.

First, let us consider opinions some Americans expressed that bridge the gap between large-city and small-community living. A 1971 survey found that numerical scores for general sense of well-being were below average among residents of the largest United States cities, but steadily improved among residents in smaller cities, suburbs, towns, and rural settlements. Asked whether they feel it is safe to walk in the streets at night and whether it is necessary to lock one's front door, according to Campbell, Converse, and Rodgers (1976:246), residents of settlements in three of the size categories responded as follows:

Safety Level	Largest Cities	Suburbs	Rural Areas
Streets safe at night	43%	80%	86%
No need to lock doors	19%	44%	63%

Despite the relatively unfavorable positions of the largest cities, the authors found community size "is not a direct measure of any attribute" (p. 246), meaning by attribute various small-scale concerns such as the ones above. One reason is that interviewees from the largest cities included large proportions of blacks whose general levels of satisfaction were low, for reasons other than big-city living. Nevertheless, various opinion polls show a consistent tendency for Americans to say that they would prefer to live in small towns.

However, Glenn Fuguitt and James Zuiches (1975) have revealed that an important contingency factor is probably at work in these preferences. They studied the preferences of people living in large metropolitan cities (over 500 thousand in population), medium-sized cities (50 to 500 thousand), smaller cities (10 to 50 thousand), towns and villages (under 10 thousand), and in the country outside any city or village. Only 9 percent said they would prefer to live in a large metropolitan city (20 percent of them actually did so) and 16 percent in medium-sized cities (24 percent actually did so). But only 9 percent expressed a preference for rural living more than 30 miles from a city of over 50 thousand. Most striking in this study is that 55 percent of the sample said they would prefer to live in rural areas or settlements with populations up to 50 thousand, *provided they were within 30 miles of a city of over 50 thousand people* (pp. 494–95). The advantages of rural living included less crime, good air and water, and better conditions for children. But higher wages, better jobs, and contacts with a variety of people were among the reasons given for wanting to live in larger places (pp. 499–500). The majority preference is evidently based on the wish to have the best of both worlds, in a culture where there is a distinct antiurban bias. The tentative conclusion is that negative feelings about big-city living may be less frequent or intense than the surveys seem to indicate.

We are still touching only indirectly on the question: What are the effects of magnitude on inhabitants' small, active scales?

Whatever their preferences may be, large numbers of people are attracted to metropolitan areas of maximum size, resulting in the continued existence of metropolitan cities. True, there are internal migrations within many of them, as from central cities to suburbs and new satellite cities, but so far, at any rate, there has been no reduction in the number or size of metropolitan areas. Job opportunities are obviously the major factor here, even in the presence of large-scale unemployment.

Major metropolitan areas seem to continue to grow because millions of people find them preferable to smaller, and especially to rural, places. Exploitation and social abuse are not confined to metropolitan cities which often provide the hope of better opportunities to a greater degree than places of lesser magnitude.

We need to review some concepts bearing on the effects that city magnitudes have on the inhabitants. First, classic models of city growth phases (Burgess's concentric zones, Hoyt's sectors, and Harris and Ullman's multiple nuclei) describe different environments in American cities. Based largely on the spatial distributions of aggregate socioeconomic data, these models are culture-bound and do not fit a great many cases (Herbert 1973:70–72). This last limitation has rendered them apparently ineffective in countering the tendency to generalize about cities as if they were not internally differentiated.

Second, Barrie Greenbie (1976) provides a concept whose components should, at this point, be somewhat familiar. He labels two segments of the potential range of an individual's active scales. A person's small, active scale, Greenbie calls the individual's "proxemic space." Larger active scale ranges he calls "distemic space." Greenbie's ideas are based on empirical urban studies, not on abstractions. Proxemic space is where individuals find security and identity on the basis of similarities. Distemic space is where dissimilar individuals and groups can facilitate the various forms of cooperation that, in the modern city, are essential for survival in proxemic space.

Greenbie thinks that proxemic and distemic space must operate together. When they do not, the humanity of cities is threatened; for example, in the case of two types of exclusive proxemic space: voluntarily walled-off middle- and upper-class suburbs and involuntarily walled-off ghettos (1976:148). Both are real or potential disaster areas, because the inhabitants of each can actually survive only through relationships with nonexclusive and diverse social elements. Greenbie's version of the industrial city stereotype is that gross social-class hierarchies emerged, maximizing distemic space, and reducing proxemic space to "beleaguered enclaves" (p. 122). His point is that for humane life in cities to be sustained, city dwellers must be able to live in distemic space at the same time that they live in proxemic space. Accepting the importance of proxemic space, Greenbie (p. 153) places special emphasis on distemic space which "defines the real city. The city is not only a physical space, a geographical place, but also an intricate hierarchy of conceptual spaces which vary greatly in the minds of its dissimilar citizens" (p. 153). He is arguing that different groups will perceive different environments while occupying the same space, and he advocates a systematic understanding of those perceptions and spaces (pp. 168–69).

Third is Kevin Lynch's concept of the "image of the city." His pioneering venture into the subject of mental maps of cities was based on interviews with residents of Boston, Jersey City, and Los Angeles. His main thesis—that city dwellers need clear "imageability" in their surroundings—does not concern us at this point. What is pertinent is that his inquiries into how people saw *paths, nodes, boundaries,* and *landmarks* in visual terms was involved in their sometimes identifying districts.

Districts are the relatively large city areas which the observer can mentally go inside of, and which have some common character. They can be recognized internally, and occasionally can be used as external reference as a person goes by or toward them. Many persons interviewed took care to point out that Boston, while confusing in its path pattern even to the experienced inhabitant, has, in the number and vividness of its differentiated districts, a quality that quite makes up for it. As one person put it: "Each part of Boston is different from the other. You can tell pretty much what area you're in" (1960:66).

As we shall see later, there are objectively verifiable differences among the same districts of Boston as variously perceived by Lynch's informants. The Boston districts have fairly clear visual identity. "Jersey City has its districts, too, but they are primarily ethnic or class districts with little physical distinction. Los Angeles is markedly lacking in strong regions, except for the Civic Center area" (p. 67). Lynch points out that, in all three cities, some regions are "introvert, turned in upon themselves," some are connected to others, while some are isolates; and some are distinctive to inhabitants but not visually distinctive to others (p. 71).

In 1962, part of the author's study of Tripoli, Lebanon, replicated some of Lynch's interview procedures. The results emphasized the importance of districts (only a minor topic in Lynch's book) in the minds of the inhabitants. The conclusion was that the informants selected districts as the major distinctive features of their city on the basis of visual, physical features (Lynch's emphasis) and on the basis of associated social and behavioral features (Gulick 1963:197). Tripoli has a *madina* (see below) and surrounding, newer districts including a European-style business district, a port district, and several residential areas.

Jersey City is a segment of the megacity of New York. Los Angeles is a world city in its own right, and Boston is a runner-up. Tripoli is a medium-sized Third World city of about 200 thousand people concentrated at very high density in only about 1.5 built-up square miles. In one way or another, large magnitudes are involved in all these cases, but in none do the interviewed inhabitants react to these large magnitudes as if they were undifferentiated. While all informants were cued to think comprehensively, one of the conclusions drawn from the Tripoli study is that their images are strongly influenced by their own experiences—a limiting factor.

Limited views, possibly suggesting limited impacts of large magnitudes, are clearly indicated by other studies in this genre. For example, Lynch also studied teenagers' spatial reactions in cities in Australia, Poland, Mexico, and Argentina. He says:

The Salta [Argentine] children play within part of a circle which is only 1/2 kilometer across. Their friends are close by. . . . Since the Colonia Universitad streets are so inconvenient, even for "hanging out," the Tolucan [Mexican] children go to the city parks and the city center at least once a week and know them reasonably well. Children in the Polish housing projects keep consistently within their project bounds . . . only slightly larger than the Salta territory (1/4 to 1/2 square km). Their knowledge of the rest of the city was scattered and random. Their counterparts at the heart of Cracow and Warszawa roam the densely active central areas; their territories are more individualized and confident. The Ecatepec [Mexico City] children fixed their action space in the nearby streets and their school. At the same time, they will spend an hour to an hour and a half in a crowded bus to travel to the center of Mexico City. They know its major elements: the subway, Chapultepec Park, the Zocalo, the Zona Rosa, and some even commute regularly. The Australians, however, are the most mobile, ranging over ground five square kilometers in extent, [but] despite this spatial range, [they] seem to be exposed to a more restricted variety of people, activity and place. They are less familiar with the center of their city . . . and seemingly less at ease in traversing those sections of the metropolis that are unlike their own. . . . Girls are more often kept at home or must travel in pairs, while boys are, at least in theory, free to roam. Some of the Melbourne boys do so, but primarily within the western working class suburbs. The Tolucans and Saltese, who are within walking range, visit the center or the large parks but rarely travel elsewhere, despite their expressed freedom to do so. The [Polish] children . . . have relatively good public transport to the center, but complain of being cut off. The colonia of Ecatepec is truly isolated save for its public transport link—a long, crowded, and relatively expensive ride. The children have little understanding of their highly amorphous municipality, which is an archipelago of isolated colonias (K. Lynch 1977:22–24).

Lynch illustrates very well how the impacts of magnitude are mediated through various proxemic and distemic spaces. Of course, one would expect young and inexperienced people to have only limited command of their urban environments, most especially the larger ones, but such limitations are not peculiar to youngsters. For example, in Los Angeles, upper-middle-class white adults had a much more comprehensive view of the city than working-class blacks had (Gould and White 1980:102–4). So, the impact of magnitude is mediated not only through different spaces but also different social identities and related social experiences.

Nor is it only *maximum* magnitude that has differential impact; minimal magnitude can have it, too. In a study probably modeled on Lynch's methods, Bob Anderson discovered important differences between his fellow students and nonstudent residents in Chapel Hill, N.C. The settlement has a population of about 45 thousand, including about 23 thousand university students. (When the latter are not in residence, the effects on distemic space are very noticeable.) The municipal area is about nine square miles, much of which is not built up. Yet the impact of this small-scale setting is not uniform on its inhabitants. University students perceive the campus and immediately adjacent areas, including bars and shops, in considerable detail. Nonstudent residents see the campus in relatively undifferentiated terms but see a wider range of other features in the settlement than the students do (Hart 1977). These findings are not surprising and are readily explainable. They illustrate the preeminent importance of individuals' proxemic and distemic spaces *regardless of the orders of magnitude of the cities in which those spaces occur.*

One is tempted to wonder if the whole idea of impact of urban environment on the inhabitants isn't so oversimplified as to be either useless or misleading. Clearly, magnitude is not an undifferentiated mass with uniform effects. We must look more closely, then, at the subenvironments contained in urban magnitudes as embodied in three cities—Cairo, Ibadan, and Boston—all of which have been studied comprehensively in terms of their internal, varied subenvironments.

THREE CITIES

Cairo

"The Anatomy of Metropolitan Cairo," chapter 12 of Abu-Lughod's 1971 book, is one of the most comprehensive published delineations of the subenvironments of a megacity. It contains vivid descriptions of the 13 subcities Abu-Lughod's quantitative and qualitative analysis led her to designate. A map shows locations of the subcities and many photographs illustrate them.

Each of Abu-Lughod's subcities is a composite of statistics from Cairo's 200-plus census tracts. She is careful to point out that these "differ from American census tracts in that they are usually more than statistical units. Some, especially in the oldest quarters of the city, are physically and functionally derivative from the ancient *harat* and *durub* [neighborhoods] which have a long tradition of social cohesion" (p. 183). For each tract, the 1947 and 1960 censuses provided quantitative data such as percentages of literate females, unmarried females, employed females, and females in school (all relatively unusual); literate males, unmarried males (likely to be migrants), unemployed males; handicapped or infirm people; and population densities per unit of area and per room. She found, through factor analysis, that census tracts similar in these terms tended to be contiguous. On this basis, plus historical information and her own qualitative observations (for example, on customary clothing and street behavior), she arrived at the 13 subcities. She arranges them into five categories: rural fringes (Subcities III, VI, IX, XIII); interior slums (Subcities I, X, and XII); urban working class (Subcity IV), urban middle class (Subcities II, VIII, XI); and upper middle or upper class (Subcities V, VII) (p. 218).

Abu-Lughod further reduces these data to three subcultural categories: rural/urban, traditional urban, and modern urban. The diversity of residential architecture includes: six- to ten-story apartment blocks with balconies (some sleek and luxurious but most drab, with disintegrating surfaces); traditional two- to three-story houses with invisible, interior courtyards; village-style, flat-roofed houses of sun-dried brick; walled enclosures in regular, straight rows (the City of the Dead, tomb-compounds occupied by living people in the enormous cemeteries between the Medieval City—Subcity X—and the Muqattam Hills); the baroque mansions of Garden City and Heliopolis; and Western European-style suburban houses of Ma'adi, complete with lawns and trees, built by and for British colonials, but now homes of upper-class Egyptians.

Landmarks familiar to foreign visitors are scattered here and there in this urban structure. The airport is on the edge of Subcity III, a "northern agricultural wedge" that has, in the past ten years, been built up with high-rise apartment blocks for lower middle-class people. Khan el-Khalili, the tourist trap for hunters of oriental jewelry and other metalware, is part of Subcity X, the Medieval City. Few, if any, tourists are aware that Subcity X is also the home of Al-Azhar, the premier theological school of the Muslim world, that has in recent decades become a full-fledged modern university; the shrine of "Our Lord" Husayn (as Muslims call him), grandson of the Prophet Mu-

hammad; and a traditional urban ambience comprised of intellectual talk in
cafes (see Berque and al-Shekaa 1972) and intense small-scale commercial life
as epitomized in the novels of Najib Mahfouz. Subcity X had a population of
475 thousand in 1960, representing a smaller increase over 1947 than occurred
in newer parts of the city. Abu-Lughod feared for its ultimate survival because
its subsistence on small-scale crafts might be doomed (p. 193). It is surely
destined for more vicissitudes, but what they will be, no one knows.

According to the 1976 census, Subcity X had an average population density
of 62 thousand people per square kilometer (range: 36 to 104 thousand). Subcity
X is a *madina*, a characteristic preindustrial Middle Eastern city with inward-
facing courtyard houses and narrow, twisting alleys.

By contrast, the 1976 population density of Abu-Lughod's Gold Coast (Subcity VII) was only 6.8 thousand people per square kilometer, a low density for
Cairo but relatively high by American urban standards. In Subcity VII are
many landmarks familiar to foreign visitors: Garden City; the American and
British embassies; the American University in Cairo; Qasr el-Nil Street; Tahrir Square and the Egyptian Museum; the Nile Hilton, new Semiramis, and
New Shepheard's hotels (with the adjoining Corniche along the river); and the
island of Zamalik, half of which is open land originally the British colony's
sports fields, the other half residential (mostly upper-middle and upper-class
apartment blocks). At the southern tip of Zamalik rises a 30-odd story cylin-
drical structure, one of the many hotel and office skyscrapers on the east and
west banks of the Nile built since 1971. Gold Coast is Abu-Lughod's own term,
borrowed from Chicago to convey the idea of wealth and privilege, and not
used by the Egyptians (p. 204). However, Garden City, the true name of part
of it, *is* called that in otherwise Arabic conversation. Abu-Lughod's Gold Coast
was once the "foreign-ville" of Cairo, and for a vivid feeling of it as such one
can read Ken Follett's World War II adventure, *The Key to Rebecca* (1981),
contrasting with Najib Mahfouz's *Midaq Alley*, a contemporaneous World War
II fictional account of life in Subcity X. The Gold Coast, still frequented by
foreigners, mostly transients, is also home to about 40 thousand people, mostly
Egyptians.

Cairo's 13 subcities comprise several different worlds, all mediators of the
city's great magnitude. All bear witness to Cairo's being many environments,
not an undifferentiated mass. However, as noted earlier in this chapter, impacts of environmental pollution affect the whole city.

We can sense the small-scale flavor of Cairo life from realistic, though fictional, works written originally in Arabic by Egyptian authors. This opening
of an allegorical short story evokes the ambience of one of the most popular
shrines in Cairo. The scene is a huge mosque containing the tomb of Sayyida
Zaynab, sister of Husayn and granddaughter of the Prophet Muhammad, located near the border of Abu-Lughod's Subcity X (Medieval City) and Subcity
XI (transitional belt):

As a boy my grandfather . . . used to come to Cairo with the family . . . to
visit the Mosque of al-Sayyida Zaynab and seek her blessings. As soon as
they reached the marble doorstep of the mosque, his father would push him
down on his knees and . . . the boy would cover it with kisses. . . . If one of
the pedantic theologians happened to see him and his family he would turn
his face away from them in disgust, condemning the evil times and invoking

the aid of God against such idolatry, heresy and ignorance. The majority of the people, however ... could understand how much these simple peas-ants had been looking forward to their visit, and that they could find no other way to express the warmth of their feelings of adoration and love for the Saint. . . . When he was a young man my grandfather moved to Cairo in search of work [and] wanted to live as near to his cherished mosque as possible (Haqqi 1973:1).

Here is the bureaucratic mind at work in a police station apparently on the border of Subcity I (Boulak—traditional urban) and Subcity II (Shubra—mixed traditional and modern):

His entry irritated Sergeant-Major Farahat. As though someone had aimed a punch at the tip of his nose, he turned on the man and thundered at him:
"What's up with you?"
"There's nothing up with me, Effendi. It's that bastard of a boy who threw a brick which broke the pane of glass of the shop window . . . genuine Belgian pre-war crystal."
"What shop's this?"
"The Friendship and Fraternity Grocery in the main street."
"I know it—the one on the corner opposite the garage?"
"That's it, may God prosper you. May the Lord never bring down upon you. . . ."
"And which window was broken—the one on the street or the other one on the lane?"
"The big one, Effendi, the one on the lane."
"Then it's not ours," said Sergeant-Major Farahat. . . . "It's Boulak's."
"How's that, Bey, when the house is in your district?"
"The side that overlooks the lane is under Boulak."
"Please, Effendi—"
"I've told you, it's nothing to do with us. Go to Boulak station" (Idris 1967:14).

Finally, we see a cul-de-sac neighborhood in the heart of Subcity X (Medieval City):

In the early morning the Midaq Alley is dreary, and cold. The sun reaches it only after climbing high into the sky. However, life begins to stir early in the morning in parts of the street. Sanker, the café waiter, begins activity by arranging the chairs and lighting the spirit stove. Then the workmen in the company office start coming in twos and threes. Presently Jaada appears carrying the wood for baking the bread. Even Uncle Kamil is busy at this early hour, opening his shop and then having his nap before break-fast. Uncle Kamil and Abbas the barber always have breakfast together from a tray placed between them containing plates of cooked beans, onion salad, and pickled gherkins (Mahfouz 1966:33).

Ibadan

Ibadan is set in the middle of the Yoruba cultural area of western Nigeria, and the city's indigenous base is Yoruba. Ibadan includes an indigenous section and the originally British colonial sections, and it has evolved into a national city now that it is the capital of western Nigeria. Its population, about a million in 1967, is now approaching 1.3 million.

Unlike some West African indigenous cities, Ibadan is not very old. It was founded in the course of regional wars in the early nineteenth century. However, its social structure has deep and ancient roots. The old residential area is irregular in shape, built partly on hills, and set within a roughly circular city wall approximately three miles in diameter. Within the wall are Ibadan's principal markets, its ceremonial center, the enclaves of various non-Yoruba ethnic groups, and the residential compounds of the Yoruba farmers, traders, and craftsmen who form the city's core. Outside the walls, for three to four miles to the west and north, are several discontinuous settlements that include private and government housing projects, factories, an agricultural training school, barracks and administrative areas, and two universities (Mabogunje 1967a:52–53).

Residential areas of the old city consist of one-story houses or compounds of houses, made of sun-dried mud (occasionally brick) with sloping, sheet-metal roofs, variously rusty in color. Several roads pass all the way through. Near their major intersection are the city hall, the central mosque, and the central market, which, in the absence of a hereditary chief's palace, "still forms the focus of traditional city life" (Mabogunje 1967a:37). Barbara Lloyd made a special study of the quarter (Oje) which comprises this central location. It had, at the time of her study, 15 residential compounds, ranging in population from 40 to 400 people (B. Lloyd 1967:67). Each compound has a *bale*, the eldest male member of the resident lineage, who arbitrates disputes, oversees members' welfare, and allocates lineage farming land (p. 66). Each lineage owns its compound in the city and farming land outside it. The latter sometimes includes a village or part of one. There are lineage religious rituals, particularly concerning ancestors, although most people are at least nominally either Muslims or Christians. The Oje chief adjudicates disputes in the central market, owned by descendants of the original chief (p. 62).

While only 10 percent of the men living in Oje are farmers, probably a quarter of them who list other occupations are also part-time farmers. Among their other occupations are construction work and driving various kinds of vehicle. Of the Oje women, 84 percent are trader-craftswomen, primarily vendors of cooked food for which there is much demand (p. 70).

Here is how daily life begins in "downtown" Ibadan:

Old men accustomed to sleeping little, and women who must call at a corn mill or the wholesale food market at Oritamerin before starting the day's trade, begin to rise about 5 a.m. Soon they are joined by men destined for work at the farm or in distant parts of Ibadan, and women who cook the family breakfast or sell cooked foods to others. Before 8 a.m. even the unemployed young men and children not yet of school age are awake, and Oje begins the day.

In most compounds a man is formally greeted by his wives [34 percent of the men are polygynous] and children. He in turn greets each of them, often using special pet names. . . . Most Muslim men wash quickly . . . and hurry to the mosque for prayers. . . . Among Christians, it is common for the whole family to gather in the parlour for a brief service. Often, this is the only opportunity throughout the whole day for the entire family to be together. The father may work at some distance and buy his breakfast along the way. . . . Women whose trading duties allow . . . cook breakfast and eat with their children; those who attend early markets may rush through the household chores, sweeping and drawing water, then buy some breakfast to eat in the stall where mother and small child spend the morning. A woman who sells breakfast food, will have a hurried snack, or often none at all, tie her small child to her back, and set off, tray on head to offer others the convenience of a ready-cooked breakfast (B. Lloyd, 1967:74–75).

Set within this Yoruba context are enclaves of other Nigerian ethnic groups—Hausa, Ibo, Ijebu—who are specialized craftsmen and merchants. They are not farmers because they do not have the local land rights that the Yoruba do. The Hausa quarter, Sabo, is the subject of a book by Abner Cohen, discussed later.

Surrounding Ibadan is a hinterland of five rings of periodic markets supplying the city with farm produce and other commodities (Hodder 1967:174–75). These goods are sold in Ibadan's daytime markets, where most of the buyers are women, many of whom cook foods that they consume or sell at the 20 night markets in the old city. B. W. Hodder adds some perspective to the picture Barbara Lloyd draws:

> This kind of night market, in which women connect their local communities with the town's main sources of foodstuffs, can only be understood in the context of the local Yoruba habits of feeding. The bulk of the working class population eats food that has not been prepared in their own homes. The normal practice is for all members of a family to eat breakfast at a cooked food stall ... to have the midday meal at least partly prepared at home, and ... the evening meal either in the local night market or to bring food from the market into the home to eat. Yoruba food, moreover, takes a long time and much energy to prepare; and it is most economically prepared in larger amounts than any one person or family can eat at a time. The explanation of this phenomenon of outside cooking and eating, however, is also bound up with the fact that women put trading first in their interests (Hodder 1967:184).

Hodder's last point anticipates discussions appearing in chapter 5: the interconnections between women's and men's work and other aspects of urban social life.

Ibadan's hinterlands include the Yoruba farming and market areas, the intercity commercial networks of people like the Hausa, and the hometown/Ibadan connections of the city's elite (P. C. Lloyd 1967:144–47).

> Traditional Ibadan is centered on Mapo Hill. Within a mile and a half of the doric columned city hall lie most of the compounds of the Ibadan people—a densely packed agglomeration of small houses.... Outside in their numerous suburbia—the government residential areas, the University campuses—live the elite. The focus of their life is Kingsway Stores. The growth of Kingsway into the modern four-story, air conditioned emporium, opened on the second anniversary of national Independence, symbolizes the development of the elite ... from the mid–1950s. Although the Nigerianization of the bureaucracies proceeded quickly, the number of non-Africans also increased. As the expatriate administrative officers left, the technicians and advisors arrived (P. C. Lloyd 1967:129).

The elite are primarily civil servants who replace the British colonials who built the first suburban developments. They are predominantly Yoruba, but not *local* Yoruba (P. C. Lloyd 1967:134). They are well educated, Western style; they live, variously, in mansions built for the British, in single-family bungalows, and two-story, three-bedroomed houses that line the roads. Those who are better off own cars. Having "a car sharply divides those who are able to live in the suburban residential areas from those who must live in the crowded town; it distinguishes those who may visit widely separated friends from those who cannot" (p. 130). Nuclear families predominate, with a Victorian tradition of woman's place being in the home, but with a recently evolved strong expectation that women be employed outside the home, in spite of their average completed parity of six children. And most families have in residence a junior, nonnuclear relative who is attending school in the city (pp. 140–44). The elite maintain ties with former school friends and hometowns, but they do not (unlike the Ibo and Ijebu craftsmen) form clubs and associations. Although the University of Ibadan has become a performing arts center, most of the elite, many of whom are its graduates, are not involved in its affairs. On the whole, the elite have few associations of their own (in this respect they are superficially similar to many suburbanites in Japan), and virtually no contacts with life in central, traditional Ibadan (p. 148), yet they have numerous friendship ties—facilitated by the automobile and ties with their hometowns to which many of them hope to retire.

At various points in the book that has been the source of all this information on Ibadan, the authors wonder if, in the future, the elite will become less transient and the traditionals less localized. Meanwhile, the city's impacts on its residents are highly diverse.

Boston

Walter Firey's *Land Use in Central Boston* (first published in 1947) is one of the best on the subenvironments of a major city. The following portrait of Boston is based on this aspect of Firey's analysis.

Central Boston has not grown in population since Firey did his study in the early 1940s. However, the city and its surroundings have changed immensely, and we need to be aware of datedness in Firey's material. His depictions of Beacon Hill, the North End, and the South End are not entirely outmoded, but the Back Bay has changed significantly since his study.

We begin with Firey's figures (1968:173) on population densities in Boston in 1940:

Area	Households with over 1.5 Persons per Room (%)	Persons per Inhabited Acre
Back Bay	4.8	202.8
Brighton	3.4	72.5
Charlestown	4.1	255.1
East Boston	7.6	203.4
Hyde Park	3.3	31.2
Jamaica Plain	2.3	46.4
North Dorchester	2.2	103.0
North End	15.8	924.3
Roslindale	1.1	48.4
Roxbury	3.8	147.9
South Boston	4.6	196.8
South Dorchester	1.2	69.2

Area	Households with over 1.5 Persons per Room (%)	Persons per Inhabited Acre
South End	6.4	349.3
West End	4.5	369.7
West Roxbury	0.6	27.8

Source: Walter I. Firey, *Land Use in Central Boston* (Cambridge, Mass.: Harvard University Press, 1947).

This list is not complete, and it does not include Beacon Hill. East Boston is the location of Logan International Airport, and the housing one glimpses briefly on the way from the airport to the harbor tunnel is characteristic of other districts such as South Boston, Charlestown, and Dorchester. Brighton is the site of the Harvard Stadium and Harvard's Graduate School of Business Administration. Dorchester and Roxbury have experienced a great influx of blacks, and serious conflicts between them and working-class whites in South Boston over school busing have received national attention in recent years. Jamaica Plain and Roslindale are almost "suburban" in character, with separate, single-family houses on their own grounds. The West End of the 1940s was totally demolished in the 1950s and has been replaced by widely spaced, high-rise apartment buildings. In spite of this radical change, the population density is about the same as it was (Blake 1977:91).

Brookline, Cambridge, and Waltham—three parts of the Boston area well known to many people for various reasons—are not included in this list because they are separate municipalities from Boston.

When Firey did his study, the old West End adjoined Beacon Hill and a section of the downtown business district called Scollay Square which, in turn, adjoined the North End and two historic landmarks, Faneuil Hall and Quincy Market. Scollay Square was a wide street, with side streets, containing hamburger joints, cheap bars, tattoo parlors, peep shows, and two burlesque theaters. It was demolished in the 1950s and replaced by the Government Center. The Faneuil Hall and Quincy Market areas have been refurbished as tourist attractions, and the adjoining downtown business district changed virtually out of recognition between 1960 and 1986. A score of new skyscrapers now dwarf what were, in the 1940s, the only noticeably tall buildings in the city (the Courthouse Annex, the Federal Building, and the United States Customs House). At least one observer (A. Lewis 1986) has noted that the concentration of huge skyscrapers in a small area on narrow streets has a negative impact. Other changes in Boston's downtown business area include the conversion of decrepit wharves into deluxe condominiums and the migration of Scollay Square's porno delights (expanded and updated) to another part of the business district.

On the summit of Beacon Hill stands the Massachusetts state capitol whose gold-domed, red brick center section is a masterpiece of late eighteenth-century American Georgian architecture. Much of the residential part of Beacon Hill is in keeping with this structure. As of 1940, Beacon Hill residents included members of several upper-class lineages and a substantial number of unmarried women, many with high-status professional jobs. There were informal organizations such as those connected with Christmas rituals, and a formal neighborhood organization, a prototype of countless others in United States cities, dedicated to keeping out "undesirable elements." At various times, commercial interests threatened the integrity of Boston Common, the park adjoining Beacon Hill, two historic churches, and four old cemeteries. The Beacon Hill people successfully defeated all those interests, contrary to the rational utility assumptions of the Chicago school of urban sociology, as Firey (1968:97–167) emphasizes.

Beacon Hill includes venerated buildings and land. Not so the North End, except for the Old North Church from whose belfry the route of Paul Revere's ride to Concord and Lexington was supposedly signaled on 18 April 1775. At that time, there were no Italians in the North End. In fact, Italians did not start coming until about 1900. Since then, it has become the main Italian area of the city, with markets, churches, mutual aid societies, and *paesani* groups. There are street processions for saints and other rituals and, in general, a very strong sense of ethnic solidarity (Firey 1968:181–87). Younger people do move out—indicating assimilation to Anglo-American values, but the smaller number moving in—up to 1938—were mostly Italian. Firey emphasizes that low rents (accompanied by very crowded conditions) could not have been the major reason people remained in the generally rather dilapidated North End, for even lower rents were, at that time, available elsewhere in Boston. And, again up to 1938, Firey notes (p. 215) the great increase in Italian land ownership in the district: 1902 (19.08 percent); 1922 (51.70 percent); 1938 (57.98 percent). Italian ethnic values and sentiments kept the North End a residential area, and so it remains today.

In contrast to the highly organized and self-aware communities of Beacon Hill and the North End (very different from each other in most ways), the South End is an "anomic," rooming house area. It has been discussed in connection with single-room occupancy (SRO) and the significance of areas of American cities that accommodate those members of the society bereft of families because of accidents that can befall people in the American kinship system. That large-scale concept is Firey's (pp. 291–92).

The South End has had its vicissitudes. From 1855 to 1870, it was an upper-class area, and most of its red brick, bow-fronted houses date from that time. While many have fallen into ruin, many others survive, and sections of the South End have, since the days of Firey's study, been declared historic preservation areas. In 1979, on account of this last development, a Muslim Sufi religious order had difficulty in getting a permit to place a Koranic inscription on imported Iranian tiles on the bow-front of its South End house. As part of the eventually successful process, the order held open house, during which all the neighbors were invited to inspect the tiles laid out on the floor of the prayer hall into which the second floor had been converted. That particular street was no longer a neighborhood of SROs, but of householders dedicated to historic preservation.

CONCLUSION

Implicit in much of the foregoing material has been the assumption that large-scale magnitudes (potentially if not actually overwhelming and destructive to the human psyche) are everywhere reduced to small-scale magnitudes that are manageable and liveable. The reduction, cushioning, and filtering processes are real, but their existence by itself does not guarantee humanness in city life. As Greenbie says, successful city life must involve constructive interplay between proxemic and distemic spaces. Such interplay is often lacking at the present stage of the evolution of cities.

SUGGESTED ADDITIONAL READING

Caplow, Theodore, Sheldon Stryker, and Samuel F. Wallace. *The Study of San Juan, Puerto Rico.* Totowa, N.J.: Bedminster, 1964. Features photographs and other materials on 25 diverse neighborhoods in San Juan.

Cohen, Aaron. *Rio de Janeiro.* New York: Crescent, 1978. This book consists almost entirely of photographs; the text is essentially captions for the pictures. Nevertheless it is informative, and the remarkable aerial shots show the variegated texture of *favelas*, middle-class houses, and high-rises, all in the same scene.

Conzen, Michael P., and George K. Lewis. *Boston: A Geographical Portrait.* Cambridge, Mass.: Ballinger, 1976. One of a series of books on major American cities. Maps, diagrams, and fine photographs, two of which show Scollay Square before and after "renewal."

The Great Cities. Amsterdam: Time-Life Books. These books are characterized by marvelous photographs and texts that include a historical sketch and vignettes of modern life. Four of the books are:

Athens, by William Wyatt Davenport and Time-Life editors; photographs by Constantine Manos and Michael Freeman (1978).

Cairo, by Malise Ruthven and Time-Life editors; photographs by Robert Azzi (1980).

Istanbul, by Colin Thubron and Time-Life editors (1978).

Jerusalem, by Colin Thubron and Time-Life editors; photographs by Jay Maisel (1976).

The Ambience of Cities

Fictional literature, both serious and popular, includes many books whose authors convey a vivid sense of urban place, of what it is like to live and work in a particular city. One of these books is Ken Follett's *A Key to Rebecca,* set in Cairo. Some other cities featured in the books (all private investigator mysteries) of current, in-print authors are Boston—Robert Parker; Chicago—Sara Paretsky; Detroit—Elmore Leonard; Los Angeles and region—Ross Macdonald and Sue Grafton; Miami and region—John MacDonald and Elmore Leonard; and Washington—Margaret Truman. These authors know their territory and, on balance, love the cities in which their stories are set.

Mental Maps of Cities

Studies of how city-dwellers see and feel their surroundings were greatly stimulated by Kevin Lynch's *The Image of The City.* Another work in this genre is:

Downs, Roger M., and David Stea, eds. *Image and Environment: Cognitive Mapping and Spatial Behavior.* Chicago: Aldine, 1973.

4
Evolution

In chapter 3, we reviewed some of the major changes occurring in twentieth-century cities. People who witness these changes are having direct experiences with urban evolution in process, for some of the changes—such as the development of megacities—are new and unprecedented in the history of the world.

However, without some perception of time depth, it is too easy to become fixed in warped perspectives. Some aspects of present-day cities are very new; others are very old; still others are in between. All of these aspects exist together. To understand the nature of cities as fully as possible, it is necessary to understand how and when various important aspects of urban life came into being. We also need to comprehend, insofar as possible, the different ages of cities.

ORIGINS

The oldest archaeological remains of settlements believed by experts to have been cities are very small sites by modern standards for "urban." Therefore, we must reconsider the question of what—apart from relatively large size— *is* urban. The general view among most archaeologists is that there are important qualitative differences between small sites considered to have been cities and others considered to have been, in contrast, peasant villages. The single most important presumed difference is that among the inhabitants of the earliest cities were people who wielded power over others, including others living beyond the settlements themselves, while the earliest peasant villages had no such powerful people. Archaeological evidence for this power is indirect and based on inferences drawn from the quality and quantity of artifacts. These artifacts include the presence or absence of monumental architecture, the abundance or rarity of grave goods made of precious materials, and distribution patterns of trade goods among different sites.

The world's oldest urban remains are in the Fertile Crescent of the Middle East and adjacent areas. The lowest (earliest) strata at Jericho, in the Israeli-occupied West Bank of Jordan, date from about 8350–7350 B.C. (Mellaart 1975:48). The oldest excavated parts of Çatal Hüyük, in south-central Turkey, date from about 6250–5400 B.C. (p. 98). There are signs of early agriculture at Jericho, and Çatal Hüyük is contemporaneous with Jarmo, Iraq, one of the oldest agricultural village sites. In both supposed city sites, evidence of craft production and trade is extensive.

Two major theories exist about the origins of the world's oldest cities in the Middle East. The older, more conventional one says that the first cities evolved in the process of imposing expanded political and economic controls on already established regions of agricultural villages (cf. K. Davis 1980). This theory is attractive. There is much evidence to support it, and there are today numerous small cities whose elites control peasant village hinterlands. Such cities have existed for a very long time; one of the earliest of them was Uruk, Iraq, dating from approximately 4000 B.C. (Adams and Nissen 1972).

The other theory about the origin of cities was inspired by sites like Çatal Hüyük and the oldest strata at Jericho, contemporaneous with, or older than, the oldest village sites in the area and older than the other urban sites. Could it have been, then, that cities—or at least some cities—evolved without the presumed preparatory stage of extensive regions of agricultural villages? Yes, say some scholars, prominent among whom is Jane Jacobs. Jacobs's thesis is that cities are places where human beings have originated some of their most important ideas, including that whole complex of ideas and techniques called agriculture. Her vision of cities is one of heterogenetic settlements. According to Robert Redfield and Milton Singer (1954), heterogenetic cities are places where creativity and innovation are generated to a significant degree. Jacobs postulates a city that would have been a precursor of Çatal Hüyük. Her city hypothetically came into existence as a trading center for preagricultural hunter-gatherers who were trading obsidian. A form of natural glass produced by volcanic processes, obsidian was an extremely important material for knives, projectile points, and other implements. Jacobs names her city "New Obsidian" and writes an intriguing, ingenious, and factually plausible narrative of how such a city could have developed from hunter-gatherer traditions and could then have become the place where the seminal concepts of agriculture were first invented. Agriculture then, for all its importance, was not the salient invention, or occurrence, of the Neolithic Age. "Rather it was the fact of sustained interdependent, creative city economies that made possible many new kinds of work, agriculture among them" (1972:42).

We do not have to choose between the two theories. Both may be correct. Some cities may have originated as trading centers for hunter-gatherers while others may have originated as trading and administrative centers for agricultural regions. The former may have evolved into the latter, but we do not know this. What we do know, with reasonable inferential certainty, is that the earliest cities of which we have knowledge were characterized by the presence of some inhabitants who had influence beyond their immediate localities. The lives of those particular inhabitants were defined by something larger than minimal active and receptive scales.

Let us recall the "urban essentials" discussed in chapter 1 (Gulick 1974b). They include the differentiation of local inhabitants into elite and nonelite categories, the elites having larger active scales of life than the others, scales involving them directly in regional relationships that link the respective settlements to wider areas than their own. We can postulate that phenomena resembling these urban essentials were the mainsprings of the evolution of the earliest, primordial cities. In the same historical connection, it has been observed that human activities tend to be hierarchical, as reflected in the spatial organization of specialized settlements such as cities (Trigger 1980:148).

PRIMORDIAL CITIES

We can now move forward in time and consider more detailed evidence of the early development of cities.

Robert Adams and Hans Nissen's chronology (1972) of the Uruk region covers over seven thousand years, virtually the entire time span over which cities have existed, not counting those millennia before about 6000 B.C. when some cities may have developed on a hunter-gatherer ecological base. The region is a desert with watercourses, whose southern edge is formed by the meandering Euphrates River which at that point runs generally west to east. The Uruk region as studied measures roughly 28 miles from west to east and 46 from north to south. The Uruk urban site itself is in the southern part of the region, about six miles north of the river. Typical of the Middle East, this region's water supply is precarious and therefore vulnerable to drought and human factors such as weakness or strength of political controls affecting the maintenance of irrigation and drainage canals. One of the most striking features of the Adams and Nissen book is its series of schematic maps, identical in size, showing the watercourses and settlements in the region at various points in its history. At times densely settled, at other times the region has been almost empty. This simplified chronology (derived from a chart on the end papers of the book) offers some fine examples of regional ecology and of the vicissitudes of a city:

Before 5000 B.C. to about 4000 B.C.: Villages developing into villages-and-towns. Local enclaves of small-scale cultivation along minor stream branches—herding, fishing, shellfishing.

About 4000 to 3000 B.C.: Villages and small and large towns developing into increasing clusters of villages and small towns, with Uruk approaching urban size.

About 3000 to 1700 B.C.: Uruk rapidly attains maximum size, but rural abandonment begins; followed by numerous walled cities, with smaller settlements neglible; followed by cities and towns along major waterways, with a partial return of village settlements along minor branches. Beginning of the period sees first evidence of canal systems, followed by intervals of large-scale, centrally administered irrigation, combined with herding and fishing.

About 1700 to 300 B.C.: Progressive abandonment of cities and larger towns. Shift toward dispersed small town-village pattern followed by reemergence of towns and villages, with Uruk again becoming an important city. Ecology is mixed large- and small-scale irrigation, date plantations, and fishing.

About 300 B.C. to about 700 A.D.: Instability of settlements; they disappear in some places but grow to maximum size in others.

About 700 A.D. to the present: Cities and towns almost disappear; virtual absence of permanent settlements in region.

Adams and Nissen (1972) relate these vicissitudes to the effects of complex interactions between ecological and political factors. Macroscale phenomena were of crucial importance, for the Uruk region was successively a part of many hegemonies of greatly varying size and character: the early dynastic periods of Ur and Akkad and the Babylonian and Neo-Assyrian empires (second and first millennia B.C.); the Achaemenian, Seleucid, Parthian, and Sassanian empires (559 B.C. to 651 A.D.); various Islamic political entities including the Umayyad and Abbasid Caliphates and the Ottoman Empire (661 to 1918 A.D.); and the regimes of modern Iraq. During that long period, Uruk itself waxed and waned repeatedly. During Uruk's career, its much greater and more famous neighbor, Babylon, grew to its zenith and then was abandoned, while Baghdad, another neighbor, did not come into existence until both Uruk and Babylon had fallen into permanent ruin.

Baghdad, in turn, has undergone great vicissitudes since its founding in the eighth century A.D. Established on the order of a Muslim caliph, it became the instant capital of an empire, only to be almost completely ruined by conquest a few centuries later, and then rebuilt in a different form from the original. In the mid-nineteenth century, Baghdad was described as a rather out-of-the-way, grubby provincial capital. A century later, the city had become the capital of an oil-producing nation and since 1918 has grown more than ten times in population and geographical area. By the end of the twentieth century, it is expected to increase by tenfold again.

Southern and central Iraq is, then, one of the oldest persistently urbanized regions in the world. However, its cities have by no means been continuously occupied; rather, they have come and gone, in some cases gone for good. To borrow Louis Wirth's famous phrase and use it in a somewhat different sense from his, the example of Iraq suggests that once urbanism is established as a way of life in a region, it will persist there as long as it is politically and ecologically advantageous for the inhabitants; but particular cities in that region are very likely to be replaced by others in different localities (cf. K. Davis 1980:141). There is no reason for assuming that a city will continue to exist for an indefinite period of time in the same place. True, a few cities have persisted for a very long time, but, like Baghdad, they have changed beyond recognition during their careers.

VICISSITUDES

Although Baghdad is part of an area that is probably the oldest urbanized region in the world, the city itself is not the world's oldest continuously occupied urban settlement. That unique status may belong to Jerusalem, the first reference to which dates from nineteenth-century B.C. records. The city is an interesting case for a number of reasons, not the least of which is the probable cause of its long persistence. Jerusalem is

> the only city of consequence in the world which enjoys none of the physical features that were the normal attributes of a great town in ages past—strategic location, abundance of water, proximity to caravan routes and rich natural resources. Jerusalem commands no great river or important highway and overlooks no great harbour. It was never the key to the conquest of prized territory. It had certain qualities not given to all—beauty, an equable climate, a modest water supply, pure air and a luminous quality to its light which must have awed the ancients as it does the modern visitor. But these were not sufficient to have made it anything more than a feasible and attractive site of early settlement (Sharon 1973:15).

However, Jerusalem is not at all the same city it was three thousand or more years ago. The original City of David (an archaeological site requiring excavation to be seen) was not inside the present walls of the old city but outside them, to the south. The present walls are only about five hundred years old, although parts of them rest on Herodian foundations (first century B.C.). One portion of those foundations is the Western Wall, sacred to Jews, which is part of the retaining wall built to hold landfill that enlarged the Temple Mount, the platform on which the Jewish second temple was built after the Babylonian exile. Jerusalem's most famous present-day landmark, the Dome of the Rock, is in the same location (called *al-Haram al-Sharif* by the Muslims) and is in a sense a successor to the second temple, but not in the eyes of Jews or Christians. Its inscriptions, dating from about 700 A.D., declare the oneness of the God of Abraham but the primacy of Muhammad's revelation. Its surviving the tender mercies of the Crusaders is remarkable. Furthermore, despite their zeal, the Crusaders were not able to establish lasting agreement among Christians as to the precise locations in Jerusalem of various important events in the life of Jesus because the ground level of Christ's day was already below grade at the time of the Crusades. It is even farther below grade now. For the most part, the present arrangement of houses, streets, lanes, and cul-de-sacs of the old city is an example of preindustrial Middle Eastern cities of which a number of other examples also exist. There are probably many morphological continuities between this and more ancient urban forms, but none of the specific domestic structures is of "Biblical age." After all, Jerusalem has been, like most old urban sites, repeatedly destroyed, its inhabitants killed, enslaved, or dispersed.

In what sense, then, is Jerusalem the "oldest continuously inhabited" city in the world? While it is certainly a credible candidate, there is no very clear answer to the question: Continuity of what? Aside from the discontinuities in architecture and morphology already mentioned, there are others. In particular, the Jews who have moved to Jerusalem from all parts of the world in the twentieth century are different genetically and culturally from the Jews who were forced to leave it 19 hundred years ago. Is Jerusalem, indeed, really the same city it has always been? We can say only two things in answer. First, Jerusalem today is more or less in the same location (in contrast to Uruk *vis-à-vis* Babylon and Baghdad). Second, Jerusalem is the same city symbolically in the minds of successive, evolving aggregations of Jews, Christians, and Muslims. The second factor probably determined the first.

If religious symbolism and sentiment are what have kept Jerusalem going through all its vicissitudes, we need to bear this in mind in considering the persistence, however long or short, of other cities. However, there is no doubt that Jerusalem is an exceptional case. Furthermore, we cannot help wondering what Jerusalem would be like if Jews, Christians, and Muslims had traditionally treated one another more humanely than they have. What would Jerusalem be like if all three had behaved toward one another in the spirit of this passage from the Koran, which Muslims believe consists literally of the words of the God of Abraham? God's command is:

Say: We believe in Allah and that which is revealed unto us and that which was revealed unto Abraham, and Ishmael, and Isaac, and Jacob, and the tribes, and that which Moses and Jesus received, and that which the prophets received from their Lord. We make no distinction between any of them, and unto Him we have surrendered (*The Koran* 2:136).

Rome is another very old, continuously inhabited city. Dating from the first millennium B.C., it is newer than Jerusalem, but somewhat more of the ancient city remains, as is the case with Athens. Dominated by the symbols and sentiments of one religion for more than half its history, Rome has been more important as an administrative center than Jerusalem. Much of its architecture was deliberately modeled on pre-Christian Roman forms, but otherwise, the same question of continuity arises. Morphologically, how much does it resemble the Rome of the Caesars? Answer: very little. The physical remnants of classical, imperial Rome survive for the most part only because they were, until recently, buried under the detritus of centuries of destruction and rebuilding. That huge monument to inhumanity, the Colosseum, too big to be buried, probably survives because of its long-time usefulness as an enclosure for tenements. Like Jerusalem, Rome has been several times sacked, looted, and depopulated. It has been a continuously inhabited city primarily in the sense of its continuously felt symbolic importance for many people.

Jerusalem and Rome have persisted as long as they have in the same locations because of the symbolic interests of many people in maintaining their identities. Had it not been for those interests, would these old cities still exist? We only know that they have persisted in spite of repeated destruction and depopulation, the likes of which have permanently destroyed other cities. Cities come into existence, increase and decrease in size, and otherwise change in character in connection with the needs of their inhabitants and people of their regions.

Fox's city types (see chapter 1) succinctly suggest what those needs are. *When* those needs were first given urban expression in various parts of the world is one of the subjects of this chapter. The goal, however, is not a précis of the world history of cities but rather a comprehension of the concept of vicissitude to provide a much-needed perspective on certain trends observable in present-day cities.

Two additional examples of major vicissitudes, ancient and modern, are in order. In the middle third of the first millennium B.C., money in the form of gold and silver coins was invented in the Aegean area. At the same time, the classical civilization of Greece spread from the Greek mainland to the coasts of Asia Minor, Sicily, and southern Italy. The spread was effected by the establishment of a large number of small cities, mostly seaports specializing in export and import of various Mediterranean products. The innovation of money and the force of arms made possible this rapid expansion of mercantilism. Each of these small states issued its own coins, fairly standard weights were recognized, and some, such as the *tetradrachms* of Corinth and Athens, circulated throughout the central and eastern Mediterranean.

Some of the overseas Greek cities became powerful enough to rival the homeland. In 413 B.C., Syracuse, Sicily, inflicted such a disastrous defeat on Athens that it never recovered its classical glory. However, Athens survives today, whereas Syracuse is a dead archaeological site. And so are most of the other once prosperous and vital city-states. A few—such as Taranto, Messina, and Catania—evolved into modern Italian cities, but others have left no trace at all on the ground; all that remain are their coins (N. Davis 1967). These cities were destroyed by one another, or by earthquakes, or by the larger scale forces of Rome, Carthage, the Hellenistic states that succeeded Alexander the Great's empire, and others. Of course, other seaport cities developed in the Mediterranean area; it had become an urbanized region like Mesopotamia, but the careers of individual cities were subject to vicissitudes—sometimes drastic and fatal ones.

Megacities provide the modern example. At least half of the 22 largest, listed in chapter 3, have been established since the sixteenth century in places where previously there had been no cities at all. Most of them were originally colonial cities. What will their future be? As we have already seen, disaster has been predicted for them if they continue to grow. What are the alternatives to disaster? No one knows specifically, but there are sure to be vicissitudes of various kinds.

The general orientation of modern Americans seems to be that it is natural for cities to grow steadily in size and prosperity, and that if they do not, they must be intrinsically defective. This attitude is understandable, given the enormous growth in population and technological development since the Industrial Revolution, and in spite of all the wartime destruction elsewhere in the world. The natural course for cities, according to this view, is bigger and better forever. Should any countertrends appear, they are regarded as symptoms of something fundamentally wrong with cities. In America, such trends have recently appeared in the form of inner city problems, massive unemployment and decline in Frost Belt cities, and overdevelopment of cities dependent on the petroleum industry. These problems are better regarded as examples of vicissitudes than as demonstrations that cities are inherently impossible environments for humane life. The historical evidence indicates that vicissitudes are normal in the careers of cities and that people keep building new cities and rebuilding old ones in accordance with a wide variety of needs. This book is based on the point of view that contemporary urban problems are vicissitudes of evolution, not evidence of the fundamental hopelessness of city life.

PHASES OF URBAN EVOLUTION

So far, we have considered (1) the origin of cities and their earliest developments and (2) the concept of vicissitudes that provides a necessary perspective on urban change, past and present.

Modern cities are products of evolutionary pasts that took place over periods of time varying greatly in length. Traces of these pasts can be found in most cities, and their presence constitutes a reality of modern life. As we survey today's cities, we can discern some very general characteristics that have evolved through time with major impacts on the receptive scales of the inhabitants. These traits can be considered as types of macroscale urban life and as phases of evolution. However, the idea of *type* must be used only in a very general sense. Likewise, the idea of *phase* must not be applied rigidly; the phases discussed here have not replaced one another in a neat succession. They have simply evolved chronologically.

The European conquests that began in the fifteenth century A.D. and the industrialization that in later centuries accompanied the conquests had profound and radical consequences for life in cities all over the world. Indeed, it is reasonable to think about the evolution of modern cities in terms of two epochs: before and after about the year 1500 A.D.

Prior to about 500 years ago, all cities in the world were preindustrial, meaning not only that they obviously existed before modern industrialization, but also that they had the general characteristics that Sjoberg (1960) identifies with this urban category. Preindustrial cities continued to exist after 1500; Sjoberg's formulation is based on post–1500 descriptions, and there are still a few preindustrial cities. However, evolution has gone far beyond them, resulting in four city types and evolutionary phases: colonial, Western industrial, revolutionary industrial, and Third World.

CITIES BEFORE 1500 A.D.

As we already know, cities originated earlier in the central Middle East than anywhere else. Most scholars think that this phenomenon occurred because agriculture originated there.

Most specialists think that because all cities originated in the context of well-established agricultural regions, they developed everywhere on an agricultural base (cf. Braidwood and Willey 1962). In only five world areas outside the Middle East and the Mediterranean area did cities develop from their own independent agricultural bases. Four occurred in the first millennium B.C.: Middle America (Mexico and Guatemala), Peru, and a few places in India and China (Braidwood and Willey 1962:330). The fifth area consisted of scattered locations in sub-Saharan Africa, but cities evolved there much later than the first millennium B.C. The Harappan civilization in the Indus River Valley (modern Pakistan) had urban manifestations as early as the third millennium B.C. However, this development may have been derivative from the Middle East, and no continuities have been found between it and first-millennium-B.C. cities in the area.

As the Roman Empire expanded, cities deriving from the Eastern Mediterranean and Middle East were established in Western Europe and Northwest Africa. Also derivative (in this case, from India and China) were new cities in Southeast Asia (McGee 1967:29).

While trade and agricultural processing were fundamental activities in these cities, they also were often seats of political power and ceremonial centers as well. There is much argument about the priorities among these characteristics as prime movers of ancient urban life, but, as in the much older primordial cities of the Middle East, there is no doubt about the religious, symbolic presence. In areas as different and unconnected as the Roman Empire and Southeast Asia, 15 to 20 centuries ago, there were cities whose forms symbolized the cosmos and, thereby, apparently provided significance and structure to the everyday lives of their inhabitants (Fustel de Coulanges 1956; McGee 1967; Rykwert 1976).

As for indigenous American Indian cities, specialists continue to argue about whether the pyramid complexes in Mexico and Guatemala were cities and political/economic centers of states (see Price 1978:174–75), or simply non-urban ceremonial centers. Probably, some of them were both. For example, Cobá, Yucatan, was a Maya Indian city before the Spanish conquest. An analysis of the trees now growing there, together with archaeological remains, indicates that radiating from the ceremonial center were residential zones of several social classes, with the elite living nearest the center, very much as they have done in postconquest Latin American cities (Folan, Fletcher, and Kintz 1979). More familiar to travelers in Mexico than Cobá, is Teotihuacán. This is not the same as Tenochtitlán, the Aztec city the Spaniards destroyed and on whose ruins they built Mexico City. Rather, it is several miles north of the present perimeter of modern Mexico City and well known primarily for the Pyramid of the Sun and other ceremonial structures. Extending in all directions are remains of apartment compounds whose residential population is estimated to have been from 75 to 125 thousand and possibly more (Millon 1973:45). Teotihuacán was not a victim of the Spaniards. Its existence seems to have begun (on a regional agricultural base) at about the beginning of the Christian era. About 800 A.D., it was abruptly abandoned for unknown reasons.

Using Fox's terminology, many of these cities had an important regal-ritual component in their cultures, and many also had important administrative and mercantile components. In Jerusalem and Rome, influential people were guardians and enhancers of cultural traditions at various times (rather than inventors and innovators), and so those cities (among others) would qualify as "orthogenetic," according to Redfield and Singer (1954). Many preindustrial cities were fortified, and probably all had markets, these having been two essential features of the ancient urban community, according to Max Weber (1962:84ff.). In some preindustrial cities, a break from the regal-ritual-orthogenetic pattern occurred, notably in new cities in northern Europe in the tenth and eleventh centuries A.D. because of the rise to prominence of mercantile middle classes. Merchants were equally devoted to making profits and endowing city institutions in which they had great pride (Pirenne 1925:149 ff.).

We have been able to indicate some of the variations that existed in Sjoberg's preindustrial city category. The information is, however, extremely sketchy and fragmentary. The diversity of cities that existed before the year 1500 A.D. was probably much greater than available information indicates. In any case, we are certainly not justified in thinking there was a uniform type of preindustrial city up to about five hundred years ago. The most we can safely think about is that several apparently similar aspects of urban life recurred in different places at different times, along with many variations. In other words, we may not think in terms of *the* preindustrial city evolving into *the* industrial city during the past 500 years, because there had been no such monolithic thing as *the* preindustrial city, just as there is no such monolithic thing as *the* industrial city today.

CITIES SINCE 1500 A.D.

When the first European explorations and conquests began in the late fifteenth century, there were cities, some already old and others quite new, in the areas mentioned above. Everywhere, cities were fewer than they are now, and all were small by modern standards. Furthermore, there were large areas of the world where there were not, and never had been, any cities: all of North America and Australia, almost all of South America, most of Europe, and many other places. Such was the urbanized world shortly before the beginning of three momentous sets of events that have radically changed it during the past five hundred years: (1) the invasion and colonization of most of the rest of the world by Europeans; (2) industrialization, beginning in Europe; and (3) the population explosion, first in Europe and then in the rest of the world. During the twentieth century, these trends have themselves evolved along the following lines: (1) decolonization of geopolitical areas but expansion of multinational corporations; (2) development of postindustrial technology (nuclear and electronic); and (3) the beginning of systematic mass efforts to reduce population growth.

Now, as we focus our attention on the past five centuries of urban evolution in different parts of the world, we need to have in mind another aspect of vicissitudes not discussed previously. Vicissitudes involve not only discontinuities such as those we have emphasized, but continuities also. Consider the excavated houses and streets at Pompeii and Herculaneum near Naples, dating from the first century A.D. Had they not suddenly been buried under volcanic ash, they would long ago have been demolished and replaced, many times over, by newer buildings, as has been the fate of domestic architecture everywhere. By being specially preserved, these particular buildings tell us something important: the inward-facing courtyard house, characteristic of the Mediterranean area and much of the Middle East, has been there for at least two thousand years. Thinking of all the cities that have been wholly or partially destroyed and then rebuilt in the same location, how many have been rebuilt in essentially the same style as before? The sparse information available indicates different responses under different circumstances. For example, after World War II, the Polish government rebuilt at great expense several blocks of baroque houses in the center of Warsaw that had been completely destroyed by the Nazis. The houses were rebuilt in all their ornamental glory, exactly as they had been before the war. This symbolic project took precedence over other rebuilding in the city where, 15 years after the war, there were many empty blocks once full of buildings. Warsaw's rebuilding was the creation of continuity for a purpose.

A very different example is Beirut, Lebanon. In the nineteenth century, commercial and political interests saw to the complete demolition of the old walled town, a warren of Middle Eastern lanes and cul-de-sacs, and its replacement by a modern, European-style business district (laid waste in the civil war that began in the 1970s). Then-modern residential districts were, at the same time, built on formerly open land on the edges of the new central business district. These events were discontinuities of form for another set of reasons.

The old, mixed residential-commercial part of Baghdad (now threatened with demolition) was very much intact up until the 1950s when about 200 thousand people lived there. Compared to new residential areas on its peripheries, it seemed very old indeed. But it was not. It was built after the 1830s when the city was destroyed by a flood. However, the styles of houses and street layouts were the same as those that had existed before the flood. This rebuilding was continuity of a very direct form.

Typically, there are conflicting interests in cities, some for demolition to make room for new building, others for maintaining what exists. In the long run, demolition and replacement characterize urban evolution, but the replacements can be of a nature that means long-term continuities of various kinds.

Because of the interplay of continuities and discontinuities, it would be inaccurate to think of "the" preindustrial city's having been replaced, in recent times, by "the" industrial city. Consider New York and Chicago, two of the largest, most industrialized cities in the world. Both are famous for the constant demolition of important landmarks and their replacement by "innovative" structures, most of which are directly related to industry and industrialized commerce. Yet both cities also have extensive residential areas whose inhabitants are described as living on a very small ("parochial") effective scale. Such patterns of life, if not the architectural styles involved, are continuities from life in times and places unaffected by industrialization. In other words, industrialized cities like New York and Chicago are internally diverse in morphology and the patterns and styles of inhabitants' lives. While some of their characteristics are unequivocally consequences of the industrial and postindustrial revolutions, others are not. Therefore, while it is certainly convenient to use terms like "preindustrial" and "industrial," it is dangerous to become fixated on them if we are seeking understandings of the fullness and variety of urban life. This point has been made before, but it needs to be reemphasized. Sjoberg (1960) contributed a composite portrait of the preindustrial city, but his generalizations are fragmentary and downplay special features in various parts of the world. His interest was in the similarities, rather than the differences, among those cities. Furthermore, many preindustrial features of city life have been maintained in company with features that are consequences of industrialization. We therefore refer to industrial cities with the understanding that this term implies a great variety of mixes of historically preindustrial and postindustrial features. The three momentous sets of events that have radically changed the world during the past five hundred years have radically changed the urban world in many ways, but they have not transformed all of it into something totally different from what it was before. There are many urban continuities, as well as innovations. "Evolution" means on-going life through adaptation. Adaptation has different expressions. It sometimes fails, resulting in extinction. It sometimes innovates, resulting in new or modified forms. It sometimes maintains the status quo when unchanged forms are able to survive over long periods of time. *We must think of the evolution of cities in all of these terms.*

Our review of urban evolution during the past five centuries in the major areas of the world is presented in this order: Third World, Western industrial, and revolutionary industrial. The reason for considering Third World evolution first is that the European explorers and conquerors established colonial cities in what is now the Third World before Western industrialization began.

THIRD WORLD: LATIN AMERICA

When the Portuguese and Spaniards invaded South and Central America, they brought with them general notions of sixteenth-century European cities, and some of them encountered the indigenous cities of a few of the native Americans. The Spaniards destroyed Tenochtitlán but maintained the urban site by building Mexico City in its place. They tried to destroy Cuzco but could not dismantle its massive walls of tightly fitted polygonal stones, so they rebuilt Cuzco using those walls as foundations. Hence, there was some degree of continuity between Native American and Ibero-American urban cultures. Actually, many new Latin American cities besides Mexico City and Cuzco were built on indigenous urban sites; in addition, entirely new cities were founded—where the invaders needed them. The latter were, in particular, ports, mining towns, and centers of conquest control (Borah 1980:47; Hardoy 1975:21). Although many of the earliest cities were only camps, the now classic plaza-and-grid morphology was also established very early, as at Puebla in 1531 and Lima in 1535 (Hardoy 1975:20).

> Post-conquest urbanization in Latin America . . . established from the start, the supremacy of city over countryside. The foundation of cities did not respond to the pressing need for urban services by established agricultural

settlers or to the actions of an increasingly independent class of burghers concentrated around a marketplace. Rather it followed the strategic requirement of concentrating scarce human resources in a restricted, and therefore militarily defensible, perimeter. The city did not arise to serve, but to subdue. . . .

Unlike that of the city in Europe and North America, jurisdiction of the Latin American city was not restricted to a specific area and did not leave the countryside in the hands of rural proprietors. Chartered Spanish American cities "owned" their hinterlands, both in the sense of economic proprietorship—since lands were granted in the king's name by city authorities—and in the sense of politico-administrative control. . . . The royal or viceroyal authorization granting a settlement the status of *ciudad* carried with it effective control over its hinterland, frequently with no limitation other than the extension of the jurisdiction of another city (Portes 1976:9–10).

Alejandro Portes and other specialists on Latin American cities emphasize the exploitative context in which they originated in their present form and the continuation of massive social exploitation into the present. While elites often no longer live exclusively near the central plaza, social class rigidities (resting heavily on *mestizo*/urban vs. Indian/rural distinctions) remain paramount.

Of course, it is not the cities themselves that dominate their hinterlands; it is certain people, but not most people, living in them. Among the latter in present-day Latin American cities are millions of squatters, discussed in more detail later. They are not only not dominant, they are also, in the eyes of many observers, exploited by the traditional elites who are often working in the interests of multinational corporations.

Cities are very important aspects of life in Latin America, a point that needs to be made in view of the prevailing antiurban bias of many people. Of Latin America's 20 largest metropolitan cities in 1970, 16 were founded before 1620, predating New York and Boston (Portes 1976:12–13). At the end of the eighteenth century, Mexico City's population of 120 thousand was larger than the combined populations of the North American cities of Port Royal, Philadelphia, Charleston, Boston, and Quebec (Harris 1971:25). This fact is particularly impressive, considering that in the colonial period, "Philadelphia and Boston ranked among the half-dozen leading cities of the British Empire" (Jackson and Schultz 1972:1). If we compare the 20 largest metropolitan cities in Latin America in 1970 with those of the United States in the same year, the latter, on the whole, are somewhat larger, but the same order of magnitude applies. The two largest in Latin America (Buenos Aires and Mexico City) matched New York and Los Angeles with 11.5 and 7 million people. The two smallest of the 20 in Latin America (Cali, Colombia, and Cordoba, Argentina), with 915 thousand and 814 thousand, very nearly matched the two smallest in the United States, Cincinnati, Ohio, and Paterson, N.J., with 1.3 million apiece (Portes 1976:12–13).

North Americans, long accustomed to thinking of their metropolitan areas' constant growth, should note that it has been occurring in Latin America also. Here, for example, are estimated populations (Harris 1971:25) of some cities around 1800 and 1960:

	Population	
City	*c. 1800*	*c. 1960*
Buenos Aires	40,000	6,751,000
Caracas	40,000	1,492,000
Rio de Janeiro	43,000	4,691,000
Lima	53,000	1,845,000
Mexico City	120,000	4,816,000

We have already discussed the more recent prodigious growth of several of these into world megacities.

North American cities offer similar contrasts. All of this growth reflects great increases in world, regional, and national populations, basically because of persistently high birth rates coupled with decreasing age-specific death rates. In Latin America, as elsewhere, city populations have tended to grow at higher rates than their respective national populations. To a large degree, this growth is a result of the migration of noncity people, but the reality of this kind of growth has led to a widespread misperception of fertility levels in urban and nonurban populations—that city people have small numbers of children in contrast to noncity people. In United States folklore, this misperception is expressed in stereotypes such as the "large farm family" and the "isolated, small, childless city family." In the United States, the fertility of rural areas (as defined by the U.S. Census) has generally been higher than that of urban areas, but differences have been less marked than would be expected from the stereotypes. For example, in 1950, adjusted birth rates for specified aggregates in the United States were urban whites (22.0); rural whites (24.0); urban nonwhites (30.6); and rural nonwhites (37.1). Even these exceedingly general figures imply that "there are major variations in the fertility of the populations of individual cities, even those of similar size," and variations within rural areas, too (Taeuber and Taeuber 1975:262–63).

In Latin America, the notion of relatively infertile city populations' being replenished by the influx of excessively fertile rural people simply does not hold. In Mexico, Chile, and Venezuela, from 1950 to 1960, city growth

is due principally to natural growth. Births minus deaths in the cities is a higher figure than that of migrants entering the cities. . . . Of the total growth of cities 20 thousand and over, 58.0 percent in Mexico, 66.4 percent in Venezuela . . . and 70.2 percent in Chile, is due to natural growth of the cities. Therefore, contrary to common opinion, migration has not been the principal cause of city growth. As Kingsley Davis pointed out, migration was the fundamental cause of urbanization at the beginning of the industrial revolution in the countries already developed, but for the countries developing at the present time, urbanization is mainly due to the natural growth of the population (Arriaga 1968:242).

The argument is *not* that migration is an unimportant factor in the cultures of Latin American cities. It is an important factor (see Roberts 1978:chapter 4) we consider further. Rather, the point is that relatively high fertility rates (and all they imply about gender roles and family structures) are also important factors in the cultures of cities. This feature has already been noted in reference to Karachi, Isfahan, and Guayaquil.

The Caribbean area can, for our purposes, be considered an extension of

Latin America. The Spaniards totally decimated its Native American population, and there had been no indigenous cities at all. Its island populations and cultures consist of various mixes of Spanish, French, British, Dutch, and African elements. The colonial cultures established in the Caribbean were based on labor-intensive plantations whose function was to export products for the profit of European owners. Caribbean cities developed as ports and banking centers for the export economy and for residence of its managerial elites and local proletariats (Cross 1979:114–15). Influences from tourism and multinational corporations have been added in recent decades. Neither orthogenetic (traditional high culture maintenance) nor heterogenetic (innovative flowering) functions seem to have been important among any Caribbean urban populations.

Squatter settlements are a very important feature of Latin American cities. However, although some of the most insightful research on squatter settlements has been done in Latin America, a more extended discussion of them is deferred until the end of this chapter because they are a significant aspect of urban evolution not only in Latin America but in the entire Third World.

The same is true of "primate cities." First used by Mark Jefferson (1939), this term originally applied to a phenomenon occurring widely, if not typically, in Third World nations: one city many times bigger than the second largest one. Although most of Latin American capitals are primate cities, this subject is also deferred since it applies to some industrialized as well as Third World nations. It is also related to the concept of disproportionate size and growth which, in turn, is an aspect of the megacity dimension of urban evolution.

THIRD WORLD: SUB-SAHARAN AFRICA

West Africa, with one of the most distinctive preindustrial and precolonial urban traditions in the world, is one of the least urbanized regions. In 1970, only 20 percent of its population was urban (according to local, official definitions of the word), in contrast to 54 percent of the population of Latin America and 75 percent of the population of North America (Gugler and Flanagan 1978:32). The rest of sub-Saharan Africa is even less urbanized. The exception is South Africa where there are some important special conditions: no indigenous urban tradition and a strongly exploitative colonial tradition extended into the present by means of extreme social segregation enforced by the minority of South Africans who are of European ancestry. Elsewhere, in sub-Saharan Africa, there has been decolonization, as in most parts of the Third World.

Cities were associated with the West African empires of Ghana, Mali, and Songhay early in the Christian era. Many of them were located along the southern edge of the Sahara at strategic sites on the trans-Saharan trade routes to northwestern Africa and the Mediterranean. Timbuctoo, Mali, has been until very recently a representative of this trans-Saharan urban tradition. Originally regal-ritual centers, many West African cities evolved in a form that does not fit academic and popular stereotypes of urban. Especially among the Nigerian Yoruba, for example in Ibadan, many city dwellers were farmers whose lands encircled the urban center and who commuted *out*, rather than *in*, to work. Like Eurasian preindustrial cities, indigenous African ones were organized into residential quarters (Gugler and Flanagan 1978:23). There were also very early preindustrial cities in Ethiopia and Zimbabwe.

European colonialism did not destroy indigenous cities in Africa as it did in Latin America, but it imposed various forms of indirect rule on them. In this respect *like* Latin America, it developed entirely new cities, notably ports and mining towns.

Studies of sub-Saharan African cities give immense emphasis to the importance of migration in their growth. In the course of these studies, migration itself has been subjected to much analysis, with results like the Wilsons' concept of scale (see chapter 2). Earlier studies of migration depicted it as involving great stress and dislocation for the actors, and concepts like "detribalization" came into vogue, together with accounts of predominantly male populations segregated in company towns. As migration studies became more sophisticated, complexities were revealed, such as the widespread practice of migrants' maintaining their ties in rural areas (Little 1974:19), and some individuals' being more predisposed to successful adaptation in cities than others (p. 51). Migrants who at first came to towns only for short periods may subsequently stay for longer and longer periods as they become increasingly involved in the money economy (p. 33). African urban studies have led the way in amply demonstrating that migration is not a simple, one-way process, and one of their most notable contributions is the richness of their data on migrants' voluntary associations in cities (p. 96 and passim).

As decolonization has taken its course everywhere except South Africa, the racial segregation that separated Europeans and Africans in cities has evolved into social segregation among the Africans themselves (Little 1974:65). This situation reflects, among other things, differential success in participation in the money economy, which, in turn, raises the point on which Kenneth Little concludes his book: Africans are continually making adjustments in their urban and rural adaptations because they often have different stakes in both (p. 106). In Africa as elsewhere, cities are components of regional systems, and this larger-than-local scale has affected the everyday lives of inhabitants in ways of which they may not always be aware.

THIRD WORLD: EAST AND SOUTHEAST ASIA

Preindustrial cities in East and Southeast Asia originated in the first millennium A.D. The first city in Japan of which there is clear record was Nara, dating from 710 A.D. All that remain of the old city are some splendid temples and shrines, but it was originally much more extensive than it is now. Nara was Chinese in conception (see a description of preindustrial Chinese cities below), and its origins are embedded in the whole process by which Buddhism and Chinese writing were established as cultural patterns in Japan (Kornhauser 1976:54–55). Subsequently, port cities were established over several centuries, and after 1600, with the consolidation of Tokugawa political power, the castle town of Edo (now Tokyo) began to grow into a primate city. In addition to religious centers like Nara, ports, and castle towns, Japanese preindustrial cities included post or stage towns on highways, market towns, and resort towns. All have undergone many changes and enormous growth since 1868 when Japan embarked on its course of systematic industrialization (pp.

70–85). A study of a central Tokyo neighborhood which attests to the vigor of small active scales in the midst of one of the most massive and intense cases of regional industrial urbanization in the world appears in chapter 2. Edward Norbeck's restudy (1978:305–8) of Takashima, a former fishing village now completely surrounded by industrial development, confirms this vigor.

Research on three Tokyo neighborhoods in 1972 and 1977 yields valuable insights on migration and small-scale life. While the picture is not idyllic, it supports other, generally positive, observations in Tokyo. There is evidence that Japanese urban life does not depersonalize or isolate. Migrants follow charted paths, and kinship and friendship ties remain strong. This pattern is all part of a generally group-oriented culture (J. White 1982:4–6). While there are now serious tensions because of the overloaded public transportation system, the concept of planning is ancient in Japan, and a consistent principle in the culture is that "cities are entities to be organized by humans for human ends" (pp. 22–23). Further details from this study appear in chapter 6. Meanwhile, the following description is reminiscent of the opinion survey of New York residents cited in chapter 3:

> The hectic pace, dirt, noise, and coldness of Tokyo dwellers disturbs migrants; on the other hand, they generally conceded that it is easier to make a decent living, and that the obverse of human warmth in smaller communities was a prying, constraining lack of privacy compared to the fresh air of Tokyo. In many cases, still, negative evaluations were made: about half of the Tokyo study's migrants wanted to move from their present residence. But very few of them wanted to move to non-urban areas, and many did not even want to leave Tokyo (p. 83).

The Japanese are beginning some new developments that may perhaps be regarded as postindustrial urban evolution. Specifically, there is the construction over the past 20 years of Tsukuba, a completely new city about 37 miles north of Tokyo. Tsukuba is a "science city," where a new university has been established and 43 government research agencies relocated. Tsukuba was meant to replace the outmoded physical plants of those agencies; this has been accomplished. The goal of helping to disperse the population of Tokyo has not been achieved. Although about 23 thousand people have moved to Tsukuba proper, many who are employed there (as highly skilled and trained professionals) prefer to continue living in Tokyo and other cities from which they commute daily. Tsukuba lacks many of the amenities available in older cities although its housing quality is very good (Bloom and Asano 1981:1239–40).

Is Tsukuba a harbinger of a future radical departure from the inner city/ suburban complex associated with industrialized cities, namely the decentralization of important urban occupations and residences of their employees in new cities of moderate size? Some observers claim that this phenomenon is beginning in the United States, but the totally planned and government-sponsored accomplishment of Tsukuba is perhaps unique except possibly for a science city in Soviet Siberia about which very little information is available (pp. 1230–31). Other governments are working on somewhat similar ideas. Egypt, for example, is gradually developing several new cities on the edges of the Nile Delta in the hope that people will, in large numbers, come to live in them rather than in Cairo. This goal is, however, very far from being accomplished at this time. In the People's Republic of China, 12 satellite cities were built on the outskirts of Shanghai between 1958 and 1980 (E. J. Perry 1980:26). It remains to be seen whether efforts of this kind really are new stages in urban evolution or, as is generally the case with the "new towns" in Great Britain, only variants of industrial suburbanism.

Japan is, like the much less industrialized Latin America, one of the most urbanized regions of the world. Southeast Asia is, like sub-Saharan Africa, one of the least urbanized (McGee 1967:23). As with sub-Saharan Africa, however, Southeast Asia's earliest cities were preindustrial, and colonial cities were later added to them. Hindu/Buddhist states established the preindustrial cities that were, in many respects, derivative from India. The remains of one, Angkor Thom in Kampuchea, is a temple complex whose architecture symbolically represents the Hindu concept of the structure of the universe (p. 37). Among the much newer cities, Bangkok also has an important regal-ritual component in its culture (complexes of Buddhist temples strongly associated with a sacred sovereign whose capital the city is). Much more, however, goes on in Bangkok, and to call it a regal-ritual city would be to stereotype and oversimplify it.

Most of the major cities of the region are, like Calcutta and Bombay, colonial in origin. They include Rangoon, Hanoi, Ho Chi Minh City (formerly Saigon), Singapore, Manila, Jakarta (formerly Batavia), and Surabaja (McGee 1967:53). All are primate cities originally founded to serve the exploitative interests of various European countries and originally reflecting those interests to some extent in layout and architecture. All have recently experienced decolonization by various means. Among the characteristics they share with other Third World cities are large numbers of squatters.

One of their special characteristics is the significant component of Chinese people in their populations. One early microurban study of the Chinese living in Singapore (Kaye 1960) set forth two facts substantiated in other places. First, the Chinese adapt much better than do most Westerners to extremely crowded living conditions. Second, a large proportion of the Chinese living in Southeast Asian cities were not born in China, yet they maintain Chinese ethnic identity (McGee 1967:168). Hong Kong is a special case. Still a British colony, it will be reunited with China in 1997, and, though very cosmopolitan, it is basically Chinese in culture. Important research on the ability of Chinese to live successfully in very high domestic density has been done in Hong Kong (Anderson 1972; Mitchell 1971).

Since the defeat of United States armed forces in Vietnam and Kampuchea, there have been mass media reports that the present governments of those countries have been forcing many or most of their city residents to move to rural areas. Whatever the truth about the extreme cruelty, indeed genocide, these policies have been reported to involve, this deurbanization cannot be ignored. Among many questions one would want answered are: What have been the effects on the cities? Is there anything that could be learned from these effects that would be useful in our search for greater insights into urban life?

Another process at work in Southeast Asia (and possibly elsewhere) has been called "diffuse urbanization" (Hackenberg 1980). This development of networks of market and service towns in areas previously devoted to subsistence farming reflects national goals to increase domestic food supplies by industrializing and to strengthen national trading positions through the augmented export of agricultural products. Government intervention and multinational corporations are involved (p. 403). The following comments make the process sound very much like postindustrial urban evolution:

> Urban structures and systems of communities do not develop from the top down. . . . Complex settlement patterns evolve from the bottom up. But— this evolution does not take place unassisted. Prerequisites include (1) substantial investment in infrastructure (highways, irrigation, electrification) by government; (2) acceptance of Green Revolution technology (high-yield seed varieties, mechanization, fertilizer, herbicides and pesticides) by both large- and small-scale farm operators. Subsequent acceleration in demand for credit, technical support services, and communications provides the environment for a dispersed system of rural service centers (p. 404).

What sort of cities will diffuse urbanization produce? How will it affect already existing cities? Hackenberg does not address such questions because most of this kind of development appears to be in planning or incipient stages.

Papua New Guinea's position relative to Southeast Asia is parallel to the Caribbean's position relative to Latin America. It had no precolonial cities, and its precolonial cultural traditions were never involved in the Hindu/Buddhist/Muslim traditions of Southeast Asia, just as Caribbean aboriginal cultural traditions were apparently unconnected with those of the continental mainland. Its cities, too, are all colonial in origin; but beyond this, superficial resemblances end. A unique feature of Papua New Guinea is that its indigenous population was not decimated by the colonizers (who were mostly Dutch, German, and British). Furthermore, the indigenous population constitutes one of the few remaining substantial aggregations of "primitive" people in the world, their cultures about as far removed from anything urban as most people can imagine.

Papua New Guinea's urban settlements (defined primarily in terms of the presence of foreign people and their institutions) totaled about 281 thousand people in 1971, 75 thousand of them in Port Moresby (Levine and Levine 1979:35, 109). Founded in the nineteenth century, the cities' original inhabitants were almost entirely foreign, with some indigenous people living in servants' quarters and later in barracks compounds on the peripheries. The indigenous urban population has greatly increased recently, and at present most are first-generation migrants who very frequently move back and forth between the cities and rural areas (p. 33). About two million people, living in 12 thousand essentially independent villages and speaking seven hundred different languages, occupy the rural area (p. 8). Culturally diverse in many ways, all villagers have in common lives characterized by very small-scale dimensions. One might suppose, therefore, that their adaptations to city life would not be successful, but actually the Levines present a rather balanced picture of this transition. Predictably, new adaptive social forms have been developed, based on traditional modes. Most notable among these is *wantok*, cooperative relations among co-ethnics, on which Hal and Marlene Levine place considerable emphasis.

Employment of the *wantok* idiom among Papua New Guinea townsmen is not only adaptive in terms of mediating the urban environment by providing community and personal security, but can also be useful in the work situation. The existence of *wantok* ties with workmates can function as a basis for cooperation on the job . . . (although the goals of these *wantok* groups may sometimes conflict with those of the institution within which they work). . . . [S]uch ties between workers and people outside the institution can . . . provide for better extension services (as, for example, when the government bureaucracy is thus made more open to public access), while . . . it may lead to preferences which interfere with the very working of the institution in question (as when the police avoid arresting their *wantok* and thus damage their reputation with the wider urban population) (p. 81).

Here again, a vignette of city life casts doubt on the validity of the impersonal, anomic stereotype of cities.

THIRD WORLD: INDIA

With the world's second largest national population (including three megacities) and having been the source of Southeast Asian urban life, India warrants a discussion of its own. As noted earlier, urban life in India dates continuously from the first millennium B.C. Some Hindus claim that Varanasi, their pilgrimage city on the Ganga River, is the oldest continuously inhabited city in the world, but archaeological remains have not substantiated this claim one way or the other.

Like Latin America, sub-Saharan Africa, and much of Southeast Asia, India was invaded and colonized by various Europeans but overwhelmingly by the British. To the many preindustrial cities (such as Varanasi, Old Delhi, and Agra) were added the three "presidency towns" (colonial cities): Bombay, Calcutta, and Madras. Bombay and Calcutta, as well as being world megacities, together with other Indian cities are of scholarly interest because of their spatial expressions of the Indian caste system (see Hazlehurst 1970). We have already discussed Lynch's study of the Agra shoemakers in this connection.

At the macroscale level, India can be seen as a very large national urban region, and Wallace Reed (1970) has analyzed some of the major linkages in this regional system. Delhi, India's capital since 1911, is a major link. Delhi was not one of the presidency towns; rather, it had once been an Islamic preindustrial imperial city like Cairo, Isfahan, and Istanbul (Noe 1984). Like them, it has a *madina* with a major citadel, palace complexes, and ornamental open spaces. To this was added New Delhi. Huge, grandiose modern governmental buildings (reminiscent of Washington, D.C.) were built, along with tree-shaded streets of single-family houses, designed for British officials, set in lawns and flower beds (reminiscent of al-Ma'adi, the originally British suburb of Cairo, and Ramat-Gan, a suburb of Tel Aviv, established in Palestine by European Jews). More recently, high-rise hotels, apartment and condo blocks, and squatter settlements have proliferated. See A. D. King (1976) for a theoretically oriented analysis of the spatial relationships of Old and New Delhi, with implications for Third World cities generally.

Reed's study of India's urban system concentrates on locations of head and branch offices of major corporations and establishes that the largest cities— such as Bombay, Calcutta, Delhi, and Madras—are the major concentrations of power and decision making (1970:130). This situation is a variant of the primate cities phenomenon. Because primate cities, by their very nature, attract relatively more migrants than do smaller cities, characteristics and problems of migrants and migration tend to be magnified in the larger ones.

THIRD WORLD: THE MIDDLE EAST

The Middle East is comparable to Latin America in being one of the most urbanized regions in the Third World. However, it differs in other respects from Latin America and the other areas discussed. As we already know, it has a much older and more extensive preindustrial city tradition than the other areas, and the effects of European political dominance in the nineteenth and early twentieth centuries were varied. In only a few instances did they clearly resemble the conspicuous colonial city evolution elsewhere.

The preindustrial urban tradition has, as usual, been encapsulated in a stereotype: "the Islamic city." Understandably impressed by the morphology of the preindustrial parts of Middle Eastern cities, some specialists in the history, art, and architecture of the area have attempted to show that it is a uniform type consequent on the theological and social tenets of Islam. Other area specialists remain unconvinced. Do the courtyard houses, the narrow, crooked, often dead-end residential alleys, and the concentrations of shops according to specialities along roofed-over streets really reflect Islam? How many of them actually antedate Islam, having evolved earlier and directly from the primordial cities discussed previously? No one knows for sure, and the arguments go on.

However, certain things are reasonably clear. The preindustrial portions of modern Middle Eastern cities, which once admirably served the social and ecological needs of their inhabitants, have been extensively demolished, and those that remain intact are threatened. This situation is ironic since it is largely Middle Easterners who have demolished and threatened. Jean-Claude David (1979:137) and R. I. Lawless (1980) discuss some of the details of the threatened demolition and plans and efforts to control it. The *madina* (from an Arabic word for city) is the only uniquely Middle Eastern part of the cities, yet cultural distinctiveness as a political rallying point is a frequent theme of many of those Middle Eastern city dwellers who have forsaken the *madina* to live in European-style villas and high-rise apartment blocks. Having once housed the entire population, those *madinas* that survive to any great extent are now mostly occupied by poor people and recent migrants who cannot afford to live elsewhere. The process has been going on for some time. In Jerusalem, upper-class Muslims moved from the *madina* to new neighborhoods outside it in the late nineteenth/early twentieth century (Kark and Landman 1980); in Tripoli the same was happening at about the same time (Gulick 1967b:28).

The primary motivation for this internal migration seems to have been the desire to be "modern and fashionable," rather than "backward and medieval." The actual demolition of *madinas*, usually with scant regard for needs of the dispossessed inhabitants, has been because of various economic and political interests. Where *madinas* survive, one has the impression that the city must be extremely old, virtually timeless, but this impression is deceptive, for the *madina* is an architectural/morphological complex that evolved as an adaptation partly to the desert-oasis ecological environment and partly to a cultural tradition that accepts the juxtaposition of religious and mercantile public functions and emphasizes the importance of private family life. This complex is probably pre-Islamic, but it has been continually renewed (with Islamic embellishments such as mosque architecture) until recently. Some Muslim architects, like Hassan Fathy (1973), encourage the new construction of traditional morphology. Much of the old Jewish Quarter of Jerusalem has been rebuilt by the Israelis in this mode, but the prevailing style is derivative from the West.

Most Middle Eastern cities are old by North American standards, but they are not, among themselves, equally old. One cannot easily guess their absolute or relative ages from their appearance. The *madina* of Damascus is much newer than its supposed original settlement site was. Alexandria and Beirut date from pre-Christian times, but the former's *madina*, such as it is, does not impress one with great antiquity, and the latter has none at all. Baghdad, Cairo, and Isfahan date from the early Islamic period (eighth to ninth centuries A.D.), but their *madinas* are not that old. Casablanca and Tehran have *madinas*, but the cities as such are only about two hundred years old. A few cities are less than a hundred years old—Tel Aviv, Ankara, and Abadan, for example. For the most part, Middle Eastern cities present palpable evidence of enormous twentieth-century population growth in the modes of industrial and postindustrial technologies, grafted onto *madinas* which, to the extent they survive, represent long continuities of certain ecological and social needs.

One part of the Middle East where *madinas* are especially well-preserved is Morocco. This situation is no accident; it is related to the more intense French colonization of Morocco (and Algeria and Tunisia) than occurred in most other parts of the Middle East. After they established their colonial control of Morocco in 1912, the French set out deliberately to restrict Moroccans to the *madinas*, building adjacent, but separate, new European-style cities for foreigners like themselves. Abu-Lughod calls this "urban apartheid" and points out that since Morocco has gained its independence, the Moroccans have, in their turn, tended to segregate themselves, with the upper and upper-middle social classes moving into the areas originally reserved for foreigners (1981:135ff and 259ff).

Confined in relatively small oases separated by vast, sparsely inhabited territories, the Middle East urban population is concentrated in large cities. In the mid–1970s more than 140 cities had 100 thousand inhabitants or more (Clarke 1980:44). By the late 1970s, at least 13 had a million or more: Alexandria, Algiers, Ankara, Baghdad, Beirut, Cairo, Casablanca, Damascus, Greater Khartoum, Istanbul, Tel Aviv-Jaffa, and Tunis. Riyadh and Amman are fast approaching this company, having been nothing more than small towns at the beginning of the twentieth century (p. 45). Much of this growth has been generated by migration from rural areas and between cities of different sizes. Migrant residents in cities vary from about 50 to 90 percent (especially in the oil boom areas of the Arabian Peninsula and the Persian Gulf) to about 15 to 30 percent, especially in the Fertile Crescent and Egypt (Findlay 1980:58–59).

Once again, the question arises whether the enormous growth of cities is caused mainly by the influx of many highly fertile rural people who more than replenish the relatively infertile indigenous city population. And once again, the answer must be carefully qualified. In Beirut, Edwin Prothro (1961:45) and David Yaukey (1961:53) independently discovered substantial differences in numbers of children and fertility rates between Christians and Muslims. Furthermore, both found that fertility rates of uneducated Muslims, urban and rural, were high and about the same, while those of educated city Christians and Muslims were relatively low. Many migrants are highly fertile, but so are some indigenous city dwellers. Joseph Chamie (1981:85) has recently criticized Yaukey's methodology, but he, too, shows clear differences among Christians and Muslims in Lebanon living in both cities and villages.

In Egypt, Abu-Lughod (1965:236–37) notes that urban and rural birth rates have been high and essentially the same, and that the number of live births to women living in Cairo decreases as their education increases, taking duration of marriage into account (see also a more recent study of Cairo schoolgirls and their mothers [Bach et al. 1985]). Since the great majority of Cairo women are uneducated, it follows that many of them have numerous children.

Vincent Costello says that Middle Eastern countries differ: in Egypt, Libya, and Lebanon, urban and rural fertility patterns are about the same, but in Turkey, Iran, Syria, and Saudi Arabia, urban rates are lower (1977:55). The reasons are obscure, but in conclusion, he writes:

> Natural increase caused mainly by declining mortality is of greater significance than in tropical Africa, the sex-ratio imbalance is less blatant and the urban population much less transient. Most cities are old rather than new creations and they have a local core of indigenous inhabitants. These people have some of the same values as the migrants, in particular the importance of family ties, and for the most part they have the same religion, Islam (p. 56).

All indications are that Middle Eastern city environments sustain strong family life patterns, neighborhood support systems, and communal religious activities, not only in the remaining preindustrial quarters but in the newer sections as well. Most Middle Eastern cities also show the effects of industrial and postindustrial technology, reflecting influences from Europe, North America, and Japan. Their respective national governments are important vectors in these influences, but Middle Eastern people have always been highly suspicious of their governments which, more often than not, have been corrupt and inefficient. Therefore, government plans and policies with respect to industrialization and urban evolution are characteristically uncertain of execution. Furthermore, government-sponsored plans have, to a major degree, been made under contract with foreign firms whose awareness of the felt needs of Middle Eastern city dwellers is doubtful (see M. H. P. Roberts 1979:148–203).

The violent horrors in Beirut during the 1970s and 1980s seem to belie the positive themes of the preceding material. This situation requires comment. Like Belfast and Londonderry, Beirut has become divided into hostile parts. In each of these cases, war on a much larger scale than the cities themselves is the cause. In Beirut, the large-scale problem has many ingredients, including exploitation of the traditional Lebanese sectarian groups by one another; immigration of hundreds of thousands of Palestinian refugees deprived of a homeland; invasion and destruction by Israel; Syrian occupation; and inability or unwillingness of the United States and Soviet Union to exert their power effectively in the cause of peace. These factors affect Beirut disastrously, but all are quite removed from the city itself in origin and potential resolution.

If life in Beirut has become a nightmare for many people, it is not because of any intrinsic fault in the city itself. Indeed, that people continue to live there probably attests to the resilience of their support groups and support systems (Munro 1987), as has been observed in Londonderry as well (Bailey 1978).

WESTERN INDUSTRIAL CITIES

The earliest industrial cities evolved in the eighteenth century from preindustrial ones in Western Europe and Great Britain. Soon thereafter, North American colonial cities like Boston, New York, and Philadelphia also began to evolve industrially, and other industrial cities proliferated. Industrial cities also evolved in places like Australia where a Western European expatriate population and its economic and political interests were predominant.

The technological processes that began with the Industrial Revolution have themselves evolved by rapid stages into the high-tech electronic processes of the late twentieth century, and this evolution has taken place conjointly with the further and continuing evolution of industrial cities themselves.

Two major trends characterize the recent evolution of Western industrial cities: (1) proliferation of residential and commercial suburbs and (2) transformations taking place in the central or inner cities. These macroscale phenomena have had profoundly important effects on the small-scale lives of most Western industrial city dwellers. We need to remember that a highly selective perception of these evolutionary events was the primary source of the bipolar moralistic model. In reviewing these trends, London is a good, extended example, supplemented by material from other cities.

London has inspired more thinking, theorizing, and experimentation in regard to urban life than probably any other city in the world. It has been the scene of countless novels, short stories, plays, movies, and TV shows. Its nineteenth-century early industrial squalor has had wide repercussions to this day through the reactions of Karl Marx, Friedrich Engels, Charles Booth, Charles Dickens, and others. By contrast, its magnificence (The City and Westminister), its elegance and sophistication (South Kensington and Mayfair), its cosmopolitanness (one of the greatest varieties of ethnic cuisines in the world), and its raunchiness (Soho) have inspired many and attract millions of visitors. Repulsion and attraction, misery and delight; these words highlight the many subenvironments of the great magnitude of London. So, too, does this vision:

> More than just a huge city, it is a collection of villages each with a distinct personality. . . . They range from the quiet and rural—like Barnes and Richmond—to the bustling and cosmopolitan—like Bayswater and Soho. These villages give some idea of how big London is and what infinite variety it can provide (Crookston 1978:7).

Peter Crookston's book, designed for visitors to London, features vignettes of 21 "villages," but four areas of London—Bethnal Green, Greenleigh, Dagenham, and Stockwell—are not mentioned at all. Most visitors depart from London without ever having heard of these areas or of many more, also not mentioned by Crookston and his associates. Social scientists have studied these four areas carefully, as we shall see.

Far from being consummately British, London's inhabitants are highly diverse racially and culturally. James Watson (1977c) has edited a collection of essays on non-British ethnic groups in Great Britain, most of them with members in London: Sikhs, Pakistanis, West Indians, West Africans, Poles, Italians, and Greek and Turkish Cypriots. In his essay on the Chinese, Watson says the vast majority is associated with family restaurants.

[They] have built up their catering establishments with remarkably little help from institutions or individuals outside their own ethnic community . . . [so they] live, work, and prosper without changing their way of life to suit British social expectations. . . . The focus of Britain's Chinese Community . . . is Gerrard Street in London's West End, known to the immigrants as . . . "Chinese People's Street" the core of an incipient Chinatown complex and . . . an interesting urban development in its own right. . . . [I]n the mid–1960's, several Chinese restaurants opened in rapid succession on Gerrard Street . . . [serving] authentic dishes previously unavailable in Britain and . . . almost exclusively to the growing Chinese population . . . but the proprietors soon learned to accommodate outsiders. Nevertheless, Gerrard Street's restaurants continue to be the major gathering places for Chinese all over Britain and . . . Europe . . . [as] arenas for social exchange between widely scattered peoples and groups (1977a:181, 192–93, 196).

Somewhat like the Hausa in Ibadan, the Chinese in London belong to far-flung networks of people of their own culture and keep themselves quite isolated. Perhaps the impact of those cities' magnitudes on them is minimal, because they contain themselves in their own environments.

Large-scale diversity and its small-scale expressions occur in other ways. Theories about where people choose to live in London may sound silly, but experienced real estate agents believe in them. For example:

[U]pward-mobility people like to live on hills (Hampstead, Highgate, Kingston). . . . There is the north-south hypothesis, . . . that people from the north of England prefer north London, while people from the southeast like south and west London. [T]he point-of-entry idea . . . says that you tend to live in an area vaguely served by the station or terminal where you first arrived in London. Thus Australians, arriving at Heathrow, discovered Earl's Court, the Continentals like the purlieus of Victoria, and the Irish quarters of London are defined as being however far you can walk from Euston carrying two suitcases—Islington, Camden Town . . . Bloomsbury (Mary Kenny 1978:23).

Two experiments in urban life for which London is notable are (1) "new towns" (attempts to establish small-scale, work-and-residence communities on the fringes of the outer metropolitan area) and (2) public housing intended to replace slum dwellings. Among the many reactions to government housing policies, there are now an estimated 30 thousand squatters in London—predominantly young adults and two-thirds single males. Various regulations that favor family residence units make it difficult for them to find homes in more conventional ways. Squatting is, to a considerable degree, also a protest against government policies:

One-third of the city's housing is between 50 and 100 years old. As a consequence, vast inner city tracts have experienced normal . . . building obsolescence, urban decay, and slum clearance, resulting in residential abandonment and neighborhood decline. In London . . . the "contagion of abandonment" has been a particularly sinister urban phenomenon, claiming not only decrepit structures but also structurally sound and habitable dwellings. Well-intentioned, but ill-conceived government redevelopment schemes have resulted in the systematic depopulation of entire districts, while budgetary problems, construction delays, and sheer mismanagement of housing stock have left buildings standing in conspicuous vacancy for years. Displaced populations are often "interred" in grim government shelters awaiting the promise of rehousing at some unspecified future date (Kearns 1981:127).

About 200 thousand homeless families in London were on housing council waiting lists in 1981 when an estimated 100 thousand government-owned houses in the city stood empty, many vacant for five to ten years because of the predatory violence by which residents fear they may be victimized. The same factors led to abandonment (and eventual demolition) of the Pruitt-Igoe project in St. Louis and depopulation and desolation of the South Bronx in New York City.

Most squatting is in government-owned properties, and despite the insecurity of illegal occupancy, the squatters' typical practice of renovating their quarters—and their neighborhoods—has brought the phenomenon virtually to the point of being recognized as a legitimate adaptation to the environment (Kearns 1981:150).

Meanwhile, for many decades, other vicissitudes have affected small-scale environments in London, some of them carefully studied. The findings of those studies, supplemented by observations made directly in the early winter of 1979, follow.

Bethnal Green is one of the old parts of the East End, an easy walk from the Tower of London. Among its earliest residents were Huguenot weavers, refugees from France. It is still a working-class area. In the nineteenth century, its typical housing was two-story row-houses, grossly overcrowded and unsanitary (Young and Willmott 1975:35). By the 1920s much of the housing in Bethnal Green and the East End had so deteriorated that the government embarked on a massive rehousing program involving demolition and relocation in new accommodations. Young and Willmott (1957) studied Bethnal Greeners in their old location and in a new housing project (Greenleigh) farther east. They discovered in the old location a strong kinship system whose pivotal figure was the mother (or senior female) of the household, known as "Mum." They also discovered great attachment to proxemic space, in particular the local pub. As noted in chapter 1, Young and Willmott's book entered the literature at a time when urban life in general, and slum life in particular, were assumed to be disorganized and anomic, and the book inspired extensive reconsideration of those ideas.

In early 1979, Bethnal Green was a very lively place. Like all London residential sections with a recognized identity, it has a "high street," where shops providing daily necessities are concentrated in easy walking distance of home. Bethnal Green's high street features second-hand clothing vendors on the sidewalks. The adjacent blocks are fronted by high- and low- rise public housing, some empty lots (sites of demolished buildings), and a few streets of two-story row houses. In 1979 they were in very good repair, often with brightly painted front doors. They were probably the best of the nineteenth-century housing stock, selectively preserved. At an intersection of two streets of these houses, there were pubs on three of the four corners, as well as more on the high street. The mediation of large magnitude through a small-scale subenvironment is very much in evidence in Bethnal Green. It has obviously survived the destructive effects of renewal Young and Willmott observed.

Dagenham is a fast half-hour train ride eastward from the Tower of London underground station. One emerges from the above-ground station onto a high street catering to working-class people. There the resemblance to Bethnal Green ends. Dagenham is wide of sky with no features on the horizon and no building over two stories high. From the station, double-decker city buses take one through uniform residential streets, eventually to another high street. The houses are almost all the same: grey brick, two story with sloping roofs, arranged in various ways so that each has a back garden and a front yard, with definite neighbors. There are no garages or carports, and many cars are parked on the sidewalks. At the second high street is a large, barnlike pub, rather different from the Bethnal Green pubs which are domestic-looking structures except for their brightly colored ornamental street-level facades.

Dagenham was built between 1921 and 1938, to house 100 thousand people and replace their deteriorated East London housing (Willmott 1963:6). Willmott emphasizes the planners' lack of sensitivity to the social needs of the inhabitants (East Enders), including the lack of public meeting places and only nine pubs for the entire settlement!

Young and Willmott discovered that Bethnal Greeners who moved to Greenleigh suffered great social deprivation, separated from their kinship networks and local ties. However, they realized that they could not ignore that Greenleigh residents had been there no more than three years. So Willmott undertook his study of Dagenham where there were younger adults who had been born there. One of his major findings is that many, though not all, native-born Dagenhamites were involved in East End-like networks, including the central role of Mum (Willmott 1963:29–36), despite Dagenham's physical layout's being less conducive than the East End's to operating such networks. So, once again, we see the massive magnitude of the city expressed in the form of diverse subenvironments with no deterministic effects on the inhabitants.

Many people believe that the magnitude of the Western industrial city is felt at its maximum in "the inner city." Usually, the inner city is thought of in monolithic terms. To counteract this notion and to elucidate a number of inner-city problems in London, Graeme Shankland and associates selected the Stockwell area, on the south bank of the Thames, for intensive study. One criterion for selection was that the area be reasonably representative of inner London, with different housing types, social classes, and ethnic groups (Shankland, Willmott, and Jordan 1977:9–10).

Stockwell, in the Borough of Lambeth, then had a population of about 50 thousand. Stockwell's housing includes oases of elegant early nineteenth-century houses in squares and crescents; working-class row-houses in various states of repair; suburban-type semi-detached villas; and a large variety and number of public housing projects (high-, medium-, and low-rise). The latter range from projects popular with their residents to others so unpopular that many of the apartments, even quite new ones, were vacant and boarded up in 1979. Shankland and colleagues found that the most popular projects have a small-scale visual impact on their residents despite being very large in terms of number of units. Vandalism and neglect are more pronounced in those of large visual scale (but not necessarily maximum size) with extensive areas of public space for which no one feels responsible (pp. 156–59). Another factor in popularity or unpopularity of housing types of all kinds is population density, most particularly density of children per acre and ratio of children to adults. Where these densities are high, so are vandalism and various forms of annoyance. The oases are the least dense, and high-rise projects are the most dense. High density of children, and the annoyances associated with it, are related to family stress and negative perceptions of neighbors (pp. 47–49).

Very poor and deprived people live in Stockwell, but only "in particular pockets of it" (p. 74). Among these are many of the 26 percent of the study sample who want to move from Stockwell but cannot afford to do so (p. 117). Of the 74 percent who want to remain in Stockwell, 38 percent cite nearness to job as the main reason. Another 20 percent mention attachment to the district and nearness of family and friends.

The evolution of London and its major parts is summarized succinctly in these figures (Young and Willmott 1975:41):

Year	Inner London	Population in Thousands Greater Outer London	Outer Metropolitan London	Total (London Region)
1861	2,808	414	1,013	4,235
1931	4,397	3,907	1,899	10,203
1971	2,723	4,656	5,290	12,699

The trends in London's recent evolution are basically similar to those in other Western industrial cities:

(1) Growth of central or inner city stalled or reversed
(2) Continued growth of suburbs and peripheral areas, resulting in continuing metropolitan area growth
(3) Migration from inner city to suburbs and peripheral areas of businesses and industries, including those that hire many unskilled, semiskilled, and other nonprofessional workers
(4) Migration from inner city to suburbs and peripheral areas of working- and middle-class residents, often members of minority racial/ethnic groups, in large numbers
(5) Migration *into* inner city of lower-class and underclass residents, usually members of minority racial/ethnic groups subject to prejudice and segregation by the majority, resulting in inner-city "ghettoization."

The conjunction of large numbers of poor, uneducated people and inadequate employment opportunities has resulted in very serious social dislocations in inner cities. Violent crime is the most publicized of these ills, and its increase in British cities has been especially notable. Brixton, adjacent to Stockwell, has been the scene of lethal and destructive race riots involving police and immigrant blacks from the West Indies.

In 1985, youths from Liverpool attacked Italians at a soccer match in Belgium, resulting in 38 deaths. Commenting on this event, a British journalist wrote that British society has produced a breed of youth for whom soccer is a surrogate form of violence. Although football hooliganism is by no means unknown elsewhere in Europe, it is uniquely violent, mindless and widespread in Britain. . . . [P]eople . . . are frustrated, unhappy, lonely and bored to the point where violence is a pleasurable release . . . from a society—or at least an area of that society—that has failed to offer them stimulation, friendship, employment or hope. Has Britain, then, alienated its unemployed or underprivileged youths more starkly than in other Common Market countries? [This] seems an inadequate explanation. What may distinguish Britain, however, is the persistence of an insular jingoism . . . a persistent sense of British superiority "on the continent" by being tougher and nastier than the locals (R. Cohen 1985:31).

Britain's inner city problems—basically comparable to those of other Western industrial cities—are exacerbated by consequences of the disintegration of the British Empire since World War II. Having evolved as the center of a vast empire, with London as its capital, the country and its cities are now painfully adapting to a greatly diminished political economy.

Ironically, these negative vicissitudes occur at the same time as commercial redevelopment, "gentrification" (residential revitalization by middle-class people which sometimes, unfortunately, dispossesses low-income residents of the formerly deteriorated housing), and an office glut caused by overbuilding office skyscrapers for speculative purposes (in 1985, 20 percent or more of office space in many United States cities was vacant).

To some extent, these Western industrial urban phenomena occur in Third World cities, too. In Egypt, for example:

In utter frustration, the chairman of the parliamentary committee on housing walked out on his job recently, grumbling, "Dwellings without dwellers and dwellers without dwellings." With these words, Milad Hanna spotlighted one of Egypt's most serious problems—housing. New high-rise apartment blocks are empty, while 500,000 people have no homes except tombs, tents and tin shacks. Another 2.5 million are crammed together, with whole families living in single rooms (El Mahdi 1986:8).

The Egyptian problem grew gradually, the result of unforeseen consequences of government policies and, in the case of the vacant luxury housing, private sector speculation.

Just as data from London encapsulate some of these recent evolutionary phenomena, so does recent information from Chicago:

In the few square miles that most visitors see of this city, all seems prosperous. A Bloomingdale's store is going up across from a new Neiman-Marcus. Free-spending conventioneers flood here, and local yuppies jam expensive bistros along the well-known "Gold Coast" neighborhood. But "Chicago's development has become a tale of two cities," says Robert Brehm . . . of Bickerdike Development Corp., whose offices are sandwiched between boarded-up storefronts on the city's West side. The gleaming new office towers downtown mask a steadily eroding base of manufacturers with large payrolls and of small businesses with growing payrolls.

[O]ver the last decade, 1,344 factories, or 19%, closed in the city. Between 1978 and 1983, manufacturing employment, once Chicago's bread and butter, dropped 27%.

For the workers and entire communities left behind by employers there are anxiety, anger and depression . . . 26% of jobless steelworkers in Southeast Chicago were forced to move because of reduced pay, 15% had one or more cars repossessed and 44% didn't have any health insurance. "My feeling is one of tragedy," says Alice Peurala, the president of United Steelworkers Union Local 65 (Helyar and Hanson 1986:1, 23).

There is no lack of theorizing on the causes and possible cures of these problems. One book-length example is Sam Bass Warner's history of Philadelphia in which he develops his concept of the "private city."

The quality which above all else characterizes our urban inheritance is privatism. By and large the productivity and social order of the metropolis flowed from private institutions and individual adjustments. So did its weaknesses. Privatism left the metropolis helpless to guarantee its citizens a satisfactory standard of living. Privatism encouraged the building of vast new sections of the city in a manner well below contemporary standards of good layout and construction. Privatism suffered and abetted a system of politics . . . so weak it could not deal effectively with the economic, physical, and social events that determined the quality of life within the city (1971:202).

The other example is Michael Macdonald's polemical exposé of the American downtown renaissance of the 1970s and 1980s (such as the recent refurbishing of downtown Boston, Chicago, and other cities). His theme is that the glitter is a cosmetic cover-up of social decay and disintegration which he describes in detail. Macdonald accounts for "America's dying cities" in terms of general cultural flaws, and he proposes cures: "The draft, drug control, tax reform and full employment—these federal programs and a revival of civic interest, in voting or voluntarism, can help restore equity and stability to America and save its cities" (1984:385).

In one important respect, Warner's and Macdonald's views coincide with those that inform this book: urban problems are expressions of general cultural and societal problems rather than being intrinsic to cities.

REVOLUTIONARY INDUSTRIAL CITIES

The revolutionary governments of the Soviet Union and China are founded on Marxist/socialist ideologies and dedicated to remaking human society in terms of them. The largest and third largest countries in the world, they have by far the most autocratic and centralized governments of all the major countries. Planning and control are conspicuous parts of their autocracies. Established by twentieth-century revolutions, both have subsequently experimented with comprehensive plans—the Soviet Union's several five-year plans and China's Great Leap Forward, Cultural Revolution, and the recent Revisionisms-of-Mao. Both suffered millions of people killed, dispossessed, and dislocated in the era of World War II, and both governments reportedly have killed millions of their own citizens for ideological reasons. These traumas substantially affected urban and rural residence patterns and movements.

There are almost no social science data (urban or otherwise) from China and the U.S.S.R. There is nothing comparable to the kinds of research done in Third World and Western industrial countries mainly because the Soviet and Chinese regimes have not allowed foreigners to do fieldwork in their countries. What has been done by their own citizens seems to be extremely circumscribed. For example, there is a relatively extensive literature on time-budget surveys in the Soviet Union (Bater 1980:135–43). James Riordan, Ivan Trufanov's translator (1977), found only 50 publications on urban life in the U.S.S.R. in 1970, and they were constrained by "taboos and limitations" (p. ii). Trufanov himself, commenting on Western urban studies (e.g., the Lynds, Wirth, and Redfield), puts them all in their place by saying that they "show a clearly expressed vindicative tendency designed to uphold the class interests of the bourgeoisie" (p. 27), or, as in the case of Young and Willmott, they are simply descriptive reports without comment or criticism (p. 32). He does give credit to bourgeois urban social studies for their rich descriptive data but says "Marxist theory alone can provide a correct understanding" of urban phenomena (pp. 34–35).

Permissible Chinese opinions may be more open. At any rate, Elizabeth Perry, who accompanied a carefully controlled delegation of United States mayors to China in 1979, found that "Chinese authorities were quick to point out the shortcomings of their system, and seemed anxious to hear about alternatives . . . [and] expressed . . . a desire to learn from abroad in alleviating the failings" (1980:26). Western social science research, though ideally objective, is nevertheless filtered through various screens of bias and ideology. Perhaps it is fair to say that the Soviet and Chinese screens have an exceptionally fine mesh.

The source material used in this book is somewhat more abundant for China than the Soviet Union, but yet very limited. The most comprehensive and systematic study (Whyte and Parish 1984) was done, not in the People's Republic, but in Hong Kong, based on interviews with people who had recently come from the republic.

While the Soviet Union and China have some general characteristics in common, the specialists agree that the differences far outweigh the similarities, for their preindustrial cultures and histories were very different, and their Marxist revolutions have taken different courses.

Soviet Union

Before serfdom was abolished in tsarist Russia, the migration of peasants to cities was severely limited, and even after that, efforts were made to limit migration. After the 1917 revolution, urban populations declined for a number of years, but in recent decades, they have been growing enormously. In 1926, 48 percent of the urban population lived in cities of not more than 50 thousand people; by 1977, the percentage was below 33. Meanwhile, the largest cities grew prodigiously. In 1959, only three (Moscow, Leningrad, and Kiev) had more than one million people; 20 years later, 18 cities had over one million, and now there are probably 21 (Bater 1980:78). Moscow grew from 1.8 million in 1917 to 7.5 million in 1974 (Riordan, in Trufanov 1977:iii). As is true everywhere, the attraction of people to cities is an amalgam of job opportunities (in this case, in the Soviet system of socialist industrialization) and the opportunity to enjoy the variety and stimulation available in cities. Soviet cities have the same structural problems as all other rapidly growing ones, such as housing shortages and transportation insufficiencies. Most of the information on these subjects is presented from the macroperspective of aggregate statistics.

Early Soviet residential planning established the superblock, accommodating about a thousand to 15 hundred people, as the basic unit where residents live within walking distance of everyday necessities like schools and shops. Some measure of local autonomy was ideally supposed to contribute to a neighborhood ethos. Several superblocks were to be combined into the *mikrorayon* (small district) with a population of 8 to 12 thousand and additional services (Bater 1980:28). Since World War II, the *mikrorayon* has become functionally so important that half the Soviet urban population now lives in units of this type, described as having a radius of 50 to 100 meters. Theoretically, several adjacent *mikrorayons* are organized into larger residential complexes with green spaces and access to public transportation (p. 102). The ideal is to maximize the efficiency and other benefits of small-scale daily life without isolating it from the city as a whole. As to the realities of sense of community, James Bater says:

> If by social justice in housing we mean the equitable allocation of available living space it may be fairly said that the situation in the Soviet Union is far better than in most countries. But the average allocation remains small, the quality of that living space is still below that common in Western Europe and North America and the differential allocative procedures that give housing perks to privileged elites remain intact. . . . [T]he recent upsurge in cooperative apartment ownership could well establish a trend toward greater residential homogeneity, albeit at a micro-scale, than the customary egalitarian admixture the typical mikrorayon produces. . . . [T]hat representatives of the various strata of Soviet society live in a particular mikrorayon, indeed, in the same apartment building, does not necessarily result in social interactions between members of those various strata. In short, there is some way to go still before the goal of social justice in housing is fully realized (p. 111).

As might be expected, the ideal of the *mikrorayon* as a provider of consumer and cultural services is very often not realized (p. 119). This failure does not mean that a structure like the *mikrorayon* is not potentially effective in increasing the humanity of life in cities. It does mean that Soviet experiments with it so far have been hampered by such problems as very rapid growth, inadequate coordination and financing, and the uniform application of norms without modifications to suit a variety of demographic realities (pp. 119–20).

China

China has an ancient urban tradition and, among some of its traditional intellectuals, an antiurban bias.

> Traditional cities were highly organized, managed, and planned in detail . . . walled [primarily to symbolize the authority of the imperial state], in a regular and consistent pattern, with great gates at each of the cardinal points of the compass, from which broad, straight avenues ran to the opposite gate, intersecting in the middle of the city where there was often a drum tower, a plaza, a cluster of official buildings, or a Confucian temple. . . . Each quarter tended to be functionally specific . . . warehouses . . . retailing . . . academies . . . military. . . . Most people lived in the same structures which housed their work activities, and within each quarter . . . were regular lanes organized into neighborhoods, a system often used to control the urban populations. The emphasis was on order, and on planned management (Murphey 1980:19).

This city was a variant of the preindustrial (Sjoberg), regal-ritual (Fox), and orthogenetic (Redfield/Singer) city. Rhoads Murphey emphasizes that the elites of traditional Chinese cities were concerned essentially with maintaining the status quo and managing the agrarian base of the culture (pp. 21–22).

Between 1842 and about 1946, Chinese versions of colonial cities were added to this preindustrial base. These so-called treaty ports, in which foreigners had special privileges, were often new cities. They "represented something new to the Chinese experience, since they were essentially replicas of the modern Western commercial-industrial city, complete with its institutions of banking, insurance, telecommunications, corporate structures with limited liability, joint stock companies, and the protection of impersonal law" (Murphey 1980:26). Industrialization began in the treaty ports along with a new class of "treaty port Chinese" who profited from the new ventures but were increasingly alienated from their Chinese traditions (pp. 25–27). Among the latter were the partisans of Chiang-kai Shek, defeated by the Communist revolution Mao led in 1948. Among the erstwhile treaty ports are some of China's largest cities today including Guangzhou (Canton) and Shanghai.

Partly because cities were associated with the old imperial culture or foreign influences, Mao's policies had a strongly antiurban bias (p. 35). It is not surprising, therefore, that the Maoist regime adopted a policy of controlling city growth by the practice of *hsia-fang,* "sending down" urbanites to work assignments in rural areas (p. 100). Murphey thinks that sending down has probably helped somewhat to limit overcrowding and unemployment in cities and to scale down the overambitious career aspirations of many young people (p. 104). He also describes how the enforced rustication has been resisted and evaded in many ways.

Chinese cities grew greatly in the middle third of the twentieth century, and a few are now among the world's largest; 21 have over a million people apiece, and 125 are between 100 thousand and a million (p. 74). However, official policy toward this growth is ideological, reflecting the antiurban tradition: cities must become producers rather than the consumers (exploiters) they used to be (Murphey 1980:80; Whyte and Parish 1984:15). Early in the revolution, strong voices favored dispersing large portions of urban populations, but the more moderate sending down policy prevailed. It, and strictly controlled household registration, have purposely limited inmigration. Martin Whyte and William Parish (p. 19) say that growth of the largest cities has effectively been slowed, while medium-sized ones have been allowed to grow more rapidly. The idea is to spread out large urban centers more evenly.

Among the important consequences are greater social stability than in Western industrial and Third World cities, a balanced sex ratio, less frequent isolation of individuals from families, and workers' residences located as close as possible to their workplaces (Whyte and Parish 1984:20–21). The policy of locating workers' housing and service facilities close to their workplaces has been carried farther than in the Soviet Union whence the policy was partially derived (Murphey 1980:82).

As in Soviet cities, small-scale everyday life is formally organized. The Chinese organization consists of neighborhood and residents' committees, the smallest units in municipal government. Guangzhou, for example, is organized into five hierarchical levels:

(1) The entire city
(2) Six districts, plus some rural counties, in each of which live several hundred thousand people
(3) Each district divided into wards responsible for from two to ten thousand families
(4) Each ward subdivided into 4 to 12 residents' committee units, each of which supervises 100 to 800 resident families
(5) Each residents' committee unit subdivided into 5 to 20 residents' small group units, each of which looks after 15 to 40 families living in a single building or in several adjacent houses (Whyte and Parish 1984:22)

China has a long tradition of government attempts to control people through various local organizations; under the Japanese occupation, this took the form of police control through organizing households in hierarchical multiples of ten (Sidel 1974:21–22). Added to the traditional control and mutual aid elements, these committees attempt to "teach the entire population a different way of relating to their world, to 'remold their world outlook,' as the Chinese say" (p. 63). Ruth Sidel's discussion (based on personal observation in several cities in 1971) has a generally favorable and sympathetic tone, well summarized as follows:

The organization of life in China's neighborhoods can perhaps best be viewed as a total community support system, one fostered and maintained by the residents of the neighborhoods themselves. As life in the Fengsheng Neighborhood demonstrates, the people . . . have a myriad of ways in which they can interact: within their courtyard, where residents talk informally, communally clean the courtyard, plant and prune the greenery, admire one another's children, and discuss the latest political events; within their study group, where people read together, discuss politics, and evaluate their own and others' attitudes and contributions, and are in turn evaluated; within the residents' committee, in which members are encouraged to help one another . . . ; within the neighborhood, where people work cooperatively to provide preschool care . . . work for the unemployed in local factories and . . . health care; and finally within the place of work, which provides not only study groups but a larger central focus, an avenue to contributing to the society, a parallel system of providing human services, and a setting for warm social relationships (pp. 147–48).

Intimacy and warmth are two of the three notable characteristics of the system, in Sidel's view. The third is control, which means group pressures of various kinds on the individual to conform to societal norms, subordinating individualistic interests to group interests as defined by the norms. Whyte and Parish (1984:76) repeatedly emphasize the importance of this control factor, combined, though, with "rich supportive networks."

Murphey adds further perspectives on this subject. Neighborhood organizations are designed not only to implement local administration but also to facilitate "mass mobilization" for various national goals. They settle disputes and control deviant behavior. "No individual is free from these constraints, even in seemingly trivial matters such as the internal cleanliness of houses or the play activities of younger children" (Murphey 1980:88).

Elizabeth Perry's report on the United States mayors' visit to China in 1979 mentions three big problems that "seemed particularly vexing: overpopulation, unemployment, and inadequate housing" (1980:26). If problems are vexing, they are probably too big for the neighborhood organizations to handle, even though they probably enforce the following encouragements to practice family planning: completely free medical care and education only for a couple's first child and the opportunity to move to a larger apartment after the birth of a first child only (p. 26).

After reviewing some of the housing shortage problems, Perry says:

While dislocation accompanying these new housing developments is substantial, the strength of Chinese community organization helps to cushion the blow. Anomie is avoidable when one moves into a neighborhood whose residents meet frequently in small groups charged with ensuring the welfare of all members. This community spirit, operating both in the back streets and the new high rises, explains how one can walk through areas of Chinese cities that are *physically* more dilapidated than the worst American slums, yet which evidence none of the *human* dilapidation so common in our own inner cities (p. 27).

In short, the evolution of modern Chinese cities has generated important social structures that reportedly solve reasonably well some of the serious problems that beset Western industrial cities. As for the Soviet *mikrorayon*, the sparse information available suggests that it may not provide supportive functions to the same degree as the Chinese neighborhood committee, but it is apparently intended to achieve similar ends.

In November 1985, the author and his wife visited China as members of a study tour cosponsored by the Family Planning Commission of the People's Republic and The Population Institute of Washington, D.C. The cities of which we saw the most are Xian, Chengdu, Beijing, and Shanghai with populations of approximately 3, 4, 9, and 11 million apiece. Particularly impressive are the orderliness of enormous crowds of pedestrians and the flow of bicycles; the predominance of new mid-rise (maximum 7 stories) and high-rise (maximum 16 stories) apartment blocks; and the ubiquitousness of new building—construction cranes are features of the skyline everywhere. Whyte and Parish (1984:232) say that the government has an explicit ideal of orderliness, but that it is a goal for which there must be continual striving.

From the North American perspective ("sick cities," crime in the streets, housing project violence, disagreeable pedestrian behavior, and gridlock traffic jams), Chinese cities appear in a very favorable light. If Chinese cities work well in contrast to Western industrial ones, why do they? Limitation to small size is obviously not the answer. The answer lies, rather, in the organization of the society and the values that accompany it and in how the People's Republic in many important ways is in continuity with the long history of dynastic China. The republic's highly centralized and authoritarian structure—from the Central Committee which governs the whole vast nation through a hierarchical system of units, subunits, subsubunits, and so on, to the neighborhood organization to which every family belongs—is not in principle very different from the dynastic system. Under the latter, the emperor was the guarantor of the harmony of the system, ensuring safe borders, safe travel, and the efficiency of canals and riverways for irrigation and transportation. The small-scale end of the social system was used, among other things, for recruiting and supervising the *corvée* labor necessary to maintain the system.

Today, neighborhood committees exercise comparable social controls for implementing slogans displayed on public walls and billboards, in which a prevailing theme is, essentially, "Work for the Progress of Society!"

This system does not now, and never did, encourage egotistical competitiveness. Rather, it gives the individual a place and a role in various group endeavors and identities of which the family is the most universal. These continuities from the past, reinforced rather than displaced by the Communist regime, are the foundation of behavior in public and private urban space.

Besides its policies and procedures for strictly controlling migration into the largest cities, the People's Republic is also developing satellite cities and satellite agricultural areas around them. The republic is creating systematically organized urban hinterlands (in contrast to hinterlands that evolve haphazardly elsewhere). All of this is occurring in the context of the national family planning program whose goal is to stabilize the total population at 1.2 billion in about the year 2000.

The resulting Chinese conceptualization of "the city" is different from that of the West and is reflected in the way urban population data are presented orally to visitors in China and as they appear in Kaplan, Sobin, and de Keijzer (1985):

Beijing. The city proper extends over 6,486 square miles, divided into ten districts (four urban) and nine counties; 42 percent of its 9.3 million population is agricultural.

Shanghai. Total population is 11 million, extending over 2,355 square miles; the city core of 5.4 million people occupies 58 square miles.

Chengdu. Total population is 3.85 million, comprising two city districts with 1.4 million people, three suburban areas, and two outlying prefectures; total area is 1,490 square miles.

The modern Chinese conception of a large city is that it consists of a dense residential, commercial, and industrial core; smaller residential, commercial, and industrial satellites; and agricultural townships whose produce is, ideally, sufficient to feed the city (minimizing the need for expensive long-distance transport of foodstuffs). We visited Evergreen Township, one of the six whose mission is to feed Beijing. Besides its family planning services, primary school, and old peoples' home, we were impressed by the intensity and ingenuity of its farming techniques. The latter included plastic (instead of glass) greenhouses with brick or earth walls and rolls of matting to retain the solar heat when there is no sunshine.

Another ideal is that people live as closely as possible to their workplaces, a continuity with traditional Chinese culture still noticeable: the small merchant or craftsman living on the same premises as his shop. The massive flow of bicycle and bus traffic indicates that this ideal is only partially realized.

Street and sidewalk behavior seems very orderly. Chinese cities are laid out in a rectilinear pattern of very wide, tree-lined avenues. This traditional arrangement contrasts very sharply with preindustrial urban layouts in Europe, the Middle East, Africa, and South Asia. This contrast is very clear in Beijing, Chengdu, and Xian but less so in Shanghai which originated as a European colonial port. Between the major avenues that form a grid are lesser, parallel streets, and between or behind them are the narrow, twisting alleys and cul-de-sacs that characterize traditional residential neighborhoods. Although many of the latter are being replaced by high-rise apartment blocks, the pattern of a grid of major avenues not only remains but is being extended. In Xian, for example, it extends beyond the massive city wall and moat, much of which remains intact. In Beijing, on the other hand, the city wall was recently demolished to make way for a circumferential subway and beltline.

Traffic along a major avenue flows through five parallel linear zones. In the center is the motor vehicle road. On each side of it, separated by a low divider, is a bicycle path, frequently as wide as the roadway. Finally, there are two sidewalks for pedestrians. In Chengdu, during a typical morning rush hour, there were traffic lights and a policeman on a platform in the center and elderly women with small red flags who controlled the bicycle flow. The motor roads were always full, the bike paths packed 10 to 15 abreast, and the sidewalks dense with pedestrians. People, bikes, and other vehicles continually met each other head-on and at various angles. The author was aware of only one accident, a bicycle collision. He turned to see what a woman's angry screams (very unusual) were about. Her bike was lying on its side, and she was berating a man who had a child on his handlebars. After a minute or two, during which he made some responses to her, he picked up her bike and set it on its wheels and kickstand and pedaled off. No one else seemed to pay any attention, and traffic flowed around them.

The flow of bicycles is steady and moderately paced. No one tries to zig-zag ahead of others. In head-on or angled encounters, an unspoken other-awareness enables people almost always to pass by or around each other. The same is true of pedestrian traffic which can be body-to-body and 20 deep on the sidewalks of shopping streets like Nanjing Road in Shanghai. There may be occasional jostling, but one does not encounter, as on American streets, self-absorbed individuals who stride along apparently oblivious to others and force one to change pace or dodge abruptly.

Obviously, we are observing learned behavior. What is learned and how is it learned? It surely must involve maximized deference for others and minimized individualism, both traditional. "Informants noted disciplinary concern with training children to be obedient, diligent, respectful of others, helpful, and cooperative, rather than aggressive, all values that were stressed by parents of an earlier era" (Whyte and Parish 1984:170). In any case, the vitally important point is that extremely crowded behavior in Chinese urban public space is manageable and livable to a degree that contrasts markedly with Western industrial cities.

Motor traffic consists mostly of trucks and buses, with a relatively small number of cars, many of which are taxis. Motorcycles are very few. There is a great deal of crossing over the center line (real or imaginary) in the face of oncoming traffic in the other direction, with frequent tight squeezes. Horns are blown very frequently, but usually not repeatedly as in anger or impatience. On one occasion, when a pedestrian, about 50 yards ahead, stepped into the bus path without looking, the driver tapped his horn, and the pedestrian backed to safety. The horn seemed to be saying, "I am coming," not "Get out of my way."

Nevertheless, the Chinese perceive vehicular traffic as a serious problem. Traffic jams in various bottlenecks occur, as do fatalities. Beijing's *China Daily* carried a story on 8 November 1985, headed "Road Deaths Soar," which said that traffic accidents killed 548 people in Shanghai in the first 10 months of 1985, more than in all of 1984. City police were reported to be taking emergency steps—heavier penalties and removing objects obstructing traffic.

Traditional Chinese housing consists of one- or two-story houses on narrow alleys. While much of it remains, it is not (we were told) preferred. Much traditional housing has been or is being replaced. The new housing consists of apartment blocks ranging from about 4 to 16 floors. Most typical are six-story blocks without elevators. Less common, but hardly rare, are taller buildings with elevators. We saw none as tall as those in Hong Kong which are often 30 stories high.

All of the above is public housing. High-rise public housing in the United States and Great Britain is a troublesome phenomenon, the subject of much discussion and controversy. Many of the public spaces (corridors, elevators, and lobbies) are no one's responsibility and are often the scenes of rapes, assaults, robberies, and murders. Some attribute this to building design (see O. Newman 1972). Others have pointed out that in American urban public housing—and to an increasing degree in British—residents are, in overwhelming numbers, members of oppressed and disadvantaged ethnic and racial minorities, and their concentrated desperation is as much at fault as building design. Although China has about 50 non-Han "minorities," they nowhere constitute the massive urban populations that blacks and Hispanics do in American cities. Nevertheless, one cannot help wondering about the livability of Chinese high-rises. The officials whom we interviewed denied that there was a serious crime problem connected with these apartment blocks. It is impossible to judge the true situation. Whyte and Parish devote a chapter to crime and social control, but they emphasize the serious inadequacy of detailed, verifiable information on crime (1984:247). Chinese high-rises probably are not so seriously problem-beset as high-rises frequently are elsewhere, for several reasons. One is the absence of large concentrations of disadvantaged, desperate people. Another is the presence of housing associations which provide extensive surveillance; this includes serving as the first level of judicial authority in cases of actionable offense. A guide in Beijing said he lived in an apartment in one of three 12-story buildings. The 300 households living in these buildings constituted the local housing association. Such associations, or workers' associations where workers in a particular establishment are living adjacently, assign households to apartments. Decisions may be made in open discussion or according to specific criteria which reflect, among other things, the "one child per couple" principle. One-child couples receive priority status, although an extra room is provided for each child if there are two of opposite sex aged ten or more. Provision is also made for at least one grandparent, where possible. Grandparents are vital as babysitters, especially when both parents are employed, and their presence is also compatible with traditional Chinese culture which emphasizes the importance of three-generation families.

Chinese apartments are very small and would probably be intolerable to most Westerners. E. N. Anderson, Jr. (1972) and Robert Edward Mitchell (1971) in their studies of high-rise apartment dwellers in Hong Kong argue persuasively that because of a variety of Chinese traditional values, domestic crowdedness that would be extremely stressful for Westerners is not so much so for the Chinese. Unfortunately, we do not know how generalizable these findings are. The people whom Whyte and Parish interviewed frequently mentioned serious conflicts over sharing the tiny kitchen (1984:81).

In Shanghai, we visited a neighborhood family planning clinic, a kindergarten, an old peoples' day center, and an apartment in a five-story apartment block (one of many). The neighborhood, Tianshan Xincun, is one of 127 such units in the central city whose population was given as 8 million (rather than 11). In the nearly 700 blocks of buildings along tree-lined streets and paths are 8 middle and primary schools, 9 kindergartens, 2 hospitals, 11 clinics, as well as cinemas and libraries. Eighty shops and commercial institutions in the neighborhood serve its inhabitants, most of whom work in or near Tianshan Xincun in shops, textile and steel mills, and various light industries.

Officials gave the following demographic data for Tianshan Xincun:

Year	Population	Households	Persons per Household	Living Space per Person
1977	38,768	10,277	3.77	8.33 m^2
1984	49,995	13,727	3.64	10.58 m^2

The one-child-per-couple principle is, we were told, on the whole now being successfully applied. The ideal picture being suggested to us was a household consisting either of a married couple and one child or a married couple, one of their parents, and one child.

We visited one of the latter families. We reached the apartment by a stairway with its own private entry (not a long corridor); the space consisted of a small kitchen and toilet/bath, two bedrooms (filled with furniture), and a balcony. The parents were a computer science professor and a teacher, living with their infant son and the wife's mother. Though very crowded, the apartment was well furnished. This household was obviously a high-status one. The immediate neighborhood (in the true sense of the word) featured closely-built apartment blocks in easy calling distance and with easy access to the ground. Red markers on many doors denoted a high grade from the health inspector. Retail outlets were abundant, as they are elsewhere. The feeling was that formal surveillance, as well as the informal policing provided by ground-level activities, is abundant.

Some officials we met considered their major urban problems to be traffic jams, pollution, noise, housing shortage, and shortage of services (such as restaurants). They could not arrange these problems in order of importance, and they did not respond to the question of how they were trying to meet the problems. We have already commented on the traffic jams. Air pollution is indeed evident; it is composed, in Northern China, partly of very fine dust from the Gobi Desert (about which nothing can be done) and partly of soft coal smoke which presumably could be abated. The building boom is an obvious response to the housing shortage. The list does not include the kinds of social problem Western urban officials would surely include, ones that lead to such despairing comments as that New York City is ungovernable and that Mexico City and Calcutta are growing out of control and are already "unlivable" for most inhabitants.

What the Chinese scene shows is that it is possible for human beings to live humanely in extremely large and dense cities. While no other national groups in the world would or could become culturally or politically Chinese in order to improve their cities, perhaps we can achieve this end by learning from the Chinese experience and adapting what we learn to our own cultures. While Whyte and Parish say that such learning would at best be complicated and problematic (1984:368), they would likely agree that the Chinese urban scene shows that megacities need not necessarily or inevitably be megadisaster areas.

Could something like the Chinese and Soviet small-scale support and control units be adapted to Western and Third World cities? As they are today, these units are the creatures of highly centralized, autocratic governments (whose interests they serve), and this form of government would be unacceptable to Westerners in terms of their values. Furthermore, the Soviet and Chinese national power structures rationalize the neighborhood organizations with a communal ideology that is antithetical to the more individualistic ideologies of the West, and, in China at least, the communal ideology also has deep roots in its traditional non-Western culture. Whether Chinese- or Soviet-style support and control units could be established in Third World cities generally is a moot question. Most Third World people habitually view their governments with fear and hostility, owing to their inefficiency, corruption, and inadequate provision of public services. They have neither the powerful social control ideology of the Soviet Union and China or the Chinese tradition of a benevolent autocracy. Besides, Third World city dwellers are proficient in creating their own small-scale support systems.

Nevertheless, there are some Third World experiments with systematic neighborhood structures linked to the municipal government. A notable example is in Brasília, the new capital of Brazil that was created out of nothing in the 1960s. The city's resident population of about 600,000 lives in five-story apartment blocks of 24–48 apartments each. A cluster of 11 such buildings constitutes a superblock, and four superblocks constitute a unit. Each superblock elects two representatives to the unit council, which has direct access to the government, and each unit has its own schools, clinics, and a small shopping mall. How well the system actually works is not clear to outsiders, and the people involved are mostly middle class. The menial workers in Brasília live outside the city in eight or nine satellite towns, some of which are squatter settlements. The total population of the satellites is about 800,000.

One thing is clear, however. The cities of about one-quarter of the world's population are actually organized in terms of units whose likes exist in the West only on paper or, at most, in small, rare, experimental versions. How would Constantine Doxiadis's (1975) hierarchy of "ekistic units" (house, house-group, small neighborhood, neighborhood, small polis), which is suggestive of the Soviet and Chinese units, actually work if it were established on a massive scale in Western industrial cities? No one knows, but in the Soviet and Chinese systems we can see something like it in operation, and we can see something of what that operation entails. In chapters 5 and 6, we focus on the small-scale support systems of Western industrial and Third World city dwellers that *are* compatible with their own values, even if they are frequently not so effective as they ideally could be.

MEGACITIES REVISITED

The megacity phenomenon is the most recent trend in the evolution of cities, fueled by the unprecedented size of the human population and innovations of postindustrial, electronic technology. Three important components of this phase of evolution are primate cities, suburbs, and squatter settlements.

Primate Cities

In many Third World and Western industrial nations, one city is many times larger than the city of second largest size. This is a "primate city," a term Mark Jefferson (1939) first used. The primate city is frequently regarded as an abnormal, parasitical, or disproportionate phenomenon. One reason is that the reality of primate cities violates George Zipf's "rank- size" rule: if the rank order of cities in a nation is plotted on one coordinate of a graph and their populations on the other, the distribution will be described by a straight line (Sills 1968, vol. 13:319–23). This was the case in the United States in the early twentieth century and in India more recently (Wilsher and Righter 1977:52). The implication that the presence of the rank-size rule is evidence of the operation of some natural law in human settlement patterns has never been demonstrated as fact. But there is no doubt about the primacy factor. Here are some of the world's primate cities as of 1970 (p. 55):

City & Country	Population Ratio to Second City
Lima-Callao, Peru	14.1
Budapest, Hungary	11.0
Buenos Aires, Argentina	10.6
Santiago, Chile	9.2
Manila, Philippines	8.1
Paris, France	7.5
Tehran, Iran	6.7
Havana, Cuba	6.1
Copenhagen, Denmark	5.9
Bucharest, Rumania	5.6
Vienna, Austria	5.2
Dublin, Eire	5.0
London, England	3.7
Colombo, Sri Lanka	3.5
Seoul, South Korea	2.9

There are many more. All Latin American countries have a primate city (Harris 1971:178), most of them capitals. Notice that the Western industrial cities listed are also national capitals. The phenomenon is only partly related to Third World "overurbanization," which is, in itself, a misnomer.

Primate cities are the result of many combined attractions, most particularly a wide variety of job opportunities at all status levels, frequently related to the exceptional concentrations of political and economic power. Very often, primate cities' growth rates are proportionately greater than rates of smaller cities. Some governments have attempted to discourage or prevent migration to primate and other cities without notable success. Centralization of bureaucratic functions in the national capital is one cause of primate cities, and some countries are trying to distribute these functions more widely.

Some governments, too, are trying to offset the results of primate city attraction that deprive many of their citizens of essential services. For example, before the Islamic Revolution, Tehran had about 10 percent of the Iranian population but about a third of all its physicians. The previous regime in Iran did try to counteract this imbalance by requiring all recent medical school graduates to practice for two years outside of Tehran and other large cities. It cannot be denied that the attractions of cities that have maximum magnitude have serious consequences. Nevertheless, the attraction is real for most people, suggesting that their small-scale, everyday life adaptations in cities are, on balance, rewarding. There is some, but not very much, evidence of massive, large-scale voluntary emigrations of people away from large cities to nonurban areas. Movements are overwhelmingly in the other direction, although they are indeed complicated by much back-and-forth movement, evidence that many people maintain ties in more than one place. Sub-Saharan Africa provides some notable examples, as noted earlier.

Unfortunately, very few studies provide specific information on migrants to cities who have returned to their places of origin, but one study bears out the generalization about the attractions of cities: George Foster's longitudinal study—being continued by Robert Kemper—of the Mexican village Tzintzuntzan. Between about 1945 and 1974, 900 Tzintzuntzeños emigrated, a third of them to Mexico City. During the same period, probably fewer than 50 returned permanently to the village (Kemper 1977:46, 53). A minority of returnees came back to the village because of adaptational failure in the city such as loss of jobs or ill-health of children. Others returned to take care of elderly relatives. Most returned because they wanted to, not to seek refuge.

The idea of "disproportionateness" comes to a head in two ways. One is in the form of *megalopolis*, the classic case of which is the urban conglomerate extending from Washington, D.C., to Boston and including two world cities (New York and Philadelphia) and three runners-up (Baltimore, Boston, and Washington). The word caught on in some circles, evoking in exaggerated form the same horrors as world city: urban sprawl and consequent environmental despoliation, megasuburbia with consequent magnification of all suburban social problems, exacerbated traffic and transport difficulties, and various irreversible threats to public health connected with waste disposal, water supply, air pollution, and even weather changes because of additional amounts of heat discharged into the atmosphere. We do not discount these matters, and there may indeed be limits of urban size beyond which human beings cannot live for very long. But, as yet, no consensus on this matter has been reached. Meanwhile, the tendency to perceive cities in increasingly larger magnitudes (Standard Metropolitan Statistical Area [SMSA] to Consolidated SMSA to world city to megalopolis) must be considered critically. Its great value is its transcendance of administrative subdivisions whose existence impedes the handling of problems, such as those mentioned above, that cannot be administratively contained. On the other hand, the think-big tendency, in magnifying big problems, masks the social and environmental diversities that are encompassed. Anyone familiar with the Boston-to-Washington area knows how internally varied it is, that it is very far from being a single environment.

The large-scale perspective epitomized by the word megalopolis obliterates the small-scale realities in which most people actually live. This is not the first time this matter has engaged our attention, nor is it the last.

The other way in which disproportionateness is perceived in urban evolution is in the idea of overurbanization as an abnormality, to which the idea of primate city is related. Overurbanization is a Western industrial ethnocentrism: "abnormal" cities are those whose male industrial work force is significantly smaller than the typical male industrial work force of Western industrialized cities (Sovani 1969:325). The idea is that the normal pulling force of migration to cities must be the attraction of industrial jobs, because this was prototypically the case in the industrialized West; another idea is that cities which are not predominantly industrial are "parasitical." This notion ignores the informal, marginal employment so important in Third World cities (see chapter 5).

Suburbs

Some specialists like to point out that there have been forms of suburbs (and squatter settlements) for many centuries. However, the phenomena with which we are concerned are recent developments. Industrial suburbanization began in Europe in the nineteenth century and has been continuing since; North American and Japanese suburbanizations are primarily twentieth-century processes. The process is integral to cities and would not exist except for cities' prior and continuing existence. These important facts are often glossed over. Some assert that suburbs are the antitheses of cities because most of the people moving to them have wanted, for various reasons, to leave the inner cities where they had lived. That set of motivations does not make suburbs noncities. What suburbs are is a set of variants of a particular kind of urban environment.

Suburbanization is a specific of Western industrial cities because it depends on complex systems of mass transport and a level of societal affluence that only industrial cultures possess, and this, in turn, makes the privately owned automobile and single-family house accessible to a very substantial proportion of the population. Early suburbanization involved the great separation of place of residence (suburban) from place of work (center city) and the necessity of commuting between them. Commuting to and from work by automobile or other vehicle is still the typical mode even though, in recent decades, an increasing number of workplaces have been established in suburban areas.

The magnitude of suburban growth, and related changes in center cities, can be seen in statistics from the United States and Great Britain. In 1970, suburbanites constituted 38 percent of the population of the United States, while central metropolitan urbanites and nonurban people constituted 31 percent each (Fava 1980:133). Reynolds Farley (1976:7) gives some aggregate figures on populations of the 15 largest United States metropolitan areas:

| | Total Population (in 1,000s) | | | Growth Rates (%) | | | | | |
| | | | | Total | | Whites | | Nonwhites | |
Area	1950	1960	1970	1950–1960	1960–1970	1950–1960	1960–1970	1950–1960	1960–1970
City	1,797	1,823	1,815	+1	0	−7	−12	+58	+42
Ring	906	1,545	2,143	+71	+39	+70	+36	+76	+91

These figures encapsulate several major trends: the end of center city growth but with decrease of whites and increase of nonwhites there; predominance of whites in ring areas (primarily suburbs) with the increasing presence of nonwhites there also. The deterioration of many Western industrial center cities, including high crime rates and high unemployment, is related to the departure of relatively affluent whites, who move to suburbs, and the concentration of nonwhites who, because of racial discrimination, tend to be undereducated, underskilled, and unable to move elsewhere, even back to the rural areas whence many of them came. The ultimate causes lie in societywide phenomena, not in any intrinsically or primordially unlivable characteristic of cities.

This discussion brings us to the last major point about suburban evolution. Suburbs are not all the same; they certainly vary within the same society, and they may vary significantly among different societies. The popular image of a middle-class "bedroom community"—with absent fathers, frustrated mothers, and consequently maladjusted, as well as isolated, families—is a stereotype, though there is a serious element of reality in it as far as women are concerned (Fava 1980). Usually associated with this stereotype are landscapes filled with essentially uniform single-family houses, and nothing else, built on seemingly endless miles of uniform streets. Such landscapes do exist, but there are others. For just one example, consider the differences between Levittown, a suburb of Philadelphia, and Vällingby, a suburb of Stockholm. Levittown more nearly resembles the physical stereotype, whereas Vällingby emphasizes moderate high-rises, with consequently higher residential densities. David Popenoe devotes a book (1977) to these two suburbs and how they have changed since their construction in the early 1950s. H. E. Bracey, too, devotes an entire book to comparing two suburban subdivisions, one outside Bristol, England, and the other outside Columbus, Ohio. Almost half of the British suburbanites mentioned access to nearby open country as a desirable feature of their suburb, whereas few Americans did. Many of the Americans expressed satisfaction with the closeness of shopping facilities in terms of a 20-minute drive in their private cars, whereas the Britishers' criterion of satisfaction was a 10-minute walk (Bracey 1964:29–39). One is tempted to see different national cultural values at work among the residents of these two suburban milieux.

David Thorns examines a number of attempts to establish types of suburb, each based on a single criterion, finds them all wanting, and sets forth his own typology based on permutations of three pairs of criteria: middle class/working class; planned/unplanned; and industrial/residential. An industrial suburb is one in which a larger proportion of its residents work inside it than outside it; in a residential suburb, the reverse is true (Thorns 1973:83).

Having once been considered by the affluent as refuges from the evils of inner-city life, American suburbs have recently been developing some of the problems from which refuge was sought. We know the main reason: suburbs could not indefinitely be kept immune from societywide problems, any more than inner cities could. Recent headlines from American newspapers dramatize some of the problems:

"Suburbs Face More Ills Already Troubling Cities"
"The Explosive Growth of Suburbia Leads to Bumper-to-Bumper Blues"

"The Suburban Life: Trees, Grass, Plus Noise, Traffic and Pollution"
"America Moved to the Suburbs, and So Did the Integration Battle"

In his review of Kenneth Jackson's *Crabgrass Frontier*, Richard Polenberg notes that there are

about 70 motor vehicles for every 100 persons [and Jackson] offers a perceptive analysis of "The Drive-in Culture of Contemporary America," a culture based on the interstate highway system, the garage, the motel, the drive-in movie, the shopping center, the fast-food franchise, the mobile home and the gas station. . . .

It is this contemporary drive-in culture that Jackson blames for "the loss of community in metropolitan America," by which he means the tendency for social life to become "privatized," and the "reduced feeling of concern and responsibility among families for their neighbors and among suburbanites in general for residents of the inner city" (1986:B–4).

Polenberg finds Jackson's book a "comprehensive and scholarly account of how 100 million Americans have come to believe they can enjoy all the advantages of the city, and yet get away from all the noise and dust."

Critiques of American suburbia are not new, and one active reaction was the construction of carefully and thoughtfully designed "new communities" for three decades following World War II. Two of the best known are Reston, Va., and Columbia, Md. Two others, mentioned in other connections in this book, are Park Forest, Ill., and Forest Park, Ohio. Raymond Burby and Shirley Weiss (1976) directed an extensive evaluation of new communities in the early 1970s; they found that although many of the attractions were realized, there were also a number of ways in which expectations were not met.

New community development generally had much less impact on social perceptions and participation than many planners had anticipated. Community identity, satisfaction with family life and the community as a place to raise children, neighboring, and participation in community organizations were not much different in new than in conventional communities. . . . [R]esidents' perceptions of their quality of life . . . were equivalent in both settings (p. 9).

What is wrong? The problems that beset suburbia and inner industrial cities alike are problems of human values and spirit more than they are problems inherent in physical environment. While good planning of that environment is certainly to be encouraged, it cannot directly affect the inhabitants' cultural patterns (see chapter 8).

Squatter Settlements

Squatter settlements occur throughout the Third World, and there are terms for "squatter settlement" in the language of every country concerned.

Estimated percentages of squatters in the populations of the respective cities, mostly from the 1960s, provide some idea of the magnitude of the phenomenon: Ankara (50); Mexico City (40); Kuala Lumpur (37); Lima (33); Algiers, Oran, and Annaba (30); Baghdad, Santiago, and Jakarta (25); Istanbul (21); Rio de Janeiro (20). Growth of squatter settlements has been accelerating. In 1950, Rio had 203 thousand *favela* dwellers; in 1964, 600 thousand. In 1946, Manila had 23 thousand; this number had increased to 767 thousand in the ensuing 20 years or so. Squatter settlements are not limited to major or primate cities but occur in Third World cities of all sizes. They continue to grow, generally at a faster rate than total urban populations do (Dwyer 1975:18–19).

The majority of squatters are recent migrants from rural areas, and some writers treat the subject as if it were simply an aspect of migration. This approach is very misleading. Many squatters move from center-city slums, among them those who have the knowledge and organizational skills to establish the settlements. Portes provides figures from sample studies in various Latin American cities on percentages of people living in "peripheral lower class settlements" who were born in the city itself. They range from 8 percent of a sample in Bogotá to 51 percent of a sample in Buenos Aires. Four studies in Santiago, Chile, yield these percentages: 29, 35, 51, and 42 (Portes 1976:57).

Why should there be this internal migration and why are knowledge and organizational skills important? One reason lies in the contrasts Latin American observers, in particular, have noticed between center-city "slums" and peripheral squatter settlements. In Lima, the center-city *corralon* (slum) is typically the home either of the most recent migrants or of the hopelessly destitute. Physically, *corralones* stagnate and decay, while the *barriadas* (squatter settlements) gradually are improved, either through self-help of the inhabitants, government assistance, or both. Migrants who first settle in the *corralones* very frequently move later to *barriadas* where, instead of renting degraded housing, they can build their own and gradually improve it (Harris 1971:221–22). Another reason is that many squatter settlements have been founded in an organized manner; a group selects a tract of unoccupied or unclaimed land and moves into it quickly with building materials. The Turkish term *gecekondu* means built overnight.

Squatter settlements vary considerably in detail, but all have important characteristics in common. They are built on land not owned by the settlers and occupied rent-free. The landowner (often the government) can evict them and destroy the settlement. This kind of destruction has happened, but many squatter settlements are allowed to stand because they are recognized as solutions to acute housing problems that the government usually cannot afford to handle by means of planned housing. Furthermore, squatters characteristically improve their dwellings, and many settlements have evolved through the years from shack towns with minimal public facilities to well-built communities with basic water, sewer, and power facilities and their own infrastructures of shops and services. These developments require political organization, and strategies vary depending on the differing nature of the larger political structures in their respective countries (see Leeds and Leeds 1976).

The settlers themselves build squatter dwellings, using the most inexpensive materials available, preferably those that cost nothing: used lumber and sheets of corrugated iron, flattened steel barrels, reed matting, and so on. Such construction can be adapted to changing family needs; small shops can be added to dwellings; and in general, these structures have great advantages over the notorious inflexibilities of public housing. Indeed, consequences for squatters forced to move into public housing can be tragic, as in Rio de Janeiro according to Janice Perlman (1976; especially chapter 7).

Squatter settlements represent a set of strategies millions of Third World people undertake to establish themselves at minimum expense as near as possible to opportunities for work. Regarded as malignant and dangerous growths by some, others take them as evidence of hope and life against tremendous odds. Most indications are that squatters are not "dangerous radicals" threatening their respective societies, but essentially hopeful people making the best, as they see it, of the socioeconomic-demographic realities of their lives. However, as Peter Lloyd (1979:209), who emphasizes this point of view, says, squatter settlements are mainly creations of the past three decades, and their long-term success will depend on further societywide developments that prevent the squatters' hopes from turning into despair.

Meanwhile, like the suburbs that they resemble only in their predominantly peripheral locations around cities, squatter settlements are a major feature of the on-going evolution of cities, particularly, though not exclusively, megacities.

SUGGESTED ADDITIONAL READING

Brown, L. Carl, ed. *From Madina to Metropolis: Heritage and Change in the Near Eastern City*. Princeton, N.J.: Darwin, 1973. The range of Middle Eastern city styles, from *madinas* to modern housing projects, are well illustrated by the photographs and drawings accompanying the informative text.

Hamblin, Dora Jane, and Time-Life editors. *The First Cities*. New York: Time-Life, 1973. Part of *The Emergence of Man* series, this book is colorfully illustrated with photographs and imaginative drawings that take the reader back to the beginnings of cities in the Middle East. Included is a map of obsidian-trading cities from 8000 to 2000 B.C., a phenomenon that inspired Jane Jacobs's imaginary early city, "New Obsidian," discussed in the text.

Kenny, Michael, and David K. Kertzer, ed. *Urban Life in Mediterranean Europe: An Anthropological Perspective*. Urbana: University of Illinois Press, 1983. Subcultural varieties, migration, and modernization in Greek, Italian, Spanish, and Yugoslavian cities.

Lewis, David, ed. *The Growth of Cities*. New York: Wiley-Interscience, 1971. Illustrated with photographs and drawings of urban subjects as diverse as *madinas*, squatter settlements, and high-rise apartment complexes.

Skinner, Elliott P. *African Urban Life: The Transformation of Ouagadougou*. Princeton, N.J.: Princeton University Press, 1974. Illustrated with maps and photographs. Emphasizes the drastic changes that people of the capital of Upper Volta (now Burkina Faso) are consciously undertaking as the city evolves from a preindustrial town.

The Architecture and Vicissitudes of Cities

First-class bookstores in most major cities have at least one counter devoted to books about the city in which the store is located. The books tend, like those below, to be profusely illustrated. Historical changes in architecture and streetscapes are frequent themes. These displays are well worth careful browsing at least.

Banham, Reyner. *Los Angeles: The Architecture of Four Ecologies*. Baltimore: Penguin, 1973.

Block, Jean F. *Hyde Park Houses: An Informal History, 1856–1910*. Chicago: University of Chicago Press, 1978.

Holt, Glen E., and Dominic A. Pacyga. *Chicago: A Historical Guide to the Neighborhoods: The Loop and South Side.* Chicago: Chicago Historical Society, 1979.

Kay, Jane Holtz. *Lost Boston.* Boston: Houghton Mifflin, 1980.

5
Livelihoods

The vast majority of human beings survive by any means they can. Nearly everyone hopes and strives for means that produce more, but most must settle for what they can get. The means of survival are tiring—physically and mentally. They are sometimes emotionally pleasing, but typically they consist of routine work that is frequently drudgery. Most peoples' work, being their means of survival, is self-justifying and sufficient for such needs as ego-maintenance and even ego-enhancement.

However, for a few people in the world, work for survival is not enough. For them, work-or-starve is not the immediate challenge that it is for most people. Such persons probably more frequently live in cities than in rural areas, and one of the results is the existence of city-dwelling intellectuals and theoreticians who are not representative of most city dwellers and whose approach to work begins at a level quite abstracted from that of work-or-starve. Among these persons were contributors to the bipolar moralistic model of cities and corollary theories. The model idealizes everything rural, including rural work which consists of farming, arboriculture, animal husbandry, and various crafts connected with these activities. The model defines them as good because they are integrated directly with nature and holistically with human life.

To put this idealization into realistic perspective, we need to keep in mind a theme repeated in chapters 3 and 4: the migration to cities of millions of rural people seeking more productive means of survival. They continue to migrate—on the work-or-starve principle—even when their urban work is exploitative and exhausting (cf. Bunster and Chaney 1985:40).

Urban work, being part of urban life generally, is far more diversified, and, in characteristic fashion, the bipolar moralists have focused negatively on only certain aspects of it. The major flaw in the moralistic model is not that the phenomena it emphasizes are imaginary. They are not, but the context in which the model puts them is unrealistically distorted.

We begin this chapter with consideration of alienation, a widely accepted negative characterization of urban work. As the presentation unfolds, we find that a more balanced view of reality does not change black into white. The facts are too varied to allow for such a simplistic outcome.

ALIENATION

Alienation is an umbrella term encompassing several different conditions. Jon Shepard (1971) has studied on-the-job alienation among factory and office workers, each divided into three categories: traditional crafts, mechanized work, and electronic work. The factory workers are maintenance craftsmen in an automobile factory, assembly line mechanized workers in the same factory, and control room monitors (electronic) in an oil refinery. The office workers are traditional clerks and secretaries, mechanized clerical workers such as key-punchers and proof-encoding machine operators, and automated electronic workers such as computer console operators and software personnel (programmers and systems analysts). The office workers are employees of insurance companies and a bank.

Shepard devised three scaled indexes of alienation:
(1) Powerlessness—absence of freedom and control in conducting one's work
(2) Meaninglessness—lack of knowledge of the relationship of one's job to other jobs and to the organization
(3) Normlessness—lack of clear standards for achievable promotion.

Shepard finds a generally similar response among comparable categories of factory and office workers. With some exceptions, for which he accounts, mechanized workers are highest in alienation scores, electronic workers next highest, and craftsmen lowest. A major exception is among office workers: secretaries and clerks are higher in alienation from their jobs than computer software personnel.

Because mechanized workers come closest to being stereotypic and, some might say, quintessentially "urban" workers, let us look at them more closely.

The following percentages of workers in each category registered scores above the midpoint of the various alienation scales (pp. 98–99):

Alienation	Factory	Office
Powerlessness	94	58
Meaninglessness	73	63
Normlessness	61	49

In contrast, here are percentages of workers in various categories who registered alienation scores the *fewest* of which were above the midpoint (pp. 98–99):

Alienation	Factory	Office
Powerlessness	19 craft	9 computer software
Meaninglessness	45 automated 46 craft	34 computer software
Normlessness	33 automated	37 computer software

Given the present-day decline in mechanized industrial jobs, can there be some basis for hope that this particular kind of alienation may be declining, too? Perhaps, but another kind of alienation—alienation from one's own emotions—is becoming evident in the increasingly important bureaucratically structured service businesses in American cities (see chapter 7).

Shepard carries his analysis a step further, beyond the on-the-job scene and into dimensions of life not confined exclusively to work. He postulates that the less people feel alienated from their work, the more they evaluate themselves in terms of their work. In contrast, the most alienated workers will tend not to evaluate themselves in terms of their work but to see it as a means to the end of various nonwork activities (pp. 38–39). Taking this analysis yet another step further, Shepard cites an earlier publication: "[D]ifferences in job satisfaction can be attributed to four factors: occupational prestige, control of work, work group integration, and the degree to which an 'occupational community' exists among workers while off the job" (pp. 126–27)

Shepard's points are, in a sense, updatings of ones Peter Berger made some time ago. Berger (1964:217) saw as one of the major effects of industrialization the sharp separation of work from private life where one's authentic self and true identity are centered. He also suggested three varieties of work in terms of "human significance": (1) work that provides primary self-identification; (2) work that is a direct threat to self-identification; and (3) work that neither fulfills nor oppresses but is of necessity endured (pp. 218–19). Existence of "occupational communities" is especially important in the cultures of cities.

Largely implicit in Shepard's presentation is exploitation, an important factor in alienation. If one had to choose only one kind of human behavior that causes the most misery to others, exploitation would probably be a leading candidate. It permeates much of life, but at this point consideration of it is confined to on-the-job work.

Barbara Garson interviewed and observed people employed in various routine jobs. The theme of her book, *All the Livelong Day* (1975), is the continual struggle of these employees against the effects of exploitation. Some of Garson's informants were employed in a city (New York) and had jobs identifiable with those Shepard studied (clerical and keypunching). Garson, who herself had had clerical work experience, emphasizes the isolation of employees in these jobs even when many of them work in the same room. They cannot talk while they work, and their work is not cooperative (p. 152). Devices such people use to endure the tedium include fantasizing and, among keypunchers, impromptu racing (p. 155). Garson points out many ways in which management could make routine work more pleasant, but as long as corporate goals are being met and as long as there is a labor pool from which it can refill the ranks of its often high-turnover employees, there is little incentive for management to do so. Garson concludes that managements ". . . create jobs that are far too complex for robots, but . . . far too regimented for chimpanzees. So they are stuck using human beings. . . . For workers it's a dilemma too. Real work is a human need, perhaps right after the need for food and the need for love. It feels good to work well. But it feels bad to be used" (p. 219).

Garson sees a "possible though not simple" solution in socialism and workers' control, but she also points out that factories in the Soviet Union can "feel the same" as those in the United States because in both countries managers exploit workers for their own ends (p. 212).

Many of the workers Garson studies have jobs they would prefer not to have, but which they must take because of financial need. To what extent is this true generally? Some observers give the impression that it is very general indeed, but a connection with alienation may not be easy to establish. One complicating factor is that workers who at any given time are alienated may not necessarily be people who originally took their jobs only because of financial need. For example, professionals and paraprofessionals in health services characteristically enter their careers with very high ideals and hopes for accomplishment. They do not enter their careers solely to earn money. One of the major causes of "burnout" (a complicated form of job stress and ultimate termination) among them is their inability to sustain those high ideals as their employment proceeds through time (Cherniss 1980:160). These workers also often suffer from a form of normlessness, as Shepard uses the term:

[E]ven the professional staff are deprived of the personal gratifications that result when one's accomplishments and professional growth are recognized through increases in responsibility and status. In fact, in fields such as teaching, practitioners remain in the same status unless they go into administration. To do so usually means an end to the person's career as a practitioner (Cherniss 1980:170–71).

Shepard, Garson, and Cary Cherniss provide only tiny glimpses into the nature of work in cities, and the cities are exclusively American. However, all three are keenly aware of the major issues, and their small-scale studies are intended to have large-scale implications. Shepard emphasizes the variety of urban work, that not all city workers are alienated, and the complication that alienated workers do not all experience alienation in the same way. Garson stresses the variety of stratagems people use to make large segments of their less-than-ideal lives bearable, and she emphasizes that much of workers' stress lies less in the work itself than in the ways in which it is managed. Cherniss's emphasis on the importance of the high idealism and professional ambitions that initially inspire many people leads one to reflect on two (among many) striking contrasts: (1) highly skilled workers suffer, not because they are unable to earn a living, but because earning a living has become very unrewarding in noneconomic ways; and (2) villagers in all parts of the world seek unskilled, low-paying jobs in cities because they know they can earn a better living there than at home. Many of those erstwhile villagers are squatters in Third World cities and have been observed to be unalienated from their work. Perhaps this quality of life is because their expectations are limited to survival. If so, this may be because most of them are materially deprived members of societies that have only recently developed cash economies (see Eames and Goode 1973:96–97ff). Or it may be because, for most people everywhere, the primary importance of work is its efficacy as a means of survival.

Some dimensions of alienation lie beyond the job scene. One is the very high rate of unemployment among youths living in United States and other Western industrial inner cities. They belong, in disproportionately large numbers, to subcultural or racial groups which have been subjected to social discrimination and deprivation: notably blacks, Puerto Ricans, and Mexican-Americans.

The study by Joan Moore and associates (1978) of Mexican-American youths in Los Angeles is particularly useful on this subject. Moore, whose research associates included members of the East Los Angeles *barrio*, describes four subcultures found in it: (1) "square type I," recent immigrants from Mexico who accept the types of work available and aim for eventual house ownership and increasingly stable work; (2) "square type II," born in Los Angeles but unable to participate in the Anglo system; family-centered, stable laborers, not very attached to the *barrio*; (3) "squares" who have left the *barrio* and entered the Anglo system, sometimes in conjunction with mixed marriages; and (4) "*barrio*-oriented deviants" (pp. 158–60).

The *barrio*-oriented deviants are convict-drug addict-neighborhood gangs. This group is a very small component of the *barrio* and even more so of the Mexican-American population of Los Angeles, now about one-quarter of the total (Moore et al. 1978:13). Precedents for these gangs, operating in "symbolic challenge to the world" (p. 36), go back at least to 1943 and the riots between zoot-suit *pachucos* and wandering gangs of Anglo military servicemen. Basically, these "home-boys" are united by familial and territorial attachment to the *barrio*, reinforced by the scarcity of jobs for them in the dominant Anglo system (p. 33). They therefore "find jobs" in hard drug traffic and the violence that goes with it. When confined in prison, they encounter another phase in the drug-traffic-violence mode, perpetuated after their release.

Moore et al. refer to these gang members as deviants because this is how the majority of their fellow Mexican-Americans, in the midst of whom they live, regard them (pp. 150–51). That this is an alienated subculture among Mexican-Americans, and among Los Angelenos in general, there is no question. There is also no question that what they do is a kind of urban occupation and a means of livelihood. The impact of this occupation is felt among Los Angelenos generally in the form of widespread terror of random, cruel, and seemingly motiveless violence. John Godwin's book on this subject includes descriptions of the horrendous effects of gang violence in the same *barrios* of East Los Angeles as those Moore et al. analyze (Godwin 1978:109–10). The Los Angeles case is, of course, only one. There are many others, and people other than Mexican-Americans, such as the unemployed or underemployed youth in British cities, are the principal actors in them.

Another expression of job-related alienation is seen in certain very restricted areas of cities. For example, there is the Warmoesstraat of Amsterdam. Maurice Punch's monograph about it is primarily concerned with the nature of police work there. Warmoesstraat is no longer what it used to be—a stable Dutch red light district (Punch 1979:186). The area is now one whose style is of "predatory criminality associated with the anonymity of an inner city area ... with its mixture of urban decay and impersonal spaces" (p. 20). No longer homogeneously Dutch (and therefore essentially predictable for the police), the area now has a large element of foreign criminals earning their livelihoods. Warmoesstraat is a melting pot of members of various ethnic groups and other persons such as runaways. While it features picturesque bridges, it is also a "colourful mixture of cafés, sex-shops, porn-clubs ('erections guaranteed or money refunded' . . .), Chinese restaurants, bars, clubs, discos, and pre-eminently, prostitutes" (p. 65).

In this context, Punch (pp. 88–93) considers police work an occupation that involves learning to cope with horrifying and unpleasant sights and situations. The job also involves learning the territory and differentiating among (1) legitimate residents and shopkeepers, (2) disreputable users of the area who nevertheless belong (such as prostitutes and alcoholics), and (3) illegitimates such as muggers and thieves (p. 128). The dilemma for the police is how to cope with a rising crime rate in the midst of increasing tolerance for unorthodox behavior in the general culture (p. 180). The frequent result is alienation, expressed in a certain amount of brutality and corruption (p. 78).

Another dimension of alienation is its diversity in terms of social class, occupational status, and gender. Lillian Rubin's study of working- class women and professional-class wives brings some of the issues into focus:

[A] major problem in professional families may be just this issue . . . work time and off-work time are so fused as to leave little room for free time that is not also spent in work. . . . For the professional . . . there is not the separation between working and living that so often characterizes the working-class experience (1976:190).

Here we encounter a situation in which work is so all-consuming that it alienates the worker from all other aspects of life. The Protestant or work ethic, with its sharp distinction between work as a virtue for its own sake and leisure (idle and sinful) has been a concomitant of this orientation among many people in Western industrial cities. Trufanov, from his Marxist-Leninist point of view, condemns it as a bourgeois orientation (1977:12), but it is understandable among single-mindedly profit-oriented employers (cf. Chinoy 1964:76–79). Observations of certain kinds of employees bear out that the work ethic is in operation. Famous among these workers is the American middle-class suburban business executive, of whom William H. Whyte says: "Work, then, is dominant. Everything else is subordinate, and the executive is unable to compartmentalize his life. Whatever the segment of it—leisure, home, friends—he instinctively measures it in terms of how well it meshes with his work" (1956:146).

On the other hand, Rubin also reminds us of a common working-class orientation in which work is dichotomized from the rest of life. Whether such compartmentalization is to be seen as alienating or liberating depends on many factors, including the nature of the work and the values and expectations of the workers.

Sidel (1978:2), who studied eight working-class, employed women living in New York City, emphasizes the "inhumanity" of their work: routinization, job insecurity, and inadequate wages for their needs. However, she also mentions noneconomic rewards interwoven with economic motivations and alienations: "Work is seen both as a financial necessity and as a means for personal gratification to all of these women" who also discuss "its frustrating, monotonous, alienating aspects" (p. 158).

It is understandable how such studies might reinforce negative views of work in cities that accompany the antiurban biases of special concern in this book. It is also understandable why some people look wistfully at livelihoods among nonurban people and are sometimes tempted to declare that they are the only truly human ones. One favorite is the hunter-gatherer mode of survival. Here there seems to be no powerlessness, meaninglessness, normlessness, or exploitation; here work seems to be its own reward: the practice of skills necessary for survival.

However, most of the world has long since evolved into forms of community where survival entails more than food and shelter, and interdependence that is far more complex than is necessary among hunter-gatherers. Furthermore, the studies cited do not present a monolithic picture. Not everyone—even in large, bureaucratically managed factories and offices—is alienated from work. Millions of people like Sidel's subjects get personal gratification from their work over and beyond its economic compulsions and constraints.

Finally, we must question whether alienation is a consequence of Western industrial city environments—whether, in other words, it is city-specific. While city-specific phenomena like long distances and difficult transportation between workplace and home can contribute to alienation, much of the problem lies in the nature and management of the workplace itself, and here Western industrial bureaucratic culture, not cities in themselves, is the paramount factor. As Peter Berger says:

> To deal with "the problem of work" . . . is to deal with peculiarly modern phenomena. The focus of the "problem" is the question of "meaning." . . . [Meaning] *becomes* problematic as the result of specific transformations within the society. . . . [T]wo developments are of decisive importance in this connection—structurally, the extreme intensification of the division of labor occasioned by the ongoing industrial revolution; ideologically, the secularization of the concept of vocation. . . . [T]he industrial revolution has brought about an ever-increasing fragmentation of specific work processes, removing the worker further and further away from the product of his work. . . . [T]his is only the external part [of the problem] . . . there is also an internal part . . . for most of history men have *been* what they *did*. This did not mean they particularly *liked* what they did—the problem of "job satisfaction" is as modern as that of the "meaning of work." . . . Nevertheless, [work] provided a self-identification for the individual that was stable, consistent, and recognized . . . a firm profile (1964:213–15).

MARGINALITY

Just as alienation is, according to many observers, a hallmark of Western industrial urban livelihoods, marginality is widely thought of as a hallmark of Third World urban work.

The idea of marginality has become particularly associated with migrants to, and squatters in, Third World cities. Marginality is reinforced by the attitudes of indigenous elites and middle classes and by theories of modernization based, in part, on Western industrial economic assumptions. One of the most thorough critiques of marginality theory appears in Janice Perlman's book on squatters in Rio de Janeiro and the unfortunate consequences of their relocation. Her summary of marginality follows:

[M]igrants are seen as uprooted, anomic individuals or families from the countryside, knowing no one in the city and having no place to go. They never adapt well to urban life and are generally anxious to return to their home towns. They seek out others of their kind and isolate themselves in parochial, ruralistic enclaves where they live in filth and squalor. Instead of using the wider context of urban agencies, institutions, and services, the contact which would help them and also have a modernizing impact, they prefer to stay within their ghettos and protect their traditional values and life styles. Within these shantytowns ... is a huge void created by the transition process. Social disorganization has resulted—evidenced in family breakdown, anomie, lack of trust and cooperation, secularization, rampant crime, violence and promiscuity.

As the self-defeating traits of the culture of poverty replace the maladaptive traits of the culture of traditionality—or supplement them as the case may be—the squatters become highly pessimistic and fatalistic. They show total inability to defer gratification or plan for the future. They are regarded as parasites or leeches on the urban economy, and as a drain on the limited resources for city services and infrastructure. Favelados are seen as lazy, not placing a high value on work, and contributing little either to production or consumption. ... [T]hey are considered politically non-interested, non-participant and non-supportive of the system (1976:129).

Perlman's major objective is to refute this "myth of marginality," as far as the squatters' behavior is concerned, and also to show how the assumption by policymakers that the myth is true can have very negative effects on the squatters (p. 91). Along the way, she gives considerable attention to the influence of Western economic ethnocentrism on formation of the myth:

The idea in economic terms is that through urbanization, industrialization, the spread of mass media, and the widening of educational opportunities, many segments of the population can be brought from the subsistence sector into the modern economy. Marginal populations will then become consumers, expanding the internal markets and stimulating further development (p. 111).

Many problems with the modernization literature stem primarily from a notion of staged development following the Western model and the assumption that characteristics of the entrepreneurial elite and mobile middle class are necessary prerequisites for modernization everywhere (pp. 113–14).

Modernization theory, as Perlman and others see it, is not only ethnocentric, it is also macrocosmic to the point of disparaging crucially important microcosmic dimensions of the squatters' adaptations to city life:

Modernization theorists ... agree that strong family ties, extended kinship networks, or "loyalties to family and clan" ... hinder individual mobility, constrain individual achievement, limit an individual's economic advancement, and take precedence over the individual's loyalty to his nation. All of these ties slow the development of modern citizenship (p. 113).

Have these modernization assumptions, that supposedly pertain to the industrialized West itself, possibly contributed to the alienation so many observers think is characteristic of Western industrial city work? Be this as it may, marginality theory has prevented many people from perceiving the positive adaptational aspects of squatters' lives. Writing generally about Latin America, but in the context of her study in Mexico City, Larissa Lomnitz characterizes this adaptability in strong terms:

Marginals occupy the bottom of the social scale in society: They have literally nothing. Their only resources are . . . kinship and friendship ties that generate social solidarity. Accordingly, a type of social structure has evolved in the shantytown that mobilizes the social resources of the settlers on behalf of survival[:] a *network of reciprocal exchange.* . . . Age-old institutions, like *compadrazgo* (fictive kinship or godparenthood) and *cuatismo* (a traditional form of male friendship), are mobilized to reinforce and strengthen the structure of local exchange networks. Characteristic residential patterns evolve, which optimize the resources of the group through various types of household arrangements. Even alcohol consumption, hitherto considered a symptom of social disorganization, can be harnessed to the objectives of group solidarity since it effectively prevents the accumulation of cash differentials among members of an exchange network (1977:3).

Of the squatters Perlman studied, 44 percent were employed in unskilled, semiskilled, domestic, or construction jobs in 1969 (p. 157). On the whole, their jobs are the least desirable in society, and many are odd jobs. In many cases, these people are prevented from working by bureaucratic harrassment such as withholding work cards (p. 158). The image of economic parasitism inherent in the marginality concept can be challenged: many of the men work in industry, construction, and transportation, mostly in the "external city economy," and many of the women work in domestic service which middle- and upper-class people consider essential to their life-styles (cf. Bunster and Chaney 1985:24–26). Unskilled workers mostly have service jobs. Typically, they are street vendors, garbage collectors, bus fare collectors, doormen, guards, street cleaners, service station attendants, car washers, street repairers, and janitors. Perlman emphasizes that these are necessary jobs, not the "drain" on the economic system that their marginal status supposedly implies (p. 153). These jobs are, on the whole, "dead end" from the point of view of many North Americans, but this is completely beside the point as far as survival of the poor in Latin American cities is concerned.

Studies of squatters in other parts of the Third World yield generally similar information. In settlements outside Istanbul, for instance, Kamal Karpat (1976:105) found 39 percent of the employed men (90 percent of the employed women) in service jobs, 17 percent in technical professions, 20 percent in construction, and 10 percent in trade. The remaining 14 percent are in crafts, agriculture, and "other" occupations. Only 7 percent of the men in his samples were unemployed. While Karpat does not discuss marginality theory, he does mention some of the squatters' contributions to the Turkish national economy: increased income to food producers, added impetus to the textile industry, and considerable investment in home improvements (pp. 102–11). One last example suggesting the central, rather than peripheral or nonessential, role of many squatters' work is that in 1957, 57 percent of the industrial workers in Baghdad were squatters (Hilali 1958:89).

All of this discussion indicates that we must be more aware that the work of many squatters in Third World cities is actually of substantial importance in the macroeconomic systems involved and that it is accomplished by means of highly effective social support systems at the microlevel. It is necessary to emphasize the positive and constructive aspects of the working lives of squatters to show that there is an alternative to the negative view that has had considerable influence on housing and other national policies. However, it would be cavalier to suggest that squatter settlements as they now are constitute a permanent solution to such massive problems as insufficient job opportunities in the rural and urban sectors, virtual absence of the low-cost housing needed by the majority of the people, and runaway inflation. No one with firsthand knowledge of squatters suggests this.

Observers who have taken the most sanguine view of squatters' accomplishments are very cautious about the future. Perlman, for instance, while stressing that they "improvise critical solutions in the short run," says "macrosolutions are clearly necessary in the long run" (1976:7). Peter Lloyd entitles his book, *Slums of Hope?*, with a question mark, because the hope is problematic. The hope is based on short-term solutions that so far have been successful, including such activities as political action for improvement of settlementwide amenities and utilities. Squatters are typically moved by "the promise of future opportunities and social mobility," but there may be increasing tension and violence if such promises fail to materialize because of generally deteriorating societal conditions (1979:216–17). Howard Handelman, noting in detail the many inadequacies of low-income public housing in Bogotá and Caracas, makes this ironical and sobering assessment:

> [A]s British architect John Turner suggested long ago, Latin America's urban poor are not only capable of building their own houses, but can also provide themselves with housing that is . . . cheaper and more to their liking than Caracas' [high-rise] *bloques*. Unfortunately, the "Turner Thesis" has also served many Latin American governments as a convenient justification for "benign neglect." The horrendous sanitary conditions and high crime rates within many Latin American shantytowns reveal the fruits of "letting the poor fend for themselves." Government resources must be spent to provide basic infrastructure and services . . . low-interest home-improvement loans, technical assistance, and low-cost construction material (1979:19).

Earlier, Handelman refers to the Venezuelan government's "total neglect of the bottom 30–35 percent" of the population of Caracas (p. 17), and therein may lie the seeds of future disaster.

Some successful squatter adaptations have already been undermined. Squatter settlements, like all urban phenomena, are varied. In contrast to the Latin American and Turkish examples, squatter settlements in Tehran before the 1978–79 revolution, have been characterized as fitting the concept of marginality (Kazemi 1980:7). Caught in the squeeze between failure of the Pahlavi regime's agricultural policies and the slowdown in urban construction in the late 1970s, the squatters' unemployment, insecurity, and general living conditions were far worse than comparable phenomena in the other cultures already discussed (p. 113). As of 1980, the Khomeini regime's response was concerned with providing food and housing, and settlers have been designated as "the weakened and disinherited" (pp. 116–17). Since the Iranian revolution is still in process, we cannot tell whether the present regime's response will become the kind of macrolevel "solution" that authors like Perlman, Lloyd, and Handelman think squatters everywhere will need in the long run.

In thinking about possible effects of government intervention in such matters, we should consider some experiences in the People's Republic of China, a very different structure of government, to be sure, from those of the countries at which we have been looking. By the early 1960s, the unemployed in Shanghai consisted mainly of immigrant peasants and educated youths who refused to relocate in the countryside. When persistent efforts to persuade them to leave failed, menial jobs in the city were found for them (L. T. White 1978:133–34). Despite the many regulations and procedures intended to control the city's growth and expansion of its households (all of which required food-rationing documents), both continued to grow and expand, and other means were attempted. For example, Lynn White says:

> [T]he lives of Shanghai's people increasingly centered around their work-places . . . by mid-1958 . . . communal dining halls had been widely established . . . for example, the Shanghai Bicycle Plant built two dormitories for 1,100 workers (800 men and 300 women). Together they constituted a single huge collective household (1978:170–71).

The government of the People's Republic failed to move large numbers of city dwellers to rural areas despite its autocratic procedures and harsh living conditions in the cities. The government's failure dramatizes that, everywhere in the world, most people who have had the opportunity to live in cities prefer to remain there. Squatters who have moved from inner-city slums and sub-urbanites who have moved from center cities are no exception to this generalization, for squatter settlements and suburbs are urban environments integrated into metropolitan areas. This preference is remarkable considering widespread antiurban stereotypes and the difficulties and unpleasantnesses that are aspects of city life. This book offers an explanation for the widespread preference for urban residence: the reality of the humanity of cities.

LIVELIHOODS IN URBAN LIFE

Two systems of accessibility and constraint affect urban livelihoods: (1) spatial accessibility of home and workplace and (2) social accessibility of employment as affected by class, ethnic or racial, and gender identities. Conceptually less global and abstract than alienation and marginality, these systems are directly connected with the morphology and social geography of cities. Nevertheless, they transcend any particular job or workplace and lie in an intermediate range of scale.

Spatial Accessibility

Mutual accessibility of workplace and home involves not only the distance between the two but also the means, time, and expense of transportation. Is being able to walk from home to work in a few minutes preferable to commuting for one to two hours by one or more mechanical means of transportation? Many people would answer yes, but we really do not know if there is any one, universal answer. There are obvious advantages to living very close to one's work—indeed, on the same premises, if possible, or at most within a short walk. But in some occupations, there also may be disadvantages, and the disadvantages of living farther away are not unerringly evident. Occupational communities—support systems based on occupational identities—sometimes involve propinquity of workplace and home and sometimes do not. People must consider many trade-offs, if they have any choice at all. There are well-known macrocosmic disadvantages connected with maximum distances between workplace and home, the most widely recognized being the many consequences of high-speed highways and traffic. Mumford (1964) sees these as being among the most important causes of the dehumanization of Western industrial cities. In addition, there are serious consequences for the quality of public services since millions of Western industrial commuters pay their local taxes in the municipalities where they live, which are different from the municipalities where they work. Experiments such as the United Kingdom's new towns, which, among other things, were intended to bring urban workplaces and rural homes close together, have not altogether succeeded. People commute into and out of the new towns; they go where there is work.

Distances between home and workplace in Western industrial cities may be longer than in Third World ones. The latter certainly have many fewer commuter suburbs. However, Third World city dwellers often have to cope with serious transportation problems. Two striking scenes in Louis Malle's film, *Calcutta*, show the crowded, rickety commuter trains and the hordes of people walking to work across Howrah Bridge in the morning. Although many squatter settlements were originally located as close as possible to work places, this is not always true. Handelman mentions that some squatters in Bogotá must change vehicles several times to get to and from work, and transportation may cost as much as a sixth of their daily wage (1979:7).

There are contrary examples, too. Cato Manor, a squatter settlement outside Durban, South Africa, was in 1958 a very good adaptational site for its 120 thousand black inhabitants because of its closeness to their jobs and the least expensive food markets. However, they were soon dispersed to make room for a "housing estate" for 17 thousand white families (Maasdorp and Ellison 1975:63, 74).

Michelson's longitudinal research in Toronto is one of the most careful and comprehensive studies bearing directly on this subject, although Toronto is a Western industrial city and not representative of all cities. Also, the people Michelson interviewed could afford to move from one type of home to another; many city dwellers have no such choices. Given these limitations, his findings are of great value. He identifies 32 specific satisfactions and dissatisfactions people had with four different kinds of dwelling. Satisfaction with closeness to work is one of the more frequently mentioned types, along with transportation and closeness to shopping areas. Dissatisfaction with long distance to work is less frequently mentioned. These people, who are able to enjoy some flexibility in adaptation, seem to attribute substantial importance to accessibility of work places, many, if not most, of which are downtown rather than in the suburbs.

	Dissatisfied with Long Distance to Work (%)		Satisfied with Short Distance to Work (%)	
Type of Dwelling	Wife	Husband	Wife	Husband
Downtown apartment	7	16	57	73
Downtown house	8	6	51	76
Suburban apartment	14	24	36	51
Suburban house	8	19	25	47

Source: Michelson 1977, approximated from bar graphs pp. 280–83, 288–91

Fewer women than men express satisfaction with accessibility of workplace, especially suburban women. (We shall return later in this chapter to the disadvantages of the suburban environment for working women.) Wives moving to downtown apartments are much more likely to be employed, and married couples with more, rather than fewer, children are more likely to be attracted to the suburbs (Michelson 1977:134, 138). These are not unexpected or unique findings, but their specificity is welcome in conjunction with aggregate data such as those on the large United States metropolitan areas that J. Thomas Black (1980) analyzes. Black documents the well-known decline of manufacturing, and many other kinds of blue-collar work, in central cities and the increase in employment opportunities in suburban fringes, with an overall increase in employment opportunities (and incomes) in almost all metropolitan areas. He emphasizes the importance of recognizing the "changing role" of cities (p. 122) and mentions the great increase in office and specialized retailing jobs in central cities (p. 99). If Toronto can be assumed to be following similar trends, the various moves of members of Michelson's sample within the metropolitan area indicate something about people's microadaptations to those trends. There are, of course, people who are adversely affected by them, some of whom we consider shortly.

Michelson draws a precise picture of people's movements within the Toronto metropolitan area. Proximity to work is one factor among many to which the movers give serious consideration. The study of the Stockwell section of south-central London (see chapter 4) provides a valuable supplement to the Toronto data. Like most North American industrial inner-city areas, Stockwell has lost many industrial and public utilities job opportunities for its inhabitants, and there is especially high unemployment among its black residents. Stockwell's residents who were working at the time they were studied (1973–76) traveled all over the London metropolitan area to their workplaces, but for the most part they did not go far afield. In 1973, almost half of them worked in central London (The City, Westminster, Camden, Hammersmith, Kensington and Chelsea, and Merton), while fewer than half worked closer to home (Lambeth, Southwark, and Wandsworth). Work journeys took less than half an hour for 71 percent of the employed people, and only 3 percent needed more than an hour (Shankland, Willmott, and Jordan 1977:85).

There were differences in the work journeys of different kinds of people in Stockwell. Women more often worked in the central area than men (60 percent compared with 40 percent) presumably because of the predominance of office and service jobs there. Men, particularly those in skilled manual jobs, more often worked further afield, in other parts of London or even outside it. This reflected their greater mobility and the geographical scatter of industrial jobs. Income was strongly related to where men worked; those working inside Lambeth earned less on average than those working further afield.

Many people who worked in Lambeth's industries and services were not local residents, but commuted from other areas, mainly further out. . . . In most firms it appeared that management, professional and senior staff were rarely local residents while, at the other extreme, most unskilled workers did live locally (p. 86).

Yet in Stockwell it is among the low-skilled or unskilled workers that the greatest mismatch occurs between skills local residents possess and jobs available to them (Shankland, Willmott, and Jordan 1977:88), and these authors (p. 87) make exactly the same point that Black (and many others) make in regard to North America: government policies should be directed to helping such mismatched people change their residences so they can live closer to jobs for which they qualify (Black 1980:121). Such policies must reckon with a macrosocietal problem in Britain and North America: a large proportion of the unskilled unemployed whose residences would be relocated are blacks or members of other racial or ethnic groups who have been subjected to discrimination.

The Toronto and Stockwell cases give some indication of the variegated dynamics of the interrelationships between home and workplace in two large Western industrialized cities. These interrelationships are also highly varied in Third World cities. Ibadan is one already familiar example. Some of the indigenous Yoruba are traders and craftsmen whose shops are near their homes in the old city center. Others commute out of town to their farms, and many women are vendors working away from home. Eating prepared foods away from home is a very common practice.

The Hausa of Ibadan live exclusively in their own quarter, Sabo, where about 30 "landlords" dominate the economy. They operate housing accommodations for visiting Hausa, and in turn, travel widely away from Sabo for many weeks each year (Cohen 1967:120–21). Sabo is part of a network of small Hausa enclaves in various parts of Nigeria, among which long-distance trade is the major specialty. The Western Ibo originally settled in three named areas of Ibadan, but many have subsequently moved away, following the "pattern of industrial and commercial development, with people attempting to live as near as conveniently possible to their places of employment" (Okonjo 1967:100). The Ijebu (nonlocal Yoruba) are concentrated in six major areas of Ibadan where they specialize in certain crafts such as metal work (Mabogunje 1967b:88–90). Finally, the Westernized elite, living in low-density suburban environments, depend heavily on the private automobile to get to their modern, institutional jobs.

Tripoli, Lebanon, has only about one-fifth the population of Ibadan and is far more compact geographically. An able-bodied person can easily traverse most of it on foot except for two sections beyond steep riverbank slopes whose buildings are more accessible by car. Tripoli has a *madina*, the traditional Islamic section of narrow, crooked alleys, courtyard-style houses, and small shops clustered by specialty, especially cloth selling, utilitarian metal work, and gold jewelry (valued by many people for investment as well as for ornamentation). Adjacent to the *madina* are three sections: in two, European-style businesses and various public institutions are concentrated; in the third are wholesale produce markets linking the city with its agricultural hinterland. These three sections and the three clusters in the *madina* all have their own names which suffice as residential and business addresses. Gulick's study, using the Tripoli telephone directory, determined the location of people who listed both business and home telephones. While this sample was highly selective, the findings make sense in terms of the city's culture and say something about home/workplace spatial distributions. Of the 50 people with business phones in the *madina*, none had home phones there, but 28 had home phones within easy walking distance and under circumstances where walking to work would be the most likely means of travel. (The *madina* is considered highly undesirable as a place in which to live, but the adjacent areas are considered fashionable.) Of the 176 businesses with business phones in the three sections outside the *madina*, 13 percent had residential phones in the same sections as their business phones, and 53 percent had residential phones in adjacent sections. In other words, two-thirds of these businessmen lived within easy walking distance of their workplaces. Tripoli's layout is such that many of its inhabitants are likely to live within reasonable walking distance of work, anyway. However, factors such as desirable and undesirable residential areas are present in Tripoli, and the type of people most likely to subscribe to two telephones (the wealthy) are able to exercise some choice. Many of them appear to have chosen maximum feasible and socially acceptable proximity of home and workplace (1967b:160–61).

Freedom of choice in this matter is the privilege of very few city dwellers in the world. Much more common are conditions like those Ximena Bunster (1978) describes among working mothers in Lima, Peru. The women's jobs are mostly in domestic work and factories and as street vendors or vendors operating out of fixed market stalls.

Market women start their working day at three or four o'clock in the morning. At that time they cook the midday meal so that their school-age children will find something to eat when they return home before the mothers, who work until five or six in the evening.

At five o'clock in the morning they set off with their babies and toddlers to [a] wholesale market where they buy their merchandise for that day. . . . [T]hey have to pay a carrier . . . to take their load to a bus [or] pay an extra fee to send it on a truck to their market.

[Stall vendors] finally arrive at their market at six-thirty a.m. They open their stands, arrange their merchandise, and eat breakfast. . . . Some manage to snatch a bite while selling. . . . The more prosperous buy lunch at a neighboring food shop; others have members of their family bring them their lunch from home. . . .

All . . . complained of the burden of their double day as workers and mothers, . . . expressed discontent at the amount of money they had to spend on bus and truck fares and on meals bought at the marketplace . . . [and] wanted the creation of day-care centers in the markets (1978:44).

One wonders if the indigenous Yoruba women vendors in central Ibadan have a more or less difficult work life, by reason of the separation of home and workplace, than these women of Lima. Note, in any case, what Deborah Pellow (1977) says about women living in the Adabraka section of Accra, Ghana, most of whom are vendors. Early in the twentieth century, the British colonial government laid out Adabraka as a *zongo* ("strangers' quarter") to accommodate ethnically diverse immigrants to the city (p. 81). Adabraka is still ethnically diverse, and most of the women in Pellow's sample are migrants from villages or smaller towns. Basically, Pellow's view is that these women are still constrained in traditional roles although no longer protected by the traditional support systems they had before moving to Accra, even though their ties to hometowns remain strong. As in neighboring Nigeria and in Latin America, the women's major occupation, outside the home, is vending (as opposed to business management which entails more power and money and is dominated by men). Vending or trade is semantically identified in Adabraka with "woman" and is not regarded by the women as a "salaried job." They associate salaried jobs with men operating in the modernized sector of Accra's economy. Pellow says the women prefer being vendors because vending is seen as part of their traditional domestic role. They simply take their preschool-age children with them to work (p. 124). Much of their vending, evidently, is in Adabraka's own centrally located market (p. 100), so the women are not very far removed from home. Pellow interprets the status of these women as being constrained by various forms of traditionalism, but she acknowledges that her views are opposed to those of other anthropological specialists on African cities (p. 45). One of the latter is Kenneth Little who notes, in an article not addressed to the constraint issue, that in Nigeria an association of market women has 300 thousand members (1978:182).

Social Accessibility

Social accessibility of work involves constraints that go beyond spatial considerations. Such constraints occur in all the urban areas of which we have sufficient knowledge. When whole groups of people endure long-term categorical limitations in their access to work, the consequences are very serious. Various forms of racial or ethnic discrimination prevent them from moving to where job opportunities are more plentiful. In the United States, migration of inner city businesses to suburbs has not benefited blacks very much because relatively few of them can take advantage of the new situation. In 1974, only 17 percent of blacks (as opposed to 41 percent of whites) in the United States lived in metropolitan suburbs, and a major reason was continued discrimination against them in the suburban housing market (Pettigrew 1980:63, 69). Mexican-Americans and Puerto Ricans live under similar circumstances. In Chicago, Native Americans live as close to friends, relatives, and their jobs as possible (Sorkin 1978:75), but their jobs are among the lowest paid, and their transiency in the city is considerable, with 20 to 40 percent moving back and forth between cities and reservations (p. 54).

The following figures show trends in white, central city/suburban populations in nine large American cities between 1960 and 1980 (Tschirhart and Kaull 1986:A–5):

City	% in Central City		% in Suburbs	
	1960	1980	1960	1980
Cleveland	71	52	99	91
Dallas	80	59	94	89
Detroit	70	33	96	93
Houston	73	52	88	80
Los Angeles	78	49	92	57
Miami	72	21	84	58
Minneapolis	97	87	99	97
New York	83	50	91	87
Portland, Ore.	94	85	99	95

One can infer from these figures for whites that the relative increase in sub-urban nonwhites, though real, is far less than that of central city nonwhites.

The 58 percent of United States blacks living in metropolitan inner cities (Pettigrew 1980:63) face formidable obstacles in increasing local employment opportunities and income. Many jobs are in black-owned businesses, "still largely 'mom and pop' with few paid employees" (Ikemma 1977:14). To counteract this situation, more black-owned inner-city business needs to be developed. In regard to Houston, William Ikemma says:

[T]he problems of a viable inner-city community-based business development are essentially . . . the same with the obstacles to inner-city (black or minority) community revitalization[:] the speculative high cost of land and property, often held by absentee-white owners, and the uncertainties of its economic profitability, in competition with the white suburban fringe areas—due to high operating costs of marginals such as security against vandalism and personal/property crimes; and also the lack of sufficient demand from the relatively low income surroundings, as well as psycho-sociological attitudes (p. 16).

Ikemma outlines various procedures, including some forms of government intervention, that might encourage more local black-owned businesses. David Manning remarks at the end of Ikemma's article (p. 18) that an expansion of black-owned businesses into predominantly white-owned areas is probably also essential. Ultimately, minority group members' greater accessibility to work will depend on their greater freedom of choice in where to live. Thomas Pettigrew sets a tone very much in harmony with the point of view of this book:

[W]hite and black Americans are more willing to reside in an interracial neighborhood if they have experienced integration previously, though the dual housing markets have long prevented most Americans from having had such experience. . . . [B]ehavior change typically precedes, not follows, attitude change. . . . [T]he most effective way to alter opposition, black or white, to interracial housing is successful living in such housing (1980:70).

Pettigrew's point is essential to the concept of the humanity of cities: city dwellers can make choices; they are not pawns of impersonal forces except insofar as thinking makes them so. One choice, which Pettigrew expresses hopefully, is to make the best of circumstances as they are. Another choice is to make the worst of those circumstances. Many people are doing that, and we cannot ignore the results, some of which are increased violence, mayhem, and murder.

Ted Gest interviewed experts on big city violence, one of whom says, "There are higher levels of frustration and anger in the cities than we have ever seen." Gest found the rage particularly evident in urban slums. Another expert predicted that poor blacks who are "frustrated by the limited avenues to success available to them in real life are likely to take the fantasy routes portrayed on television" (1981:63).

Gest stresses the plight of the unemployed in various large cities, a plight not only of native-born minority group members but also of refugees and illegal aliens. Cleveland and Detroit, older industrial cities with large, long-standing inner-city unemployment problems, ranked first and second in homicides per 100 thousand population in 1980, but Houston and Dallas, two of the supposedly most glittering of the fast-growing Sun Belt cities, were third and fourth. The need for more jobs is the central, but not the only, issue Gest emphasizes along with "broad changes in society." Such frustrations are not confined to the United States, and Gest gives brief reports of violence and fear in cities in Western Europe, the Soviet Union, Italy, China, and South Africa.

Great Britain, a country that long had a reputation for a high order of public civility, has recently exhibited similar violence. T. D. Allman (1981) focuses attention on the occurrence of the extravagant wedding of the Prince of Wales in London at the same time as a riot of desperately poor people in Liverpool's Toxteth district in which the police themselves rioted and, among other things, used a van to mangle an innocent bystander to death. Shifting his attention to Brixton, South London, Allman observes:

[T]hese people knew they lived in a country that had no place, and held no future, for them. The unemployed youths of all races mingling on the street corners knew it. And the unemployed men of all races, sitting in the same parks ... knew it. And on the side streets, the white, Asian, and black householders all seem united in the same, almost hopeless struggle—to keep what little they had in the face of a creeping devastation all around them (p. 18).

Only part of the problem, in this case, is racial/ethnic inaccessibility to jobs; another part is evolution. Great Britain's cities have become overpopulated in relation to their hinterlands which, in the days of the British Empire, extended over the entire world, but have subsequently shrunk. When we say that city dwellers can make choices, we are *not* saying that people like the Brixtonians Allman describes can freely extricate themselves from their environment solely on their own momentum and choice. What we do say is that this environment, and various alternatives to its alleviation, are the products of human will and choice, not of impersonal forces about which no one can do anything. One of many alternatives is more organized, as contrasted with unorganized, political violence, a worldwide phenomenon that is not wholly urban in occurrence. For better or worse, its motivation is often to prepare the way for broad changes in society (cf. Kohl and Litt 1974; Niezing 1974). Another alternative, which involves conflictive change but not wanton violence, consists of urban social movements whose goals have been "the redefinition of urban meaning to emphasize use value and the quality of experience over exchange value and the centralization of management" (Castells 1983:309).

As to constraints identified with gender, the basic issue is whether the heterogeneity of cities better facilitates women's accessibility to nondomestic employment than do less heterogeneous environments. We have already seen that the widespread employment of women as vendors in Latin American and sub-Saharan African cities is interpreted by some observers as being essentially domestic in nature, and therefore constrictive, and by others as being an avenue for nondomestic opportunities. This divergence of opinion reflects the extensive recent literature on women's experiences in Third World, "developing" societies. The general tenor is that "development" has not, except in a minority of high-status cases, widened women's social and occupational opportunities. On the contrary, it is asserted, their opportunities are often confined even more narrowly than they used to be within traditional male-dominated systems, especially in the cities.

As far as Western industrial cities are concerned, there is no question or controversy about the massive numerical participation of women in the nondomestic labor force, but there are many questions and controversies about the quality and status of their occupations compared to those of men. Underlying most of these discussions are serious concerns about the relative amounts of power, authority, and influence men and women exercise. These are important issues, but they constitute a far larger and more ramified discourse than can be accommodated here. We must limit the discussion to city-specific constraints, as well as opportunities.

Women's nondomestic work can also be looked on as being primarily a survival strategy complementary to that of men. Aidan Southall (1975:274), for example, refers to the development of a new middle class in south-central Africa in which husbands and wives work in the city and also on farms in the countryside. Similarly, in the Kisenyi section of Kampala, Luo/Luhya wives live in the city during slack agricultural seasons but return to their rural homes when their farm work is needed (Halpenny 1975:278). Among the Ganda, the city's indigenous ethnic group, many household heads are women. Some are dependent on men, but some are not. The nondependent woman who lives alone and controls her own household occupies a recognized status that has its own name: *nakyeyombekedde* (p. 282). Philip Halpenny thinks that women like this may be far more common than has been recognized. So there are variations and cases which do not neatly fit the general picture of women constrained. Nevertheless, the prevailing condition appears to be one of constraint. Christine Obbo (1975:290), for example, says that in East African cities, women immigrants are often harassed by authorities, treated as presumed prostitutes, and deported on that pretext.

In Middle Eastern Muslim cities, women's participation in the nondomestic labor force is less than in Latin America, sub-Saharan Africa, and probably much of Southeast Asia. On the whole, it reflects the formal subordination of women to men coupled with the social segregation of men and women outside their own domestic domains. However, while the vast majority of craftsmen and business people are men, there are some women vendors. In Cairo, they are particularly noticeable in what Abu-Lughod calls the city's rural fringe areas, where they sell their own agricultural produce. Even in Riyadh, Saudi Arabia (the most fundamentalist of all Arab Muslim societies), there are some women vendors, but their customers are women only, as are most of those in

Cairo. The distribution of women's nondomestic urban occupations is often bimodal in terms of skill and status levels, the main groups being professionals and industrial workers. Most of the women professionals are teachers; most schools are sex-segregated, and women teach girls. There is minimal contact with men. The same is true in factory work. Women workers, in sharp contrast to many women in Western industrial cities, seldom hold jobs that unavoidably involve frequent contacts with men.

One of the few studies of nondomestically employed urban women in the Middle East was made in 1975 in a textile factory in Shubra el-Kheima, an industrial settlement on Cairo's northern edge. Among the 20 thousand workers in the factory were 1,150 women, a relatively large concentration of employed women by Egyptian standards. Economic need was their most important reason for working, but another was "a socially acceptable opportunity to get away from the home environment and make new acquaintances." To get to work, the women had to leave home between four and five in the morning and walk to the bus station with a male escort to ward off abuse by other males along the way. From the station, they had a one-hour ride in company buses (presumably free from the sexual harassment for which public buses are well known) to the factory (Hammam 1981:6–7).

Domestic and transportation constraints are two of the many aspects of women's work in the industrial West that are, in part, related to urban environments. (Other problems, such as unequal pay for equal work, discriminatory standards for promotion, and sexual harassment on the job, may or may not be more important, but they do not seem to be so clearly city-relevant.)

Michelson observed in detail the tendency for Toronto women who are primarily oriented toward work to move into in-town apartments, but a very large proportion of urban women in Canada and the United States live in the suburbs. Even though suburban employment opportunities have greatly increased (to the severe detriment of many poor people living in inner-city ghettos), they are spread thinly so that

> the friction of space weighs heavily on suburban women because they have less ability . . . to make themselves physically mobile. Not only are they more likely to be bound to the home by child care, obligations to aged parents, and by general household duties but they simply have less access to the auto transport needed in suburbs, *when that transport would assist in their development as individuals in their own right* (Fava 1980:135).

Mary Cichocki (1980:151) refers to the way metropolitan morphology "discriminates against the existing life-styles and future opportunities" of women and concludes her study of working and "nonworking" Canadian suburban women by saying:

> The spatial and temporal characteristics of the women's movement behavior and associated activity patterns reveal the existence of serious inequalities in the form and structure of outer suburban areas. . . . [T]hese inequalities lie in the physical isolation of residential neighborhoods, increased distance in travel, infrequent transit scheduling, and inadequate social services in outer suburban communities. Not only does the problem require the coordination of facilities such as the provision of more day-care centers, more efficient and accessible means of transport, and better job opportunities located in time and space, but also a means to alter the perceptions and

attitudes of women themselves with respect to their roles in the home as members of modern society (pp. 162–63).

In counterpoint to the "suburbanization of jobs," with its particular constraints and opportunities for women, is the continuation, if not expansion, of certain kinds of white-collar work in inner cities which also attract many women. It has even been suggested that the substantial attraction of working women, married and single, to inner cities may be a factor in their revitalization (Wekerle 1980:201). However, in inner cities women have to contend with fears for their physical safety even more than men do. While the study by M. T. Gordon and others (1980:158) indicates that these fears are often greater than warranted by the actual frequency of attacks, their findings "suggest that women may have developed life-styles that include restrictions on their freedom and behavior and that may keep them safe by limiting their chances of becoming victims."

What relationships may there be between the existence of this fear system and an observation in France (Wekerle 1980:195) that women appear to be prevented from indulging in various kinds of public activities in Western industrial cities that men are not prevented from doing, such as hanging out in cafés and eating alone in restaurants? The French observation is very limited, for groups of women do make extensive use of urban space. Gerda Wekerle mentions the recent development in North American cities of women's protective networks—in women's buildings, coffee shops, bookstores, bars, and restaurants. For women who benefit from such networks and for some career women attracted to center cities because of the high-paying jobs, some parts of inner cities may constitute a kind of "turf." And, regardless of whether their public work is merely an extension of their domestic roles, the women vendors of sub-Saharan African cities certainly inhabit a turf, the geographical basis of a sense of community.

OCCUPATIONAL COMMUNITIES

The constraints on livelihoods in cities that figure so prominently in the preceding section are to a considerable extent connected with the identities of various aggregations of people, as perceived by themselves and others. It is ironic that while the absence or weakness of recognized identity is so often thought to be one of the drawbacks of life in cities, real and recognized identities in cities can be at the root of serious difficulties there. Actually, as many recent studies of urban ethnicity have shown, social identities have benefits and liabilities, and the actors involved must often negotiate trade-offs between them (see chapters 7 and 8). In this final section, we review a number of situations and instances in which occupational identities are the basis for various kinds of coping behavior that are, on the whole, beneficial for those involved. This material is arranged into five general categories: friendships, familistic connections, adaptations to stigmatized statuses, workers' organizations, and localized communities.

Friendships

The strength and importance of work-related friendships in Japanese cities is one aspect of Japanese corporations that has received considerable attention.

Japanese corporations have been depicted as paternalistic institutions in which various values of preindustrial Japanese culture have been adapted to industrial needs and conditions. One result is to provide employees with various communal activities in which friendships are generated. These matters have been described and analyzed at length for middle-class "salarymen" (Vogel 1971) and blue-collar workers (Cole 1971). Ezra Vogel emphasizes the intensity of friendships:

> The husband's friends are his co-workers, the wife's friends are her neighbors. These relationships are remarkably intimate. If . . . a wife has difficulty with her husband, . . . she may turn to her neighborhood friends for support and suggestions for dealing with them. . . . Most wives say that they feel freer in talking to other wives than to their husbands, and they tell other wives many things they would not tell their husbands. The same is true for the men, who generally feel freer in talking to their close working associates about certain things than to their wives (pp. 136–37).

Robert Cole, discussing blue-collar employees of a Tokyo diecasting plant and an auto parts company, notes some differences between the companies, and between married and unmarried workers, in the frequency and intensity of nonwork social activities on company premises. However,

> in both firms, the carry-over of worker friendships to off-the-job association suggests that the firm as a corporate group still tends to make work and work-established relationships central to the workers' lives. For male workers, co-worker ties take precedence over the neighborhood ties (1971:140).

Cole contrasts these Japanese observations with findings of various studies in the United States in the 1950s which emphasized the supposed dichotomization of Americans' work from other aspects of their lives.

Two quite different studies of North American workers raise questions about that dichotomy, in addition to those raised earlier in this chapter. One is the study of a tavern patronized by successful, well-paid blue-collar workers on the outskirts of a midwestern city (LeMasters 1975). Most of the patrons have in common not only a similar occupational status but also predominantly German or Scandinavian ancestry. The description of their values (about which more is said in chapter 7) does not include friendship in any detail, but "the inner core of the tavern's patrons functions as a mutual aid society: psychological support is provided in times of crisis; material help is available if needed; children are cared for; cars are loaned; and so on. In our vast, impersonal society such support and aid are highly functional" (p. 142). E. E. LeMasters does not say how many of the regular patrons of the Oasis Tavern formed their friendships on the job, but clearly the friendships he observed in the tavern are anchored in a very strong sense of occupational status identity.

In contrast to the Oasis informants are the 70 unmarried college graduates Joyce Starr and Donald Carns interviewed in Chicago in 1970–71. They do not patronize singles or other bars to any great extent. They are not particularly sociable in their neighborhoods, nor do they participate in organizations. Where they make their friends, of the same and opposite sex, is primarily at work. Work is "the setting most likely to facilitate familiarity and emotional intimacy" (Starr and Carns 1973:96). "It is the adjustment these graduates make to the world of work and their patterns of forming and dissolving friendships outside of work that provide their significant connections and sense of self in the urban milieu" (p. 97).

An altogether different contrast to the separation-of-work-and-real-life stereotype is Trufanov's declaration—unsupported by any evidence—that in Soviet cities people interact with friends about equally at home and at their workplaces, with workplace friendships increasing as occupational status increases (1977:71). This comment leads to a different dimension of friendships from that considered above: friendships on the job that do *not* extend beyond work times and places. John Swetnam (1978:147), in his study of social relationships in the marketplace of a small city in Guatemala, shows that marketplace friendships among neighboring vendors, customers, and suppliers are important in facilitating cooperation.

These observations on friendships and work are only fragments. However, aside from the stereotypes involved, there is good reason to suppose that they are instances of widespread realities.

Familistic Connections

Migrants to cities typically use a variety of personal connections to find jobs and dwellings. Family and kinship connections are among them, as has been widely observed. Less well established is the extent to which familistic connections are sustained over relatively long periods of time in the pursuit of urban livelihoods. Observations in Beirut and Cairo appear to document the importance of kinship ties in sustained work relationships (Abu-Lughod 1961; Farsoun 1970; Khalaf 1968; Khalaf and Shwayri 1966). These observations are well grounded in Middle Eastern culture, and the authors know their territory well. However, David Makofsky, citing some of these same sources for comparison, says that he did not observe the operation of such traditional connections in small workshops in Istanbul, where the majority of Turkish factory workers are employed (1977:84–85). Perhaps Turkey is different in this respect from Egypt and Lebanon. Perhaps, too, there are different phases in the relationships of kinship ties and work, so that the nature of those relationships appears to be different in different phases. Two studies of family-oriented businesses in United States cities suggest something of this sort.

One study (Chock 1981) consisted of interviews with Greek-American small businessmen in Chicago and Washington, D.C. Characteristically, they had started their businesses in partnership with brothers or other relatives, and, although a common ideal is eventually to become sole proprietor, participation of more than one kinsman in the business is likely to continue (p. 53). Phyllis Chock emphasizes that these small businessmen do not regard their work as a road to advancement in general or for their children in particular (for that purpose, professional careers are necessary) and that they do regard their businesses as essentially domestic in nature. The small businessman's self-esteem comes from maturation of a sense of being his "own boss" (p. 57). These findings sound somewhat similar to Pellow's data on women vendors in Accra. It would be very interesting—and important for insights into livelihoods in cities—if it could be shown that Chock and Pellow have observed the same dynamics under conditions that are different in many ways.

Hope Leichter and William Mitchell (1980:168) emphasize the fragility of business-connected relationships with kinfolk, mentioned by Chock, in their study of 63 familistic small businesses among Jews in New York City. Most of the businesses employed ten or fewer people and were predominantly retail or service enterprises. Cases were drawn from a sample of clients at a family service agency, and the authors acknowledge that the high incidence of financial difficulties, interwoven with tensions among kinfolk, that they discovered may bias their findings. The involvement of kinfolk in one another's livelihoods is just one aspect of the extended kinship networks of the people concerned. Leichter and Mitchell's conclusion is a succinct statement of the cost-benefit quality of these relationships:

> The general inability to segregate kinship and occupational roles when these involve the same people means that there is likely to be a great deal of carryover from one area of relationships to another. Even though business activity is a source of considerable conflict among kin, this conflict does not appear to produce complete ruptures in kinship ties. Rather, since business frequently entails the financial or other assistance of kin, it reinforces obligations of reciprocity and tends to strengthen the momentum of kin interaction (p. 175).

Jagna Sharff vividly introduces a very important study of familistic livelihoods:

> Street life on Dolittle Street is a sleight of hand. The clumps of six to 10 young men who seem to be socializing daily on the corner from early morning till late at night are not there solely for convivial reasons. Nor is the little hole-in-the-wall cigarette store near the corner selling only tobacco cigarettes. Nor is the storefront several tenements down the block just the home of a popular bachelor with lots of friends continuously dropping by. The mechanic next door is not simply repairing cars. And the mothers conversing in small groups and calling out of the windows are not occupied with housework and child care. Nor are the children simply playing. All these places and activities are both what they are and something else, too— and the something else is invariably aimed at adding to the meager resources of the neighborhood, often illegally (1986:139).

"Dolittle Street" is the fictitious name of a real street in Manhattan's Lower East Side, an area famous as the starting point for a succession of recently arrived immigrant ethnic groups, currently Hispanics. Dolittle Street people survive through a combination of regular work (factory worker, handyman, janitor, waitress), public assistance, and irregular work (stealing and fencing, working for the illegal lottery, and various activities connected with drugs). All of these jobs are low-paying and unstable. The typical family's strategy for survival is to have as many of its members as possible employed in a variety of jobs. So, as Sharff (1986:140) says, "Having a large number of children is an immensely useful short-run option pursued by the majority of households. The large family doesn't keep the poor in poverty, but rather serves as a mechanism for survival."

These people have several other important characteristics. One is mutual aid that tides over families in especially bad times, even though they also compete with one another for scarce jobs. Another is the summertime communal fishing for softshell crabs at Coney Island which provides the only seafood they can afford and is "perhaps the most joyful community activity in the neighborhood" (p. 142). The third is the parents' socialization of their children into four basic roles. There is the household "street representative," a boy who aggressively defends his family's honor and engages in other dangerous activities such as those associated with drug traffic. There is the girl who is a "young child-reproducer" whose role is to become a housewife and mother. Lives of these two are limited to the overall active scale of the neighborhood. However, some boys are raised in a nonmacho mode that results in a personality appropriate for regular wage earning. These individuals may achieve success beyond Dolittle Street; and so may the "scholar/advocates," girls socialized to be untraditionally assertive, who frequently attain "pink-collar" jobs, may attend college, and marry up and out of the neighborhood. Sharff concludes that

> the large family is a kind of social security system for the present and future of the household. The members of the family are linked in an organic network, to which each contributes according to his or her talent and means, and on which all depend—the risks of the street representative role notwithstanding—for their day-to-day survival (p. 143).

The Dolittle Street study is very important in several respects:

(1) Along with some other studies, it explicitly contradicts the portrait of poor, urban Hispanics whom Oscar Lewis presented as evidence for his "culture of poverty" concept (see chapter 7).
(2) It demonstrates the existence of poor peoples' support systems, not only in the family but beyond it (see chapter 6).
(3) It demonstrates the existence of diversified personalities and roles in a subculture routinely stereotyped in uniform terms.
(4) It documents that, contrary to middle-class values, in certain sociocultural contexts, illegal activities are recognized as jobs.
(5) Its emphasis on the felt need for numerous children contradicts the widely held stereotype of the small family as an inevitable component of modern urban life and presents a sobering challenge to those who believe that the population problem is very possibly the premier macrothreat to humankind.
(6) It is probably a microcosm of the survival strategies of millions of poor city dwellers, including Third World squatters, surviving in "marginal economies."

Stigmatized Statuses

Stigmatized occupations are important because they frequently form the basis of occupational communities, and their existence in cities is pertinent to urban stereotypes, including the bipolar model.

Let us consider the second point first. The ancient notion that cities are wicked and corrupt is partly because deviant or stigmatized activities (as defined by various people at various times) are more feasible in cities than in small, homogeneous communities. Prostitution, possibly the oldest and most universal of these activities, flourishes in cities because the large heterogeneous population provides a sufficient clientele, and clients can seek its services anonymously. The same is true of other kinds of sexual service (such as pornographic entertainment), the provision of mind-altering substances, gambling, and others. Many, if not most, city dwellers at any given time and place disapprove of these activities and at times take action against them. On the other hand, some city dwellers (and visitors) want these activities. This situation is a component of urban cultural heterogeneity and, of course, conflict. Different cultural groups define deviance and stigma differently: on Dolittle Street, working in the drug traffic is a survival strategy; among middle-class suburbanites (whether or not they are drug users) it is a crime.

Prostitution is the most ancient of these occupations. Almost always stigmatized (see an exception later in this chapter), its legal status has varied considerably. Whether romanticized or condemned as hell on earth, it is a favorite literary theme. Its professionals and clients, however, have revealed very little about it and are understandably reluctant to be studied. A recent exception to this statement is a book edited by Frédérique Delacoste and Priscilla Alexander (1987).

As an occupational community at the local level, there is firm evidence (as opposed to rumors about "red light districts") of the conspicuous physical concentration of prostitution in various cities; Punch's data from Amsterdam are one example. In Beirut, the prostitutes' quarter, demolished in the 1970s, was clearly demarcated and identifiable, complete with neon signs featuring exotic women's names. The prostitutes there were interviewed on the subject of their life histories (Khalaf 1965). Until recently, Tehran also had a distinct prostitutes' quarter (Farmanfarmaian 1970), as did Baghdad (Gulick 1967a), and, unquestionably, as did or do many, if not all, other large cities. Whether the visible localization contributes to the prostitutes' mutual aid and support—to a true community—is another matter on which little is known. The probability is that it frequently does.

Striving for a sense of self is an important aspect of life for a variety of people, besides prostitutes, who have stigmatized occupations or belong to otherwise stigmatized groups whose members often have limited occupational options. Such striving has been mentioned in connection with Greek-American small businessmen, and Chock refers to their sensitivity to the stereotype of the "little Greek with the corner restaurant" (1981:46). It is probably more pronounced among people whose stigmatization is more pronounced.

One of these groups is the burlesque strippers in Toronto. Salutin's study of them is an example of small-scale research *in* (rather than *of*) the city, as noted in chapter 2. Salutin's main interest is in how these women achieve and maintain a sense of self-worth, given that their occupation violates and is offensive to conventional morality, is therefore deviant, in many locations illegal, and viewed with contempt by many people. Their audiences are composed of a wide variety of men (and occasionally women): lonely ones and happy ones, regulars and rare attenders, and married and single men representing an extensive range of occupations (p. 173). Salutin says the strippers redefine their stigmatized work as being socially useful and requiring talent, and therefore as being good. At the same time, they conceal any personal information about themselves that might label them as being sexual deviants (in particular lesbians) in order to present an image of themselves as being sexually normal and therefore moral (p. 174). Underlying all this is the attitude that sexuality is in itself good, contrary to the Victorian ethos that has been important in North American culture.

Strippers don't end up stripping because they have skidded downward in their careers as have the burlesque comics. They chose stripping as an occupation, and their decision was based upon what they knew of the world. The experiences they have had ... formulate themselves into a common-sense rationality of how best to put their bodies to use, how best to live their lives. In their own view, they haven't fallen in status. After all, one alternative would have been full-time prostitution, which has neither the social status nor the economic payoff. . . .

To strippers, stripping is a good thing, and they do it as naturally as stenographers type. It earns them a minimum of $165 a week [around 1970], and offers what they call an "easy life" (1973:180).

This easy life is not without problems, including vulnerability to certain kinds of criminals. But the important point is that, contrary to conventional middle-class expectations, this quintessentially urban occupation is not, to its practitioners, a degrading or dead-end job.

In North American cities, organized crime is, according to Francis Ianni (1974:16), part of a phase that immigrant ethnic groups—all stigmatized— have gone through in striving for upward mobility. In New York, in the past, Jews and Italians were prominent in organized crime. They have now been largely replaced by blacks and Puerto Ricans. Ianni says that at present, successful black organized crime activists (other than those dealing in nar-cotics) may be accepted and respected in their neighborhoods very much as one would expect a small businessman to be (p. 69). Activities defined by the larger society as illegal—such as playing the numbers—are often acceptable in the ethnic community (p. 122), as in the case of Dolittle Street. Then, too, some activities connected with crime may provide essential services in their stigmatized areas. "Gypsy cabs," frequently stolen cars, are often the only taxi service available in ghetto areas because legally registered taxis will not serve them (Henslin 1968:146; Ianni 1974:246ff).

Stigmatized occupational groups are not always or necessarily racially or ethnically distinctive. Seoul "shoeshine boys" are held in contempt and ridi-culed by the larger society which excludes them from economic participation. They are part of a paternalistic, territorial structure organized in the idiom of the traditional Korean kinship system. It "fulfills the complete institutional needs of mastery of the material environment, socialization, and social control" (Kang and Kang 1978:180). Though stigmatized, the syndicate provides useful or desired services for the larger society: "shoeshines, ownership and operation of tearooms, boardinghouses, and inns of prostitution; and monetary invest-ment in various legitimate businesses," and it provides its members with access to "wealth, esteem, and power" within its own boundaries (p. 181).

Irish tinkers (also known as travellers) are often confused with Gypsies because of numerous life-style similarities, but they are not Gypsies; they are racially and ethnically Irish. Other Irish people despise the tinkers, and when some of them emigrated to England in the 1950s and early 1960s, one Bir-mingham official is quoted in a newspaper as having said, "The Tinker is a throwback to the past and has no place in the life of a modern city, where people come to live in a settled, orderly and mutually helpful society. We intend to make conditions so intolerable, so uncomfortable and so unprofitable for these human scrap vultures that they won't stop here" (Gmelch 1977:50).

Until recently, the tinkers lived in rural Ireland, moving about as tinkers, beggars, breeders of donkeys and horses, and collectors of other peoples' unwanted materials. Various macroeconomic changes have recently attracted them to the cities. Many live on welfare and begging; heavy drinking is a problem, and yet, as if in response to the Birmingham official, not to mention disparagers of informal, marginally economic work generally, George Gmelch says:

> The Travellers' scavenging serves a valuable economic and ecological func-
> tion in Irish society. Tons of steel, iron, copper, lead, and other metals would
> be wasted if not reclaimed in this way; the Travellers also recycle used
> clothing, appliances, and furniture from the middle class to the poor. Dublin
> metal merchants estimate that Tinkers account for about half of all the
> scrap metal collected outside of industry . . . [and they] also save the city
> of Dublin considerable expense each year by clearing away the hundreds
> of abandoned or dumped autos (p. 70).

As the tinkers have moved into cities, some of their traditional coping responses—such as secretiveness and excessive drinking—have increased in intensity. Also, because the women, as welfare recipients, often are the principal family breadwinners, familial discord and violence have increased (p. 160). These problems, in turn, accentuate prejudices against the tinkers. However, Gmelch emphasizes that many of them can adapt successfully to standard housing and thereby gain entrée to new occupational opportunities. If, in the near future, many of them do, we may wonder if they will continue to perform the useful jobs that they have done. If not, who will?

Other distinctive groups have carved out their own occupational niches in British cities. Jamaicans are concentrated in transportation, engineering trades, and various service occupations (Foner 1977:131). They are conspicuous as conductors in the London transport system. "Pakistanis are disproportionately represented in the textile industry, doing unskilled labor and working night shifts" (Khan 1977:75). South Asian and Caribbean people are particular targets of white racism in Britain (Watson 1977b:2), and their occupational adaptation reflects their maximum accessibility to jobs that native Britons have become reluctant to take. In this way, they somewhat reduce the threats of racial assimilation and economic competition that many Britons feel they present (Watson 1977a:194). The Chinese and Italians have specialized in restaurants and catering (Palmer 1977:250–51; Watson 1977a:193ff) as have the Greek Cypriots, but they are also willing to experiment with a wide variety of small businesses (Constantinides 1977:280). The Chinese, at least some from Hong Kong, have minimized white British racial fears by keeping themselves as isolated as possible from general British society, to which they consider themselves superior (Watson 1977a:192–93). Catering in general offers excellent opportunities for nonnative Britons, and Watson's observations should ring true to anyone familiar with everyday urban life in the United Kingdom:

> Catering is dominated by immigrants; few English work in this sector,
> except at management levels or in neighborhood tea shops. The franchised
> food outlets and hamburger chains employ Spanish, Turkish, and Italian
> workers, while most of the independent restaurants are managed by mi-
> grants (Greek Cypriot, Italian, Bengali, etc.) who recruit labor in their own
> homelands.

> So far, few Chinese of village origin have taken up occupations outside
> the catering trade. New openings and opportunities have appeared in the
> wake of the restaurant boom: travel agencies, hire cars, gambling halls,

specialized grocery shops, food processing and cinemas. Most of these services are directed at the larger community of catering workers; only a small proportion of their income derives from non-Chinese customers. The Chinese have restricted themselves to these protective economic niches largely in response to intense competition from other ethnic minorities in Britain. Corner grocery stores have long since become a monopoly of the South Asians (from East Africa and Pakistan) and the Cypriots (Watson 1977a:194).

Workers' Organizations

Generally speaking, the stigmatized groups we have considered have made the best of their urban situations—even taken advantage of them in some cases—to earn their livelihoods. Sometimes, however, the job, rather than any ascribed sociocultural identity of the people who perform it, is despised in a particular culture. A notable example is garbage collection. Stewart Perry (1978), whose book is quoted in chapter 1, studied the collectors in San Francisco, locally known as "scavengers." The concern that led Perry to study one of the two privately owned, cooperative garbage collection companies serving San Francisco is very important: the possibility that people performing a dirty, hard, distasteful, but necessary, job can be properly recompensed for their work and not be personally demeaned by it. Perry says that between 1960 and 1970, the number of unskilled refuse collectors in the United States more than doubled; the number in cleaning services rose 50 percent (p. 6); and need for this kind of work will increase (p. 188).

Trash collection is necessary to society and is the kind of work that figures prominently in the livelihoods of many city dwellers all over the world. The garbage collectors of the Sunset Scavenger Company were for several reasons definitely not demeaned by their work at the time Perry studied them in the late 1960s. The principal reason is that the collectors and drivers are shareholders in the business, earning good wages from its profits by serving about 160 thousand customers (p. 25). Their sense of involvement in the company is enhanced by their being mostly Italian-Americans, and about half are related to one another, with some sons following in their fathers' footsteps (pp. 118, 122). Other rewards of the work itself seemed more than to compensate for its liabilities: the camaraderie and good humor of the crews on the job (p. 79); working outdoors; getting to know neighborhoods well and actually following the life courses of some of the residents (pp. 112–13); being one's own boss (p. 84); and others. Perry concludes his study on a somber note. Various changes—some generated internally and others imposed from outside the organization—that were under way might transform Sunset from a cooperative "into a conventional American business firm. . . . What I was able to learn about the scavengers of Sunset makes such pressures and changes appear to threaten what is prideful and efficient in the cooperative organization" (p. 202).

Whatever does happen to Sunset in the future, it was, for at least 50 years, a successful adaptation of urban workers in a livelihood denigrated by the general society. Under what particular conditions can others replicate such success? Is the cooperative structure essential? Perry seems to think so. Yet a Chicago sanitation department garbage collector said this about his work after having described its difficulties and hazards: "I don't look down on my job in any way. I couldn't say I despise myself for doing it. I feel better at it than I did at the office. I'm more free. And, yeah—it's meaningful to society" (Terkel 1974:105).

The Portland, Ore., longshoremen William Pilcher (1972) studied are, in important ways, similar to and different from the scavengers of San Francisco. Like the scavengers, "they do not conceive of themselves as employees" (p. 23). Rather than being shareholders in a cooperative, they are members of the International Longshoremen's and Warehousemen's Union (ILWU) that became famous in the 1930s for its involvement in violent strikes under the leadership of Harry Bridges. The Portland local of the ILWU provides a community for its members very much as the Sunset Company does for its shareholders. While stevedoring is not denigrated to the extent that garbage collecting is, it has a wild, roughneck image that is at least ambivalent. Unlike the scavengers, the longshoremen cherish their image (p. 21). Very unlike garbage collecting, longshore work is highly irregular. "This involves treating the most undesirable aspect of longshore life, the unpredictability of the work, as a desirable mode of existence" (p. 84). Most of the longshoremen are "old-line Americans" with Anglo-Saxon, and secondarily, Scandinavian, surnames (p. 13). However, like the Italian-American scavengers, kinship connections among them are intense. Consanguineal kinsmen and those related by marriage constitute about 70 percent of the group (p. 85), and visiting among them is very frequent. While Perry says little about residence patterns of the scavengers, Pilcher emphasizes that the longshoremen, although a "tightly integrated social group," live scattered all over the city. Their relative affluence enables them to live very much where they want in a city that does not have clearly demarcated "good" or "bad" neighborhoods (p. 15). Like LeMasters's construction workers, who also cultivate a strenuously macho image, the longshoremen are noticeably out in the woods during hunting season. In other leisure hours, they spend most of their time "puttering in the garden, improving the lawn and landscaping, and painting or otherwise improving their homes" (p. 92).

Pilcher says "the longshoreman's job is cherished both for the inherent qualities of the work, and for the freedom that it gives him" (1972:23). A careful reading of Perry suggests he could have said exactly the same thing about the scavengers, even though their work schedule, unlike the longshoremen's, is regular. Members of both groups like their work, not only because it pays well but also because it allows them to feel good about themselves and provides them with a community. The ethos of these groups is not a throwback to the moralistic work ethic, but each group puts work into a context for its actors that provides them with recognition and freedom of spirit—"meaningfulness," if you will. It is the general absence or weakness of such qualities in the work of most of the people Studs Terkel interviewed in Chicago that, he believes, is the besetting problem of modern work in America (1974:xxii-iv). Is the problem, as Terkel (and others) perceive it, a consequence of the nature of cities—or of *some* cities? Do Portland and San Francisco provide environments more conducive to meaningful work than Chicago? If Terkel were to conduct the same type of interviews in Portland and San Francisco, would he get the same results as in Chicago?

Perhaps the work lives of the scavengers and longshoremen are concatenations of fortunate circumstances that may not be stable over very long time periods because they are vulnerable to various changes. At the end of his study, Perry was concerned about the future of the scavengers' community, owing to technological and social changes. It is possible, too, that the Portland longshoremen's community might suffer the same fate as the San Francisco longshoremen's community, now virtually destroyed by the introduction of container ships and their loading technology (Mills 1977).

Localized Communities

Perry and Pilcher minimize the role of geographic localization in the strength of the scavengers' and longshoremen's communities. In other situations, however, localization seems important.

Bhim Nagar is the Jatav neighborhood in Agra, India, presented in chapter 2 as an example of the effects of large-scale changes on small-scale structures. When Owen Lynch studied Bhim Nagar in 1963–64, the official abolition of the Indian caste system had already affected the Jatavs' work and weakened some structures in the neighborhood. Nevertheless, Bhim Nagar still constituted a support system for its members in at least two ways. One was the circulating credit system from which every member of the neighborhood's ten sections was entitled to benefit (O. Lynch 1969:187). The other was the new local temple that symbolized the neighborhood and the integration of the Jatavs into the all-India Neo-Buddhist movement among former untouchables (p. 198). Whether these unifying and supportive elements would suffice to maintain the reality of the neighborhood as such remained to be seen. Lynch says that the Jatavs' goal was to become more integrated with the city's general culture (p. 200), but one wonders if they would willingly dismantle the supportive aspects of their traditional culture without at least trying to adapt them to their new, larger scale, less restrictive involvement in the city. One would certainly expect them to do this if they perceived it as advantageous.

The perceived advantages of a livelihood-related local community is precisely what Abner Cohen (1969) emphasizes in his study of Sabo, the Hausa quarter in Ibadan, Nigeria. The original Hausa homeland was in the savanna belt of West Africa, between the coastal rain forest and the Sahara. The Hausa have subsequently spread all over West Africa, living in their own special quarters in major towns and cities. They are specialists in long-distance trade, and their dispersed quarters are the nodes of an effective communication network. Cohen vividly and succinctly describes the situation:

> The Hausa trader is ubiquitous in the towns of the forest belt of West Africa. . . . Aloof and distinct in his white robes, proud of his customs, Islamic beliefs and practices, and of his "Arabic learning," he is often regarded by the host people among whom he lives or moves as an exploiter, a monopolist, a rogue and trouble maker. When his business fortunes are at an ebb, he may pose as an Islamic teacher, diviner, barber, butcher, commission agent, porter or beggar. His high degree of mobility, skill and shrewdness in business are widely acknowledged and have earned him the reputation of having a special "genius" for trade. On closer analysis, much of this genius turns out to be associated, not with a basic personality trait, but with a highly developed economico-political organization which has been evolved over a long period of time (pp. 8–9).

In recent decades, the Hausa have felt their livelihoods threatened by various political changes, which has led to an intensification of Sabo's structure and a new direction in their practice of Islam, keeping them distinct from the Yoruba majority who have more recently been converted (pp. 13–14).

Three-quarters of the men in Sabo work in long-distance trade, specifically trade in cattle from north to south and kola nuts from south to north. Both commodities are highly perishable, and to transport and market them successfully, day-to-day knowledge of supply-and-demand conditions, speed in operations, and credit and trust are all essential. Cohen believes that under Nigerian conditions, these prerequisites are best met by an ethnic monopoly such as the Hausa's (pp. 18–20).

Sabo has three major demographic aggregations. The "settlers" form a permanent core of native-born residents and their families. They include the 30-odd "landlords" who own half the housing in the quarter and control the many operations of long-distance trade. The "migrants" are mostly single men (or men whose wives have remained in their home areas) who work for others and are uncertain if they will remain permanently in Sabo. The "strangers" are transients (p. 38). Most members of all three aggregations are involved in various phases of the cattle-and-kola-nut trade. So, too, are the 250 prostitutes in Sabo. Their freedom is necessary to provide companionship for the men (p. 61). The Hausa believe there are political and mystical dangers in marrying or having sexual relations with Yoruba women, and so these relationships are almost exclusively with Hausa women. The prostitutes are all previously married women, and many will marry again. Many of the 950 housewives are former prostitutes. In fact, there is an occupational flexibility in the matter that seems compatible with the structure of Sabo as an occupational community (pp. 57–58).

The Hausa attitude toward the status of wife is apparently a version of the one widespread in patrilineal, preindustrial cultures: she is to be secluded in the domestic sphere. However, the Hausa have been able to adapt this value to their needs:

> In Sabo society, prostitution does not carry the same stigma which it does in Western or in some other societies. The Hausa *karuwa* is idealized in the culture as a woman of strong character, intelligent, and highly entertaining . . . no great shame is inflicted on the parents or other relatives of the prostitute [in strong contrast to the Arabs] though it is nearly always the case that women leave their natal settlements when they become prostitutes [only 2 of the 250 were born in Sabo] (p. 55).

Sabo is only one of several ethnically distinct quarters in the old, traditional part of Ibadan, and the Hausa trade network is a cultural pattern of long standing (although they now use trucks and other industrialized equipment).

The localized community of the railwaymen of Sekondi-Takoradi, Ghana, presents several contrasts to Sabo. The city itself (with a population of 123 thousand in 1960) is new, a largely twentieth-century creation that grew from a fishing village and an adjacent deep water port—hence the double name (Jeffries 1978:9–10, 17–18). Railway work is, of course, industrial and not traditionally grounded. Probably the most important difference from Sabo is that the railwaymen are ethnically diversified. The strength of their occupational community is not based on exclusive ethnic identity, but rather on membership in a trade union that has played an important part in Ghana's pre- and postindependence history. National political involvement is Richard Jeffries's chief concern, and he does not say very much about the railwaymen's localization in the city. What he does say, however, is important. These skilled and semiskilled workers display "an impressively high level of job commitment and stability" (p. 16). Many of them say they would like to save enough money to set themselves up in private business. Some do, but many never do. Most of them say they would like, eventually, to return to the rural or small-town homes from which they originally came, but in fact many retired railwaymen have settled in Sekondi-Takoradi "either because of their success in developing small local businesses, or simply because they ultimately prove reluctant to leave long-established circles of friends" (p. 17).

The continuing presence of many . . . retired artisans in such residential areas as Esikado . . . contributes to the sense of corporate identity so evident amongst the skilled railway workers. Even for the majority whose stay in Sekondi-Takoradi proves more transient, involvement in this community, its shared interests and cultural life, is real and deep. . . . One major reason . . . clearly lies in their geographical concentration. Virtually all of the Sekondi-Takoradi railwaymen work in one of the two large but dense con-glomerations at Sekondi Location and Takoradi harbour. The close contact and regular communication experienced there extends . . . beyond the bounds of the work- place to their residential situation and leisure pas-times. . . . Residential areas such as Esikado are characterised by a dis-tinctly supra-tribal, proletarian ethos (p. 17).

Emerging from recent studies of factory workers in Istanbul, Turkey, is a complex picture of localized occupational communities and various supralocal identities, all very much entwined with one another. "Aktepe" is the pseu-donym of a "neighborhood" (population about 30 thousand) on the outskirts of Istanbul studied in 1970–71 (Dubetsky 1977). A. R. Dubetsky does not refer to it as a former squatter settlement, but he does mention "the old single story makeshift homes first built by the new migrants" that are being replaced by new four- or five-story apartment buildings. The latter, he says, attest to its prosperity (p. 363), and quite likely Aktepe represents an advanced stage of the self-improvement processes observed so often in Third World squatter settlements. Aktepe has an ethnically heterogeneous population, but the in-habitants' own folk stereotypes enable them to perceive themselves as divided into two contrasting communities, the "Laz" and the "Kurds." The Laz, 40 percent of Aktepe's population, are Sunni Muslims from Black Sea coastal areas. The Kurds, 26 percent of the population, come from eastern Anatolia, where there are many true Kurds, but Aktepe's Kurds are actually Turkish-speaking Alevis (Shia Muslims). The Laz and Kurdish quarters of Aktepe offer visible contrasts. The former has two mosques, the latter none; during the month of Ramadan, people in the Alevi quarter can be seen not observing the fast. In fact, many of the Sunnis regard the Alevis as not being Muslims at all because they are so unobservant. Each quarter is endogamous—a "quite different social world" (p. 362).

When it comes to the workplace, however, Dubetsky does not sustain the idea of contrasts except that more of the Sunnis have become wealthy as entrepreneurs (p. 368). The bulk of the residents of Aktepe are laborers in workshops and small and large factories, as well as owners of small retail shops. Many of these workplaces are in Aktepe itself; others are outside it but mostly within walking distance.

The ethnic and regional community structure of Aktepe carries over into the workplace, and here the processes are apparently the same regardless of community membership. Where possible, kinship ties, region of origin, and sect are used for living and for maintaining a loyal and effective work force. The owner is a patron and looks for trustworthiness in his employees, largely on the basis of their kinship ties or ethnic identity and mutual obligations with him. Since religious sentiments are very strong—especially among the Sunnis—the reinforcement of trustworthiness and loyalty has gone as far as the building of a mosque on the premises by the management of one factory, thus creating a sort of congregation (pp. 366–67). The sense of moral community, based on traditional connections, carries over from workplace to neighborhood, too, and Dubetsky mentions the establishment of various local improvement organizations by wealthier entrepreneurs in their neighborhoods (p. 368).

Dubetsky points out that entrepreneurs and patrons use kinship, religious, and regional connections as much as they can, but that there are circumstances under which they cannot. "When a high level of skill is necessary . . . management must use more objective means of hiring workers . . . and disregard region or sect" (p. 367). Under these circumstances, social class awareness is sometimes manifested; David Makofsky (1977) emphasizes class consciousness. In his study of workshop and factory workers in Istanbul, Makofsky did not find the operation of kinship and other personal status connections that others have found elsewhere in the Middle East and that Dubetsky found in Turkey. There is, unfortunately, no indication of whether the workers Makofsky studied were the same as those Dubetsky studied. If they were not, and if those Makofsky studied did not live in neighborhoods like Aktepe, then it is all the more possible that the localization of Aktepe was highly significant in the organization of its inhabitants' work. The one point of consistency between Dubetsky and Makofsky is that both found that class consciousness emerged the most strongly among highly skilled workers (Makofsky 1977:93).

Class consciousness and a work-related sense of community particularly impressed William Kornblum (1974:17) in his study of South Chicago steel mill workers. The following quotations summarize much of what he learned:

As I came to associate with second- and third-generation adults, it became almost impossible to set Serbian and Croatian ethnicity apart from the activities of native-born Poles, Italians, Mexicans, and blacks in South Chicago neighborhoods. All these groups manage their ethnic attachments within a diversity of primary groups and institutional settings which may or may not include members of other ethnic groups. Thus I soon found myself associating with people in heterogeneous primary groups formed in the churches, the steel mills, the local unions, and the ward political organizations of the area. . . . Ethnicity is not just a persistence from the past but . . . [it] may take its place among more modern criteria for forming personal attachments in contemporary communities.

Whatever their ethnic affiliations, South Chicago people share the common culture of working-class America, . . . largely shaped by the steel industry. Steel-making brings South Chicago people together in the world of work. Steel presents all the ethnic groups with similar life chances and common aspirations for future generations. . . . In their leisure lives outside the mills, South Chicago families could attempt to segregate themselves within ethnic cultural worlds, or they might associate with diverse groups of neighborhood friends, but in every case, ethnic segregation was limited by the more universalistic experience . . . of the steel industry. . . . Steel mills . . . bring together the diverse elements of different neighborhoods into work groups which in turn are aggregated in union politics. This pattern of aggregation depends on no single principle but builds upon primary relations and ethnic loyalties . . . created in both place of work and place of residence (pp. 16–20).

In Irondale where Kornblum concentrated his research, workplaces and homes are very close, and coming between them—literally and figuratively— are many corner taverns with functions very similar to those of the Bethnal Green pubs. There are ethnic and neighborhood (interethnic) taverns, and, making the rounds among them, the steelworker is able to participate in different sets of occupational, ethnic, and neighborhood primary attachments (p. 80).

Much of Kornblum's book is concerned with the union politics of Irondale steelworkers, and on this subject, Ira Katznelson stresses the separation of workplace politics and home-community politics in American urban life generally, and even in South Chicago where the two types of location are adjacent.

In the mills, these workers see themselves as labor (in opposition to the steel companies and, on occasion, to capital more generally); and as labor they are quite militant. The ordinary idiom of plant life is . . . class. There, clear majorities vote for radical insurgencies within their union. Yet as soon as these workers . . . go home, they cease to see themselves primarily as workers. On the East Side and Hegewisch, in Irondale and Slag Valley, they are Croatians, Mexicans, Poles. Here the Tenth Ward organization of the Chicago Democratic party machine, whose language is ethnicity, patronage, and services, is political king (1981:6).

Since Kornblum's study was done, Irondale has suffered adversely from the decline of the United States steel industry. Vicissitudes, caused by macroscale phenomena over which people living small active-scale lives have no control, are threatening three of the occupational communities whose communal strengths have been emphasized (the San Francisco scavengers, Portland longshoremen, and South Chicago steelworkers). This sobering reality does not, however, negate how those communal strengths were created by the will, choice, and spirit of individual people working together. They therefore can be re-created, and this process of re-creation is also an aspect of vicissitudes.

CONCLUSION

This chapter began with a reminder that urban livelihoods, like all livelihoods, are the means of peoples' survival and that therefore their efficacy for survival takes precedence over such considerations as job satisfaction and career fulfillment. For most city dwellers, efficacy for survival is the paramount criterion as far as work is concerned. Nevertheless, alienation is a problem that cannot be disregarded. We examined it in a wide variety of ramifications and found that it does not universally accompany city livelihoods, as antiurban stereotypes would have it. We proceeded to examine a variety of contexts in which city dwellers create support systems based on their livelihoods, often in the face of difficulties, constraints, and macroscale threats. In chapter 6, we extend our consideration of support systems to a wider range of urban contexts.

SUGGESTED ADDITIONAL READING

Coles, Robert, M. D. *The South Goes North.* vol. 3 of *Children of Crisis.* Boston: Little, Brown, 1971. Rich in eloquent, poignant, and insightful observations of southern migrants to northern cities.

Dwyer, D. J. *People and Housing in Third World Cities: Perspectives on the Problem of Spontaneous Settlements.* London: Longman, 1975. A detailed study of the creativity of Third World squatters, illustrated with photographs.

Levering, Robert, Milton Moskowitz, and Michael Katz. *The 100 Best Companies to Work for in America.* New York: Signet, 1985. Discusses in detail how a number of large, bureaucratic corporations have been able to overcome Shepard's criteria of alienation.

Romo, Ricardo. *East Los Angeles: History of a Barrio.* Austin: University of Texas Press, 1983. A large-scale, historical presentation of the largest Mexican-American community (population over one million) in the United States. Provides a valuable background for the specialized studies of East Los Angeles discussed in the text.

6
Connections

T he previous chapter began with a consideration of alienation from work, one of the classic concepts of what is fundamentally wrong with Western industrial culture, and therefore with Western industrialized cities, and—in the minds of many people—with "the city" in general. Our consideration of the concept did not dispose of it altogether, because outright disposal is not warranted by the information available to us; but it did substantially modify the idea of alienation as a universal characteristic of life in cities. In particular, by viewing work as an integrated, rather than segregated, part of life, we discovered a great variety of work-related interpersonal connections that, on the whole, function beneficially for the actors.

Here, we examine connections further—beyond work-relatedness—but with elaborations on several important factors featured in chapter 5, such as kinship ties, localized and dispersed networks, and others. The emphasis is on small-scale connections. Larger-scale connections are considered in chapter 7.

COMMUNITY AND THE PROBLEM OF STASIS

The word "community" implies a comprehensive system of interpersonal connections, and where the actors are conscious of their involvement in such a
system, community is a useful designation for the realities involved. In this
sense, occupational communities are discussed in chapter 5. However, the
emotional freight the word often carries in the feelings of many people can
seriously damage its usefulness. To a considerable extent, people associate
community with nostalgia for things past. The phrase, "loss of a sense of
community," as a condition of industrialized life, epitomizes this feeling. To
the extent that this feeling idealizes the static and the nonchanging, it is an
impediment to comprehending life in cities. Furthermore, to the extent that
it may impede city dwellers' adaptability to changing conditions, it can do
them a serious disservice.

Change is, ironically, one of the constants of life in cities. To be sure, there
are relatively stable social systems within these fundamentally changing environments. That city dwellers usually strive to maintain those relatively
stable systems as long as they are advantageous is also a constant in the
evolutionary processes of cities. If community were generally understood to
mean "a relatively stable multifunctional support system whose members are
ready to alter it in response to changing conditions," it would be a useful
concept. It would represent the optimum in urban social adaptation. But if
community is taken to mean "a stable multifunctional support system whose
members feel that if it is changed, it will not be a community any more," then
the concept is too inflexible. The difficulty can be seen in the accounts of
occupational communities in chapter 5. Is Bhim Nagar still a community at
all, given the profound changes that have occurred in the Indian caste system?
Is Sabo still the same community it used to be before the Hausa, reacting to
threats to their ethnic identity, embraced a religious brotherhood, membership
in which maintained their distinctiveness from the Yoruba? Answers to questions like these are likely to become mired in arguments about the meaning
of community as a static concept. If, however, we look on Bhim Nagar and
Sabo as systems of support and survival strategies, we are using a more flexible
conceptual image that allows us to take adaptational changes into account.
Lynch and Cohen present the Jatavs and the Hausa of Ibadan as adapting
their support and survival strategies to serve them under conditions of increased receptive and active scale. Their future success or failure in so doing
is what will be important. As to members of the Sunset Scavenger Company
and the Portland Local of the ILWU, Perry's and Pilcher's obvious affection
for them may increase the risk that they be sentimentalized as threatened
static communities. Instead, it is more useful to consider them as people who
will try to adapt their support and survival strategies as best they can under
changing circumstances. This endeavor will probably result in their not stay-
ing the same as they were, which might be interpreted by some people as loss
of community, when in fact they might be developing new strategies for survival and support.

The assumption made here is that adaptations to changing circumstances
in the interest of support and survival strategies is the norm of life in cities.
To facilitate the understanding of this norm, an adaptational conception,

rather than a static one, is needed. Anne Buttimer expresses such a conception well. While her immediate concern is the physical planning of urban neighborhoods, her remarks apply to the whole spectrum of urban support and survival systems:

> Livability ... cannot be defined adequately in terms of systems or states of *being*. For life in residential areas involves a dialogue of behavior and setting, or demand and supply; it is thus essentially a condition of *becoming*. In this existential view, the planner can no longer be considered solely as the manipulator of supply; neither can the academician be seen merely as the investigator of resident aspiration and satisfaction. Least of all, can the citizen be considered a passive pawn of external social or technological processes. ... For such a joint involvement in the *becoming* of residential areas, a radical new education is needed. ... We need frameworks for investigation and reflection which do not segment and ossify parts of the city. ... And we need an empathetic understanding of urban life as existential reality, as lived experience (1980:22–23).

While a static model is inadvisable for analytic purposes, we must never lose sight of the search of many city dwellers to maintain the status quo. We cannot ignore this pursuit, nor should we make value judgments of it. What we must do is assess the extent to which it works as one support and survival strategy among others, and under what circumstances.

Relative stability facilitates some successful strategies. For example, an American analysis of a British survey shows that length of residence is the single most important factor in the sense of community attachment in urban Britain outside London (Kasarda and Janowitz 1974). Shankland, Willmott, and Jordan found that in the Stockwell section of South London "a high degree of population movement almost inevitably works against other things that people value, like neighbourliness, local social contacts, mutual aid and a sense of community," especially among working-class people but less so among professional and managerial people (1977:50). These authors note with approval a plan of the Greater London Council to facilitate tenancy of different generations of families in the same housing projects (p. 151). Norman Dennis (1970:296), in his retrospective study of the devastation caused by a government relocation project in Sunderland, England, refers to long-term residence, accommodation, and adjustment as important factors in inhabitants' satisfaction with their former neighborhoods, however insalubrious the latter may have seemed to middle-class bureaucrats.

The relative stability of residence in neighborhoods in American cities is frequently found to be associated with positive indexes of social cohesion in those neighborhoods (Skogan and Maxfield 1981:148). The longer people have lived in a neighborhood, the more their social lives tend to be focused in it, and the higher the stakes they have in its well-being. People with high stakes in a neighborhood are likely to be involved in various local group activities, including those intended to deter local crimes (p. 233). The effectiveness of such neighborhood activities is, to be sure, varied. Wesley Skogan and Michael Maxfield, in their study of ten neighborhoods in Chicago, Philadelphia, and San Francisco, found that, on the whole, those with low crime rates had high neighborhood integration, of which stability of residence was one component (p. 106). On the other hand, a study of six matched pairs of neighborhoods in

Atlanta found that, while low-crime neighborhoods were more residentially stable than high-crime ones, their residents were older, a phenomenon widely observed to be associated with lower crime rates (Greenberg, Rohe, and Williams 1981:63).

While the beneficial aspects of stability cannot be guaranteed in all cases, they cannot be discounted, either. This situation is nowhere more apparent than in cases where the ranks of long-term residents are decimated by phenomena of larger scale than the neighborhood itself. A poignant example is Richard West's description of the deterioration of one building among many in a section of Upper West Side Manhattan where efforts at revitalization and gentrification are also underway:

Life hadn't always been impossible at 13 West 103rd Street. When Sally moved into her $125-a-month two-bedroom, the old five-story walk-up had just been . . . renovated. . . . She took the apartment for the same reason she stayed so long—proximity to her subway, to Central and Riverside Parks, to Broadway's stores, and to her church. Back in the middle sixties there was a comfortable neighborhood feeling on the block. She quickly made friends with many families, most of them black working-class. . . .

Over the years, Sally came to believe that the landlord was a cutter of corners. Few dollars ever trickled back for building maintenance. Worse, he hired worthless superintendents who drank a lot, repaired nothing, and for a bottle and a few bills allowed fellow winos to sleep in vacant rooms. . . . Then . . . the super began renting to junkies. . . .

Like hyenas smelling a mortally wounded animal, the pushers and junkies sensed that 13 West 103rd Street was dying. They moved over from abandoned buildings on 102nd and set up shooting galleries in 13 and 11, next door. . . . Within a year of the first junkie's arrival, the violence, police, OD's, thefts, lack of heat and hot water [because the copper plumbing had been removed for sale], and fires had emptied the building except for nibbling rats, dopers, and Sally Chambers. . . . In 1979 . . . she sent her son away to escape life around the home he had known since birth. Now it was time for her to flee (1981:24–25).

Whether those long-term residents who remain in the area and the recently arrived gentrifiers will be able to reestablish neighborhood stability remains to be seen, and it will necessarily take some time.

On the whole, the data support the case for relative stability—gradual, piecemeal change—rather than abrupt, systemic change. But stability can occur under destructive circumstances as well. One is the practice of "redlining," in United States cities, by which banks deny mortgages to blacks who wish to buy houses in areas whites occupy. Redlining is one cause of the restriction of blacks to inner-city areas from which whites have departed. Life in inner-city ghettos, despite the prevalence of violence in them, has been described in terms of a particular kind of stability:

[R]esidents of the ghetto themselves describe a life of monotonous and unremitting changelessness. Hour after hour, day after day, unemployed men stand on street corners waiting for something to happen. . . .

The most salient aspect of the stimulus deprivation in the ghetto community, the feature that gives ghetto life its quality of chronic depression, is the lack of expectation of change. There is a sense of futurelessness that makes activity indifferent, pointless, perfunctory, and invariable (Dumont 1971:55–56).

These are cases where maximized stability is the actual norm, or the condition desired by some but not all actors on the scene. And these cases raise serious questions about the nature of the communities involved.

When terms like community and stability are applied to social situations, assumptions may be made that the facts do not warrant. A more specific concept like support and survival strategy—taking into account whom it benefits and at whose expense it may operate (as in the practice of redlining)—seems to have more analytic power. Community, though, has such attractive connotations that it is unlikely to fall into disuse. And whether more specific, modified versions of it—such as "community of limited liability" and "contrived community" (Suttles 1972; chapters 3 and 4)—will gain widespread currency is an open matter.

A recent and encouraging development in the finer tuning of the community concept is Zane Miller's study (1981) of Forest Park, Ohio. Forest Park (not to be confused with Park Forest, Ill., also a social scientific study subject) is a Cincinnati suburb founded in the mid–1930s as part of the Roosevelt administration's greenbelt community program (see chapter 4). Initiated as an unincorporated settlement by a private developer, it had, by the late 1970s, grown into a fully fledged municipality with a population of about 19 thousand, mostly white, middle-class people but also 19 percent black (p. xvii).

Miller conceives the history of Forest Park as an evolution of different manifestations of community, as follows:

1935–1952:   Metropolitan Community
1953–1968:   Community of Limited Liability
1969–present: Community of Advocacy

In the first period, Miller argues, community was perceived as a mixed residential/commercial subdivision of metropolis and region, in which inhabitants would be active in civic enterprises for the general welfare (p. 46). In the second period, community continued to be perceived in terms of general civic interest to which inhabitants had obligations but in a context of residential mobility:

[V]illage officials and citizen activists all saw Forest Park as a community of limited liability. There one could . . . be born and raised, work, act out the role of citizen, and die. But few Forest Parkers actually thought of living out their lives in Forest Park. These socially- and geographically-mobile middle-class people had loyalties and ties to non-territorial communities, as well as to their residential locality, and they changed addresses routinely in response to changing job opportunities and family life cycles. Therefore, a community such as Forest Park was primarily important as a place these people could move into and out of with a minimum of social and psychological disruption and a maximum of material comfort. . . .

The idea that Forest Park was a community of limited liability led to a quest for enduring and stable property values, not an enduring and stable population. The problem was how to make the place economically viable for three parties simultaneously: the developer, who owned the undeveloped land; the residents, who bought and sold real estate or rented there; and the village government, which needed a tax base sufficient to provide a level of services attractive to middle-class people, employers of middle-class people, and merchants who catered to middle-class tastes (pp. 94–95).

Miller is concerned with the political activities of these various interest groups and how Forest Park evolved from a community of limited liability into a

> *community of advocacy,* a community of competition for power and scarce resources, a community of distrust and disbelief in established ways and institutions as channels for realizing aspirations or satisfying grievances. It was a fragmented community, turning inward to psychological concerns and to economically motivated anxieties about Forest Park's "deterioration." . . . Forest Park's civic morale sagged . . . undermined by the pressure of voluntary organizations which were parochial, inward-turning, and backward-looking, and whose "civic" activities masked an intensely narrow individualism which placed concern for each person's psychological or material well-being above the welfare of either the city government or the community as a whole (pp. 176–77).

Miller relates this evolution in part to the "me-generation" outlook, as well as to social class and racist concerns which surfaced at the same time. Prominent among the voluntary associations were neighborhood organizations named after various sections of Forest Park which had earlier been designated only by a letter of the alphabet in an attempt to focus communal identity on Forest Park as a whole (p. 145).

Miller's study is based on a dynamic, rather than static, concept of community; it examines conflicting interests without abandoning the general concept of community and is addressed to one of the central components of the humanity of cities: the symbiosis of small-scale support systems and various large-scale structures of which the microlevel support systems are necessary parts.

DISCONNECTEDNESS

Whatever nomenclature we use (community absolute or modified, stability absolute or relative, systems or networks), we are concerned with relationships among people, with interpersonal connections.

Classical urban theory holds that the urban environment is inimical to human connectedness, that, instead, anomie and anonymity prevail. However, classical urban theorists neglected that there are many different kinds of urban environment. Anomie and unwelcome anonymity *do* prevail in *some* of them.

First, let us look at some urban environments in which disconnectedness does occur. Two fairly well-documented examples are multiproblem families (families beset by a variety of serious problems) and some elderly people, all living in United States cities.

Multiproblem families are frequently concentrated in publicly owned, highrise apartment buildings. The reasons for this concentration lie in the concatenation of racism and rental policies in relation to the welfare system (Rainwater 1970:9). Such projects are notorious for the physical violence—often gang- and/or drug-related—that frequently besets them. For example, early in 1981, there had been 11 murders and 37 other casualties within two months in the Cabrini-Green project in Chicago. These incidents were the results of gang warfare which intimidated the majority of the residents and prompted then-Mayor Jane Byrne to announce plans to move into the project herself to stay "for as long as it takes to clean it up" (United Press International 1981).

What conditions generate such an environment? Lee Rainwater, in his study of the Pruitt-Igoe project in St. Louis, suggests that part of the answer lies in the high density of people who, because of their overwhelming personal problems, are unable to develop any neighborhood feelings or structures. This situation results in a social vacuum, into which move predatory, violence-prone individuals. Their intimidating presence further discourages any efforts at neighborhood formation. At the root of the situation is the disconnectedness of individual households from one another (1966:27). Rainwater says that "black slum culture" generally includes networks of extended kinfolk (1970:6), considered further in this chapter. In contrast, part of the dynamics of situations like that of Pruitt-Igoe is that too many families are concentrated there who lack the support of such networks; this particular kind of human environment generates anomie and its attendant miseries.

Just as only some slum environments are like this, so are only some concentrations of older people in cities. Firey's description (1968) of single-room occupants in Boston's South End is one example, and Joyce Stephens's study (1976) of elderly tenants in a Midwestern slum hotel is another. In both cases, problems of being elderly in present-day American culture are compounded by problems of being poor. Like Firey, Stephens interprets the plight of the elderly people she studied as a consequence of the nature of industrial society, but not specifically of urban environments. The survival strategems these people use

> are inextricably linked to the ever-present threat of deviance, which . . . surrounds these people and perpetually threatens to engulf them. A fundamental mechanism for the control of deviance is their avoidance of close relationships . . . restricting and constraining their ties and dependencies upon others [so] as to minimize the effects of deviance on their own lives. These effects include the high probability that close relationships will become exploitative associations; the constant threat of violence; and the reciprocal norms of distrust and suspicion (1976:39).

Later, Stephens notes that many of these elderly people have had life histories of alienation—that they never lived in cohesive social communities to any great extent (pp. 90–91). Nevertheless, they are "survivors" (p. 94), but their survival strategies do not involve the networks of trust and support that most people need, seek, and find in cities.

Arlie Hochschild's study (1973) of 43 old people living in a small apartment building near San Francisco, while it exhibits some marked differences from Stephens's findings, also seems to illustrate a major point Rainwater and Stephens make in very different contexts: people who are predisposed to alienation and disconnectedness are likely to carry these characteristics over into urban settings which, in themselves, are not preordained to be generators of alienation and disconnectedness.

> The few whose family ties were feebly held together by Christmas cards and graduation notices did not "make up for it" by plunging themselves into Merrill Court affairs. They . . . remained aloof from the subculture as well. Moreover, those who had especially strong and rewarding family ties . . . were among the most active in Merrill Court society (Hochschild 1973:95).

MINIMAL CONNECTEDNESS

Hochschild's main point is that most residents of the apartment house have formed a community of pseudo-sibling relationships in which there are rivalries and differences but "not alienation and not isolation" (1973:63). The ability of these elderly people to form a new kind of community in an apartment house was unexpected, hence the title of Hochschild's book, *The Unexpected Community*. Hochschild sees life in Merrill Court as a relatively successful adjustment to the bad social conditions nonaffluent elderly Americans generally face (p. 139).

Unlike the elderly people Stephens studied, most of Merrill Court's residents appear to have been predisposed toward forming supportive relationships. But while predisposition seems important in this matter, it may not necessarily be a determining factor. This contingency is suggested by studies of three social situations in which support and survival strategies have been generated, perhaps even more unexpectedly than in Merrill Court.

Harvey Siegal (1978) reveals one of these situations in his book on single-room occupancy (SRO) tenement and welfare hotels in New York City. Contrasting the single-room occupants with many slum and ghetto dwellers who have a sense of hope and collective vigor, Siegal characterizes them as "socially terminal," without kinfolk or estranged from those who exist, bereft of material resources, living on public assistance, and afflicted with mental and physical ill-health (p. xx). Yet, under these seemingly most unlikely circumstances, a fabric of support strategies has been woven. There are "helping pairs" of people who live together, providing mutual support for their addictive needs (pp. 137–38). Then there are relatively permanent groups of drinkers made cohesive by a variety of reciprocated services (pp. 139–40). And, possibly unique to SROs, Siegal thinks, are quasi-familial groups headed by "matriarchs," each of whom cares for a group of men in various nurturing ways. These women enjoy high status and may perform functions beyond those associated with a particular group. A matriarch may serve as an ombudsman for other residents of the building and may also develop a symbiotic social control relationship with the building's manager (p. 143). Siegal discusses some other social groupings, but these examples will suffice. Unfortunately, we do not know why there is such a contrast, if not contradiction, between the findings of Siegal and Stephens.

Elijah Anderson describes a second situation in which support strategies have been unexpectedly generated in his book about the "extended primary groups" who congregate at Jelly's bar and liquor store in South Chicago. These black men are not typical South Side residents or ghetto area blacks, for

> most are viewed as marginal or deviant within the larger black population, and in many circumstances they see themselves as deviant or as lacking in moral responsibility by wider community standards. These . . . men . . . hang out and participate with others they know to be drunkards, beggars, and thieves. . . . Most . . . are not involved in continuous responsibility for nuclear families . . . [and] many . . . come up short with regard to general "decency" (1978:31).

Yet, these men have evolved into three groups with collective and personal identities. Each has a relatively stable core, although many persons' identities shift from one to another. The actors themselves call the three groups the "regulars, hoodlums, and wineheads" (p. 38). They are socially stratified. The regulars generally hold regular jobs and look down on those who do not. The hoodlums, who live by various means implied by their name, are generally disdainful of more conventional people. The wineheads are the lowest in the hierarchy, not welcome to remain on the premises of Jelly's for any longer than they need to buy their bottles. Even though individual "memberships" in these groups are precarious, each type of identity provides some basis for trust within it (p. 52). Thus, the rudiments of community have been generated among people who, as far as we can tell from Anderson's account, previously had no such predisposition.

The third example of an unlikely support system comes from a study of 31 deinstitutionalized state mental hospital patients who had been returned to their home district in Boston. The district is

> the economically depressed, defensively "tough," predominantly Irish-American, working class community of 38,000 . . . [called] "Carney." It is . . . a good test case community because, although notorious for its violent rejection of outsiders (throughout the Boston school busing controversy), Carney boasts a proud tradition of taking care of its own (Scheper-Hughes 1981:91).

While many of the ex-patients resided with relatives of various degrees of closeness ("testifying to the potential strength of the working class extended family in Carney," says Scheper-Hughes, p. 94), Carney did not otherwise recognize the ex-patients as its "own." This behavior occurred principally because "the insane" are generally stigmatized and because the deinstitutionalization program and its personnel are associated with "deeply resented outside forces," at the time aggravated by the school busing controversy. So, the ex-patients avoided most public and private gathering places in Carney and formed supportive relationships among themselves to the extent that "they depended almost exclusively on each other for material, economic, psychological, or moral support" (p. 98). This case is another where predisposition was a factor, for the ex-patients had previously been associated with one another in the hospital.

We have examined some interfaces between connectedness and disconnectedness in cities, as revealed by empirical studies. Results of the examination refute the assertion implied by the bipolar model, namely that the urban environment, by its very nature, results in social disorganization and anomie. At the same time, the examination also has shown how, under certain circumstances, those negative conditions can occur.

CONNECTEDNESS

Now we turn to circumstances under which urban connectedness is widely recognized and well documented. These circumstances can be grouped into two broad, sometimes overlapping, categories: territorial support systems and dispersed support systems. In the former, geographical propinquity in itself appears to be an active factor in the system; in the latter, support networks appear to function well under circumstances where geographical propinquity is either not a factor at all or only to a small extent.

The most clear-cut and extreme conception of urban territorial support systems is probably that conveyed by the common image of preindustrial cities: cities totally subdivided into quarters with unambiguous boundaries, each of which constituted a complete community in the fullest sense of the term. It is impossible to know whether there ever were such totally subdivided cities in former times. What survive today in those portions of some cities that have continuity with their preindustrial past are a few clearly defined quarters interspersed with areas that cannot be so identified. For instance, it is said that Jerusalem—meaning primarily the old part within the walls—may have as many as two dozen clearly defined, very homogeneous neighborhoods (Safdie 1979:20), but this case is said to be virtually unique, with no evidence that the whole old city is totally subdivided. Indeed, up until 1948, Muslim Arabs lived in the Jewish Quarter; the subsequent destruction of its houses contributed to the tragedy of the Arab-Israeli conflict. In other Middle Eastern cities whose *madinas* survive from preindustrial times, there are some distinctive quarters, but they appear to be islands surrounded by areas that are not territorially organized. As noted earlier, the siege conditions recently prevailing in Jerusalem, Beirut, Belfast, and elsewhere have intensified territorial communalism, not only in formerly preindustrial cities but in postindustrial ones as well.

These last examples are modern urban territorial communities with a vengeance. They are not, however, typical or representative of territorial support systems generally. Before considering the latter in more detail, we need to note that some observers of modern, industrialized cities think of them as complete fabrics of territorial social organization—at least they seem to do so in idealistic terms. A case in point is Peter Berger's definition of city that begins with a paraphrase of Wirth:

[A] city is a relatively large, dense, permanent settlement of heterogeneous individuals and groups of individuals organized to perform, or facilitate the performance of, locality-relevant functions in an integrated manner and to ensure integration with the social system of which the city is a part (1978:9).

While there is no denying that the territorial component in urban support systems can be extremely important, there is considerable doubt that it is ever as comprehensively or purposefully expressed as Berger says, except possibly in the formal neighborhood organizations of cities of the Soviet Union and People's Republic of China (see chapter 4). However, there may be many cities like Sheffield, England, where 85 percent of an interview sample said they had a named "home area" in the city (see chapter 2).

In the current literature on urban and community-level studies, two words stand out as being the most useful umbrella terms for the support system phenomena that concern us: "neighborhood" implies a territorial entity; "network" implies conscious connectedness among people. Neighborhood and network are not necessarily or always mutually exclusive. Indeed, neighborhoods that figure most prominently in the consideration of support systems generally include networks. At the same time, however, there also are supportive networks that are not territorially localized, networks in which physical propinquity is not a salient factor in connectedness.

The words "neighborhood" and "network" are in common and imprecise use, and attempts to define them rigorously for purposes of social science analysis have often turned out to be too narrow. For example, Suzanne Keller (1968) reviews at length the great variety of expressions of neighborhood behavior depending on culture and social class. What actors consider appropriate neighborhood behavior differs greatly in different cultures and different classes within the same culture. Neighborhood connections are more important to some people than they are to others. Recent research in Pittsburgh reinforces and enriches in specific detail Keller's point about neighborhood variety (Ahlbrandt 1984). Consequently, a priori definitions of neighborhood frequently do not fit many relevant realities, limiting their analytic usefulness. These problems are important, but need not trouble us in this book. Where we find support systems with a territorial or spatial component in the supportive behavior, we label them neighborhoods.

The movement to tighten the concept of social network for research purposes seems to have originated among urban scholars as they began to realize that most conventional categories of social organization were insufficient for the social realities to be found in cities. Network began to be used to refer to connections that do not clearly fit into such categories as family, voluntary association, formal group, or even informal group. J. A. Barnes, an early practitioner of network analysis, sees the network largely in terms of individuals' social ties that cut across their memberships in other organizational categories (1969:54). Network analysis is a research technique that involves exceedingly meticulous observations of connections that are subjected to graphic and mathematical analyses by which the boundaries and intensities of the network are determined. In this book, network as an umbrella term is far broader. In fact, it is subsumed under social connection systems like family and voluntary association.

Neighborhood and network, along with derivative verbs like neighboring and networking (see Klieman 1980: chapter 1), sometimes have emotional and ideological connotations that their use in this chapter is not intended to have. For example, to some people, neighborhood connotes parochialism and reactionary politics, while to others it is the quintessence of the human dimension in city life (Keller 1968:7). Network is currently in vogue in a context that goes beyond the idea of supportive connection and into the area of advocacy and adversary relations, as in Klieman's guide (1980) to, and handbook for, a wide variety of innovative women's networks in the United States. While these emotional, ideological, and political connotations reflect realities, they are specialized realities and do not encompass the comprehensive meanings of neighborhood and network as used here.

NEIGHBORHOODS

An urban neighborhood is a physical microenvironment set in a system of diverse, other environments. How inhabitants react to the neighborhood and how it may have environmental effects on them are subjects of great importance that have received significant attention from scholars.

Amos Rapoport (1977) points out that the concepts of territory and territoriality (both pertinent to neighborhood) have been understood in oversimplified fashion and have different types of dimension. His five-element model is perceived primarily from an individual's point of view:

(1) *Home range.* The usual limit of *regular* movements and activities defined as a set of settings or locales and their linking paths. Members of particular groups tend to have home ranges more alike than those of other groups.
(2) *Core area(s).* Areas within the home range most commonly inhabited and used—possibly daily—and best known.
(3) *Territory.* A particular area or areas owned and defended—physically or through rules and symbols—to identify an area as belonging to an individual or group.
(4) *Jurisdiction.* "Ownership" or control of a territory for a limited time and by some agreed-upon rules, such as right-of-way over paths for specific events but not all the time.
(5) *Personal distance or personal space.* Spacing among individuals in face-to-face interaction, the bubble of space surrounding individuals (the subject of some research). In urban contexts personal space affects crowding in public areas, pedestrian movement and pavement use, and possibly acceptability of public transport; generally, however, it is a microscale rather than mesoscale phenomenon. Personal space is also *portable*, whereas the other elements, especially (2) and (3), are expressed in the built environment (pp. 278–79).

Rapoport's core area and territory most nearly coincide with neighborhood, and the model makes clear that territoriality is not only coterminous with neighborhood, but is also wider and narrower than neighborhood.

The home range is made up of behavior settings, one of which is neighborhood. An acquaintance of the author who lives in Chicago and commutes to and from work for a total of four hours a day provides a specific example. Her home range consists of three behavior settings, each involving different people: (1) home and neighborhood; (2) workplace and professional and other associates; and (3) a group of "regulars" who use public transportation at the same times she does. The transportation setting—so characteristic of Western industrial urban life yet largely ignored as a significant behavioral or life space—is a setting with its own rewards for each person.

Unfortunately, there is very little systematic research on home ranges, but Rapoport does cite Lamy's research in Paris. Lamy studied the home ranges of working-class people, managers and professionals, and upper- and middle-class people. Lamy found the working-class home range was, except for workplace, focused in the neighborhood—shops, friends, church, and hangouts were concentrated there. The managerial-professional neighborhood included some friends and some shops, but other friends, shops, and all other behavioral settings were outside the neighborhood. The upper- and middle-class neighborhood contained nothing but residences; all other behavior settings lay outside the neighborhood, some outside the city itself (Rapoport 1977:304).

Lamy's findings highlight important socioterritorial variations in different people's experiences of neighborhood. These differentials may be of such importance that the generally accepted concept of neighborhood may be too narrow. This notion is the thesis of Tridib Banerjee and William Baer (1984) whose research in Los Angeles leads them to propose the more comprehensive concept of residential area in preference to neighborhood unit.

Greater dispersal of home-range behavior settings does not necessarily mean deprivation of support systems. Some people want close residential propinquity, but not others whose support systems do not depend on it. Availability of transportation and relative ease of access are probably important factors here. Let us reconsider two working-class populations: the Bethnal Greeners Young and Willmott studied and the "blue collar aristocrats" LeMasters studied. All of the latter owned automobiles and depended on them completely to get to their favorite hangout which was not a neighborhood tavern. In sharp contrast, the Bethnal Green pubs were all neighborhood centered, within easy walking distance of everyone's home. While differences between social classes in neighboring locales have been observed, there are differences within the same social class as well. Let us reconsider another example: Japanese corporate employees. In Rapoport's terms, the men's home ranges are oriented toward their workplaces and various after-hours hangouts, and hardly at all toward their neighborhoods, but their wives' home ranges are concentrated in the neighborhood (Vogel 1971:102–10).

Michelson has identified what is possibly the common denominator underlying such seemingly contradictory differences. He concludes, from a wide variety of sources from different cultures, that the crucial factors in active neighborhood interactions are (1) actors' perceptions of homogeneity with those who live close to them and (2) an awareness of mutual needs that can be met in terms of propinquity (1976:190). On superficial inspection, this common denominator seems obvious, but its ramifications are far reaching. Each factor exists in different intensities; one or the other, or both, may be absent from any particular locale; and perceptions and needs of different persons living in the same locale may be different. These permutations go a long way toward explaining the bewildering variety of neighboring patterns that have been observed.

Howard Hallman encapsulates this variety in five chapters of his book (1984). One part of the book, "The Many Faces of Neighborhood," includes chapters on five such faces: neighborhood as a personal arena, a social community, a physical place, a political community, and a microcosmic economy.

Among neighborhood needs that different people perceive differently is the need to reduce interpersonal overload (Baldassare 1979:165). Social overload in cities is a concept that derives ultimately from the thinking, originally published in 1903, of Georg Simmel (1971). More recently, Stanley Milgram (1970) has explored it empirically, as noted in chapter 3. At this point, we consider only Rapoport's ideas about neighborhood housing styles in relation to overload. Rapoport compares a variety of neighborhood layouts in several different cultures. The sharpest contrast is between a Western industrial suburb with single-family houses, each set in unenclosed but private open space, and what he calls "the inside-out" arrangement typical of Middle Eastern *madinas*: closely adjoining courtyard houses with no exterior open space except the street. Rapoport (1977:337) argues that these architecturally dissimilar arrangements serve the same functions in the context of their respective cultures' symbolic systems: they enable residents to isolate themselves, thus reducing overload, at the same time facilitating interaction if and when it is desired. Thus, differing intensities of neighboring can be accommodated at different times, and households with differing neighboring needs can be accommodated in the same locale.

According to Mark Baldassare, the experts generally disagree about the effects of high density of neighborhood population on residents. He suggests that a reasonable guideline to overcrowding in American urban neighborhoods would be more than 12 housing units per acre. He believes that high-density neighborhoods have costs (overloading of services and land) and benefits (diversity and stimulation) for residents (1979:130–36). Among people he interviewed, fear of crime is mentioned more frequently by those living in high-density neighborhoods, whose residents tend to be lower-income people, but it is not clear what basis in reality this fear has (p. 152). Baldassare disagrees with Milgram that most people *randomly* turn off encounters in order to cope with overload. Rather, he hypothesizes that people minimize those contacts they value less than others and that high density does not adversely affect friendships and group affiliations (pp. 165–66).

Whether architects, engineers, and planners can create house and street patterns that will help maximize all the positive potentials of neighboring is important and controversial. Many scholars, including Michelson (1976) and Oscar Newman (1980), have addressed the question. A major reason why it is controversial has already been mentioned: many important variables related to cultural and individual needs are very difficult to control for. Banerjee and Baer's book (1984) is an empirically grounded effort by planners to meet this challenge.

Also controversial is whether some built environments are intrinsically destructive of the positive aspects of neighboring. Here again, the difficult-to-control-for variables are present. For instance, residents who do not seek or need neighborhood interaction may dislike contrived cul-de-sacs and "banjos," in which some form of neighborhood interaction is (deliberately) unavoidable. Park Forest, Ill., affords striking examples. Its layout of cul-de-sacs and short residential streets appears to encourage intense sociability in some neighborhoods but not in others (Whyte 1956: chapter 25). Where there is intense sociability, it indeed provides social support. It also, however, can make life miserable for residents who, for whatever reasons, deviate from the powerful pressures to conform to the common denominators of suburban life-style (pp. 358–59 and passim).

In contrast, high-rise apartment houses, seen by some as a diabolic violation of humane life, are not necessarily that for everyone who lives in them. True, multiproblem families, when concentrated in large numbers in such buildings, are notably weak in forming support systems—with often dire results. But for other high-rise dwellers, this is not true. Michelson found that although suburban Toronto residents did have many more neighborhood contacts and ties than downtown high-rise apartment dwellers, the latter were by no means deprived of social contact; rather, their supportive contacts were made more from nonlocal communities of interest (1977:158, 173, and passim).

In all of these considerations, we must bear in mind two paramount needs: opportunities for people to form support networks when and if they want them and the absence of barriers to such formation (Michelson 1977:28). On the whole, city dwellers seem quite adaptable to their built environments in their striving to fill these needs.

The kinds of support typically provided in neighborhoods have been much studied, cataloged, and described. Baby-sitting, borrowing and lending tools and supplies, watching houses that are temporarily vacant, assisting and comforting at times of death or serious illness are all well known and facilitated by physical propinquity. Companionship and sociability are also facilitated by it, and their expression has a particularly localized quality when it occurs outside the walls of private houses. Especially notable in this regard are neighborhoods where street life is very active and intense. Careful and vivid analyses of active street life have been done in cities as diverse as New York (Jacobs 1961), Chicago (Suttles 1968), Cairo (el-Messiri 1978; Nadim 1975), and Beirut (Joseph 1978). Since active street life is strongly associated with particular social class characteristics, we defer more detailed discussion of it until chapter 7.

Social cohesion in neighborhoods can be achieved in a variety of ways besides the mutual aid functions already mentioned. One is through religious institutions when they are present and locally identifiable. Among the many documented examples are nuclear members of a Catholic parish in a southern United States city (Fichter 1954), Hindu temples such as the one in the Jatav neighborhood in Agra, India (O. M. Lynch 1969), neighborhood mosques whose cohesive social importance has been noted in Mombasa, Kenya (Stren 1978:206), neighborhood religious fraternities in the old part of Seville (Gregory 1982), and the fiesta of the patron saint of the home village of squatters in Lima (Lobo 1982:166).

Neighborhoods can sometimes organize for political purposes. For example, in Chicago, "block clubs" are quite common; they negotiate with government agencies for better public services (Suttles 1972:56–57) and struggle against unwelcome elements such as drug pushers and gang bangers (Keegan 1987:1:1). Similar organizations have been widely observed in squatter settlements in cities in all parts of the Third World. One of these is "Mathare 2," a neighborhood of about two thousand people outside Nairobi, Kenya. Marc Ross (1973) wrote a book about the political integration of Mathare 2, accomplished through the excellent leadership of a village committee of 11 men and 11 women. The committee adjudicates local disputes, runs a nursery school, supervises the local water supply, manages a savings and credit cooperative, and negotiates continually with a basically hostile government to protect the precarious interests of the inhabitants (pp. 100–13 and passim). Mathare is, like many squatter settlements, illegally located, and two of its inhabitants' major income sources (beer brewing and prostitution) are also illegal. So the police continually raid the neighborhood (p. 148). The committee serves to mitigate the effects of the raids through payoffs.

The Iranian city bazaar, a network of covered commercial streets in the *madina*, is a particular kind of neighborhood characterized by a cohesive system of interrelated families. In times of crisis, such as the Islamic Revolution of 1978–79, the bazaar functions very effectively as a communications center, in this instance, for antigovernment activities (Touba 1985:135). In 1978 in Shiraz, Iran, the bazaar communications network reached shopkeepers outside it, resulting in small shops all over the city being closed, at very short notice, in protest demonstrations.

The last aspect of neighborhood we consider is the defended neighborhood. Gerald Suttles developed this concept, although he did not originate it. While it is widely applicable (for example to squatter settlements and the Middle

Eastern *madinas*), urban scholars primarily associate it with Western industrial cities and their current security crisis.

The defended neighborhood is most commonly the smallest area which
possesses a corporate identity known to both its members and outsiders.
Functionally, the defended neighborhood can be conceived of as the smallest
spatial unit within which co-residents assume a relative degree of security
on the streets as compared to adjacent areas. . . .

The defended neighborhood may be large or small . . . [but] is generally
expansive enough to include a complement of establishments (grocery store,
liquor store, church, etc.) which people use in their daily round of local
movements. . . . [T]he defended neighborhood is primarily a response to
fears of invasion from adjacent community areas (1972:57–58).

The best known indicators of inner-city defended neighborhoods are "street
corner gangs [that] claim a 'turf' and ward off strangers or anyone else not a
proper member of the neighborhood . . . vigilante community groups, militant
conservation groups, a high incidence of uniformed doormen, and frequent use
of door buzzers and TV monitors" (p. 34).

Some good illustrations of defended neighborhoods appeared in an article
on New York City's ten safest neighborhoods (as determined statistically and
impressionistically in 1981). "These neighborhoods . . . aren't confined to any
one borough or to a single ethnic or income group." Many factors make a
neighborhood safe, "but they certainly include community pride and cohesiveness, well-defined boundaries, and perhaps most important, the willingness of people to look out for one another" (R. Young 1981:30).

Looking out for one another typically involves citizen patrols, as Randy
Young shows. Defended neighborhoods, like ethnic groups, illustrate an irony
of urban life. While humaneness is supported and augmented within their
boundaries, they are responses to some inhumanities that are also aspects of
the heterogeneity of life in cities.

NETWORKS

Donald Warren (1981:171) has delineated the types of network from which
individuals in American cities customarily receive help: household, kinship,
co-workers, voluntary associations, neighbors, friendship. In addition are formal organizations, such as health and law enforcement services. Some networks do not fit exactly into any of these categories, but Warren's categories
are pragmatic and operational, and useful as guides to thinking about networks in all cities, not only American ones.

The pervasiveness of urban networks is indicated by their inclusion in several different contexts in this book. Co-workers' networks are a major topic of
chapter 5. Networks of neighbors, households, kin, friends, and others are
discussed here and in chapters 7 and 8. The remainder of this chapter covers
household, kinship, and friendship networks.

Household and Kinship Networks

Household and kinship networks should be kept conceptually separate. While
it is true that most households everywhere consist of nuclear families, there
are also many that do not consist of kinfolk at all. Furthermore, many kinship
networks extend beyond any single household. It is a serious mistake to equate

the household with the family. This must be emphasized, because many social scientists, particularly those observing cities, have made this equation and drawn inferences from it that need to be corrected. An important part of the problem is that censuses use the household as the basic enumeration unit and record various and sundry kinfolk (as well as nonkinfolk) as constituting the members of a household. For the most part, the kinfolk are combinations of parents and children. What censuses do not do is show connections and networks among different households. From this fact, some unwary observers have inferred that kinship networks, notably those in Western industrialized cities, are confined to single households. It has taken the efforts of pioneering scholars like Elizabeth Bott (1971) and Bert Adams (1968) to show that this is not true. Bott, in her network study of 20 urban British married couples, delineated several categories of kin living outside the couples' households: those with whom some contact was maintained; those with whom there was no contact but about whom there was some personal knowledge; and those whose existence only was known. Couples' kin connections consisted of the first two categories. For the three couples whom Bott describes in detail, those connections consisted of 69, 22, and 21 individuals (50, 42, and 23 percent, respectively, of the couples' extra-household relatives) (pp. 120–21).

Adams studied 799 young adults living in Greensboro, N.C., in 1963–64. His explicit purpose was to challenge the then-predominant image of the isolated nuclear family household in industrial cities. Because his research methods were quite different from Bott's, his findings are not precisely comparable, but they have a similar impact. Here are some figures from a table in Adams's book (1968:29) on the importance of kin in the young adults' total scheme of things.

| Sex | Occupational Stratum | Mobility | No. | *Importance of kin (%)* | | |
				Very Important	Somewhat Important	Relatively Unimportant
Male	White collar	Upward	75	39	52	9
		Stable	98	34	52	14
	Blue collar	Stable	60	45	40	15
		Downward	22	27	50	23
Female	White collar	Upward	85	52	36	12
		Stable	122	64	33	3
	Blue collar	Stable	94	60	32	8
		Downward	26	31	54	15

Adapted from table II–3 in Bert N. Adams, *Kinship in an Urban Setting* (Chicago: Markham, 1968), p. 29, by permission.

These findings are consistent with those of other researchers in Western industrial cities as to the relatively greater importance of kin networks among women and to a lesser extent among working-class people. Adams devotes most of his attention to relationships of the young adults to their parents and siblings and emphasizes the importance of long-distance communications—especially telephone and mail—in maintaining contacts in dispersed networks.

Before discussing kinship networks further, we should complete our consideration of the household as such. Households are the basic domestic units of a settlement. The majority consist of a core of kinfolk, but this is not true of all households. Indeed, in the United States in 1980, 27.8 percent of all households were nonfamily units (United States Bureau of the Census 1981:40). This figure represents a considerable increase over the previous 20 years, and it may be true that nonfamily households are significantly more frequent in the postindustrial United States than in the Third World. For example, one component in the relatively high frequency of United States nonfamily households is the emergence of the urban commune, a reflection of the counterculture movement, that consists of various combinations of unrelated people who set up housekeeping together. An interesting feature of this movement, at least as seen by one observer, is the effort often made to develop an explicitly family feeling in the household (Kanter 1979:117 and passim). Many communal households do include children and parents, but they are in company with various others, and the domestic units are not nuclear or extended family households as generally understood (Raimy 1979).

Single-person households constitute another important component in nonfamily households in the United States. Some of these, as we have already discussed, are comprised of "socially terminal" people, living in SRO hotels or rooming houses and only marginally sustained by support systems. Others, however, consist of such people as young adult professionals launching their careers. In 1980, 23.5 percent of United States men, and 17 percent of the women over age 18 were single, an increase over the previous 20 years. A very small, but meticulously studied, sample of middle-class households in North London, England, revealed that 25 percent of households in one part of a housing project were nonfamily households, mostly consisting of single persons (Firth, Hubert, and Forge 1970:77).

There are recent indications that increasing frequencies of single-person and childless-couple households are becoming territorially significant. A notable case is Chicago where the housing construction pattern since 1970 reinforces the trend to white single-person and couple households. About half of the 30 thousand new housing units built between 1970 and 1975 were in 28 of the city's 840 census tracts—all on or near the lakefront, in neighborhoods that include most of Chicago's single areas. Singles occupy 63 percent of the units in these lakefront tracts; childless households occupy 87 percent (De Visé 1979–80:34). Pierre De Visé infers from the statistical data that single adults are attracted to areas where other single adults are numerically predominant, thus increasing their chances of making advantageous social contacts. More affluent single men seek areas where single women outnumber them, and single women seek areas where affluent men congregate. However, De Visé does not see this localization tendency as an expression of uniformity; he thinks three different types of people congregate in these areas: "the marriage-shy nomads and loners; the spouse-seeking and root-seeking singles; and the unmarried couples in relationships of varying durability, conventionality, and sexual orientation" (p. 35). The phenomenon De Visé writes about also occurs on a larger scale. San Francisco, for example, has an unusually large number of single men and women (398 thousand out of a total of 592 thousand). Their presence undoubtedly contributes to the large number of nonfamily households in the city and is also related to San Francisco's large homosexual population (Wolf 1979:74–75).

Nonfamily households are found elsewhere in the urban world. For example, Samir Khalaf and Per Kongstad report that, at the time of their study, in the Hamra section of Ras Beirut (where the American University of Beirut is located), about 20 percent of a sample of 533 households consisted of single men or groups of unrelated people, mostly professional colleagues or students (1973:63). Beirut had then the reputation of being one of the most "Westernized" cities in the Middle East, and many of Khalaf and Kongstad's informants were associated with Westernized businesses and institutions. Even in the much less Westernized city of Isfahan, Iran, the 1966 census showed 6.23 percent single-person households and 4.39 percent belonging to something other than single-person and kinship households (Gulick and Gulick 1974:455). The Gulicks' Isfahan study yielded a subsample of 7.67 percent single-person households. Interviews revealed details that the census did not: every one of the single-person households in the sample was housed in a compound of rooms, and in most cases the single individual was related to other residents of the same compound (pp. 455–56).

Household arrangements are survival and support strategies, and a household's composition, at any given time, is a function of them. Nothing is sacred, or exclusively familial, or otherwise immutable, about household composition. Indeed, within only one year, there were changes in the composition of 44 percent of the household compounds in the Isfahan study (Gulick and Gulick 1974:451).

Average household sizes (per some territorial or population unit) are frequently given in the literature, but only limited inferences can be drawn from such figures as to household composition, not to mention functions. For example, according to the 1980 census, the average household size in United States central cities with populations of over one million was 2.51 persons for all, 2.80 for blacks, and 3.25 for people of Spanish-speaking origin (United States Bureau of the Census 1981:45). What may we infer from these data about racial/ethnic differences in households as survival systems? For comparison, the 1976 census of Egypt revealed that overall average household size in Cairo was 4.8 persons. The range of average household sizes among the city's 26 districts was 4.0 to 5.0. Within this very narrow variance in such a crude index, faint glimmers of sociocultural significance can be seen, but they are only very faint. Consider Qasr al-Nil; it includes Garden City, Tahrir Square, and the island of Zamalik—an area of upper-class residences, extensive and handsome open spaces, and Cairo's newest and finest hotels. Qasr al-Nil's average household size is 4.0, with an average of one person per room in four rooms. In contrast, Boulak, one of the poorest and most densely populated parts of the city, has an average household size of 4.6, with an average of 2.5 people per room in an average of 1.8 rooms; and Darb al-Ahmar, which encompasses part of the old *madina* and part of the Northern Cemetery squatter settlement, has an average household size of 5.0, with 1.9 people per room in 2.6 rooms. When one realizes that Qasr al-Nil has houses and apartments of palatial size and design, while residential conditions of the utmost crowdedness and squalor have been observed in Boulak and Darb al-Ahmar, one should appreciate how greatly the imagination must be stretched to bring reality to the statistics. Furthermore, we must always remember that average-household-size figures indicate very little about household composition, familial or otherwise, and nothing at all about interhousehold networks.

Nevertheless, it is not easy to ignore a major revelation of these average-size figures: Cairo households are much larger than households in central cities of comparable size in the United States. Many factors are involved in the difference, only one of them that Egyptian urban married couples tend to have more children than American urban couples.

Average-household-size figures from some other Middle Eastern cities are worth a brief comment. The figures were assembled from a variety of sources that used observations made in the 1950s (Gulick 1969:132):

City/Country		Average Household Size
Amman, Jordan	Christian	5.60
	Muslim	7.00
Beirut, Lebanon		5.76
Tripoli, Lebanon	Christian	5.70
	Muslim	6.70
Tunis, Tunisia	Christian	4.80
	Muslim	4.80
	Jewish	5.01

In these figures, we catch a glimpse of religious/ethnic differences, a major topic in chapter 7.

The 1947 censuses of Egypt and Iraq yielded average household sizes for Cairo (4.7) and Baghdad (9.2) (Gulick 1969:133). The Cairo average is virtually the same as that of 1976, a notable finding, considering the city's enormous growth (about 150 percent) between the two dates, and the housing shortages and overcrowding that were a major concern and complaint of Cairo residents in the 1970s and 1980s.

Why the great difference between Cairo and Baghdad and the enormous average household size of the latter? The question cannot be answered in terms of household composition differences because there were no data on them in the two cities at that time. Furthermore, the Baghdad figure is an average of averages of the ten official quarters of the central city, ranging from 11.0 in a quarter comparable to Darb al-Ahmar to 5.3 in a quarter somewhat comparable to Qasr al-Nil (Gulick 1967a:253). The difference probably results from different housing styles. In Cairo, in 1947 as well as in the 1980s, the great majority of households lived in apartments in multistoried walk-ups or taller high-rise buildings. In central Baghdad, there were no high-rise residential buildings; everyone lived in one- or two-story courtyard row houses. Such houses can accommodate more people than the typical high-rise apartment, as well as several different households. However, depending on the definition of household being used, census enumerators might well record as one large, complex household, living inside one front door and sharing one courtyard, residents who actually constitute several household units based on food and budget sharing. So, differences between Cairo and Baghdad in 1947 may arise because of architectural features that in one case inhibited formation of large, complex households but in the other case encouraged it. The differences may also have come from ambiguities in observation or definition.

This discussion raises two important issues. One is the limited usefulness of census figures, regardless of how official and comprehensive they may be. Limitations involve not only data-gathering inaccuracies, but also meaningfulness of enumeration units. For example, census tracts and similar geographical entities, such as those in Cairo and Baghdad, may not represent sociocultural distinctiveness, and therefore comparisons among them based only on census figures may be meaningless. By the same token, an emphasis on such arbitrarily defined units may obscure the existence of socially significant geographical areas. Within the same city, some official census districts may represent cultural distinctiveness and reality while others may not. Basta, Beirut's Sunni Muslim district, is not an official unit, and therefore no statistical data on it, as such, are available. On the other hand, Ashrafiyah, Beirut's Maronite Christian quarter, is an official unit and also a significantly distinctive subcultural entity.

The second important issue is the architecture of domestic housing, a highly significant component in the physical structure of cities and therefore of various urban environments.

Now let us move closer to a bridge that will connect the concept of household with that of kinship network. The first step across the bridge is a consideration of household composition which cannot readily be inferred from household size. Considering kinship households only, worldwide data show that the majority of households everywhere consist of some variant of the nuclear family— parents and their dependent children. There is some cultural variation, to be sure, but not nearly so much as might be expected from stereotypes about the typicality of the nuclear family household in one culture and the extended family household in another. The term "extended family household," as generally used, refers to some combination of parents, their children, and grandchildren living in the same menage.

A few examples suffice. Raymond Firth, Jane Hubert, and Anthony Forge (1970:77), in their study of middle-class households in Highgate and a North London housing project, found 4 extended family households out of a total of 90. Of the remainder, 57 were nuclear family households, 13 were married couples only, and the rest were various other combinations of relatives and nonrelatives. In Beirut's Hamra district, Khalaf and Kongstad (1973:62) found a similar frequency of extended family households—3 percent. Even in cultures where the extended family (often confused with extended family household) is said to be typical, nuclear family households actually predominate. Owen M. Lynch found that in the Jatav quarter of Agra, only about a quarter of the households were composed of joint families (meaning either three-generational families or sets of adult siblings, without parents, but with spouses and children). These households, he says, were unstable, tending to break up into separate nuclear family households when the inheritance from the oldest generation was divided (1969:173).

To understand nuclear and extended family households sufficiently as support and survival systems, one must be mindful of cultural values (extended or joint family households are idealized in Indian cities but not in Western industrialized ones) and how kinship networks are continually changing because of birth, death, marriage, and divorce. Families, like individuals, have life cycles; this is a shorthand way of stating a much-studied, highly complex subject that lies beyond the main concerns of this book. We are concerned, however, with notions such as the association of the infrequency of urban extended or joint family households with a presumed disintegration of kinship systems because of industrialized urbanism. Enough has already been said to dispel any idea that kinship networks are unimportant in cities. That they change and adapt is a different matter from disintegration. Even Richard Sennett (1974b), whose overall image of middle-class families in late nineteenth-century Chicago is gloomy, discusses at length the relative advantages (and disadvantages) of intensely nuclear and extended kinship networks in that quintessentially industrial city.

Family life-cycle phenomena must be taken into account if we are to understand functions of various kinship/household arrangements as support systems. For example, a married couple household may consist of (1) newlyweds who have not had children; (2) a man and a woman of any age who have never had children; (3) a man and a woman whose children are grown and live in their own separate households and with whom their parents may have various dependent or independent relationships; or (4) a remarried man or woman who has had children by previous spouses. Only to describe a household as three-generational or extended does not make clear the nature of the relationships of the senior generation, in particular, to the others. The senior grandparental generation, usually a married couple or the surviving spouse of one, may include the original and continuing head of the household, a true patriarch or matriarch. This situation has been idealized and dramatized— but very frequently not put into practice—in Third World households. On the other hand, the grandparental couple, or surviving spouse, may have been taken into a household established by a son or daughter, to be cared for in old age—a dependent, even low-status role. This arrangement, not uncommon in Western industrial cities and Third World cities, too, is so different from the first that some observers would prefer not to call it an extended family household but rather something like "nuclear family with dependent parents." Yet a genealogical chart of the household, or list of its members' relationships, would not show anything about the dynamics of the relationships involved.

We close this discussion of household/kinship with a review of two studies— both done in Middle Eastern cities—in which investigators tried to obtain more specific information on household size and/or composition than is usually found in the literature.

First is Fuad Khuri's study of families in Chiyah and Ghobeire, two satellite municipalities of Beirut, on either side of the road leading out of the city toward the highway over the mountains to Damascus. The inhabitants are (or were before the disastrous civil war that began in 1975 and the Israeli invasion of 1982) mostly Maronite Christians and Shia Muslims. Khuri's analysis involved three different income levels, and his other data on households are highly relevant here. His categorization of 4,587 households, containing 5,054 nuclear families, follows (1975:113):

	Low Income		Middle Income		High Income	
Household	N	%	N	%	N	%
Single person	16	1	11	1	21	4
Nuclear family	2,384	76	681	75	340	61
Nuclear family and maids	7	0	26	3	101	18
Nuclear family & dependent parent	338	11	144	16	80	15
Two nuclear families	359	11	38	4	12	2
Three nuclear families	25	1	2	0	2	0
TOTALS	3,129	100	902	99	556	100

That high-income people should have more live-in maids than others is to be expected, but high income is only a relative term. These are not rich people by Lebanese standards. Having a live-in maid is far more common in Middle Eastern, than in Western, cities, and it may have affected the household-size figures discussed in connection with Cairo and Baghdad. In most of the households consisting of two nuclear families, the families are headed by a father and son (the classic patrilocal or virilocal residence pattern), but substantial numbers are headed by mother and son, father and daughter, and brother and brother. Mother and daughter, sister and sister, and brother and sister are other combinations. The number and variety of combinations is far greater among low-income people than among those of other income levels. All of these arrangements represent survival and support strategies. Of the single-person households, Khuri says the individuals are mostly high-income, older people. One advantage is that by living alone, those who are well off can manage their affairs as they see fit (1975:114). They can afford to remain somewhat independent of the networks to which they belong. This option is likely to be more available in urban than in smaller, more closed, rural settlements.

There is not nearly enough information on this subject for us to discern whether, in cities of particular cultures, there are unchanging norms over time in such distributions of household arrangements as Khuri's. Observed at a particular time—the dependent parents and older people in the multiple-nuclear-family households will die relatively soon, resulting in fewer such households. But will new households composed of nuclear family plus dependent parent and new multiple-nuclear-family households replace them, resulting in essentially constant proportions of household types over time? Whatever the answer might be (if we had one), would it come about because of constant striving toward ideal patterns of household composition, or would it be the outcome of pragmatic strategies of budget- and space-sharing, or both? These are fascinating and important questions to which no clear answers are available.

Meticulous retrospective studies, such as Sennett's on nineteenth-century Chicago and Flandrin's on seventeenth- to nineteenth-century Western Europe, provide some suggestions. These studies point clearly to the numerical preponderance in the past of nuclear family households. Jean-Louis Flandrin

(1979:68–69), moreover, uses fragmentary evidence that frequencies of nuclear and extended family households have fluctuated through time in rural and urban areas in Western Europe. Furthermore, in table after table, Flandrin presents average-household-size figures, ranging between four a d six, from seventeenth- and eighteenth-century urban and rural Europe. Large by late-twentieth century urban American standards, these are consistent with twentieth-century Third World magnitudes. The point, once again, is to encourage skepticism of the sentimentalized image of large, complex households in the past, supposedly eroded away by the baleful influences of modern urbanism.

The second study, directed by John and Margaret Gulick in Isfahan, Iran, has already been cited. While residents of Chiyah and Ghobeire lived in high-rise apartments, the subjects of the Isfahan study lived in one- or two-story houses. The houses were of two basic types: old style, with rooms arranged around a courtyard (Rapoport's "inside/outside" house); and new style, a one- or two-story rectangle with an attached walled enclosure, usually containing a garden or carport or both. An early discovery in the research (1971–72) was that both types of house very frequently accommodated more than one household. Using a term widely employed in African studies, the Gulicks designated each house as a compound and proceeded to gather information on household size and composition in the context of compound size and composition. The following figures give some idea of the ways in which the two types of unit are combined (1974:446–48):

Households per Compound	Frequency of Compounds	Relatedness of Households in Compound	Average Number of Persons	
			per Household	per Compound
1	55	—	6.91	6.91
2	49	(26) both related	4.64	9.29
		(23) neither related		
3	18	(9) all related	4.09	12.77
		(2) 2 related, 1 not		
		(7) not related		
4	10	(6) all related	4.30	17.20
		(1) 3 related, 1 not		
		(1) 2 related, 2 not		
		(2) not related		
5	8	(3) all related	4.18	20.88
		(1) 4 related, 1 not		
		(1) 3 related, 2 related		
		(2) 2 related, 3 not		
		(7) 3 related, 2 not		

TOTAL: 287 households in 140 compounds

If compounds had been mistaken for single households, one could easily arrive at average "household" sizes like those reported for Baghdad in 1947. One can also see that average household size occurs in at least two modalities, 6.9 and 4.18 to 4.64, within this same working-class population. Larger households, living in one-household compounds, were composed mostly of married couples (and their dependent children) who tended to be older and longer married than other members of the sample who were also still in their child-bearing years.

The definition of household in the Isfahan study follows that used by the Iranian census: a commensal unit, that is to say, a food-sharing unit whose members presumably use the same food budget. It is a good operational definition, though not a perfect one, for members of different households in a compound would eat together on occasion, notably wives eating together when their husbands were away.

The 287 Isfahan sample households were of the following types, again conforming to census usage (p. 455):

Households	N	%
Parents & unmarried children	190	66.20
Parents & married children with or without grandchildren	30	10.45
Married couple, no children	23	8.01
Single person	22	7.67
Other	22	7.67

For analysis, these data are combined into two categories: simple households (single person, married couple, nuclear family) and complex households (where there were dependency relationships or mutual support systems beyond a single nuclear family). The 242 simple households ranged in size from 1 to 12 persons, the average being 4.38; the 45 complex households ranged from 3 to 19 people, average size, 7.44. The average size of all households was 4.86, virtually identical to the average size for Cairo. Nuclear families prevail as the cores of households in the same cultural context where extended kinship networks also prevail.

The Isfahan sample presents a reality of intensive kinship networks, with economic needs and pragmatic arrangements being prominent factors in the various combinations of related and unrelated tenants in the compounds. By analyzing the lengths of marriages of nuclear families living in various arrangements, some tendencies in family life-cycles appeared. Newlyweds frequently live in the same household as the bride's or groom's parents, sometimes also with siblings. When one or both parents die, the couple may continue living with siblings or may establish itself as a single nuclear family household which, as time goes on, may take on dependent parents or siblings of the husband or wife (p. 463).

We have already cited Adams on the importance of the dispersed kinship networks of people living in a moderate-sized United States city. There is no reason to think his sample is unusual in this respect. Edwin Prothro and Lutfy Diab, in their study of women in two Middle Eastern villages and four cities (Amman, Damascus, Tripoli, and Beirut) also cite other studies making the same point and summarize their conclusions as follows:

[A] large majority of younger wives who have parents and parents-in-law living in the same village or same city neighborhood seem to pay and receive from each at least one visit a week, with visits to and from other relatives added in. The visiting pattern is affected by proximity . . . but is as strong in the cities as in the villages, or in the upper class as in the lower class. . . . Visits to relatives were so frequent and so expected that those wives who did not report visits of at least once a week usually felt that some explanation was called for. . . . The overall impression that emerges from the data on visiting is that there is an enormous amount of personal contact and a strong "social and psychological extended family" indeed (1974:72–73).

Visiting is only one aspect of extended kinship connections in Middle Eastern cities. Among middle-class people in Beirut, for example, there is also shared ownership of small manufacturing establishments, retail stores, and commercial enterprises (Farsoun 1970:262). Samih Farsoun refers to the "functionally extended family" in this connection, for, consistent with other findings, the residential extended family is very unusual. Furthermore, Farsoun says, "most of the partnerships and corporations of urban Lebanon are partnerships of siblings, cousins or other extended kin, and . . . even the corporations are most often nothing more than legal protection for wholly family-owned or extended-kin owned establishments" (p. 263). Farsoun points out that kinship groups are sufficiently large to provide technically competent members to fill important positions, and he asserts that the same is true in all Third World countries. These urban kinship structures thus perform vital survival and support functions, extending into the political sphere as well.

A different, but very striking, instance of the importance of Third World urban extended families comes from a study of about five thousand households in the Mexican cities of San Luis Potosí, Mazatlán, Querétaro, Tampico, and Mexicali (Selby and Murphy 1982). Samples from each city were divided into households that had sent members to work in the United States (a minority) and those that had not. Henry Selby and Arthur Murphy's analysis hinges on categorizing all households into five domestic life-cycle stages. Stage 4 households are the primary senders of members to the United States; they are nuclear families in which all the children have reached wage-earning ages. They "are able to rise socially and economically by incorporating distant relatives into their households and retaining married children and their spouses" (p. 13). The ideal is to establish a three-generation residential household. It is not easy to accomplish, but sending a member to the United States, whose remittances will further augment household resources, is one way—a risky one—for facilitating the process (p. 14).

Although the support systems of squatter settlements all over the world have been noted, their kinship networks have been slighted in the literature. An exception is Susan Lobo's study (1982) of squatters in Lima, Peru. Here, the basic kinship network is, in anthropological parlance, an ego-based bilateral kindred. Being ego-based, no two kindreds are identical (though many overlap in membership) except where the same kindred is shared by a set of full siblings. While these kindreds are not corporate groups that can be perpetuated over time despite complete change of membership, they are reinforced by the *paisano* residential clusters where many of them overlap (pp. 90–91). These are clusters of people who migrated from the same region.

We have been considering various dimensions of kinship networks at some length because their great importance has been ignored or minimized in traditional urban stereotypes. Now we reach the point where kinship networks must be seen in their interrelationships with networks of nonkin of various kinds. We consider several examples briefly.

In a squatter settlement outside Mexico City, "kinship is the most common social foundation for reciprocity networks . . . [yet] kinship affiliation is neither necessary nor sufficient for network formation, as one frequently finds mixed networks of extended families with jointed families or with nonkin neighbors" (Lomnitz 1977:156). Networks have various intensities, from extended families each of whose members pools resources with all other members, to small non-kin networks, often composed of women friends who exchange things with each other, sometimes, eventually, bringing husbands into the network (p. 157).

Kenneth Little, in a review of the literature on urban social organization in sub-Saharan Africa, refers to

> the apparent ease with which, despite the continuous coming and going of people, strangers in the town are able to discover their friends and kinsfolk, or husbands and wives to trace their deserting spouses. The explanation is . . . "that each individual African is involved in a network of social ties which ramify throughout the urban community and extend both to other towns and to the tribal areas" (1974:76).

Citing Peter Gutkind, Little says that urban African networks occur in two different but overlapping types, kin-based and association-based. As in the case of work-related friendship networks like those considered in chapter 5, these networks often meet in bars.

Kinship connections operate vigorously in cities when they are the basis for functional support systems. In some cases, this function is so important to the members that they consciously form themselves into corporations. Dennis Gilbert (1981) has studied two upper-class kin corporations in Lima, Peru. They have an internal structure, and their functions are economic and political. Individual members are assured a career and income, and the corporation preserves intact, through time, a large capital estate (pp. 754–55).

In New York, and apparently in other United States cities, a substantial number of Jews belong to family circles whose membership, like that of the family corporations in Lima, consists of all descendants of an ancestral married couple. Their functions, generally, are to provide fellowship, mutual aid, and, often, death benefits (Mitchell 1978:42).

In both cultures, kinship ties on both parents' sides are recognized. This bilateral or cognatic system produces an unwieldy group of people who normally cannot be held together for more than one generation. The corporate structures provide rules whereby the group can be perpetuated far longer. Cognatic descent is not exclusively associated with modern, industrial or industrializing societies. Indeed, the Ga core group of central Accra, Ghana, is cognatically organized (Kilson 1974).

Boujad, a city of 18 thousand inhabitants in Morocco, is, like many communities there, centered on the shrine of a local saint (Eickelman 1974:279). In considering whether the core of social interaction in Boujad is or is not uniquely urban (he decides it is not), Dale Eickelman emphasizes a key concept, *qraba*, which means "closeness." "As used by urban and rural Moroccans, *qraba* carries contextual meanings which range imperceptibly from asserted and recognized ties of kinship, participation in factional alliances, ties of patronage and clientship and common bonds developed out of residential propinquity" (p. 283).

Sefrou, another Moroccan city, has a population of 30 thousand and is a half-hour bus ride from the famous city of Fez. Hildred Geertz's analysis of kinship ties in Sefrou focuses on a particular extended kinship network (the Nas Adlun) which has 145 adult members, of whom 36 still live in their ancestral quarter in the *madina* (1979:320). The remainder are scattered in various locations in new houses outside the *madina*'s walls. Individual members of the Nas Adlun range from very poor to very wealthy which contributes to an important aspect of the network's functions as a support system:

> Although distinctions are made in Moroccan speech between what we would call "kinsman" and what we would consider "nonkin" on essentially biogenetic grounds, the operative, everyday, acted-upon premises do not rely on sharp and simple distinctions among family, friend, and patron. . . . In American culture the three are viewed as contrasting or even conflicting forms of personal relationships. . . . For many Moroccans, however, the social ties of friendship and patronage intergrade with family, and many of the same norms apply to any of them (pp. 315–16).

From situations in which kinship networks interdigitate with nonkin networks, we move to other kinds of connections. We have already mentioned a number of them, and it will suffice to consider a few more in the process of concluding this chapter.

Nonkin Networks

Probably the most widely recognized nonkin network is a group of friends. Many survey studies have tried to assess the relative importance—in terms of supportive reciprocities—of such categories as kin, neighbors, and friends. The results do not lend themselves to easy generalization, partly because of cultural differences. For instance, H. E. Bracey's findings on two suburbs in the United States and England include these generalizations: the Americans seem to find it easier to meet new neighbors, but few have made close friends; the Americans do not discard friendships as readily as the British do when they move, partly because more of them own cars and can maintain contact; and British housewives frequently express a frustrated need for one close friend (1964:110–14).

A study of a housing project in Sheffield, England, reveals that 59.4 percent of the informants have contact at least twice a week with relatives also living in the project, and half of those who have friends saw them during the previous day or two (Black and Simey 1954:109). Willmott, in his book on adolescent boys in Bethnal Green, found that a large proportion of them spend their free time with groups of friends or companions, often including "best friends." Few of these groups have leaders, and thus they do not resemble gangs, but are, rather, true peer groups (Willmott 1969:29–34).

Michelson found that suburban and downtown high-rise-dwelling housewives in Toronto do not differ significantly in the amounts of contact they have with "the three people they feel closest to." However, those living in the suburbs are more likely to have met their friends in the local neighborhood, while those living in high-rises are more likely to have met their friends in nonlocalized situations. Furthermore, the most frequent contacts of people moving to downtown apartments are with friends rather than neighbors; the reverse is true for those moving to suburban houses (1977:153–57).

The information on Middle Eastern cities in this chapter seems to emphasize kinship almost to the exclusion of other network forms. Eickelman's study, however, suggests the existence of nonkin connections there as well. There is very little published information on them, but they are vitally important. In particular, the *shillah* in Egypt and the *dowreh* (circle) in Iran are well recognized by people who know the cultures well. These are closed, usually nonlocalized, groups of friends who get together regularly at one anothers' homes in turn.

Among upper-class Iranians, *dowrehs* exercise political and economic influence. Frequently, they have a patron-client structure. The more powerful members use the less powerful ones for transmitting or obtaining information, in return for using their influence on behalf of the less powerful members.

> Many Iranians are frequently members of more than one *dowreh*. An individual may belong to a political group . . . [and] may also be active in any variety of other *dowrehs* organized for social, cultural, recreational, or intellectual purposes. With the overlapping and interlocking quality of membership which does exist, a message inserted into one *dowreh* will quickly fan out through the entire network. Moreover, *dowrehs*, especially those organized for the last three purposes above, frequently cut across social class lines. As a result, a message will fan out not only within a given social class, but also between social classes (Zonis 1971:240).

Activities associated with *dowrehs* "center around the acquisition of a sense of security" (p. 241).

Networks of the *shillah/dowreh* type are not easy for outsiders to observe and may be far more prevalent than would seem to be the case in the literature. A recently reported variant is the *tafrita* of traditionally oriented women in the city of San'a, North Yemen. The *tafrita* is an afternoon gathering in someone's home—in the absence of men. There is entertainment, smoking, chewing of *qat* (a mild drug), and a general sense of euphoria (Makhlouf 1979:26). While the *tafrita* is manifestly entertainment, it is also a bonding ritual occasion that serves the latent function of emphasizing a sense of community among participants (p. 27).

Of the many kinds of reciprocal assistance and support that perpetuate friendships, the patron-client relationship is not usually thought of in terms of friendship. However, Michael Kenny (1966:136) says that "the element of real friendship often enters" the patron-client relationships of people in the Madrid parish of San Martín. Patronage/clientage is, throughout the Third World, a very important means by which people cope with bureaucratic institutions.

CONCLUSION

This chapter closes with some examples of networks that ramify very widely in their respective cities and, to some extent, illustrate innovative support and survival strategies.

In three southern California cities (Santa Barbara, Santa Paula, and Oxnard), Susan Keefe (1980) observed Mexican-American and Anglo-American networks of friends. She refers to them as "personal communities," meaning "groups of people on whom an individual can rely for support and/or approval" (p. 52). These personal communities are spatially dispersed and constitute, in these cities, personal interaction that is "organized and thriving" (p. 70).

> Mexican-Americans have larger ... personal communities than Anglos mainly because of ... [having] many relatives in town. Mexican-Americans ... exchange aid with a larger number of people. Moreover, Mexican-Americans are more likely to have multiplex ties with their contacts, which along with kinship ties are assumed to be the "strongest" or most "intense" kinds of relationships.... Finally, Mexican-Americans have fairly dense personal networks in which most of the members know each other....
>
> Anglos, in contrast ... have small, nonkin personal communities. About half the Anglos surveyed have no relatives in town at all. The rest have one or more.... Anglos appear to be more inclined ... to maintain relationships with nonkin. While the Anglo networks are small, they are ... long-term and durable. There is commitment to a high proportion of these ties in exchange and emotional support relationships. And the networks have a high density, indicating that most members know one another. Thus, Anglos ... maintain enduring, mutual aid relations with a close-knit group of people. They are not isolated nor do they lack an interdependence with others despite the comparative absence of nearby kinfolk (p. 71).

Cuban women exiles from the Castro regime, living in the Washington, D.C., metropolitan area, have developed a network system that helps them maintain their ethnic identity at the same time that they modify, but do not relinquish, their traditional women's roles (Boone 1980). The majority of the women are married and have children (traditional) but are working in service jobs ranging from secretary to college professor (not traditional). Most live in the suburbs and commute to work (1980:236). Of their support system Margaret Boone says:

> In the heterogeneous locale of the modern metropolis, [the ethnic group] domain becomes especially important for family and individual security. Support is provided among Washington Cubans along widely ramifying network lines, and less so within discrete, localized ethnic groups. In fact, Cubans in Washington do not self-consciously belong to one national identity group. Although efforts to create a sense of unified Cuban ethnicity have been made, associations have met with apathy especially on the part of the more wealthy suburbanites (p. 247).

Poorer Cubans in the area apparently have their own, more localized support networks.

The communication network (the "grapevine") operates in a wide variety of ways. For example, in their traditional role of keeping close tabs on their daughters—even after the latter are married—the women are in continual touch, mainly by telephone, with relatives and friends not only in Washington but also in other cities and even in other countries (p. 254). Considerable social control is exercised in this way. Women who have the time to do so care for others' children, using the grapevine, when necessary, for in many cases they are not neighbors. These are but two examples. Basically what the grapevine does is to transmit information about Cuban family members, create a sense of belonging, and also check behavior felt to be inappropriate to the ethnic group and status level of the participants. When higher-status people, especially, move to Washington, the information is spread by the grapevine, and the newcomers are "at once enmeshed in a network of Cubans" (p. 262).

William and Joan True (1977) discovered a network system of an altogether different kind in their marijuana-use research in San José, Costa Rica. With a population of about 440 thousand, San José has a central section, including a park, which is the main communication and transportation node of the city. From it, bus lines radiate to the residential outskirts like spokes. To get from one peripheral area to another, it is necessary to go into the center and from there take another bus to one's destination. The Trues found their 82 subjects by starting at known hangouts in the center of town and, from there, tracing personal networks to wherever they led. They led to all parts of the city (p. 132), and the authors were strongly impressed by how wide ranging, and not geographically restricted, these networks were (p. 133).

In this chapter we have considered various important forms of urban connectedness, starting from the microperspective. That cities are rich in interpersonal ties should be beyond doubt, and readers of this book will certainly be able to think of many more examples than those presented. Nevertheless, the stereotype of isolated, anonymous city dwellers remains, and it continually needs to be counteracted.

SUGGESTED ADDITIONAL READING

Gutman, Robert, ed. *People and Buildings*. New York: Basic, 1972. An extensive collection of essays by experts, this book aims for greater collegiality between architects and behavioral scientists, with the ultimate goal of enhancing positive urban interconnectedness.

Lyon, Larry. *The Community in Urban Society*. Chicago: Dorsey, 1987. At many points, Lyon's presentation runs parallel to that of this book. However, he goes into far more detail on studies of communities and how to organize them. His data come entirely from the United States.

Schoenberg, Sandra Perlman, and Patricia L. Rosenbaum. *Neighborhoods that Work: Sources for Viability in the Inner City*. New Brunswick, N.J.: Rutgers University Press, 1980. Based on field research in five St. Louis neighborhoods, this important study tests the viability of each one by evaluating it in terms of four propositions on what constitutes a neighborhood community.

7
Subcultures

A subculture is the system of learned behavior and values possessed by a particular aggregation of people who are also members of a larger society which contains many other, different subcultures. A subculture has its own identity and customs, but its members also share many of the cultural patterns of the larger society.

THE SUBCULTURE CONCEPT

Although anthropologists and others have examined the concept of culture exhaustively, the idea of subculture has not been developed with any precision. For example, no systematic work has been done on what the range of intensities of uniqueness of subcultures may be. The nearest approximation to such precision is found in studies of ethnicity. In this chapter, ethnicity is one kind of subculture, but there are other kinds, too. Behavioral research related to specific urban environments is, in general, underdeveloped, and so is precision in understanding subcultures. Perhaps these two kinds of underdevelopment are connected. The subculture idea cannot be adequately comprehended unless different subcultures are studied in relation to one another; the best environments, by far, in which to do this are urban; but too few relevant urban studies have been done.

This state of affairs is surprising since it is the presence of subcultures in cities that renders them heterogeneous, and heterogeneity—as a general, rather than abstract, quality—is one of the very few characteristics of cities on which there is universal agreement.

The task in this chapter is to make the concept of urban heterogeneity as concrete and nonabstract as possible. Doing so should enable us to comprehend the interrelatedness of heterogeneity with other urban phenomena, many of which have already been discussed. It should also give insights into one of the most formidable challenges to the humaneness of urban life. That challenge is to find ways in which the hostilities and inhumanities can be mitigated while, at the same time, support and survival strategies are maintained. This issue is basically the same one as that which lies behind discussions of the question: How can a pluralistic society be made to work? But, we put the question in terms of the structure of specific cities rather than society in the abstract. Underlying this challenge is a paradox: while support and survival systems typically flourish within urban subcultures, hostility and inhumanity frequently typify relationships between different subcultures.

One of the most comprehensive and insightful studies of the subculture concept, specifically related to cities, is Claude Fischer's *To Dwell among Friends* (1982). Fischer presents analytic discussions based on empirical data—interviews conducted in several locations (urban and nonurban) in Northern California. After a consideration of personal networks, whose richness in urban settings he conclusively documents, Fischer devotes several chapters to subcultures of various kinds. Explicitly challenging the urban negativism of the bipolar moralists, Fischer says:

> The counterargument . . . is that urban life is marked not by the breakdown of *community*, but by the build up of plural *communities*: a diversity of cultural groups, each its own variation of the national culture. My term is "subcultures." These subcultures are founded on many bases other than kin and locality—on ethnicity, occupation, lifestyle, and so on. . . . And though these social worlds cannot be as all-encompassing as the total community of yore, people do find fellowship, guidance, and meaning in them (p. 194).

Fischer discusses at length the paradox of urban subcultures: they are bolstered by urban life but at the same time are set into tension with one another. However, the tension is in public interaction and we should not extrapolate from such interaction, "whether it be reserved or hostile . . . to private inter-action and even to personality—seeing urbanites as dispositionally cold or rancorous—when there may be . . . little correspondence between public and private acts" (p. 235).

In the remainder of this chapter we look at several different kinds of sub-culture, all of which have received empirical recognition in urban studies. The three categories of subculture—each comprised of different specific subcul-tures—are (1) universal subcultures, (2) collective life-styles, and (3) bureau-cratic subcultures and problems of scale. Most of these subcultures have already been mentioned, discussed, and exemplified in various contexts in previous chapters. The emphasis here is less on subcultures in themselves than on the important fact that they coexist in urban life.

UNIVERSAL SUBCULTURES

The two best-known universal subcultures are ethnic and social class groups. They are universal in that virtually everyone belongs to an ethnic group and a social class, if not in one's own perception then in that of others. For example, while everyone agrees that blacks and Hispanics in American cities are mem-bers of distinct ethnic groups, there may be some question about whites whose ancestors came from Great Britain and northern/northwestern Europe, a few of those ancestors having been the "founding fathers." Many of these people do not think of themselves as ethnic, but others do and may refer to them by such terms as Anglos, honkies, or WASPs.

Less generally recognized as subcultures are gender and life-cycle groups. They intersect and overlap with the others, and one way of comprehending the resulting coexistences is by using a matrix such as this:

	Groups			
Gender	Ethnic	Religious	Social Class	Life Cycle
Female	A	B	C	D
Male	E	F	G	H

One example of how actual groups fit into these categories is the Italian-American boys' gang William F. Whyte (1981) studied in Boston which fits into categories E and H. Another example is the Tokyo suburbanites who belong in C and G; Ezra Vogel (1971) emphasizes the social status and distinct social worlds of these men and women.

The categories are conceptual sorting devices, not watertight compartments. In American cities, physiological distinctiveness (race) is seen by most actors as an aspect of ethnic subcultural identity, even though race and culture are unconnected in origin. Religious distinctiveness in a given urban situation is often a component of ethnic or social class identity, and is so treated in this chapter. Joseph Fichter, however, treats religion as a separate subcultural category because the actors he observed often consider it to be one. And indeed, Fichter's sociological study (1954) of a Catholic parish in New Orleans is a sectarian, not an ethnic, analysis. On the macroscale, Charles Shanabruch's history (1981) of the Archdiocese of Chicago from 1833 to 1924 is a detailed account of, first, the proliferation of "national" (ethnic) parishes and the intensification of interethnic rivalries, followed by the careful welding, under the leadership of George Cardinal Mundelein, of a sectarian structure whose unity overrode its ethnic components.

Ethnic Subcultures

Multiethnic studies focused on single cities highlight the coexistence of subcultures and diverse ethnicities. We have previously considered four of them: Pons on what is now Kisangani, Zaire; the study by Lloyd and others of Ibadan, Nigeria; Abu-Lughod on Cairo; and van den Berghe and Primov's analysis of Cuzco, Peru.

Probably the most detailed and comprehensive such analysis of a North American city is Nathan Glazer and Daniel Patrick Moynihan's *Beyond the Melting Pot* (1970)—a historical, political, and sociocultural portrait of the blacks, Puerto Ricans, Jews, Italians, and Irish of New York City. The point of the title is that the once-widespread notion that all immigrant groups in the United States would or should become homogenized in a cultural melting pot is a myth. Attachments to ethnic identities, with their costs and benefits, continue to be real.

> The positive aspects of ethnic attachment should be recognized; the general approval of efforts to build up black pride and self-confidence and self-assertiveness will encourage this. This is perhaps the most difficult point to make, for we believe it would be a disaster for the city if ethnic divisiveness is fostered. But we can *accept* the reality of group existence and group attachment, yet not allow it to become the sole basis of public decisions. The city should not be a federation of nations, with protected turfs and excluded turfs (p. lxxxv).

Foremost in Glazer and Moynihan's concerns are the serious and complicated problems related to the massive influx into New York of blacks and Hispanics. The authors' strategy is to present these two as subcultures whose arrival in the city was actually the latest in a succession of ethnic arrivals. All the newly arrived groups faced poverty and discrimination; all coped with them in terms of their distinctive cultural patterns—the Irish by highly effective political organization, the Italians by close-knit neighborhoods. Blacks and Hispanics are on their way (Glazer and Moynihan mention that many more blacks and Hispanics are prosperous middle-class achievers than is generally recognized), but the problems of adaptation—including residential displacement of other groups—continue to be of major proportions.

On a smaller scale, Gerald Suttles (1968) offers a meticulously detailed analysis of the Italians, blacks, Puerto Ricans, and Mexicans living immediately adjacent to one another in the Near West Side of Chicago. Each group has its own territory and space-use behavior. Associations of personal trust occur primarily within ethnic, age, and sex groups. Nevertheless, these different groups live in close proximity to one another in ways that, despite many conflicts, express a generally understood moral order.

Glazer and Moynihan and Suttles repeatedly make the point that, though ethnic groups have distinctive subcultural patterns, they are also internally diverse. This existential diversity contradicts the uniform stereotyping of ethnic prejudice. Two important portrayals of intraethnic diversity are those of the Chicanos of East Los Angeles (Moore et al. 1978) and a black neighborhood in Washington, D.C. (Hannerz 1969). The Moore study is discussed in chapter 5.

Hannerz did a field study in a Washington black neighborhood which, unlike many others in the city, had always been inhabited by poor blacks. He says that the "Winston Street" people see themselves as comprising two categories: "respectables" who, according to themselves, are allied to mainstream American morality, and "undesirables," whom the respectables characterize in terms of "drunkenness in public, spontaneous brawls, unwillingness to work, sexual licence, and occasional trouble with the police." The undesirables, in turn, characterize their opposites as "stuck up," "house niggers," and "Uncle Toms" (1969:34–35). Not content with this obviously stereotypic dichotomy, Hannerz probed more deeply and discovered four life-styles which he calls the "mainstreamers," "swingers," "street families," and "street corner men" (p. 37). He stresses that these groups are approximations of reality and that there are Winston Streeters who are not oriented closely to any of them.

Mainstreamers conform more closely than the others to general middle-class American values. They are predominantly homeowners. Husbands are present in the households, employed (many in white-collar jobs), and interact closely at home with their wives.

Swingers tend to be younger than mainstreamers (teens to 30s). They are frequently younger siblings, and some will eventually become mainstreamers. Many are unmarried. Unemployment is not a serious problem among them, but they change jobs and domiciles frequently. They are not home-oriented and spend much of their leisure time at parties and places of entertainment. Their personal networks are loosely knit. Some swingers, when they become older, will join the street families rather than the mainstreamers.

· [The street families] are childrearing households. This means that there is practically always an adult woman in the household who is the mother of all, most, or at least some of the children there, and whose age is somewhere between the upper twenties and the fifties. . . . The women may or may not have a husband who is a member of the household—among the street families on Winston Street, between one-third and one-half are headed by women without husbands (p. 46).

Street families' average income is lower than that of mainstreamer families, with many below the poverty line. The men and women—if employed—are in unskilled manual work, and dependence on welfare payments is considerable. They are of the same age as the mainstreamers. Hannerz calls them street families because "they are conspicuous in the open-air life of ghetto street corners and sidewalks. Probably it is their way of life, and the complementary life-style of the streetcorner men, which most closely correspond to an outsider's image of typical ghetto life" (p. 46). Although not all of them conform to the mainstreamers' stereotype of them, it is the street families, and street corner men, whom mainstreamers regard as "undesirables."

Hannerz's street corner men follow the same life-style as Liebow's, but Hannerz places them in a wider context. He identifies them as the street family men who are frequently unemployed and typically peripheral to, if not wholly absent from, households.

Melvin Williams, in his study of a poor black section of Pittsburgh, differentiates "mainstream," "spurious," and "genuine" subcultures, the first being similar to Hannerz's of the same name. The genuine black subculture, he says, "comes close to" Hannerz's street families, but this is "not adequate for people who are the keystone of black culture in urban America" (1981:8).

Poor Blacks have responded in a variety of ways. The "genuine" ones have defied pervasive influence of "mainstream" values and have persisted in demonstrating a style that often defiles and denies those values. Thus, their behavior is distinctively expressive rather than instrumental, in terms of the goals and rewards of mainstream society. The "spurious" . . . linger in a "no-man's land." They are often bitter about both the behavior of "genuine" Blacks who, they rationalize, "keep us down," as well as the attitudes and institutional restrictions of the mainstream that keep them out. They refuse to be the one and cannot be the other, so they are marginal and/or isolated, but the tolerant bosom of the ghetto provides a place for them in spite of themselves. The "spurious" are often the hard drug addicts, amateur poets and novelists, or chronic prison inmates (who fail to "beat the system") (p. 9).

The four Winston Street life-styles can be seen as ethnic subsubcultures or as social class groups within an ethnic subculture. Either definition is acceptable. The point is that different ways of life within the same ethnic group are identified. Outsiders typically regard the ethnic group in question in uniformly negative, stereotypic, prejudicial terms. Hannerz and others like Moore, who have produced similar findings, demonstrate empirically that uniform stereotyping has no factual basis. Potentially such knowledge can be used to enhance the humanity of interethnic relations. Williams's "genuine" subculture, however, is a product of oppression and a possible perpetuator of stereotyping.

One of the most notable full-length studies of an ethnic minority in a Third World city is Abner Cohen's book (1969) on Sabo, the Hausa quarter in Ibadan, Nigeria. Its socioeconomic characteristics are discussed in some detail in chapter 5. Beyond his descriptions of Sabo life, Cohen is concerned about the fundamental raison d'être of ethnic groups. He argues two alternative hypotheses: that the prime mover of the maintenance of ethnic identity is either (1) economic survival or (2) symbolic group support. His conclusion as far as Sabo is concerned favors the first alternative. This important conclusion encourages caution in accepting at face value the sentimentalized portrayals of ethnicity popular in the United States.

In most cases, motives for ethnic group maintenance are apt to be multiple and mixed. For example, S. Frank Miyamoto, in the 1984 introduction to his book on the Japanese community in Seattle (first published in 1939), places the great solidarity of the community into a wider context. The source of strength was adherence to Japanese cultural patterns and economic self-sufficiency. Both features were intensified, if not caused, by the anti-Japanese prejudice of the surrounding majority that obstructed integration and assimilation (p. xxiii). The Japanese community of Seattle was severely disrupted by the infamous relocation program of 1942, in which the United States government moved West Coast Japanese to concentration camps in the Southwest. Even so, 60 to 70 percent of its members moved back after World War II, joined by Japanese from elsewhere in the United States (Leonetti and Newell-Morris 1982:23).

Beleagueredness—coupled with internal solidarity—is a prominent theme in other studies of ethnic subcultures. The experience of Jews in American cities illustrates this point. In 1870, Harlem, in uptown Manhattan, was a partly rural section receiving an influx of immigrants. By the early twentieth century, the largest ethnic group in Harlem was composed of over 100 thousand Jews. But by 1930, only about five thousand Jews were left—blacks having replaced them (Gurock 1979:146–49).

Meanwhile, Boro Park, a section of Brooklyn, N. Y., became a larger and denser Jewish community in the 1960s, when blacks and Hispanics displaced Jews from other areas of the city and the issue of ethnic identity was, in general, intensified (Mayer 1979:40–41). It is now a fully organized Orthodox community that nevertheless has elements of general American middle-class culture (p. 7). The vividness of Boro Park's Orthodox identity is well conveyed by this description:

> During the Christmas season Boro Park presents a curious image. . . . Its streets are dull and unlit in comparison with the streets that are its official borders. . . . [T]hose streets and avenues near the periphery are richly decorated with Christmas trees and electrical ornaments on doors and window frames. It was from this observation that the first definition of the boundaries of the Jewish community emerged. . . . There were almost no Christmas decorations at all in the center itself. At the outset then, the density of Christmas decorations was used as an unobtrusive measure of the social boundaries of the Boro Park Jewish community (p. 45).

Whereas Boro Park as Egon Mayer observed it exemplifies a consolidation phase of displacement, Mattapan (a section of Boston) exemplifies a disintegration phase of the process as Yona Ginsberg (1975) saw it. Mattapan, a middle-class semisuburb with good housing stock, lost three-quarters of its Jewish population between 1968 and 1972. Ginsberg studied those who remained, and summarizes their condition as living in fear (p. vii). Those who had left were replaced by blacks from inner Boston, and those who remained were surrounded by blacks. The fears were the usual ones: increased street violence and physical deterioration. The Jews who remained did so primarily because they were satisfied with the quality of their housing and their immediate neighborhoods. An important fact emerging from Ginsberg's interviews was that the remaining Jews regarded their immediate black neighbors as respectable people like themselves, in contrast to the "cheaper class blacks" who were not homeowners (pp. 193–94). In other words, they perceived a social class commonality with their new black neighbors that ran counter to their overall feeling that Mattapan was becoming unlivable because of a black invasion.

A similar awareness of social class or qualitative differences among blacks comes through in Jonathan Rieder's interviews with Jews and Italians living in Brooklyn's Canarsie section. Rieder says of one of his interviewees:

> Middle-income blacks he saw as "just like me. . . . But if they are going to send shit from Brownsville down here, it's a different ballgame." . . . The distinction between niggers and blacks was the foundation of a ranking of the profligate lifestyles of lower-income blacks and the respectable lifestyles of middle-income blacks. Beneath the surface of apparently racial judgment was the ineluctable reality of class cultures in conflict (1985:59).

Rieder quotes two other Canarsians who see the black problem not in racial terms but in terms of class conflict (pp. 117–18). These examples of selective perception are, however, overwhelmed by his detailed account of the seething hatreds and fears of the Italians and Jews, most of whom had earlier been displaced by blacks and Hispanics in other parts of New York City. Interracial tensions were only part of their problem, which also had its roots in the societywide malaise of the 1960s.

It is encouraging in terms of improved interethnic relations that even people with strongly negative feelings about other groups can recognize that there is diversity among the others. However, it is essential to see beyond this recognition into the humanity of the otherness. Two books, one on blacks and the other on Hispanics, serve this purpose well. Carol Stack concludes her study of black families in a Middle Western United States city with this admirably concise yet comprehensive statement:

> Black families in the flats and the non-kin they regard as kin have evolved patterns of co-residence, kinship-based exchange networks linking multiple domestic units, elastic household boundaries, lifelong bonds to three-generation households, social controls against the formation of marriages that would endanger the network of kin, the domestic authority of women, and limitations on the role of the husband or male friend within a woman's network. These highly adaptive structural features of urban black families comprise a resilient response to the socioeconomic conditions of poverty, the inexorable unemployment of black men and women, and the access to scarce economic resources of a mother and her children as AFDC recipients.
>
> Distinctively negative features attributed to poor families, that they are fatherless, matrifocal, unstable, and disorganized, are not general characteristics of black families living substantially below economic subsistence in urban America. The black urban family, embedded in cooperative domestic exchange, proves to be an organized tenacious, active, lifelong network (1974:124).

Shirley Achor's study of a Chicano *barrio* in Dallas is in some ways reminiscent of Moore's book on Chicanos in East Los Angeles and Hannerz's on blacks in Washington, D.C. She delineates four different modes of cultural adaptation among barrio inhabitants, all contrasting with Anglo-American popular and academic stereotypes such as their being less competitive, more fatalistic, and less future oriented.

The "insulationists" regard the macroenvironment of Dallas as essentially hostile, avoid it as much as possible, and rely on the economic, emotional, and psychological resources within the *barrio* itself (1978:116- 17). The "accommodationists" regard *barrio* residence as temporary and are "eager to learn Anglo ways that will help them successfully cross cultural boundaries" (p. 122). The "mobilizationists" are political activists on behalf of the *barrio*. They "actively cultivate ties beyond the *barrio*, as well as preserving established local relationships. In a sense, their strategy involves pursuit of biculturalism. They seek to become effective in the Anglo world, while maintaining primary allegiance to and identification with the *barrio* community" (p. 128). Finally, there is a relatively small number of people whose life-style is maladaptive, alienated from the *barrio* and the Anglo world. Though their number is small, their impact on the larger society is notable:

Feelings of powerlessness, meaninglessness, and estrangement can lead the alienated to aberrant social behavior. For some, family life is severely disrupted. A man beats his wife and sexually abuses his own child; a mother sprays her baby with aerosol propellant to keep it from crying; a pregnant daughter vanishes in the city. For others, alcoholism or drug addiction offer avenues to welcome oblivion, or armed robbery a path to economic subsistence. . . . Social workers, police officers, and other agents of the dominant society tend to overestimate [the occurrence of alienation] because it is precisely among this group that their clients are largely recruited. The majority of the *barrio* families, who cause no problems to Anglo authorities, remain outside the purview of many caretakers. Nevertheless, these agents tend to group all *barrio* residents together into a single negative category. . . . The sustaining and positive aspects of *barrio* life are unknown to and unimagined by them (pp. 130–31).

Among the sustaining features of Hispanic *barrio* life in United States cities is the *bodega*, or neighborhood grocery store. There are 65 hundred of them in the New York City area. They are havens for sociability and suppliers of favorite ethnic foods; they are conveniently located in contrast to most supermarkets, and their proprietors cash payroll and welfare checks for regular customers (Agins 1985b:1, 13).

Popular and academic attention has been focused in recent decades on blacks and Hispanics in North American cities because they have had an overwhelming impact on those cities. Yet we must not lose sight of the many other ethnic groups whose presence contributes to the complex social fabric of Western industrial and Third World cities. Many of them have been discussed earlier in this chapter and, in various connections, in previous chapters. Among these are Native Americans, many of whom migrate back and forth between their reservations (depressed rural areas virtually by definition) and various cities. At the conclusion of his article on the high rate of alcoholism among Navajos living in Denver, Theodore Graves says:

The research also makes clear that urban migration is not the best way to solve the economic limitations of reservation life. Experience with migrants indicates that most would prefer to live and work near their reservation homes. Forcing them to seek employment in large urban centers only adds to their adjustment problems in many ways. Indian critics of BIA [Bureau of Indian Affairs] policy have often suggested that federal funds now invested in relocation might be better spent in improving reservation opportunities and promoting Indian jobs in surrounding communities (1971:309).

Like all other city-dwelling Native Americans, the Mohawks of Brooklyn have a reservation base, in their case in Canada. Although Mohawks have lived and worked in Brooklyn since 1915, all who have died there have been buried on the reservation, indicating its symbolic importance (Blumenfield 1981:294). Nevertheless, the Mohawks have made one of the most successful Native American urban adaptations. They have done it through the men's specialization in high steel construction work. New York's continual building boom has provided ample employment opportunities for them. High steel work is dangerous and requires great stamina and courage; it also pays well. Those who practice it are therefore genuinely respected and admired. The Mohawks know this, and the resulting self-esteem has enabled them convincingly to transpose their aboriginal warrior image to that of a genuine modern Mohawk warrior (Freilich 1977:170).

Generally speaking, though, the status of urban Native Americans is particularly unjust. Survivors of genocide and dispossession by European invaders, they are currently subjected to ethnic and racial discrimination despite their relatively small numbers.

Also notably unjust is the status of another relatively small ethnic subculture, that of the Arab-Americans. Unlike several ethnic immigrant groups which contributed notoriously to urban crime in the United States, Arab-Americans have been law-abiding and inconspicuous from the beginning. One of their major concentrations is in Detroit. There, the Muslim subcommunity, was, in the early 1970s, struggling by legal means to prevent the city from physically destroying their community through "urban renewal" policies. The Maronite Christian subcommunity, on the other hand, though retaining its identity, was becoming highly assimilated to American culture (Aswad 1974:13–15). Assimilation is one way, of course, to mitigate the problem of being a target of ethnic/racial prejudice. In the 1980s, urban Arab-Americans found themselves increasingly subjected to attack and to negative stereotyping in the media. Branded as terrorists because a few Middle Eastern Arabs actually are terrorists (Association of Arab-American University Graduates 1986a:1; 1986b:3), they have been the objects of harassment and occasionally, of actual terrorism in the United States, as in the case of the 1985 bombing murder of one of them in Los Angeles (Arab-American Anti-Discrimination Committee 1986a:3; 1986b:7). Basically these attacks are caused by over-zealous and uncritical support of Israel in its long dispute with the Palestinian Arabs, a dispute in which most Arab-Americans are not involved—another instance of an urban problem whose genesis is international, not city-specific.

The Melting Pot Theory

This section on ethnic subcultures began by discussing Glazer and Moynihan's cautions regarding the American ethnic melting pot. It closes with two somewhat different perceptions. The first is derived from a study of Italian, Rumanian, and Slovak immigrant adaptations in Cleveland, Ohio:

> Despite varying value orientations and strikingly different patterns of social mobility, the stories of these three communities have the same ending. The sons and daughters began to lose meaningful contacts with their parents' origins in the 1920s; during the late 1930s and the 1940s an increasing proportion married outside the group. Thus the melting pot absorbed them into the larger community of Cleveland and widened that community's limits. But even as the old ethnic mosaic of the city began to disappear, a new system of religious groupings emerged as the characteristic social order of the metropolis. Memories of place, cultural loyalties, and social relations were now articulated within the boundaries of religious groupings of Protestants, Catholics, and Jews, rather than within the ethnic community and neighborhood (Barton 1975:173).

The second perception is that members of the same ethnic subculture can undergo different "melting pot" experiences. Portuguese immigrants in two adjacent New England cities, "Perryport" and "Texton," have, in the first case, successfully adapted, in many instances achieving middle-class status. In Texton, however, they remain an isolated, negatively stereotyped ethnic enclave.

The differences are because of different conditions in the cities. In Perryport, the original Portuguese were welcomed because of their valued contribution to the city's seafaring economy. With that positive beginning, further positive adaptations were made even though the seafaring economy changed radically. In Texton, the Portuguese originally worked in textile mills, but as that industry became increasingly depressed, the Portuguese became increasingly unwelcome in a city with high unemployment (Smith 1975).

Social Class Subcultures

Not everyone would agree that social class can best be perceived in terms of culture in the anthropological sense. Milton Gordon (1978:chapter 8) has convincingly argued the point, however, and the examples adduced clearly show social classes as cultural groups rather than narrowly economic categories.

Probably the most influential analytic presentation of urban social classes is Lloyd Warner and Paul Lunt's book, *The Social Life of a Modern Community* (1941). A major classic of urban anthropology, this book is the first volume of the Yankee City Series, a one-volume abridged edition of which was published in 1963 (Warner 1963). It has long been public knowledge that "Yankee City" is Newburyport, Mass., a small seaport and manufacturing city north of Boston. By empirical means, Warner and his associates (who included 30 fieldworkers and analysts) identified six social classes in the city. They, and the percentages of the study sample belonging to them, were: upper upper (1.44), lower upper (1.56), upper middle (10.22), lower middle (28.12), upper lower (32.60), lower lower (25.22), and unknown (0.84) (Warner and Lunt 1941:88).

As part of their highly detailed analysis, they correlated these classes with the city's ethnic groups: natives (53.8 percent), Irish (23.49), French (8.73), Polish (4.03), Greek (2.45), Jewish (2.37), Italian (1.69), Armenian (1.47), Russian (0.84), and Negro (0.48 percent). By native the authors meant what would now more likely be called Anglo or WASP. Within each class, the approximate percentages of nonnative ethnics were: upper upper (0), lower upper (25), upper middle (20), lower middle (30), upper lower (60), and lower lower (40) (p. 222). The Yankee City informants actually referred to these classes by four geographical terms, lumping together the two upper and two middle classes. From this, Warner and Lunt define social class as "two or more orders of people who are believed to be, and are accordingly ranked by the members of the community, in socially superior and inferior positions" (p. 82). The criteria used in Yankee City include occupation, financial status, family background, membership in certain clubs or associations but not in others, and stereotypes of supposedly typical behavior. Warner and Lunt discovered that, though the rank-order hierarchy is clear cut, there is some mobility of individuals from one class to another.

The impact of the Yankee City study was enormous, particularly on sociology. Previously, social class had been an almost taboo subject among American social scientists because of their egalitarian ethic, but they began to discover social classes everywhere once Warner and his colleagues had brought them out of the closet. As often happens in the wake of a major, pioneering study, the specificity of Yankee City's six classes to that particular city was frequently overlooked, and there were many efforts to apply the Yankee City formulation, unmodified, to other cities. The results were generally uncon-vincing. However, one of the more successful applications of the Yankee City terminology was a comparative study of Querétaro, Mexico (population 50 thousand) and Popayán, Colombia (population 33 thousand). In this study, the data necessitated addition of a middle-middle class category. Among the more notable findings was that upper-class families in Querétaro had entered that status relatively recently, in most cases, whereas Popayán's upper-class fam-ilies constituted a "true aristocracy" with coats of arms and genealogies trace-able to sixteenth-century Spain whence their ancestors first came to America (Whiteford 1964:80).

Although the Yankee City typology of classes is no longer accepted as a general model for research, there is general acceptance of a hierarchy of classes in cities. Still, there is no agreement on a universally applicable number or taxonomy of classes.

A sociological/psychiatric team studied New Haven, Conn., an old New En-gland city like Newburyport, but at least ten times larger in population in the early 1950s (Hollingshead and Redlich 1958). Using criteria similar to Warner and Lunt's, August Hollingshead and Frederick Redlich discovered five, rather than six, classes, labeling them simply by Roman numerals. Their frequencies and general occupational characteristics are:

I. 3.4 percent "old families," wealthy, executives, professionals
II. 9.0 percent upwardly aspirant, managers, professionals
III. 21.4 percent employees and semiprofessionals
IV. 48.5 percent skilled and semiskilled
V. 17.7 percent semiskilled and unskilled.

While Class I clearly corresponds to Yankee City's upper-upper class, other equivalences can only be made in a very general way. We must conclude that there is social class variance even between these two cities that have much in common in terms of regional culture. So one would expect even more vari-ance between less similar cities, and this is one reason there is no consensus on a generally applicable taxonomy of urban classes.

Nevertheless, two loose social class generalizations have wide currency and need to be mentioned. The first is that preindustrial cities had, and may still have, two classes: a very small upper class and a huge lower class. The idea is that as preindustrial cities evolve into industrial, or Third World cities, a middle class emerges into the system. This idea is generally true but greatly oversimplified. For example, in a study of teenage girls and their mothers in Cairo in 1980–83, ten distinguishable ranking levels were identified within the range of upper middle to upper lower in Yankee City terms (Bach et al. 1985).

The other generalization is that in most Western industrial cities, the fol-lowing hierarchy can be discerned: upper class or elite, middle class or white collar, working class or blue collar, and underclass. It is well to acknowledge at the outset that "elite" and "underclass" are words that make many people angry and perhaps a bit fearful as well. The words are felt to imply destructive, invidious value judgments on large aggregations of people. Here the terms are simply categories by which to order our data. The following empirical examples of social class subcultures, for convenience only, are given in the order of these categories.

Urban elites have been studied in a number of ways. In chapter 2, we mention the existence, even in very small urban settlements, of local elites who have larger scale social ties beyond the settlement, people who have local influence and power but would not be regarded as elite in larger settlements.

Power and wealth commonly accompany elite or upper-class status, although not all upper-class people are necessarily powerful or rich and many powerful individuals are not socially elite. Nevertheless, investigations of who actually has power and influence in cities almost invariably reveal the salience of a core group of upper-class persons. An exception is Robert Dahl's study (1961) of New Haven that dissociated the exercise of power and influence from the upper class of the city, interpreting it as decentralized among various middle-class groups. This controversial conclusion, however, has been challenged by a more recent study of the city (Domhoff 1978:chapter 2), which asserts the centrality of an upper-class power elite.

Floyd Hunter published an important pioneering study in this field in his 1963 book on "Regional City" (Atlanta). Hunter used the "reputational" interview strategy by which a manageable number of the city's most prominent citizens are asked to name the other most prominent citizens. What is revealed is a set of mostly interlocking networks of powerful, influential, and socially elite decision makers.

"Colonial City" is James Haugh's pseudonym for Norfolk, Va. His focus is on the city's public-voluntary-not-for-profit sector (PVNFPS). "This research sought to discover the importance of business position, 'being Virginian,' and personal talents, demeanor and attributes in the PVNFPS of Colonial City" (1980:1–2). Like Hunter, Haugh reveals the existence of tightly knit networks of a limited number of upper-class people who wield influence in the city. One of Haugh's conclusions is that, once established, a power elite will not easily relinquish its power nor tolerate what it perceives to be threats to it (pp. 117–18).

Continuity and perpetuation is a theme Abner Cohen emphasizes in his study (1981) of the Creole upper class in Freetown, Sierra Leone. These Creoles (who are not the same as those of the Caribbean) are "a status grouping marked off from the other social groups in the country by a special lifestyle and by a dense network of social relationships" (p. 21). They

> share an homogeneous and socially enclosing culture, [and] can also be identified as a group of people who enjoy and exercise a great deal of power in Sierra Leone. This power stems essentially from the senior positions they occupy in the civil service and the professions. Their ascendancy is also secured and perpetuated by the extensive property . . . in Freetown and . . . Freetown peninsula which they control. . . . [L]ike all other elites elsewhere, they cooperate informally as a group through their culture to develop and maintain their interests, and endeavor to pass them on to their own children, so that these may succeed them and thus perpetuate their high status and privileges. Culture and power thus interact dynamically in the formation, definition, and continuity of the group in response to changing circumstances. During the past twenty-five years, the Creoles have evolved into a "state elite" specializing in the objectification, maintenance, and coordination of state institutions and functions (p. 40).

It is tempting to think of elite social classes as having the same subculture everywhere, and certainly the recurrent emphasis on the exercise and maintenance of power reinforces the temptation. For example, from a worldwide perspective, one might assume that the upper-class subcultures of Boston and Philadelphia are identical. However, E. Digby Baltzell demonstrates that this is not the case. He compares and contrasts

> two privileged classes . . . to show how and why Boston Brahmins produced a long tradition of class authority whereas Proper Philadelphians did not. . . . [T]hese differences largely reflect the very different religious ethics of the founding fathers of each city. Bostonians and Philadelphians were and still are motivated by the hierarchical and authoritarian ethic of Puritanism, on the one hand, and the egalitarian and anti-authoritarian ethic of Quakerism, on the other (1979: x).

A Look at Suburbia

Middle-class subcultures in Western industrial cities have been studied largely in terms of suburban settlements, since the enormous suburban growth of the twentieth century is, for the most part, a middle-class phenomenon. Suburban middle-class subcultural patterns of behavior in North America, Great Britain, and Scandinavia have been discussed previously in a number of connections. In this section, we consider just one middle-class study which challenged many of the negative stereotypes of suburbia so popular in the 1950s and 1960s.

Herbert Gans followed his influential study of Boston's doomed West End with two years of research as a resident of Levittown, N.J., 17 miles from Philadelphia. Gans and his wife moved into Levittown soon after it opened in June 1958. The builders' plan had been to construct a complete community of at least 12 thousand houses (three basic house types), organized into "neighborhoods" of about 12 hundred houses, each with an elementary school, playground, and swimming pool. Levittown was conceived of as a true community, not merely a suburban subdivision many of which had already proliferated around American cities.

Gans undertook his study to discover ethnographic facts about suburban, middle-class life in counterpoint to the myth of suburbia already established as fact in the minds of social critics, city planners, and others. Gans states the myth in these terms:

> [T]he suburbs were breeding a new set of Americans, as mass produced as the houses they lived in, driven into a never ending round of group activity ruled by the strictest conformity. Suburbanites were incapable of real friendships; they were bored and lonely, alienated, atomized, and depersonalized. As the myth grew, it added yet more disturbing elements: the emergence of matriarchal wives, absent husbands, spoiled children, and with it, rising marital friction, adultery, divorce, drunkenness, and mental illness. . . . [I]ndividualism was dying, suburbanites were miserable, and the fault lay with the homogeneous suburban landscape and its population (1967:xvi).

Gans had misgivings about this myth because his own impression had been that suburbanites were generally happy in their new homes, even though some of the criticisms included in the myth had some validity.

Gans says that, "given the declining influence on behavior of regional origin, religious preference, and ethnic background, the crucial source of variety in

Levittown is class and class subculture" (p. 24). However, he also says that three-quarters are lower-middle class, while the fourth quarter is divided between upper-middle class and working class—so there is considerable class homogeneity.

Of the working class, Gans found what others have found: its members are mostly blue-collar workers and of relatively recent European peasant origins. Husband and wife roles are clearly differentiated, and friendships are largely with other men and women, respectively (p. 25).

The lower-middle class includes blue- and white-collar workers and even some professionals. Husbands and wives are closer to being companions. Their nuclear families are child centered, and their social life focuses on relatives, if they do not live too far away, and more particularly on neighbors and friends met in voluntary associations and church activities (p. 28). Gans divides the Levittown lower-middle-class subculture into two groups. The "restrictive" people are suspicious of the city and of urbane upper-middle-class people and lead sober lives with little drinking and partying. The "expansive" people have less pronounced Protestant-Puritan backgrounds, are more openly sociable, and are less concerned with respectability and keeping up appearances (p. 29).

The upper-middle class includes managers and professionals, generally college educated and "trained to be interested in and to participate in the larger world" (p. 30). Their active scales of behavior are larger. Their domestic and personal lives are not sex segregated. The upper-middle class is also divided into two groups, "conservative-managerial" and "liberal-professional" (p. 31).

One can see in these group portraits—especially as Gans fleshes them out in detail—microcosms of North American middle-class life-styles in general.

Almost half of the Levittowners came from other suburban areas and a third from cities (19 percent from Philadelphia) (p. 32). The reasons for moving to and buying in Levittown were many, but predominant were the desire for more space and a good, new house. "They did not regret leaving the city, nor did they flee from it. . . . They were not looking for roots or a rural idyll, not for a social ethic or a consumption-centered life, not for civic participation or for 'sense of community' " (p. 37).

Neither boredom nor loneliness, though they certainly exist, are serious problems in Levittown (p. 228). Family cohesion has improved over previous locations (p. 220). In general, especially in his chapters 8 and 9, Gans emphasizes the vitality and lack of mindless conformity among the Levittowners, especially as he saw them, during two years, sorting themselves into various interest and friendship groups, some in the immediate home neighborhood, others more widely dispersed.

Gans's analysis of middle-class life in Levittown, while it refutes the more extreme negative stereotypes of suburbia, does not present a utopian picture. Some of his negative findings appear later in this chapter; the continuing problems of American suburban life have already been mentioned in chapter 4.

The Underclass

The last urban social class subculture is called, by some, "the underclass," and by others "the culture of poverty." Both terms are highly controversial, particularly the latter one which is virtually taboo among many social scientists.

We need to understand the ethnographic basis for underclass/culture of poverty and give some attention to why it generates so much rage—more so than does the myth of suburbia.

Richard Nathan (1986) says that people concerned with social policy at first resisted the term underclass because of its stigmatizing implications. Nathan does not mention that culture of poverty, which is in some respects synonymous, had previously aroused similar feelings for the same reason. Nathan's recent description of the underclass makes a very important distinction that the original culture-of-poverty idea did not, and so it may be more acceptable among social idealists.

"Underclass" is a shorthand expression for the concentration of economic and behavioral problems among racial minorities in large, older cities.

The existence of a distinctive underclass group is an ironic result of the success, not the failure, of American social policy. The civil-rights revolution (surely not complete, but extraordinary nonetheless) has caused a bifurcation within the black and Hispanic sectors. . . . With opportunities opened up for upwardly mobile and educated members of these groups to move to suburbs and better-off urban neighborhoods, the people left behind in the urban ghettos are more isolated. The role models of an earlier day (a teacher, postman, civil servant) have departed. . . . But the result is that the dangerous inner-city areas that fester in our land have become an increasingly serious social and economic problem. We cannot easily put our social science calipers to the task of measuring the underclass. It involves more than conventional economic and demographic indicators. The underclass condition is also attitudinal and behavioral. It is often manifest in crime and vandalism, which further isolate underclass groups. . . . [W]e are talking about a relatively small subgroup among the poor. Not everyone who is poor is in the underclass (p. 32).

Nathan reviews the genesis of the workfare idea and its evolution, through liberal/conservative consensus, into a welfare system "focused on training, education, job placement and work, including in some cases the assignment of welfare family heads to obligatory work-experience positions" (p. 32). He says that over two-thirds of the states are currently developing this new system. The test of this experiment "will be in the money put into training and other services for those who need them most" (p. 32) including women heading welfare families and jobless young men in distressed urban areas.

The culture-of-poverty concept explains why some poor people remain isolated in the ghettos. Poverty

is a way of life, remarkably stable and persistent, passed down from generation to generation along family lines. The culture of poverty has its own modalities and distinctive social and psychological consequences for its members. It is a dynamic factor which affects participation in the larger national culture and becomes a subculture of its own (O. Lewis 1961:xxiv).

Lewis itemized the traits of the culture of poverty: chronic unemployment, crowded living quarters, lack of privacy, gregariousness, high incidence of alcoholism, frequent resort to violence in quarrels, physical violence in rearing children, wife beating, early initiation into sex, consensual marriages or free unions, strong present-time orientation, relatively little ability to defer gratification and plan for the future, resignation and fatalism in the face of life's realities, and others. Lewis notes that these types of behavior occur among some people in other social classes, but in the culture of poverty they form a particular pattern (pp. xxvi-vii).

Anthony Leeds (1971) and Charles Valentine (1968) wrote two of the most thorough and stringent criticisms of Lewis's ideas. Leeds (pp. 228–29) lists all of the culture-of-poverty traits Lewis set forth in his various publications, and argues that they do not constitute a system of meanings as they should if an autonomous culture were really involved. The most serious criticism Leeds and Valentine level is that what Lewis calls the culture of poverty is not a self-perpetuating, intergenerational way of life; it is not a culture (or subculture) at all. Rather, it is an assemblage of behaviors imposed on the poor by the larger society (Leeds 1971:244–56; Valentine 1968:116).

Leeds, Valentine, and others interpret the salience of the culture-of-poverty idea to be that the poor are to blame for their own condition. The concept is, in this view, yet another example of blaming the victim. Ironically, using the culture concept is intended to obviate blame or fault: people learn the patterns of their culture and follow them because they see no alternative. However, Lewis's critics point out that people living in his culture of poverty do see better alternatives but are prevented from acting on them because they are politically powerless (cf. Liebow's *Tally's Corner*). The fault lies, they argue, in the larger society which deprives the underclass of power and resources and at the same time views the poor as being behaviorally defective and requiring reform. Of particular concern to critics was the impact of ideas like Lewis's on important policymakers. One of the latter was Daniel Patrick Moynihan who concluded that the principal source of poor blacks' social inadequacies was the deteriorated black family. The country cannot afford "a large lower-class that is at once deviant *and* dependent" said Moynihan. His proposed solutions would force conformity of the poor to " 'stable working-class' norms as defined by middle-class moralists" (like Moynihan) or the poor would "be coerced into a semblance of conformity and forcefully punished for their deviations from respectability" (Valentine 1968:36–37).

Stack's book on poor black family life, among other things, presents the "deviant" not as deteriorated but as an alternative to middle-class family behavior. Similarly, in Aschenbrenner's study of black families in Chicago, among whom conjugal ties tend to be fragile (suggesting familial breakdown to middle-class observers), a non-middle-class support system is very much in evidence:

> Implicit in the organization of extended families is a humanistic value— that of deep involvement in the lives of many people. Among poorer families, sharing is more often in the form of small loans and gifts of money, as well as services, while in those with more financial security, often only social support and services are exchanged; in either case, sacrifices of time, energy, or money as well as sympathy and concern are expected and received. Sometimes demands cause resentments and conflicts among family members; but the sense of obligation is strong (1975:143).

Another conclusion, this one based on a study of ten families then living in the now-demolished Pruitt-Igoe housing project in St. Louis, is that

> there *is* a culture of poverty—a distinctive style of life that is shared and is apparently similar in black ghettoes all over America. . . . [S]uch a culture

does contribute to the perpetuation of poverty by compounding the problem of control over children and spouses and supporting a style of life that is rewarding within the ghetto ("living sweet," for example) but detrimental to mobility out of the ghetto (Schulz 1969:193).

The behavioral patterns of the underclass at issue are both intrinsic (self-perpetuating subcultural) *and* extrinsic (imposed by the political and economic restrictions of the larger society). In either case, they are adaptational strategies for coping with deprived circumstances; in neither case is blame or fault ascribable to the poor themselves except by ethnocentric or politically self-seeking moralists.

Poverty (chronic deprivation of a society's resources) is not new, and it is worldwide (Eames and Goode 1973). To blame poverty on the putative defectiveness of the poor themselves is also ancient and worldwide. That Oscar Lewis's intentions in postulating the culture of poverty were misread as a form of blaming the victim is evidence of the power of those biases and of the biases of those who do not want to accept social inequality as an existential aspect of the human condition (Leeds 1971; Valentine 1968; and others). Recent field studies of urban poor people present a mixed picture of the pluses and minuses of life: the high morale and vitality of Third World squatters (Mangin 1970:xxix); the violent and opportunistic, yet spontaneous, generous, and hospitable life-style of slum dwellers in Naples (Belmonte 1979:143); the interdependence of poor people and upper-class people in Cairo (Rugh 1979:90–91); and many more.

Probably the most deprived underclass people of all are those who are literally homeless, who sleep in the streets or other public places. Frequently observed in cities like Calcutta, homelessness has become much more visible than it used to be in North American cities.

The causes are controversial, but one is deinstitutionalization of many former mental hospital patients. They are not only impaired, and so not readily employable, but there is also widespread neighborhood resistance to establishing group homes for them despite laws and court orders to the contrary. Researchers doing ethnographic fieldwork among the homeless in Austin, Texas, challenged the widespread assumption that the mentally ill comprise a major proportion of the homeless. They found that only 10 percent of those they studied had been institutionalized one or more times. "These proportions are by no means trivial, as they well exceed the proportion of the Texas population hospitalized for mental illness. Nevertheless, they do not approach the one-third to three-quarters of the homeless population reported as mentally ill by the media and in much of the research literature" (Snow et al. 1986:414). These authors mention two causes of homelessness: the "non-impaired individual trapped in a cycle of low-paying, deadend jobs which fail to provide the financial wherewithal to get off and stay off the streets . . . and the decline in the availability of low-cost housing" (pp. 421–22).

The decline of available low-cost public housing in American cities, and reluctance of private developers to build more low-cost housing, despite some tax benefits, was a front page feature in *The Wall Street Journal* (Celis 1986). Poor or absent maintenance of public housing results in such deterioration that 70 thousand units are now boarded up, and a thousand are being demolished each year. In Jersey City, N.J., an applicant for public housing may have to wait up to ten years. Many cannot wait so long, and many become homeless as a result.

All major American cities provide shelters for the homeless, but the supply cannot keep up with the increasing demand. Most shelters provide nothing more than cramped, temporary quarters, but "perhaps 100 or more of the roughly 2,000 United States shelters now help some homeless to rejoin society through professional counseling, medical care, job training and placement, and links to permanent housing" (Lublin 1986:1). However, these efforts are frustrating to the staff and poorly funded, so we are brought back to Richard Nathan's comment that success of the workfare program will depend, to a large degree, on how much of a financial commitment the larger society is willing to make.

One theme of this book is that enhancing the humanity of cities requires macroscale and microscale insights and action in combination. There are suggestions of this idea in efforts being made to ameliorate the lives of the underclass subculture.

Life-Cycle Subcultures

Observations of life-cycle subcultures generally combine age and sex, and this is how, for the most part, we present them.

It is arguable whether children have subcultures apart from their parents', but serious attention has been given to city children's socialization—that is, the processes by which they learn the life-style of their parental and peer-group subculture. Garth Mangum and Stephen Seninger (1978:60) contrast middle-class and underclass modalities of learning in these terms: "Nearly everyone whom the middle-class adolescent knows in the adult world bases a sense of self-worth on his or her work role, whether in employment, in home-making, or in avocational accomplishment. Work is perceived as a source of self-respect." Of the ghetto child, they say:

> Young ghetto children are forming self-concepts while their endangered bodies learn to fend off the numerous daily threats of their surroundings. Whatever the relative strengths of the family itself, the consensus is strong that the child is not likely to be provided with a strong self-image or positive work values (p. 66).

The danger with all such generalizations—however well-grounded—is that they lend themselves to stereotyping. Fortunately, there are data that demonstrate individual variations.

Peggy Miller's highly detailed description and analysis of language acquisition by three two-year-old, white, lower-class girls living in South Baltimore is a sophisticated case in point. Miller concludes that "Amy, Beth, and Wendy traversed a developmental sequence that closely resembled the sequence previously documented for middle-class American children and French-speaking Canadian children. While there were some differences those were minor and existed against a background of striking similarity" (1982:154). The background to which Miller refers is that of processes of language acquisition, not family or neighborhood background. Such cross-cultural similarities are one way of counteracting subculture stereotypes.

In terms of the content of language acquisition, Miller observes individual and subcultural differences. First, the girls' mothers in some respects differed in what they imparted to their children.

Marlene fostered independence, appreciated Amy's athletic ability and her growing verbal assertiveness. She placed a high value on sharing. Liz valued friendliness, happiness, and politeness in a child. She tried to cope with the battles of will to which she and Wendy were susceptible. She encouraged Wendy's musical inclinations, hoped she would finish high school and, perhaps, go on to college. Nora communicated more than anything her pleasure in Beth. She had a gift for fantasy. She believed that children learn by doing and went to some inconvenience to allow Beth to "help" with adult tasks (p. 150).

So much for individual differences; at the same time all three mothers taught their daughters to defend themselves physically, when necessary, and to cope with their various strong feelings—sometimes with assertiveness, sometimes with compliance. Miller surmises that these children are learning to "use their considerable linguistic resources in different ways from children of more privileged backgrounds . . . one group needs to cope with the injuries of economic deprivation, while the other does not" (p. 151).

Janet Mancini's study of five teenaged boys living in Boston's Roxbury section explicitly challenges monolithic stereotypes of ghetto subculture. She demonstrates at length how the five boys, though they have much in common, are nevertheless developing markedly different personalities largely because of different family situations.

The portraits that follow attest to the richness and range of interpersonal "styles" composed and played by young black males within the context of an inner-city subculture. Although they share demographic characteristics, we find critical differences among the boys in *how* they relate to that cityscape, and to the people who form the fabric of their daily lives. All the boys live in poverty, but poverty alone has not made Leroy a "troublemaker," Ernie a "withdrawn kid," or Dave a "con artist." Though we may find higher rates of social disorganization in inner-city areas, integrity, conventional values, and emotional and social stability are by no means foreign, as will be evidenced by Keith the "conformist" and Hank the "together guy" (1980:2).

In contrast to these North American observations, Ximena Bunster and Elsa Chaney's in Lima, Peru, and Helen Safa's in San Juan, Puerto Rico, suggest that there can be indistinctness of youthful subcultures among poor people in Latin American cities. Safa (1974:54) says there is no teenage subculture among working-class and poor people in San Juan: small children grow steadily into adult roles. Bunster and Chaney (1985:chapter 4) devote a chapter to how this process takes place in Lima.

The boys' gang is by far the most common subject of research on urban teenagers. Frederic Thrasher's *The Gang* (1927) is one of the classics of the Chicago school of urban sociology, and Albert Cohen's *Delinquent Boys* (1955) introduced the idea of the delinquent subculture "as a collectively arrived at solution for status problems of some working-class males, . . . a type of reaction-formation against conventional middle-class values by those who are especially disadvantaged with respect to them" (Short 1969:xli).

Lewis Yablonsky (1970:187ff) has differentiated three types of boys' gangs. His concern is with gang violence, and his findings, based on research rooted in the classic studies of the Chicago school, distinguish among social, delinquent, and violent gangs. Social gangs are organized for sociability based on feelings of mutual attraction. They have a stable location, and the leader is often idealized. A good example is Boston's Norton Street Gang (Whyte 1981). Delinquent gangs sometimes resort to violence in pursuit of their goals, but their activities are not focused on violence for its own sake. The primary goal is profit attained primarily by means of burglary and robbery. Members are cohesive and, as individuals, emotionally stable. Yablonsky says that present-day delinquent gangs differ from the "criminal gangs" the Chicago school once described; they are not part of a larger, adult criminal hierarchy into which members may graduate when they are older. Delinquent ang members, if they do become adult criminals, do so on an individual basis, not as members of a system (1970:190). Violent gangs differ significantly from these types. Although they do occur in rapidly changing suburban areas, they are concentrated in what Yablonsky calls "disorganized slums," as contrasted with "stable" slums of the sort Suttles studied. Disorganized slums develop with the influx of rural populations into inner-city areas from which more stable lower- and middle-class families are displaced (p. 213). Extreme conflicts in values break down the strong family structures characteristic of stable slum areas and produce considerable numbers of sociopathic boys who form violent gangs.

> [Such] gangs appear to originate in order to adjust individual emotional problems, for reasons of "self-protection" and defense, for channeling aggression, in response to prejudice, because of the peculiar motivations of disturbed leaders or because of a combination of these factors mixed with special external conditions produced by "enemy gangs" (pp. 192–93).

Gang activities include sadistic, "senseless" attacks, with no attendant feelings of concern or guilt and no empathic human relationships. This behavior includes the "gang bang" in which as many as 15 or 20 boys forcibly copulate, in turn, with a girl (pp. 239–40). More is said below about the "subculture of violence."

Because of their impact, delinquent and violent gangs have attracted much attention, but they do not typify urban teenage subcultures. More representative, certainly of middle-class teenagers, is Levittown (Gans 1967:206–16). Levittown was designed and built for parents with young children, and as the latter grew into adolescence, they became increasingly bored and dissatisfied with the place. In the teen parlance of the 1960s, Levittown was "Endsville." Some vandalism and delinquency (but nothing to compare with violent gangs' activities) were the results, as was a serious gap in understanding between parental and adolescent generations. A major problem was the absence of places in which to congregate that were accessible to people without automobiles. A twelfth-grade essayist gave the best summary of Levittown's problem and a good solution: "I think the adults should spend less time watching for us to do something wrong and help us raise money for a community center. We're not asking for it, we only want their help" (p. 214).

> If one begins with the assumption that adolescents are rational and responsible human beings whose major "problem" is that they have become a distinctive minority subculture, it is not too difficult to suggest programs . . . a range of inexpensive coffeehouses and soda shops and other meeting places, bowling alleys, amusement arcades, places for dancing, ice and roller

skating rinks, garages for mechanically inclined car owners (all within walking or bicycling distance or accessible by public transportation), and enough of each so that the various age groups and separate cliques have facilities they can call their own. Since adolescents are well supplied with spending money, many of these facilities can be set up commercially (pp. 214–15).

Considering the well-documented importance of local hangouts for urban dwellers generally, the failure to provide them in Levittown is remarkable.

Moving on into the subcultures of people in young adulthood, we consider two cases of age/gender subcultures: young married women in Bergen, Norway, and young Dominican and other Latin American women in New York.

From 1979 to 1981, Marianne Gullestad studied a network of 15 young working-class mothers living in cooperative apartments in four Bergen suburbs. She is emphatic that their way of life constitutes a subculture, with a values-system involving some conflicts and at the same time a strong moral core. She examines family life, neighborhood, and particularly relationships with friends.

[R]estaurants and discotheques are important fora . . . whose influence on urban women's lives [has] received little attention . . . in social studies. The city is more than a collection of workplaces and neighbourhoods; it also include[s] a variety of centralized functions, among these different kinds of commercial amusements. For the women of this study, restaurants and discotheques serve as fora for acting out their identities as women (1984:20).

"Hearth and home" is one important arena of these women's lives, a traditional one in Norwegian culture. But many of them also work (at mostly low-paying, low-status jobs), and they act out their identity as "attractive women" by dancing and drinking in discotheques. Dressed in tight jeans and high heels, they demonstrate their attractiveness to themselves and others, and bring this feeling back to hearth and home. Gullestad (pp. 310–11) says "as long as they do 'nothing wrong,' going out and seeking confirmation of their identities as attractive women from men other than husbands is a way of trying to solve the tension between sexuality and sameness in marriage and household. Having gained such confirmation they can return reinforced by it to marriage." Gullestad refers to this as the "magic circle" of their lives. It does not always work, and divorce (for various reasons) is something to be reckoned with.

Gullestad's subjects live in a culture with a strongly rural, pietistic component and a traditionally male-dominated public and economic life. It does not include, however, the *machismo* of Latin American culture that is the underlying context of the Dominican bridal showers Adele Bahn and Angela Jaquez (1984) observed in and around New York City. The bride-to-be is assumed to be a virgin and to know nothing about sex. The shower is altogether different from the middle-class Anglo shower where, nowadays, the bride-to-be is frequently known not to be a sexually ignorant virgin. The Dominican version is a crash course in practical sex education and also a raucous, bawdy party for all concerned. Typically, the bride-to-be is expected to "blush and show embarrassment, horror, and astonishment at the 'dirty jokes,' 'red tales,' and 'fresh tricks' that follow" (p. 135). She may be stripped to her underwear, or even completely naked, and stroked with a vibrator or dildo. "Typically, one of the participants is dressed like a man and imitates the groom's actions on the wedding night. If no one dresses as a man, a dildo is tied around the waist of one of the guests and this 'male impersonator' 'attacks' the bride. The dildo is rubbed on her face and all over her body" (p. 135). All the while, the bride-to-be is given advice on how to please a man sexually, including performing fellatio. Decorations in the apartment living room where the shower takes place include pornographic pictures from magazines and balloons made of blown-up condoms. The refreshments include sausages, hot dogs, and other edible items arranged as an array of sets of penis and testicles (p. 134).

The whole event is a complicated reaction to *machismo*. The instructional emphasis is on the bride's pleasing the groom sexually (and in other ways), not on how he can please her. Yet despite the conspicuousness of effigies of men's genitals, many of the jokes are against men, centering on their being either impotent or cuckolded. "The jokes constitute an ideological attack on a system, and make manifest another ideology: . . . that 'he' is not so powerful after all and 'she' may have a weapon at her disposal" (p. 139).

Middle-aged women in American cities have been shown to have distinctive behavioral patterns in which gender and social class subcultures—as well as age—are intertwined. Gans writes:

> [M]ost Levittowners experienced less depression, boredom, and loneliness after the move. Even so, a minority, sometimes up to a third, report the opposite, particularly among the Philadelphians. Occasionally, these feelings stem from being isolated in the community, but usually they reflect more general problems of working and lower middle class women in contemporary society. If there is malaise in Levittown, it is female but not suburban (1967:226).

Most of the emotional problems Gans discovered were women's problems: working-class women cut off from their parents and wives whose husbands' jobs are on the road, absenting them from home much of the time. Social isolation and feeling "stuck" in the house were major sources of stress. Those who had moved from their native Philadelphia felt the isolation and lack of outside activities the most keenly, and Gans recognizes that the problems of these particular people exemplify what critics of suburbia said was wrong with all suburban lives (pp. 237–45).

Malaise is perhaps too mild a term for the quality of life experienced by 50 white working-class families living in various parts of the San Francisco Bay area (Rubin 1976). Lillian Rubin depicts these early middle-aged married couples largely in terms of unhappy childhood memories, stressful early marriages, current marriages full of sexual stress from partners' hostility and failures to communicate, economic precariousness, and truncated leisure activities because of perpetual shortage of funds. In part, these people are stressed in ways similar to the Canarsians Rieder studied: they are aware of liberalized values and actions, originating in upper-middle-class subcultures, which they are constrained from adopting. Above all, Rubin sees her interviewees as being locked into their subculture, and their children as perpetuating it.

> The most commonly heard wish is: "I want my kids to be happy." But what does it mean? "I don't know; I just want them to be happy, that's all. I want them to have everything they want, all the things we couldn't have." Even now, it's hard for working- class adults to imagine what it means to "be

happy," hard to imagine a life that's very different from the one being lived. The alternatives they perceive still are limited . . . not just by their childhood experiences but by the cumulative effect of their adulthood as well; limited not just in dreams for personal life but in occupational life as well (p. 207).

Those working-class children who do go to a four-year college go to the type of college "that, at best, will track them into lower-middle-class jobs through which they will live lives only slightly better than their parents' " (p. 209).

Rubin is emphatic that the working class is a self-perpetuating subculture constrained by the larger society. She concludes:

We tell ourselves and them, they will be able to move into the more privileged sectors of the society. A comforting illusion! But one that avoids facing the structured reality that there's no room at the top and little room in the middle; that no matter what changes people or groups make in themselves, this industrial society requires a large work force to produce its goods and service its needs—a work force that generation after generation comes from working-class families. These families reproduce themselves not because they are somehow deficient or their culture aberrant, but because there are no alternatives for most of their children (p. 211).

This statement could easily be about the basic dynamics of the culture of poverty; the big difference is that these are white working-class people, not black or Hispanic underclass people.

These images of constrained women in American industrial cities should be compared, when possible, to those of women in Third World cities. Life-styles of working women in sub-Saharan Africa are discussed in earlier chapters. Here, we briefly consider migrant women living in the poor section of Tehran. Aware of new and different patterns of female behavior and of their male migrant relatives' greater opportunities in the city than in rural areas, these women's access to larger active scales of life becomes ever more limited (Bauer 1984:287). Their lives are largely confined to their neighborhoods where personal interactions of various kinds are intense (pp. 278–79). If they suffer substantially from the type of loneliness reported for some North American urban women, there is certainly no mention of it. However, visits to extended family members or shrines outside the neighborhood are closely controlled and rarely undertaken except with men of their households or other women. Such encapsulation of women's subculture is one way of shielding vulnerable individuals from "the world of strangers" (see chapter 8), the most significant of those strangers, in this case, being strange men (p. 280).

The final life-cycle subculture we consider is that of the elderly. Previous discussions of elderly people in this book are concerned with studies of retirement homes as examples of observers' small-scale perspectives. Here, the context is different. Two studies of communities designed and created for elderly people represent social class and life-cycle subcultures.

Idle Haven Mobile Home Park is in an East Bay suburb of San Francisco. At the time of Sheila Johnson's study (1971), there were about 150 mobile home parks in the greater San Francisco Bay area, and she is aware that she was studying an example of an increasingly important type of urban settlement. Idle Haven was not a retirement community, for only about a third of the men were retired. However, nearly half of the residents were over 60, so elderliness was an important element. The 260 people living in 146 mobile homes were mostly married couples without anyone else (pp. 19–22). Occupations and income levels were predominantly working class. Idle Haven is within easy walking distance of a shopping complex, and major shopping centers, churches, and hospitals are not far away. It is surrounded by a six-foot-high fence; the residents value highly its function of keeping out all kinds of undesirable people (p. 15), as they do formal rules for neighborly behavior. Blacks are deliberately excluded from Idle Haven, typical of the national mobile home population of which fewer than 2 percent was black in 1968 (p. 50).

> Many of the residents of Idle Haven had lived for many years in Oakland— a city which by 1983 is expected to have a population more than 50 percent Negro. Since the residents of Idle Haven were both elderly and of the working class, they usually tended to live in older less affluent neighborhoods which, during the last few years have become solidly black enclaves. . . . One retired teamster said he had always expected to live in his Oakland home for the rest of his life. However, as white neighbors had moved out and black neighbors moved in, he had become an alien in hostile territory. His wife had been spat at and jostled off the sidewalk by young bloods until she was afraid to go shopping alone or on foot. Their house had been twice burglarized while they were out bowling, and acid had been poured on their lawn (p. 50).

Many others told a similar story. As with the remaining Jews in Mattapan, life in their old neighborhoods had become ruled by fear. Consequently, the attractiveness of the protected, exclusionary mobile home park was great.

Johnson emphasizes the many ways in which Idle Haven residents, sensing themselves to be largely homogeneous, construct a communal support system.

> Mobile home parks such as Idle Haven are genuine small communities, with all the advantages and disadvantages that such communities enjoy. Residents trust one another, help one another, and enjoy each other's company; at the same time—given the nature of small groups—they also gossip about each other, watch to see that no one gets more than anyone else does, and occasionally bicker among themselves. Given the financial and social needs of the elderly, such communities clearly serve an important purpose. To force them to take in all applicants would be to destroy the social fabric of the parks and to turn them into ordinary working-class neighborhoods, with their greater potential for anomie, indifference, and crime (p. 176).

"Fun City" is the ironical pseudonym for a West Coast retirement community (Jerry Jacobs 1983). Various clues suggest it is near Monterey, and that the metropolis from which many of its residents came is San Francisco. Fun City is a privately built town with a 1970 population of 5,519, of whom 5,516 were white and none was black (p. 45). The intentional exclusion of blacks is probably the main feature Fun City shares with Idle Haven. Fun City is a solidly middle-class settlement, at least half of its residents having been professionals, managers, or business owners before retirement (p. 47). They are decidedly older, too: the average age of the women is 66, the men 73. Children and young adults are conspicuously absent from both communities for different reasons. Many Idle Haven residents have always been childless, while many of the plentiful children and grandchildren of Fun City's residents live in the "metropolis" and its suburbs.

Fun City is organized around wide, well-kept streets that are remarkable in several ways: (1) they are all about the width of a four-lane highway; (2) there are no cars parked in the streets; (3) there are few cars driven on them; (4) they are all immaculately clean—no cigarette butts, gum wrappers, toothpicks, match sticks, bent beer cans, broken bottles, animal excrements, or less seemly items . . . ; (5) they are all lined on both sides with sidewalks that no one walks on; and (6) all the city's streets and sidewalks can be observed at any time of the day or night in the same state of eerie desolation (p. 1).

The streets are lined with well-kept tract houses, priced from $19,000 to $50,000 (early 1970s values). They are immaculate inside and out, but show few signs of life except for the large, late-model American cars in the carports. "Viewed from a distance, Fun City appears to be a cross between a suburban tract community being readied for habitation and a large, cleverly camouflaged used car lot" (p. 1).

Although promoted by the developers as offering "an active way of life" for retired people, Fun City is not a very active place. Jerry Jacobs estimates that on any given day, no more than about 10 percent of the population are participating in Activities Center programs and in informal activities at the shopping center. And most of these are the same people. The majority stay at home most of the time, and as many as a quarter never leave home, according to a knowledgeable mailman (p. 42).

Many residents are housebound because they are too infirm to walk to the shopping center or friends' houses, or are no longer licensed to drive, or both. They perceive themselves as being more active than they are (pp. 56–57). Many of them are close enough to children or grandchildren to receive visits from them. Nevertheless, they are ambivalent. "They enjoy having friends and relatives visit, but they also enjoy the peace, quiet, and general low-key existence that Fun City offers. In brief, their ability to cope has been reduced considerably with age, and Fun City gives them (in some ways at least) little to cope with" (pp. 59–60). The watchword of Fun City life is never giving offense, always keeping the peace (p. 73). This conflictless ideal is, in many ways, fostered by Fun City's racial and social class segregation and homogeneity, and its isolation. While some residents are truly content with these conditions, others are not (pp. 81–82).

> Fun City must be viewed as having been relatively successful in its screening operation, . . . [but] a relative failure as a retirement setting. This is true notwithstanding . . . that different segments of the population are reasonably content with Fun City. For most it has proved to be a "false Paradise." I believe that is true of segregated retirement settings in general. One has, after all, grown up in "natural settings," conflictual, stressful settings that emanate from the diversity of persons, opinions, and behaviors that one encounters in the world at large (p. 83).

Jacobs thinks that the trend toward building isolated, segregated retirement settings should be reversed by locating many more of them in natural urban settings whence most of the retired persons came. One reason why a Fun City resident referred to the place as a "false Paradise" was that its facilities did not mitigate a serious problem of American retirees: the traditional work ethic that energized their earlier years allowed no justification for leisure except as a reward for work (p. 76). How, then, to adapt constructively to a life of nothing but leisure?

COLLECTIVE LIFE-STYLES

Homosexual Subcultures

Until very recently, homosexuality was so strongly condemned in Western industrial cultures that homosexuals painfully hid its existence and most heterosexuals fearfully denied it. During the last decades of the twentieth century, however, public opinion has become somewhat less punitive, and homosexual subcultures emerged into view in some cities. On the whole, homosexual men's and women's domains are separate (for example, men's "gay bars" and women's "gay bars"), but sometimes they occur in the same location.

One of these is a portion of Jacob Riis Park, a two-mile stretch of beach on the Rockaway Peninsula, Queens, N.Y. Homosexuals predominate in 2 of the beach's 14 sections, Bays 1 and 2. Homosexuals have come to Bays 1 and 2 for several decades, but in the 1970s their presence became noticeable (Canavan 1984:68–69) through their clothing and general demeanor. Gay men outnumber the lesbians and make themselves more conspicuous. Both sunbathe and swim in the nude—at least some of them do—and heterosexuals are present who do the same.

That nude bathing is possible at all in this densely populated, public location is worthy of note. Perhaps it is because of the emergence of the "culture of civility," of tolerance within limits of publicly deviant behavior, earlier claimed as an exclusive feature of San Francisco (Becker and Horowitz 1971:4–19). San Francisco is generally recognized as a major concentration point of homosexuals, which contributes to the proportion of single and childless adults in its population. The lesbian women there

> tend to live in certain ethnically mixed, older, working-class areas of the city. . . . These areas bound each other and have in common a quality of neighborhood life, low-rent housing, and the possibility of maintaining a kind of anonymity.
>
> The central clearinghouse for rentals . . . is the San Francisco Women's Centers and Switchboard bulletin board. Several women have reported coming to San Francisco with no personal contacts, calling up the switchboard or checking their bulletin board, and following up on a request for a lesbian roommate. Through this one contact they have . . . become part of a social network and integrated into the community in a short time. Since much of the socializing in the community consists of visiting friends, women without cars try to live near each other so that gradually, within a small radius, many lesbian households may exist. One woman told me proudly that within the two-year period that she and her lover had lived at their present address, twelve lesbian households were established in a one block area nearby through word-of-mouth alone (Wolf 1979:98–99).

The San Francisco male homosexual community has been comprehensively and sympathetically, though critically, studied by Manuel Castells (1983:138–72). Castells credits members of this subculture with major responsibility for the renovation of dilapidated housing, reinvigoration of various aspects of street life, and energetic participation in politics. He is, however, concerned about the dangers of their alienation from the lesbian community and low-income nonwhite ethnic groups (pp. 169–70).

"Port City," with a population of about 600 thousand, including supposedly 50 thousand homosexuals, is located on the northwest coast of the United States (Read 1980:5). Kenneth Read focuses on a tavern, The Columbia, a generally recognized gathering place for homosexual men. Read's main interest is the patrons' behavior styles, rather than "homosexual culture," a concept he thinks is of dubious validity (p. 13). Read links The Columbia to a much wider urban context than a local homosexual subculture, indeed to a theme that goes to the heart of this entire book:

> The virtue of cities lies in their very diversity. In a mass population comprising many different patterns of life and experience, it is far easier to find others with whom you can be "at home" than in the monolithic and self-contained small community. Cities have been misjudged. Public attention has focused upon crime, violence, slums, and all the other evils that are unquestionably a part of urban life and more manifest in cities than elsewhere simply because they contain the highest concentrations of population. But there is another side to the life of cities. If there is no longer a monolithic structure of American values, if that ideal has been shattered by over a hundred years of constant change and the failure of enculturative institutions to reproduce generation after generation of people who have internalized the same verities, cities are places where all the fragments can be found, where, rather than being lost in the faceless crowd, it is possible to find a reassuring and mutually supportive place with others in the kaleidoscope (pp. 175–76).

Like Castells, Edmund White (1980) is very much concerned about homosexual political activism, gay liberation, and the like, and also about the intricate nuances of individuals' activist commitment or lack of it. That urban homosexuality in American cities is a congeries of life-styles is amply illustrated in his book. He emphasizes the great variety in New York City, at the same time stressing the "cult of success" that affects New York homosexuals and heterosexuals alike (p. 250). During his tour of American cities, doing interviews and participant observation, he notes in passing the residential concentrations of homosexuals in various cities, for example Chicago (p. 166), Boston (p. 275), and Washington (p. 295).

Especially in his lengthy discussion of homosexuals in San Francisco, White's social, as opposed to sexual, concerns become manifest. Like Castells, White notes that while homosexuals have been in the forefront of restoring old parts of the city, they have, like other gentrifying landlords, been responsible for dispossessing poor blacks and Hispanics from their former homes. Not only that, but many San Francisco homosexuals, though themselves targets of prejudice, are racists (pp. 55–58).

The Subcultures of Pastimes

Leisure-time activities have a more prominent place in urban life than is obvious in much of the urban studies literature. Street life, neighborhood activities, and the attractions of many kinds of local hangouts have vital importance in the humanity of cities. The emphasis, however, is usually on these locales as focuses for social identity and cohesion. Their importance as arenas for fun and recreation frequently receives secondary consideration, if any at all. Fun, indeed joyfulness, is found in such diverse locales as the neighborhood bars in Seville that are typical of all southern European cities, the pubs of British cities, and the sidewalk sociability of working-class areas like Chicago's Near West Side (Suttles) and Boston's West End as it used to be (Gans). Leisure-time activities and interests are prominent in the studies of the elderly and homosexuals discussed above.

But what of leisure-time activities for their own sake, and their effects on cities?

> There are groups that follow professional sports, musical genres, art forms, and the like, and they often include a core of heavily committed members (for example, the people in fan clubs that travel to their teams' away games). . . . Does urbanism encourage involvement in hobby-based subcultures? One part of the answer is clear: urbanism, in northern California, and no doubt elsewhere, supports formal institutions and services for the hobbyist. Cities have more art galleries, stores, instructional services, and museums for the artist; more tennis stores, clubs, and teachers for the tennis buff; and so on (Fischer 1982:224).

Increasingly prominent in the fabric of Western industrial cities is the great popularity of spectator sports, accompanied by new forms of large-scale communal identities and intercity rivalries, the construction and maintenance of enormous sports arenas, and accompanying problems of public crowding.

SUBCULTURES OF VIOLENCE

Though public exhibitions of violence are nothing new, the violence for its own sake of prize fights and professional wrestling is made all the more conspicuous through the medium of television, as are the impromptu eruptions among players and spectators at team spectator events in which violence is not an intrinsic feature. Without knowing what proportion of urban populations are actually involved in this behavior, we cannot assess its significance. Attempts to assess the effects of simulated violence on television have yielded contradictory and inconclusive results. In any case, the emergence of a "culture of violence" concerns some observers. Being the victim of violence is widespread in Western industrial cities. While the frequency of such violence is considerable, it is less than the publicity about it would suggest. Nevertheless, fear of it is so pervasive that it has become an urban phenomenon in its own right. That fear of violence can exaggerate its actual prevalence has been shown by research in British cities (Baldwin and Bottoms 1976:158–59). That expressed fear of violence is, to an important degree, actually fear of the heterogeneity of misunderstood subcultures is the theme of a research project in an American city (Merry 1981:14–15).

The specific concept of a subculture of violence appears originally to have been formulated in 1967 by Marvin Wolfgang and Franco Ferracuti (1982:140 and passim). These authors amassed an impressive body of data and theory from biological, psychiatric, psychometric, sociological, and anthropological sources to support their thesis that a variety of different cultures contains a subculture of violence. In other words, subcultures of violence occur cross-culturally. Participants in these subcultures are predominantly young men (p. 260). Most of these authors' extended examples of the subculture encompass rural and urban areas; they explicitly state that violence "is not the product of cities alone," but they do assert that "the contemporary American city has the accoutrements not only for the genesis but also for the highly accelerated development of this subculture" (p. 298). As far as Third World cultures are concerned, "it is not the disturbance of the social equilibrium alone that may make violence a viable way of life for many people. It is a culture, or contra-culture, that makes physical aggression a virtue, often with political or religious justifications" (p. 270). We explore these and related ideas further, in various urban contexts, and from various points of view.

Yablonsky's characterization of violent boys' gangs as sociopathic is well grounded and, considering the nature of violence, understandably judgmental in tone. R. Lincoln Keiser's study (1969) of a large "federation" of boys' gangs in Chicago has an objective, ethnographic tone, but the realities are essentially the same. He presents the "Vice Lords" as having a definite social organization including sections and subsections, and involving mutual aid among fellow members (p. 53), but their various activities are primarily violent for the sake of group and individual status. The gang bang is not, in this case, a violent sexual activity, but a fight between gangs and one of their most important street happenings (p. 29). However, activities that are far more frequent are "hustling"—any way of making money other than holding a job—and "wolf packing." Hustling includes armed robbery; wolf packing consists of one or more members' committing assault in order to enhance their status (pp. 34–35). Prostitutes, drug pushers, and gang bangers continue to bedevil the residents of working class neighborhoods in Chicago (Keegan 1987:A–1).

No single or consistent cause of violent, public behavior has been identified, but among the ingredients are hatred born of socioeconomic hopelessness and the emergence of a subcultural ethic that makes violence a virtue. Contributory factors include serious flaws in the criminal justice system (Lundsgaarde 1977; R. Starr 1985:24). In Houston in 1969, more than half the homicides went unpunished. Henry Lundsgaarde not only interprets this situation in terms of faults in the legal system, but also raises questions about the values-system of a culture which, in effect, renders homicide acceptable in a large number of cases (chapter 7).

It is instructive to compare the discussion above with Willmott's observations of adolescent boys in Bethnal Green. They had gangs, and many had been in trouble with the police, primarily for stealing (1969:144–45). But violence was another matter.

> There is, locally and particularly among the adolescent boys, a general "cult of toughness," a respect for physical prowess and for "spirit," which sometimes pushes into aggression even boys who have no special taste for it. But in practice the "toughness" is much more a matter of convention or folklore than of day-to-day behaviour. There was plenty of evidence that most boys seldom fought and disliked violence . . . systematic fighting and mob battles are a rare occurrence in the East End. A 16 year old said, "There are some who say they fight with bottles and knives and go out for big punch-ups and all that, but it's mostly talk" (pp. 152–53).

A small minority of boys was given to violence and hooliganism. Willmott ascribes this tendency to the sense of failure and frustration of being poor and unsuccessful in a culture where success and affluence are primary goals, but this "still does not tell us why certain boys respond to a poor school record and a low-status job with a sense of frustration and bitterness, while others whose experience is apparently similar do not" (p. 166).

This inconclusiveness reminds us of Mancini's delineation of different personality types emerging from different familial influences among American urban poor people. But the most striking difference is that the oppression of ethnic and racial discrimination was absent from the Bethnal Green scene.

During the last half of the twentieth century, political terrorism has become a fact of everyday life in many cities of the world. Whether or not the unprovoked murder or mutilation, or merely the intimidation, of noncombatant persons is justified by the hoped-for achievement of some worthy goal, political terrorism is a different dimension of the subculture of violence from that we have been considering. In the cities of Northern Ireland and Lebanon, terrorist acts are skirmishes in civil wars. In many cities (and countrysides) of Latin America, terrorism has been one of the weapons of urban guerillas fighting against the oppression of militaristic governments (Kohl and Litt 1974:110–11). The Palestinian and Islamic groups using terrorist tactics in European cities have adopted the only weaponry at their disposal against the overwhelming military force of countries like the United States and its allies such as Israel and the former Pahlavi regime in Iran.

To reiterate a major theme of this book: the genesis of urban terrorism as it is currently experienced is not intrinsic to city life per se. The cause and solutions of the many grievances involved lie beyond any particular city. They lie in national and international politics.

BUREAUCRATIC SUBCULTURES AND THE PROBLEMS OF SCALE

Bureaucratic organizations employ many city dwellers, but there are many different kinds of bureaucracies: governmental agencies, business firms, and educational and public and private health institutions. Given this variety, anyone who is employed by one bureaucracy (and so a member of that system) is also a client of (an outsider to) other bureaucracies. One would hope that these millions of role reversals would result in innumerable considerate and empathetic interactions between bureaucrats and clients. Instead, clients' encounters with bureaucrats are notorious for the inflexible, dehumanized behavior of the latter and the helpless frustration of the former. The urban individual or small group often experiences the full force of anonymous depersonalization in encounters with bureaucrats and bureaucratic agencies. The causes are many and beyond the scope of this chapter.

Our purposes here are to recognize that bureaucratic subcultures must be considered among all the other subcultures constituting the heterogeneity of cities and that in encounters with bureaucratic institutions, the large-scale dimensions of urban life have their major impact on the small-scale realities of individuals and small groups. The following account illustrates several of the principal issues:

> In the Berkeley Complaint Project . . . we investigated a complaint about one child and one law. An eight-year-old child with his shirttail hanging out was engulfed in flames within two to three seconds after a match touched the cloth. The surgeon . . . suggested that the victim's parents complain to the Consumer Product Safety Commission. Their letter . . . asked simply:

"Why did the shirt burn so rapidly?" One month later the CPSC replied . . . "We will take whatever action is indicated." The parents' question remained unanswered. In our subsequent field research we examined the roles of the federal flammability laws, W. T. Grant (the retailer), the National Retail Merchants Association, the American Textile Manufacturers Institute, the Senate Commerce Committee, the Cone Mills Corporation, the Department of Commerce, the White House, a presidential campaign finance chairman, the Consumer Product Safety Commission, the Federal Trade Commission, and other hierarchies organizationally related to the child [who] suffered the burns. This research uncovered an incredible amount of interaction between industry and government groups, with each organization intent on organizational survival. The relationship between these organizations and the family and child affected by their actions was minimal. . . . The parents' question, "Why did the shirt burn so rapidly?" was one that the CPSC was not willing to face. The full answer is as complex as America itself. In tracing a case such as this one, the anthropologist becomes aware of the constraints that organizations place on the people working within them, and of the importance that direct interaction has in influencing decisions. Most large organizations are not set up to be responsive to the public or, in this case, a child (Nader 1980:38–39).

That bureaucrats are frequently constrained within their own organizations is illustrated by the case of a community mental health center in a low-income, multiethnic area of a large midwestern city (Schwartzman 1980:47). The center opened in the early 1970s with great enthusiasm, based on its staff's conviction that it would really become *the* community mental health center. Soon, however, the staff was beset by internal and external criticisms—some contradictory—that seriously affected its service (p. 48). This situation came about because the federal and state bureaucracies that controlled the center conceived of it as if it were a patient in a mental hospital.
This may sound peculiar, but it is really the logical consequence of a state mental health department, encouraged by federal financial support, attempting to move out of the business of direct service, but continuing to use an institutional model of direct service to patients for establishing relations with new direct service providers (community mental health agencies). The funding bureaucracies have placed a community agency between themselves and individual patients without changing the model of the relationship, placing these new agencies in the role of a patient *in* the hospital (i.e., community) (pp. 49–50).

The removal of bureaucrats in service organizations from direct involvement with their clients is exemplified by Fred Goldner's account of his experiences as a management official of the Health and Hospitals Corporation (HHC) of New York City, a semiautonomous corporation running New York City's 17 municipal hospitals and ambulance service on a $1.2 billion budget (1984:227). Most of its funds came from Medicaid, Medicare, and Blue Cross reimbursements and from municipal tax levies. Goldner recounts his observations of the criticisms the city's mass media leveled at the HHC (for mismanagement or waste of funds, for example), frequently abetted by politicians seeking favorable publicity with one segment of the public at the expense of poor people who would directly suffer from cuts in hospital budgets and staffs (pp. 221–22). Goldner says nothing about the direct relationships between patients and staff, but his account does provide some appreciation of the predicament of an organization that must struggle for its own survival.

A different dimension of bureaucratic survival is the profit motive—the driving force of business corporations. Saving costs by replacing human workers with computers and self-service schemes is a major reason for increasingly poor service to American customers. "Personal service has become a maddeningly rare commodity in the American marketplace. Flight attendants, salesclerks and bank tellers all seem to have become too scarce and too busy to give consumers much attention. Many other service workers are underpaid, untrained and unmotivated for their jobs, to the chagrin of customers who look to them for help" says Stephen Koepp in a *Time* magazine cover story (1987:49). He carefully recounts the stresses caused by service employees' discourtesies and inefficiencies despite the increasing importance of service businesses in the American economy. Short-sighted management policies concerned only with profits, not with customers or employees as human beings, are blamed. Many people would regard this as classic bureaucratic behavior.

Koepp cites Arlie Hochschild's *The Managed Heart* (1983) for its coining of the term "emotional labor." Hochschild says emotional labor is a necessary skill in jobs requiring face-to-face or voice-to-voice contact with the public, requiring the worker to produce an emotional state in another person, and in which the employer has some control, through training and supervision, over the employees' emotional states (p. 147). Her book focuses on airline flight attendants, their training and experiences on the job. Emotional labor, while essential for maintaining public civility, may result in excessive stress and a general numbing of any feelings (pp. 187–88).

The final example of a bureaucratic subculture is a reprise on the subcultures of power and poverty, discussed earlier in this chapter, as well as an illustration of the problems involved in the interface of small-scale everyday life with the large-scale subcultures that affect it. Jack Newfield and Paul Du Brul's book, *The Abuse of Power* (1977) examines what they call the "permanent government" of New York City. Several excerpts set forth the book's main points pertinent to our concerns.

Ultimate power of public policy in New York is invisible and unelected. It is exercised by a loose confederation of bankers, bond underwriters, members of public authorities, the big insurance companies, political fund-raisers, publishers, law firms, builders, judges, backroom politicians, and some union leaders. The power of this interlocking network of elites is based on the control of institutions, money, property, and the law-making process (p. 75).

This permanent government is not an invincible conspiracy. It is only a creative self-interest of the rich. It sometimes can be beaten, as when the 50,000 residents of Co-op City waged a thirteen-month rent strike in 1975–76 that successfully conquered a rent increase. Or when neighborhood activists stopped the Lower Manhattan Expressway in 1967 (p. 76).

There are about 1500 or 2000 people in New York City who have pieces of a power that is decisive, concealed, and therefore unaccountable. And over the past fifteen years, this group, plus three mayors and a governor, has been responsible for the policies and decisions that have swept New York to the lip of ruin. These 1500 or 2000 people all know each other and deal with each other as members of the same club (p. 77).

These are the institutions that controlled the decisions which helped New York City decline and go broke: to invest billions of dollars in a World's Fair and a World Trade Center; to bulldoze and redline neighborhoods ...; to build highrise luxury housing rather than restore and renovate existing housing for moderate-income families ... to keep the Port Authority's surplus funds from being used to subsidize mass transit; to loot and ruin the Mitchell-Lama housing program that should have kept the middle-class in New York City (pp. 80–81).

Newfield and Du Brul include a chapter on organized crime—the Mafia. In our terms, it is a subculture, and

a separate permanent government in New York City. It is dangerous, corrupting, and virtually all-powerful in specialized areas like the waterfront, the garment center, and the private carting industry. It holds, through the threat of force, cartel franchises on illegal services like narcotics, loansharking, gambling, pornography, and prostitution. Its dominant role in the international heroin traffic makes the mob one of the central villains of this book. But, ultimately, organized crime has less economic and political power than the biggest banks, insurance companies, corporations, and utilities (p. 254).

Newfield and Du Brul scornfully refute the romanticized semiheroic godfather image promoted in certain media.

Low-level Mafia men walk out of restaurants on Mulberry Street without paying the bill—because they are so cheap.... Powerful mob bosses like Carmine Galente are as bestial as the most vicious elevator mugger you will ever read about.... Mafiosi are not Bogarts or Brandos. They are mean, greedy, small-minded men. "Mutts," as Joe Hynes likes to call them (p. 253).

In further comment and insight on ethnic subcultures, Italian-American leaders in San Francisco "reflect a clear awareness of the status distinctions made by the region of their ancestors' origins, even though they came a century ago. To them, the Mafiosos are southerners who are 'ignorant greaseballs'" (Wirt 1974:233n).

The following is an unusually comprehensive yet concise statement of the realities of bureaucratic life (in New York City) and problems of scale.

Almost all citizens come into contact at some point in their lives with school systems and health-care organizations; millions of city dwellers are on welfare; all are conscious of the police either as a source of protection or harassment, and some are processed through the police-courts-prison complex. Lower-level employees in these agencies—teachers, social workers, nurses, clerks, policemen, lower-court judges—most directly represent government to the governed. These contacts are fraught with tension. Low-level bureaucrats are in extremely sensitive positions, but, unlike local machine politicians, they lack the affective ties that bind party bosses to followers. They constantly interact with the public and have a great deal of power over the lives of captive clients. *The bureaucrats, moreover, are hardly ever responsible to those nonvoluntary clienteles, but are rather, accountable to their bureaucratic supervisors* [emphasis added].

The bureaucrats have difficult jobs. They must typically operate in an environment that makes it impossible for them to satisfy their professional goals. Too often the resources available to them are inadequate in part because of the dependency of cities. There are too many children in the classroom; the court caseload is impossibly heavy; not enough policemen are available in high-crime areas. Bureaucrats work in a situation in which their authority is challenged regularly and in which there is a higher than average possibility of physical and psychic threat.

To deal with these work-related circumstances, they act in ways that heighten urban conflict. Policemen may come to see and treat all young blacks as potential criminals. Lower-court judges process cases so quickly as to transform judicial decision making into administrative routinization. Social workers often penalize clients who rebel against the agency's routines. Health-clinic doctors and nurses, under the pressure of their workload, may act as if their patients were not human. As a result of this kind of activity, the gap between bureaucrat and client inevitably grows, as does discontent with a remote, unresponsive, irresponsible urban government. This process of interaction, in short, takes on a dynamic of its own that is profoundly alienating (Katznelson 1981:129–30).

SUGGESTED ADDITIONAL READING

Cavallo, Dominick. *Muscles and Morals: Organized Playgrounds and Urban Reform, 1880–1920.* Philadelphia: University of Pennsylvania Press, 1981. A very informative account of people like Jane Addams, Jacob Riis, and Luther H. Gulick who believed in the reality and hope of the ethnic melting pot of the United States.

Clinard, Marshall B. *Cities with Little Crime: The Case of Switzerland.* Cambridge, England: Cambridge University Press, 1978. This study focuses on Zürich, a city that is relatively homogeneous and where Swiss culture minimizes violence. Clinard does not deny the presence of "white-collar crime." "Little crime" is not intrinsic to this city, but rather is a concomitant of the larger society's values.

Cohen, Abner, ed. *Urban Ethnicity.* London: Tavistock, 1974. The contributing authors analyze urban ethnicity in half a dozen very different countries.

The Obvious Illusion: Murals from the Lower East Side. Photographs by Philip Pocock, introduction by Gregory Battcock. New York: George Braziller, 1980. Consists of color photographs of Hispanic murals painted on buildings in New York's Lower East Side. These murals are not sleazy graffiti, but striking and sometimes beautiful expressions of life and feelings in an ethnic slum.

Partridge, William L. *The Hippie Ghetto: The Natural History of a Subculture.* New York: Holt, Rinehart & Winston, 1973. Whether or not there is a "subculture of drugs," this book is a good description of a self-consciously drug-using group in an urban setting.

Wikan, Unni. *Beyond the Veil in Sohar.* Baltimore: Johns Hopkins University, 1982. Wikan is a Norwegian anthropologist, and the wife of Fredrik Barth, cited elsewhere in this book. In Cairo and Sohar, Oman, she had the wonderful and rare opportunity of observing the women's subcultures first hand. Her observations are a breakthrough in the understanding of women's subcultures in the Middle Eastern Cities.

The Subculture of Youth

Kazin, Alfred. *A Walker in the City.* New York: Harcourt Brace Jovanovich, undated reprint of 1951 ed.

Richler, Mordecai. *The Street*. Harmondsworth, England: Penguin, 1969.
Kazin and Richler grew up in Jewish neighborhoods in New York City and Montreal, respectively, and these books amusingly and eloquently chronicle how their lives expanded from the carefully detailed small local scale to the larger world. All of us, regardless of ethnic identity, will remember comparable experiences.

8
Agenda for the Humanity of Cities

World Bank Photo

The agenda proposed here is intended for all behavioral scientists who want to commit their urban research to deepening and extending our knowledge of how the humanity of cities may be augmented and enhanced and, correspondingly, of how the inhumanities that afflict life in cities may be minimized. It is also intended to stimulate and encourage anyone who is concerned about the quality of life in cities.

Previous chapters have presented many detailed examples of the humane and inhumane in city life, often intertwined with each other. Let us summarize six major conclusions derived from these studies:

(1) Most of the negative assumptions about the intrinsic nature of city life contained in the bipolar moralistic model are contradicted by empirical findings on occupational communities, connections, and subcultures.

(2) Destructive vicissitudes are evidence of the fragility and vulnerability of the urban fabric, but they do not mean that cities are doomed because they are inherently evil.

(3) Stereotyped groups are not monolithic but are, rather, internally diverse. Intergroup contacts, while they can generate conflict and tension, can also increase awareness of diversity and therefore counteract monolithic stereotyping.

(4) The humanity of cities can be adequately comprehended only from both the small-scale (microcosmic) and large-scale (macrocosmic) perspectives. Observing urban life from only one perspective results in a distorted view of reality.

(5) Among the large-scale components of urban life that impinge on small-scale life are powerful interest groups which tend to be greedy for profit and more power, frequently to the detriment of the lives of the powerless who may remain helplessly exploited or may respond with grass-roots movements.

(6) Megascale components of urban life exist beyond any particular city. We refer to them as societywide, national, or international factors that are not intrinsic to cities. They include overpopulation, rural socioeconomic deterioration, water and topsoil depletion, and worldwide national budget allocations that deflect huge armaments expenditures from more constructive needs and purposes. All of these affect cities, mostly adversely, although armament manufacture, from a limited perspective, can be beneficial in terms of jobs.

In previous chapters, we have repeatedly mentioned the various research methods and orientations urban scholars use. Instead of summarizing that material here, we highlight it and the urban agenda by noting some new directions proposed for urban anthropology. Essentially, they can be distilled into refining small-scale research on the one hand and, on the other, undertaking research on the large-scale dimensions of urban life.

Lawrence Watson (1981) and Owen Lynch (1979) call for greater sensitivity to the differences between "etic" and "emic" research. These terms have not been used heretofore because they are anthropological jargon. However, the actors' perspectives discussed at the very beginning of the book are essentially what is meant by emic perspectives. Etic research, in contrast, imposes a theoretical model external to the behavior being observed. The modernization model, with its marginality corollary, and the bipolar model are two etic constructs that have required emic modifications. Watson (p. 444), in criticizing his own previous research on Guajiro Indian migrants in Maracaibo, Venezuela, shows that emic perspectives on his data yield more realistic results. Lynch (pp. 20–21) reaches the same conclusion about squatters in Bombay who turn out to be far more diversified than the Marxian model of exploited slum dwellers would predict. Although he does not mention the emic/etic issue by name, Kerry Feldman (1975:365) shows that well-established concepts of the nature of squatter economics do not stand up under detailed ethnographic scrutiny that is free of older preconceptions.

The need for anthropological, and basically emic, research in the large-scale arena has been expressed in different ways. One is research on formal organizational life:

An understanding of how everyday activities, decisions, factions, and re-lationships actually work within an organization requires an analysis of informal social networks. Inside formal organizations, and often cross-cutting them, are systems of social relations that develop because people have "natural" affinities to others . . . based on class, sex, education, age, common interests, or whatever. No matter how or why they form, they are always there and affect organizational activity in a major way (Britan and Cohen 1980:14).

Applied anthropologists attempting to become cultural brokers for ethnic groups in their relations with a city power structure must study the power structure itself to be effective brokers as Carole Hill (1975:344) concludes in her research on the inadequate services provided ethnic groups in Atlanta.

While the understanding of a city's power structure involves the kinds of insight Gerald Britan and Ronald Cohen mention, it also involves a broad, holistic view. Joseph Bensman provides such a view of New York in his con-clusion to *The Apple Sliced*:

Any examination of all the types of communities, whether based on race, ethnicity, deviancy; profession, occupation, or class; or leisure, the arts or avocation; or . . . residence, spatial concentration, or ambience would sug-gest an almost uncountable number of specific communities in New York City and in the outlying areas into which these communities extend. Given these myriad of often unknown, unrelated, and conflicting communities, a central problem for the study of the city and for all urban sociology is the means by which these separate communities coexist and are integrated, at least to the extent that such integration exists. . . . [T]he basic question is, Why do all these separate communities and cultures not fly off in all di-rections or erupt in a war of all against all? (1984:341).

Megascale phenomena that are components of human nature, such as greed, fear, and hatred of the "other," are, as we have repeatedly seen, very much part of urban life, but they are not specific or intrinsic to cities, and their genesis and control are far beyond the expertise of urban scholars or, for that matter, any behavioral scientists.

What are not beyond scholarly expertise, however, are those megascale phenomena that are products of human actions, such as overpopulation and others mentioned above. Among them is deindustrialization, the decline in employment in industrial production that has reached major proportions in the United States and Great Britain, the two earliest societies to become industrial. In the 1980s, this process has involved plant closings, disastrous to many cities, and the flight of capital and manufacturing to Third World, low-wage areas. The immediate causes are the decisions of corporate executives. Katherine Newman (1985:6–12) and colleagues devote a triple issue of the journal, *Urban Anthropology*, to this subject. They emphasize the need to study and understand better the macroscale operational factors and the microscale effects.

The remainder of this chapter reviews a variety of ways in which the hu-manity of cities is asserted—bridges between subcultures, positive adaptations to distemic space, grass-roots movements, and the megascale phenomena that must be coped with rather than succumbed to.

DISSOLVING BOUNDARIES

Conflicts between subcultures are typical of urban life but not necessarily permanent. Ronald Bayor (1978:chapters 8 & 9) shows how the conflicts among Jews, Irish, Germans, and Italians in New York City that peaked between the two world wars were resolved with effective leadership (often slow in coming) and recognition that there were vital interests in conflict resolution. Gentrification processes in Auckland, New Zealand (Loomis 1980:193–95), and in a northeastern United States city (Williams 1985:270–71) have placed into juxtaposition groups differentiated by social class and ethnicity. Still in the process of change and adjustments, barriers remain among these groups. Whether the barriers would be breached remained to be seen at the times of observation.

Ethnic barriers can be weakened by attenuation and at the same time leave intragroup support systems intact. For example, among members of the nuclear Japanese community of Seattle, there has been extensive marriage to outsiders. Nevertheless, the women, in particular, maintain contacts in the interest of group solidarity (Leonetti and Newell-Morris 1982:31). In Hong Kong, Gregory Guldin distinguishes between ethnic neighborhoods and ethnic communities and illustrates them with examples of two minority Chinese groups. One is composed of immigrants from Shanghai, the other of people originally from Fujian who had sojourned in the Philippines (part of the extensive "overseas Chinese" presence in Southeast Asia and the Western Pacific). At an earlier time, both groups had their own ethnic neighborhoods (geographically concentrated multifunctional support systems). In time, the Shanghainese neighborhood dissolved, but an ethnic community, a dispersed network of kin and friendship ties, remained (1980:257). Guldin sees this process as a kind of evolution in which the intensity of ethnic ties, and changes in it, needs to be measured.

THE SPIRIT OF ACCOMMODATION

Howard Becker and Irving Louis Horowitz claim that in San Francisco a "culture of civility" eases tensions among various "deviant" groups, although it does not characterize social class and ethnic differences. Its achievement, they admit, is problematic, but it is not a figment of utopian imagination. "Accommodation requires, as a first condition, that the parties involved prize peace and stability enough to give up some of what they want so that the others may have their desires satisfied as well" (1971:15).

An innovative type of accommodation in United States cities is the communal household that does not "accord with stereotyped notions of what living in a group is like. Members of these groups haven't withdrawn from society— they don't follow a guru or require one another to hold any faith in common. Their goal is simply to live together in a way that is caring and fun" (Raimy 1979:4). These households have a great diversity of membership arrangements other than conventional family groups. Communal motivations are economic help, housekeeping efficiency, concern for the environment, and concern about personal growth. "There is one underlying motivation that is the most important reason people join or start communal households . . . 'companionship,

security, and a supportive atmosphere' " (Raimy 1979:14–15). These ties counteract the subcultural identities we have considered.

Community newspapers often heighten awareness of local issues in American cities. An unusual one is *The Tenderloin Times,* serving San Francisco's
Tenderloin district and published in four languages: Vietnamese, Khmer, Lao,
and English. Indochinese immigrants now amount to half the district's population.

> Given the diverse nature of the area, the paper has to "promote a greater
> sense of understanding of the different communities," Waters [the editor]
> says. "We've tried to break down some of the cultural barriers that exist
> just by letting people know who their neighbors are, and what kinds of
> things they went through." *The Tenderloin Times* English section, the bulk
> of the paper, often runs stories about the refugee community, while the
> Asian pages frequently explain the various kinds of social services available
> (Quinones 1986:16).

Local response to the paper has been "amazingly good," and it is highly regarded by the city's mainstream media.

Generalizing from his observations of Levittown, Herbert Gans suggests a
living arrangement that seems feasible and could be widely applicable:

> Putting together all the arguments for and against homogeneity suggests
> that the optimum solution, at least in communities of homeowners who are
> raising small children, is *selective homogeneity at the block level* and *het-
> erogeneity at the community level.* Whereas a mixture of population types,
> and especially of rich and poor, is desirable in the community, as a whole,
> heterogeneity on the block will not produce the intended tolerance, but will
> lead to conflict that is undesirable because it is essentially insoluble and
> thus becomes chronic. Selective homogeneity on the block will improve the
> tenor of neighbor relations, and will thus make it easier—although not
> easy—to realize heterogeneity at the community level (Gans 1967:172).

By "block" Gans means "an area in which frequent face-to-face relations take
place, in most cases *a sub-block* of perhaps ten to twelve houses" (p. 172).

THE PROXIMITY OF HETEROGENEITY

Morris Milgram, a developer of integrated neighborhoods, reviews what has
been accomplished in open housing and the difficulties that must be overcome
by continually vigilant organized action. Where integration has been most
successful, different groups have perceived important interests or characteristics that they have in common (1977:65).

"Dover Square" is a multiethnic housing project in a large northeastern
American city. In 1975–76, about half of its resident families were Chinese,
one-quarter black, 12 percent white, and 6 percent Hispanic. In 1976, "it had
the highest per capita rate of robberies and assaults in the city. . . . Yet in a
survey of 101 residents, 75 percent said they did not think the project was
dangerous" (Merry 1981:9). Nevertheless, 56 percent were afraid to walk
around the neighborhood at night. Sally Merry analyzes these and other apparent anomalies. The physical layout of the project makes surveillance of
distemic space difficult (discouraging the self-policing of neighborhoods Jane
Jacobs emphasizes), and members of the four ethnic groups are scattered
evenly throughout the project (contrary to Gans's recommendation of block

homogeneity combined with community heterogeneity). Merry believes that crime and fear of crime operate in Dover Square in a self-reinforcing system that is fundamentally fear of strange and unknown "others" (p. 14). Dover Square residents have more otherness than, perhaps, they can cope with, coupled with the neighborhood's being in a transitional area where economic depression is a major problem. A variety of avoidance strategies prevents residents from learning to interact with members of other groups (p. 224).

Greater intergroup knowledge and recognition of common interests despite differences are needed to reduce intergroup hostilities:

> The two successful interethnic organizations in the project are an infant care center and a day care program for older children, . . . essential for working mothers. People who work long hours are probably less inclined to devote time to organizations that satisfy only diffuse community needs or purely social or recreational ends if these organizations appear to be at all unsafe or uncomfortable.
>
> The solution to urbanites' and suburbanites' fear of the city is not . . . more locks, bars, and guard dogs, or an enhanced police presence, but greater knowledge of the city and its residents (p. 241).

Ignorance exacerbates fear of the unknown, which exacerbates intergroup fears and hostilities.

Annemarie Bleiker, comparing her own and another study among working-class people in Cambridge, Mass., finds that close friendships and kin ties are not necessarily localized, as formulated by the "proximity model" others espouse. Members of the neighborhood she studied established strong relationships among one another but retained kin ties and friendships with more distant people. A sense of commitment to the neighborhood was the bridge across ethnic and other differences such as being oldtimers or newcomers (1972:172).

CROSS-CUTTING SUBCULTURAL BOUNDARIES

We have already cited several cases in which actors' interests and the characteristics they share with members of other groups override subcultural boundaries. This situation seems most frequently to occur when members of different racial/ethnic subcultures realize that they belong to the same social class subculture. Although this process may, one hopes, reduce the virulence of intergroup prejudices, it would seem to extend and augment social ties rather than replace one type with another as is certainly the case in three cities of sub-Saharan Africa. Jos (Nigeria), Kampala-Mengo (Uganda), and Nairobi (Kenya) are inhabited by a great variety of tribal and regional groups, and all remain intact as support and identity systems for their members. However, in each city some people have also developed wider social ties. In Jos,

> ethnic groups attempt to project a favorable image. Since they intend to stay, they want to remain on good terms. They may donate their assembly hall for some civic purpose or rent it to other ethnic, social, business, or political groups. Through fines or other sanctions, they attempt to control their members' behavior so as not to damage the tribe's reputation in the community. Ethnic groups express pride in their traditions by holding public performances of plays, masquerades, and native dances. When they seek to raise money by staging formal dances, they may court community good-

will by inviting prominent individuals of other ethnic groups to serve as hosts or masters of ceremony (Plotnicov 1967:292).

Much of Leonard Plotnicov's presentation on Jos consists of interview material with a small number of individuals, of whom he says:

> Regardless of the strength of tribal loyalties and the depth of parochial village sentiments, even the most traditional men relate positively, as individuals, to Jos' conditions. For example, the Yoruba informant could express both humaneness and friendship when asked to intercede and help settle the family disputes of his Hausa neighbors. The Tiv shared the delightful pastime of African drafts [checkers] with Yoruba men of his age, and had established a joking type of relationship with an old Hausa woman who lived across the street and who was friendly with his wife. The Ijaw informant's closest personal friends reflected a variety of ethnic backgrounds, and he also demonstrated civic responsibility when he occasionally gave (upon invitation) free professional advice to the Township Advisory Council and to his church congregation (p. 291).

In Nairobi, political participation since Kenya gained independence has evolved into a complex interweaving of ethnic and social class identities.

> Social class and tribe are not necessarily incompatible with each other as principles of social and political division. In fact, the two can operate at the same time in producing political divisions in a society.... [I]ndividuals tend not only to be associated with other people of their own ethnic group but also with people from their own social status. [The] ... well educated tend to have friends who are also well educated, while poor people also associate with other poor people. At the same time, they also tend to associate with people from their own tribe.
>
> Class and ethnicity have a different importance in different areas of political life.... [P]olitical participation and information are related to class and not ethnicity, ... attitudes toward the government since independence are a function of ethnicity, ... assessments of living conditions since independence are determined by both class and ethnicity, and ... formal group membership and the belief that politicians are overpaid are related to neither class nor ethnicity (Ross 1975:135–36).

In Kampala-Mengo, residents have evolved a citywide political system, including kinship modes of interaction, not identical with any intratribal political system. At the same time, specific tribal patterns of behavior continue to operate in the domestic sphere in two structures: "a first-order one of the widest level concerning the distribution of power, authority, and economic opportunity in the single urban system of relations; and a second-order one of the urban domestic life of individual ethnic groups whose rural home systems of land tenure, marriage, residence and descent have great relevance" (Parkin 1969:192).

GATEKEEPERS AND BROKERS

Gatekeepers, and, especially, brokers, mediate between minority individuals and bureaucratic agencies. Peter Snyder, introducing his data on the gatekeepers of five ethnic neighborhoods in Los Angeles, reviews the considerable cross-cultural literature on the subject and makes a clear distinction between gatekeepers and cultural brokers. Both provide links between members of a local ethnic enclave and the larger society, but the broker has a greater role as an innovator and mediator between the small subculture and large dominant culture. The broker is able to function in both contexts. The gatekeeper is more likely to be a member of the minority ethnic group and facilitates adaptation rather than innovation.

Snyder interviewed Anglos, Arabs, blacks, Chicanos, and Native Americans who had migrated to Los Angeles. The percentages of them who know of gatekeepers in their midst are, respectively, 48, 52, 70, 43, and 61, and actual use of them is, respectively, 10, 40, 40, 30, and 10 (1976:43). The main services gatekeepers furnish are locating housing and employment and providing legal, medical, and general advice including economic counseling. The most frequently used service is giving medical advice and aid. For example,

Ms. G. was born in a small village near Guadalajara, Mexico, and came to the United States eight years ago. In Mexico she had some training as a nurse's aid and as a midwife. People came to her for medical advice, medical care, and midwifing services. Ms. G. on occasion dispenses store-bought medicines, but usually sends her "clients" to one of two Spanish-speaking doctors who she says are good and will charge only nominal fees. When asked why she does not send people to the local county public health agencies and clinics she responds, "They don't like Mexicans there. They give bad treatment. They do not speak Spanish very much and do not explain well to the people what is the matter with them" (p. 46).

Snyder interviewed 18 gatekeepers. They have an average of 15 gatekeeping contacts a week, and about half of them also have full-time jobs. So gatekeeping involves them in considerable extra work. When asked why they do it, most indicate that they don't know or they want to help their people. While some gatekeepers are busybodies or status-seekers, others are truly altruistic (pp. 46–47).

Bernard Wong's monograph on New York City's Chinatown mentions the increasing activity of cultural brokers in its behalf (1982:97). From a population of 500 in the 1870s, Chinatown now has grown to 75 thousand people, and newcomers continue to arrive, many by way of San Francisco (p. 27). The community is highly organized and has formal associational links with Chinese communities in a number of other North American cities. Its inhabitants are highly diversified. They include people whose families have been in America for generations and recent refugees from Vietnam, a few upper-class people, and many middle- and working-class ones (p. 35).

Chinese cultural brokers in New York have been motivated by several developments since the 1960s: availability of Affirmative Action and Community Development Program funds, the influence of black and Hispanic ethnic movements, and realization that they are still a discriminated-against minority. The brokers have a variety of occupations, but they are well educated, aged 20 to 40, mostly middle-class American born, and living outside Chinatown. Knowledgeable about Chinese and American culture, they are dissatisfied with the traditional leadership structure of Chinatown with its patrons and coteries of poor clients (p. 97).

BUREAUCRATIC SUBCULTURES AND THE "OTHERS"

Whether individual bureaucrats do or can mediate between their institutional rules and perceptions of reality, on the one hand, and their clients, on the other, is a crucial question for the humanity of cities. As yet, there is no definitive answer because there is very little reliable information about it, only fragmentary glimpses. One such glimpse is a study of the Boston Housing Authority (BHA) (Pynoos 1986).

Regarding processes of tenant selection, the BHA faced a situation in which "over the years, family public housing has experienced a shift from poor white tenants, either temporarily unemployed or working, to primarily welfare-dependent minority tenants" (p. 190). This change exacerbated a dilemma: whether to follow the first come-first served rule and thus treat everyone evenhandedly or to break the rules and give priority to applicants in the direst need. John Pynoos is concerned with how a bureaucratic agency wrestled with this dilemma. That it did so is a plus for the humanity of cities.

Nevertheless, gaps in empathy and understanding are enormous, and Lyle Shannon expresses this problem passionately:

Rather than to take the position that the culture of poverty must be accepted as an explanation for the failure of programs supposedly designed for the less fortunate, isn't it just as feasible to conclude that these programs were planned by persons with too little understanding, too little vision, too little scientific knowledge?

[H]ave we really planned for the movement of people from the South and Southwest to urban industrial communities? Have we attempted to help immigrants find a place in the community? Is the middle-class, suburban Welcome Wagon or its equivalent found in the inner city? Are state employment offices, the more or less official arm of the establishment for workers who are in transition . . ., located in imposing edifices, mainly staffed by middle-class, Anglo, English-speaking professionals, or are they decentralized, even decentralized to storefronts adjacent to bars and taverns? Are they staffed by persons who have the slightest ability or interest in empathizing with the less fortunate? . . . Is the neighborhood or community school seen as a community center for persons of all ages rather than an institution for children, a place to have them deposited while adult Anglos, both male and female, participate in the exciting world of professional and skilled work? . . . Are ADC [Aid to Dependent Children] mothers seen as prolific leeches on society or as loving, compassionate mothers, who, if given the opportunity to learn, may show us that they are as responsible and as capable of contributing to society as anyone else? (1979: 61).

DISTEMIC SPACE BEHAVIOR

Stressed Behavior and Its Remedies

Jonathan Freedman's landmark book, *Crowding and Behavior* (1975), refutes some long-held notions, based on experiments with rats and human beings under extremely artificial laboratory conditions, about the evil effects of high-density living. Extrapolations from these findings to everyday life in crowded cities fit neatly into the assumption that cities are inherently unlivable. Freedman's experiments and observations led him to conclude that

crowding by itself has neither good effects nor bad effects on people but rather *serves to intensify the individuals' typical reactions to the situation*. . . . Thus, people do not respond to density in a uniform way, they do not find it either always pleasant or always unpleasant. Rather, their response to density depends almost entirely on their response to the situation itself. Density acts primarily to make this response, whatever it is, stronger (pp. 89–90).

Sitting in a doctor's waiting room, taking a test in a class, waiting on line at an airport, or traveling in the New York subway are usually unpleasant experiences, and most people would agree that crowding makes them even more unpleasant. In contrast, watching a football game or a play, riding on a cable car in San Francisco, spending a day at an amusement park, and attending a cocktail party are pleasant experiences and for most people are made even more exciting and enjoyable when the density of people is fairly high. Crowding intensifies the normal reaction—making a bad experience worse and a good experience better (p. 93).

Freedman addresses his situational view of crowding stress to distemic space in New York City. While recognizing (as have others) that having to deal with too many anonymous people can have negative effects, he points out that encouraging interaction among different people is very important in connection with housing design (pp. 123–27). He also points out the vicious circle that fear of danger in distemic space can create. "[S]treets are dangerous . . . not because there are too many people on them, but because there are too few. . . . There is a self-fulfilling prophecy—you are afraid of the streets so you stay off them, so they become dangerous, thus providing a reason to be afraid of them" (pp. 132–33). Freedman makes the same point that Jane Jacobs and Sally Merry do.

Their points are valid, but there *are* serious problems regarding people's behavior in crowded distemic space. One reason may be that "once crowding is believed to produce stress, it becomes a negative influence and would be expected to have all sorts of bad effects" (Freedman 1975:82), but there seem to be other reasons as well.

Criminal violence aside, public incivility is a serious problem in Western industrial cities, and in all cities of the world (except for the revolutionary industrial ones) as far as vehicular traffic behavior is concerned.

A newspaper column notes Richard Valeriani's list in the *New York Times* (Cooper 1985:B–1) of 100 reasons why, "although New York is a swell place to visit, you wouldn't want to live there." The items include some that might well deter visitors: rampant incivility, graffiti, crosstown traffic, honking horns, cabbies and bicycle riders who run red lights, refuse and animal excrement on streets and sidewalks, diplomats who double park, obnoxious cops, Central Park after dark, men urinating in public, the subway, box radios, Times Square, potholes, and cabbies who tell you they don't want to take you where you want to go. The tone is humorous, but there is no question that the problems are real, and the distinction between legal and illegal incivility has become blurred. The following excerpts from an article in *New York Magazine* make the point forcibly:

Civility has begun to collapse just as surely as the city's services and the FDR Drive. Drivers . . . are breezing through red lights as never before. Mass transit passengers, many of them middle class, have suddenly begun smoking in subway trains and on platforms with impunity. . . . Midtown-office-building plazas, once considered an amenity of incentive zoning and a boon to strollers, have been so overrun by vagrants, drunks, and dope dealers that their owners . . . have begun closing them down or fencing them off. . . . The police department's 911 emergency number no longer automatically brings cops. When rookie transit cop Victor Sims broke up an attempted bank robbery . . . last July, the worst resistance he reported came from the 911 operator, who needed five minutes of persuasion to believe that the call was not a joke. Subways are not only twice as late and twice as likely to break down but they seem twice as filthy . . . [and] the decay, stench, and filth that permeate the system are intensifying passenger anger and disgust. . . . Last year, the police issued more than 500,000 summonses for such incivilities as leaving garbage cans uncovered, playing loud box radios, obstructing sidewalks, disorderly conduct, unleashed dogs, harassing pedestrians, loitering, and drunkenness. Seven out of ten people summoned never even bothered to show up in court. Two-thirds of the city's parking violation summonses were also ignored last year. Only 2 percent of the more than 29,000 fines assessed for illegal peddling were actually paid. With fewer people feeling compelled to obey the law, enforcement recedes. Cops turn their backs on petty crimes and misdemeanors. . . . Police and court officials insist that violent and major crimes have to take priority, but the price paid by New Yorkers for trivializing minor crimes has been a tangible coarsening of city life (Pileggi 1981:27–28).

This account comes from an article whose main theme is that the deterioration of life in New York City arises to a major degree from the city's budget crisis and its dire effects on all public services. However, Mayor Edward Koch is quoted as saying that the deterioration derives also from the general permissiveness beginning in the 1960s in which values that did make sense were indiscriminately flouted along with those that did not make sense. Of course, the presence of a large, entrapped, poverty-stricken component of the population is also a cause, but it does not account for the middle-class misdemeanors. It does seem clear that positive feedback is at work, that a system of behavior is in operation into which no corrective factors are being introduced, and therefore the behavior grows and intensifies. If the feedback metaphor is valid, then the solution begins with introducing corrective factors that induce negative feedback in which the behavior contracts and diminishes.

Roger Starr (1985) suggests a strategy focused on crimes committed mostly by members of poor, minority families, but it should be applicable to middle-class misbehavior, too. Starr recommends that each city "must pick the area or activity important to its very life that is most adversely affected by random crime. It must start by attending to that sector. As part of what it does there, however, each city must make basic changes in its police forces, courts and prisons that will help battle crime throughout the city" (p. 25). Starr chooses New York's subway system as an example of such a target sector, and proposes nine priorities for corrective change. Some are very far-reaching, such as "the whole population must support the efforts of leaders in the current crime-prone population to strengthen family structure and educate the young in the mores of an urban society, the better to survive and prosper constructively" (p. 20). Such education seems clearly to be needed, also, among other segments of the population. More specifically, Starr proposes that "the public must see that in the crime target area, no breach of law is so trivial that it can be ignored"(p. 20). Starr ends on this note:

There will be times in the future, as . . . in the past, when the price of the effort to repel the criminal threat to the traditional city will seem too high. People will ask themselves why they should defer more humane uses of public funds . . . to build jail cells, buy advanced technical weapons for the police, and install bigger computers to keep track of the repetitious crimes of habitual offenders. Why not simply move to the country, taking what can be carried of the great achievements of urban civilization? That's exactly the problem. What are the greatest achievements of urban life? Surely one means the rewards of talking to many different kinds of people, the ready presence of uncountable varieties of goods and services, the treasure houses in which both the world's fine art and its popular culture are displayed and performed, the parks, the institutions of learning and health, the architectural landscape—to take a few samples. They cannot simply be dispersed and yet remain the same. If the city is to be deprived of them by loss of civil peace, love of those same treasures demands that attention, ingenuity, and resources be dedicated to restoring it (p. 60).

Neither Nicholas Pileggi nor Starr is nostalgic for some mythical, nonurban past. On the contrary, both are concerned with vicissitudes, though neither uses the term. They are concerned with on-going urban evolution, using, as it happens, New York City as their example. The points they make and the issues they raise are applicable to other cities as well.

Colin Ward (1978) is also concerned about vicissitudes of urban distemic space. His subject is the adaptation of children to life in cities, in particular British industrial cities which have been suffering negative vicissitudes since World War II. The violence and neglect featured in the lives of many poor urban children come in part from lack of positive adaptations to vicissitudes.

Watch the scrimmage at the bus stop when the city child comes out of school, interview tenants on a housing estate terrorised by its children, learn that the annual cost of vandalism in England, Scotland and Wales is, at a minimum estimate, well over 114 million pounds, or read that one out of every eleven children in the city of Atlanta will be murdered if he or she stays there, and you will be in no doubt that the city has failed its children. It fails to awaken their loyalty and pride. It fails to offer legitimate adventures (p. 203).

Citing a personal conversation with Roger Starr (then housing administrator of New York), Ward shows his awareness that the city does not do anything, but rather the people who inhabit it do things. Starr told Ward that he was mystified by the way urban land values remain high even when the land itself has become derelict (p. 203). Obviously, such land should be reappraised at its real market value, and then it would become available to poor people who can realize their "aspirations for housing at human densities, for domestic and public open space, for low-rent premises for small businesses, and for all those activities which are the very essence of urban civilisation but show a low rate of return on capital invested" (p. 203). Ward discusses many ways in which children's activities that allow them to discover their own skills have been facilitated by using vacant city land. These projects include vegetable gardens and raising chickens for the experience and earning money.

Real involvement in the adult city world is another goal for children on which experiments are being made in Great Britain. For example, a schoolteacher in the inner city of Sheffield arranged for her class to visit an unusual house about which they were curious. Visits to the elderly owner and the library revealed that the house was 200 years old and scheduled for demolition to make room for a parking lot. "This distressed the class because they had become involved with the old lady and her husband and because they had come to see that it was valuable to have one building that was in some way special in their district" (p. 185). Against considerable odds and setbacks, the children eventually saved the house. The headmaster of their school said they had enjoyed their involvement and realized that "democracy depends on 'us' being able to tackle 'them' about 'our' heritage. . . . But to my mind the most important thing is their realisation that they can actively play a part in shaping their surroundings, that what *they* say about where and how they live will be listened to and that the key to their future lies in their own awareness" (p. 185). Multiplied thousands of times, such new learning might well be the corrective feedback factors that the urban distemic space behavioral scene needs.

Ward sees a special problem in the restricted use of distemic space that is the experience of most girls and women, and his view of this restrictiveness has wide implications:

The problem of the girl in the city is a male problem. If she is deprived of her fair share of environmental contact because she has household tasks which her brothers are able to evade, the answer is a more equitable sharing of these tasks in the family, especially since her mother too probably feels oppressed by the same assumptions. If it is because of a patriarchal religious tradition, the patriarchs have to change. If it's for fear of sexual exploitation, it is the exploiters rather than the girls who have to change their ways. And if the liberation of girls brings in its train an explosion of female crime, it is the equation between anti-social acts and bravery which has to be broken. The environmental liberation of girls, far from implying that the girl in the city should become hard and tough in the way that the city boy aims to be, demands that the boy too should pride himself on those allegedly feminine qualities of care and tenderness. One of the discoveries that Urie Bronfenbrenner made in Moscow, was that the taboo on tenderness had not infected the children of that city: ". . . I recall an incident that occurred in a Moscow street. Our youngest son—then four—was walking briskly a pace or two ahead of us when from the opposite direction there came a company of teenage boys. The first one no sooner spied Stevie than he opened his arms wide and, calling . . . 'hey little one!', scooped him up, hugged him, kissed him resoundingly, and passed him on to the rest of the company who did likewise, and they began a merry children's dance, as they caressed him with words and gestures. Similar behaviour on the part of any American adolescent male would surely prompt his parents to consult a psychiatrist."

The liberation of the city girl from the expected norms of passivity and docility implies also the liberation of the city boy from the pressure to be a predator (pp. 158–59,163).

The messages carried by our discussion of stressed distemic space behavior are: its causes are many; the stress appears to be a self-reinforcing process; a considerable variety of corrective inputs must be made into the process; and much thought, care, and experimentation has been devoted to the design of such inputs.

Public Space/Proxemic Space

Distemic space is usually, though not necessarily, publicly owned. That ownership is one of the reasons why there are distemic space behavior problems: too many people using the space ignore norms of conduct that most would presumably follow under other circumstances.

Given the unprecedented size of cities in the world today, crowded distemic space is here to stay. Therefore, new norms, variously appropriate to each of the different cultures of the world, are needed to make inhumane distemic behavior exceptional rather than commonplace. Various conscious experimental efforts to achieve this goal are discussed above.

There is also evidence of what is probably largely unconscious behavior on the part of individuals and small groups to make distemic space more manageable for themselves. The effects are not necessarily benign or even neutral for others, and therefore the behavior in question may not suggest solutions to the macroproblems of distemic space. Indeed, some of them may be part of the problem.

Lyn Lofland, in *A World of Strangers* (1973), devotes two chapters to "privatizing public space." These chapters

focus on some of the devices that urbanites use to avoid the world of strangers and thereby reduce the necessity to use or even acquire complex urban know-how. . . . [E]ach transforms public space . . . into private or semiprivate space. Each allows its user, for long or short periods of time, to a greater or lesser degree, to avoid the difficulty and the challenge that are the essence of the city as a world of strangers (p. xi).

We have previously considered some of them, such as creating "home territories" in bars, shops, and some open spaces and "concentrated urban villages" (pp. 119–35). These are essentially transformations of distemic into proxemic space, and we have said that a good portion of the humanity of cities exists in them.

The same cannot be said, however, for the creation of "dispersed villages," by which Lofland means the urbanites' use of the automobile to move to various places where they are personally known in such a way that they "almost never [have] to enter any truly public space" (p. 136). Lofland does not connect this behavior with the traffic problems mentioned above, but it may well be connected, particularly if it is true that the city of strangers stimulates some actors to play fantasy roles (p. 158; Sennett 1974a:175). "Traveling in packs" is another device of urbanites for taking their privacy along with them:

They use public space with abandon, in such a way that, for example, a group of adolescents can choose to play running games in an air terminal. They feel free to indulge in backstage behavior, calling each other by name, yelling at one another across the expanse of the setting, using obscene language and laughing loudly at private jokes. And they express proprietary attitudes. If their numbers are plentiful enough, they may even force others to depart, as when the overflow from a convention invades a city's nightspots (Lofland 1973:139).

Lofland's chapters on defensive body management and adventuring in the city are highly descriptive of actual behavior, and so are instructive, but they do not move us much toward coping better with crowded distemic space beyond asserting that a desired goal is cosmopolitan persons' "need to know a great deal more than the simple fact of common humanity about the people who surround them" (p. 176).

John Ottensmann (1978) has reviewed a dozen published studies that indicate predictability in the presence of street life in social class and density contexts. The clear conclusion is that street life and neighboring are associated with working-class, high-density areas; lack of street life is associated with low-density, middle-class areas. In the former situation, proxemic space extends into public space; in the latter, it does not. Ottensmann emphasizes that his study is preliminary and that research in a greater variety of scenes is needed. Research on whether people accustomed to street life at home are or are not better adapted to problem-prone crowded distemic space would be valuable. Not all users of crowded distemic space create problems there.

The development of more other-oriented caring in distemic space behavior must not wait for some miraculous efflorescence of utopian mass altruism, for such a miracle will probably never happen. Other-oriented caring combined with individual self-interest is a real motivation; it exists, and it can be put to use, as Raquel Ramati's *How to Save Your Own Street* (1981) attests. Ramati describes streets that actually have been saved; hers is not a visionary "how-to" book but a practical one based in part on her own experiences in New York City. She says:

> Streets take up about a third of the land area in our cities. Yet many Americans think of streets as places to avoid or endure, not as places to enjoy and remember.
> The most obvious reason for this waste is that cars, buses, and trucks dominate the street and often seem more important than people. Fortunately, this is not a completely accurate image. Many streets . . . have yet to be reduced to mere roads, and increasing numbers of people are determined to keep their streets from such a fate.
> [T]he nation's urban policies have . . . begun to emphasize the revitalization of existing neighborhoods. Streets are their core and countenance. Making sure that streets take on a new life is basic to this neighborhood strategy.
> [N]eighborhoods and streets form existing resources. . . . [W]e all have a stake in making the most of what exists—conserving and improving upon and maintaining investments made over the years. Streets, not to mention the buildings edging them, are a reflection of such past expenditures. Caring for them, we conserve a reflection of ourselves, of our fellow citizens, and of a shared cultural heritage.
> [N]o one else is going to undertake and pay for this process unless you (. . . an owner of a building along the street, a community leader, a government planner, a city commissioner, an architect, a real estate developer seeking a zoning change, or any individual or group having an interest in their street) take the lead, create a constituency, and learn how to tap the resources of both government and the private sector (pp. xi–xii).

Scattered in Ramati's book are references to open areas other than streets—parks and derelict, vacant land (often resulting from the abandonment and demolition of buildings). That parks are an urban amenity is universally agreed, but it is not widely enough recognized that many of them, such as Golden Gate Park in San Francisco and Central Park in New York, exist only because of the foresight, courage, and persistence of dedicated persons in the past, or, as in the case of London and other European cities, the noblesse of bygone aristocracies.

Established parks have the same needs and problems as other distemic areas, such as maintenance and control of crime and incivility. But the expense of meeting these needs is not a sufficient reason for not creating additional parks to accompany the continuing growth of cities. Joseph Shomon's book is primarily a practical guide on how to acquire and maintain additional urban parklands. He is concerned with the loss not only of undeveloped land to urbanization but also of already existing city parkland to highways and other construction.

> The deterioration of urban lands and waters is part of the greater problem of environmental deterioration in the United States. . . . When urban design is dominated by the profit motive, some very sterile and monotonous urban patterns are likely to result. . . . There is growing recognition that if our cities and suburbs are to be livable and pleasant, some semblance of openness and naturalness, even some measure of wilderness, are essential (Shomon 1971:6–9).

Shomon (pp. 96–104) briefly describes two successes in New York City: the Jamaica Bay Wildlife Refuge in Queens and tiny Paley Park on East 53rd Street, Manhattan.

Paley Park also is featured, among many other "small urban spaces," in William H. Whyte's richly illustrated book (1980). He leaves no doubt that they are immensely enjoyed by many people, and he raises the question of why there are not more of them:

> The biggest single reason is [that] . . . many businessmen have an almost obsessive fear that if a place is attractive to people it might be attractive to undesirable people. So it is made unattractive. There is to be no loitering—no eating, no sitting. . . . [B]enches are made too short to sleep on, . . . [and] spikes are put on ledges; most important, many needed spaces are not provided at all. . . .
>
> Who are the undesirables? For most businessmen, curiously, it is not truly dangerous people. It is the winos . . . [and others who are] a symbol, perhaps, of what one might become but for the grace of events. . . .
>
> The preoccupation with undesirables is a symptom of another problem. Many corporation executives who make key decisions about the city have surprisingly little acquaintance with the life of its streets and open spaces. From the train station, they may walk only a few blocks before entering their building; . . . some don't venture out until it's time to go home again. To them, the unknown city is a place of danger. If their building has a plaza, it is likely to be a defensive one that they will rarely use themselves (pp. 60–61).
>
> The best way to handle . . . undesirables is to make a place attractive to everyone else. The record is overwhelmingly positive on this score. . . .
>
> Seagram's management is pleased people like its plaza and is quite relaxed about what they do. It lets them stick their feet in the pool; does not look to see if kids are smoking pot on the pool ledge; tolerates oddballs, even allowing them to sleep the night on the ledge. . . . The place is largely self-policing, and there is rarely trouble of any kind (p. 63).

In nine years of studying New York City plazas and small parks, Whyte found a serious problem in only one, and in well-used places, none whatsoever.

> The exception is a plaza on which pot dealers began operating. The management took away about half the benches [and] . . . constructed steel-bar fences on the two open sides of the plaza. These moves effectively cut down the number of ordinary people who used the place, to the delight of the pot dealers. . . .
>
> [I]t is characteristic of well-used places to have a "mayor," . . . a building

guard, a newsstand operator, or a food vendor. . . . [Y]ou'll notice people checking in during the day—a cop, bus dispatcher, . . . street professionals, and office workers and shoppers who pause briefly for a salutation or a bit of banter. Plaza mayors are great communication centers, and very quick to spot any departure from normal. . . .

One of the best . . . is Joe Hardy of the Exxon Building. . . . Joe is very quick to spot real trouble. . . . Teenage groups are an especial challenge. They like to test everybody—with the volume knob of their portable radios as weapon. Joe's tactic is to go up to the toughest-looking person in the group and ask his help in keeping things cool . . . (pp. 63–64).

Whyte treats these small parks and plazas as extensions, if not parts of, the streets and sidewalks they adjoin. And so, his observations and critiques are concerned with street life, and it is very important to be aware that this is not the street life of working-class, ethnic subcultural residential areas, but of business district streets, distemic space that is not the turf of any particular group. These passages epitomize the humanity of cities, and its ramifications. Here we have macroscale behavior (corporate decisions) affecting microscale everyday life adversely and positively, and we catch a glimpse of the corporation not as an anonymous mass but as an organization of fallible individuals like the street-ignorant executive. Here we have the self-fulfilling prophecy working for good and ill. Here we have caring, or at least personal curiosity, humanizing an otherwise anonymous scene. Probably most of the people frequenting these midtown Manhattan open spaces on weekdays are office workers and retail business employees enjoying lunchtime and other break periods away from nearby buildings; many are regulars, and so the scene is not completely anonymous.

William S. Paley, whose foundation created and maintains Paley Park, expressed the hope that such parks would spread and multiply (Shomon 1972:104). The result would be more corrective factors introduced into the feedback system of distemic space behavior. Another example besides Paley Park is First National Plaza in downtown Chicago where people sitting on benches and parapets can look at a large mosaic mural by Marc Chagall, paid for by a private foundation.

Formal parks and plazas have always been typical amenities of Mediterranean and Latin American cities, serving very much the same functions as those noted above. A famous example in North America is Jackson Square in the French Quarter of New Orleans. The streets of the quarter are laid out in a grid pattern, and the square is actually a plaza surrounded on three sides by important buildings: the cathedral, two ornate structures that once housed important government offices, and two rows of elegant residential buildings once the homes of upper-class families (all reminiscent of Latin American cities). The French Quarter survives from preindustrial, colonial times, thanks to the efforts of many people, and it would be foolish and futile to try to reproduce it elsewhere. But to create spaces and opportunities for the kind of public sociability it provides is a necessity for the present and future humanity of cities.

Elegance is nice, but it is not a necessity for the humanity of distemic space. Three examples will suffice. One of them is the "adventure playground" that originated in Copenhagen and has spread widely in Europe and Great Britain

(Lambert and Pearson 1974). Instead of immobile play equipment set in concrete, the adventure playground provides natural ground and shrubbery; lumber, bricks, and other construction materials; and the appropriate tools. With these items the children can build, tear down, and rebuild to the limit of their imaginations. The other two examples consist of the conversion of derelict urban space to vegetable gardens and small livestock farms. The ultimate goal is enlarged community life, based on productive work. The two examples are the Inter-Action Centre, Kentish Town, Borough of Camden, London, and the Bronx Frontier Development Corporation, New York City.

Ed Berman founded Inter-Action in 1968. City farms and self-help gardening clubs are only some of its activities, the others being a wide variety of educational programs and activities and community building projects. These creative efforts have produced positive humanity where it did not exist before, using derelict land. "According to Berman, the caretakers of the surrounding [housing projects] say that vandalism has plummeted since the opening of this City Farm. That in itself is surely recommendation enough" (McKean 1977:50). Charles McKean describes many other organizations in Great Britain that use abandoned land to create jobs for the unemployed and build multidimensional community lives for participants.

The Bronx Frontier Development Corporation has been active in the South Bronx since 1976. By 1984, it had reclaimed 80 abandoned lots and helped convert them into garden plots by providing topsoil produced from manure from the Bronx Zoo and various Bronx riding academies and discarded vegetables from the Hunt's Point Terminal Market. The corporation has other activities, including coordinating the many other gardens in the South Bronx (Flanagan, c. 1984). Another such reclamation organization is Glie Farms Inc., founded with corporate venture capital; it grows herbs for New York restaurants (Agins 1985b:1, 25).

Planning

Many city and regional planners seem unconcerned with everyday life in distemic space. The result can be that carefully made and well-meaning plans may lead to unsatisfactory outcomes. A case in point is the South Commons urban renewal project in Chicago. Designed with a mix of high- and low-rise buildings intended for upper- and lower-income families and, implicitly, a variety of racial/ethnic groups, the project did not facilitate social integration. On the contrary, various groups segregated themselves from the others, partly because of their differing patterns of using distemic space. Furthermore, unwanted visits from youths living in the area surrounding the project became a problem. They regarded the project as an intrusion on their territory.

Deborah Pellow raises these issues with respect to what was wrong with the planning process. One possibility is that mistaken idealism led to accommodating too much heterogeneity in a small space. Another is that needs and interests of the surrounding population were disregarded. Pellow argues for anticipatory research focused on the location and the people who will live in a development. No social impact assessment or cultural profile was made for South Commons (1981:23).

There is a problem with designer/user separation. . . . What an architect views as kitsch, the masses, for whom the architect is designing, may regard as perfection. And what the architect regards as attractive and functional, the users may find discordant to their needs and tastes. The public space at South Commons, the mall, which few would use, is a case in point (p. 24).

The architectural profession is prone to fads, and when they are followed on a large scale, as in housing projects, the result can be highly adverse, particularly when the architects' priorities are set on professional ambitions, rather than on livability of the buildings. The LeCorbusier fad, for example, inspired the Pruitt-Igoe project and other housing disasters (Fishman 1977; Kimmelman 1987). Architects' and planners' ignorance of, or insensitivity to, their clients' cultural patterns can reach almost unbelievable depths, as in the case of Indian professionals' failure to design in terms of other Indians' housing needs for accommodating extended family and gender-segregated residential patterns in Bombay (Choldin 1976:312–13).

It would be inaccurate and unfair to convey the idea that all architects and planners are deficient in such knowledge and sensitivity. For example, there is an increasing amount of research on precisely what are the impacts, positive and negative, of high-rise dwellings on various categories of people (Conway et al. 1977; Gillis 1983). There are also sophisticated, sensitive, and thorough studies of the interrelations between people and the constructed environments in which they live (Porteous 1977; Rapoport 1982). A section of Amos Rapoport's first chapter is called "users' meanings and designers' meanings"; in it he shows how divergent they can be (pp. 15–19). Equally insightful is a book-length critique of British urban planning policies and projects which invokes the great need for openness, opportunities for choice, listening to those who will use or live in the buildings, and identifying the rights and needs of silent, as well as vocal, client populations (Eversley 1973:324).

GRASS ROOTS

Grass-roots efforts involve the mobilization of ordinary people to achieve group interests against more powerful organizations such as corporations and government bureaucracies. In much of the literature, grass-roots groups appear to be the good guys against the bad guys. While this is frequently so, small groups also are quite capable of pursuing selfish ends to the detriment of other small groups, and bureaucracies are not always as monolithic as they appear to outsiders. On the latter point, we have noted the dilemma the Boston Housing Authority faced regarding two conflicting policies both of which were in the public interest. Furthermore,

many governmental decisions involve ambiguous legal and moral considerations ... when the public interest and interests of organized interest groups are in conflict. Often an administrator's personal interest is involved. In these situations, the ethical considerations are more hazy and complex, and the governmental administrator may have to assess:
1. The impact of interference by politicians and pressure groups on the administrative process;
2. The waste of public resources and the degree of public accountability for actions affecting individuals and groups;
3. Provisions for equal citizen access to government services even to those who cannot afford them;

4. The impact of secrecy in governmental decision-making upon the public and upon rational discussion of alternative public policies; and
5. The use of insider knowledge for private gain (Murphy 1977:33).

With these cautions in mind, we proceed to an overview of the grass-roots dimension of the humanity of cities. We have previously referred to grass-roots efforts in a number of contexts. One of the most important of these references is squatter settlements in Third World cities. Connected with squatter settlements is the serious and technically pragmatic effort to rationalize the processes of self-built house construction using cheap, locally available materials and structural features that are pleasing and suited to the environment (Fathy 1973; Turner 1977). Such efforts have been vigorously opposed by those who gain from corporately built housing.

Manuel Castells's *The City and the Grassroots* (1983) gives detailed accounts of citizens' struggles against urban power structures from sixteenth-century Europe to twentieth-century America. An example of the type of struggle Castells chronicles is the sustained tenants' movement in New York City that has gone through many phases throughout this century, seeking not only equitable rents but humanization of the entire landlord/tenant relationship (Lawson et al. 1986). The protracted nature of this struggle carries an important lesson: the quick fix is not to be expected when the power structure remains intact.

Existing grass-roots movements can be inhibited by factors less obvious than direct opposition. For example, Bryan Roberts (1973:281–85) shows that consumer cooperative and neighborhood organizations in Guatemala City, while providing opportunities for social support, are too localized to have any impact on large-scale political issues that affect the actors. Different reasons among the actors for participation can also deter sustained action. Karl Hess, who for several years tried to establish hydroponic gardening in the Adams-Morgan district of Washington, D.C., attributes what he sees as the limited effectiveness of the Adams-Morgan Organization to the conflicting motivations for participation among early members.

> The counterculture people were ... looking for a new way to make social decisions ... without social exploitation of one group by another. The idea of a town meeting—with people who make decisions being responsible also for carrying them out, and not merely for getting someone else to do it—was understandable and inspiring to them. ... Blacks in the neighborhood had a clearly different view. The rhetoric of participation was accepted and so was the form. But the reality behind it was ... power. Blacks ... wanted ... to have the power to make those decisions—to have power *in*, not power *to change*, the system. Whites who do not understand this can make fearsome mistakes in assessing the meaning of black-white alliances for social change (1979:41–42).

In 1985, the author was a member of a group that visited Adams-Morgan and talked with a spokesperson for the Adams-Morgan Advisory Neighborhood Commission (ANC). A brochure said there are 30 ANCs in the District of Columbia, established by Congress on the model of the original Adams-Morgan Organization. Each ANC has an elected council which can lobby for public issues. ANCs receive a 30-day notice on all district government actions that may affect them and have 30 more days to react. The ANC coordinates a variety of community activities and services, and it has direct access to the mayor and city council of Washington. Regardless of motives for participation, these are much needed innovations in bringing ordinary, mostly poor and disadvantaged, people into direct communication with the government.

Lack of two-way communication between people's small-scale everyday lives and the large-scale bureaucratic context of those lives contributes greatly to inhumanity in cities. The Hatikva Quarter in Tel Aviv, for instance, has a stigmatized reputation as a violent, lawless slum. While it awaits government "rehabilitation," Hatikva is "under-administered" (Marx 1982:39), meaning that government services are supplied poorly and irregularly.

> Authorities tend to know little about local affairs, and occasionally treat the area as if it were foreign territory. Thus the police from time to time raid the area, arrest a few drug pedlars, and then withdraw. Because they lack local contacts, authorities depend on local political brokers whose influence depends on the patronage they can offer to clients. Few such people have a permanent following, but the authorities often assume that they lead factions (p. 39).

A large proportion of Hatikva's population consists of Jews from Yemen, Iraq, and other Middle Eastern countries (Deshen 1982:32), and the Jews of European origin who dominate the society tend to look down on Oriental Jews.

Hatikva lacks a grass-roots movement such as the Adams-Morgan ANC that emerged from a deteriorated socioeconomic situation. Emanuel Marx tells us some of the reasons why:

> The inhabitants do not perceive joint interests and therefore do not join forces. Sources of employment, and even most entertainment, are located outside the area, and people disperse daily in all directions. Neighborhood networks are the potential basis of political organization for the inhabitants. But they engage in mutual aid and cannot unite because there is no communal issue to rally around, and no single authority to oppose. The rehabilitation project could have become a focus for local organization, but its community workers quickly made the residents of each neighborhood dependent on their assistance. Central government works against voluntary associations that could represent the inhabitants. While associations can be set up relatively easily, they are then co-opted by the authorities and thus lose their power. Or if they persist in remaining independent, the authorities fear them and put obstacles in their way (p. 44).

The essentials of the Hatikva situation are not peculiar to Tel Aviv. The seemingly benign cooptations of bureaucrats that sabotage grass-roots movements are found everywhere. Consider the case of Karl Hess and his associates when they sought funding from the National Science Foundation (NSF) for a science center that would provide an infrastructure for their project to develop local food production in Adams-Morgan. The NSF sent a sociologist to look into the project and turned it down cold. Hess's group "did not meet the government-approved definition of a neighborhood self-help program" (1979:46). Even at NSF such programs focus on enhancing neighborhood people's ability to obtain welfare assistance more effectively, not to produce their own wealth and future.

> Government programs aim at getting money for poor people. Our hope was that knowledge would in the long run be more useful, provide more money, and eventually strike at the system-causes of poverty. We felt, and continue

to feel, that poverty is actually a lack of skill, and a lack of the self-esteem that comes with being able to take some part of one's life into one's own hands and work with others toward shared—call them social—goals (p. 46).

In a quite different way, the efforts of Nora Harlow (1975) and her colleagues to establish and maintain a cooperative day-care center and school in Morningside Heights, New York City, were continually obstructed, though not killed, by a variety of bureaucratic maneuvers. The center was to be in a storefront owned by Columbia University which owns most of Morningside Heights and (in conjunction with other large institutional owners) has succeeded in evicting more than ten thousand residents to make way for nonresidential buildings. Court suits and demonstrations held up total demolition (p. 3). One example of the obstructing behavior they encountered follows:

> The district consultant for city daycare was the first . . . to pay us an official visit. . . . A sweet middle-aged woman who sat on a tiny nursery chair with her knees up to her chin and talked to us about better ways to make play dough and about hiring professionals who really knew about children and about applying for government funding. . . . We would not learn anything from this woman or teach her anything. Her group was hierarchical, written record-making, money-exchanging, impersonal; our group was circular, verbal, work-exchanging, personal. . . . Our district consultant was pleasant over the phone. She asked if we were still opposed to hiring teachers and getting funded and she said that most of the last fifty violations could be disregarded. The rules were being changed. She said she would record our violations as "in the process of correction." . . . (1975:144–48).

Harlow and Hess, and their associates, are well-educated, sophisticated, middle-class people who, though they have no political power, have political know-how and are not handicapped by racial/ethnic discrimination. Try to imagine the countless unrecorded obstructions experienced by people who lack the advantages of Hess and Harlow.

Harlow mentions mass evictions in Morningside Heights, and we have previously mentioned other such cases of urban inhumanity, notably the demolition of Boston's West End. We should add two verifiable nineteenth-century examples: massive demolitions of poor peoples' neighborhoods to make way for railroad stations in London and Baron Haussmann's boulevards in Paris, both now regarded as historical treasures. The feelings of the nineteenth-century dispossessed are as forgotten now as they were probably disregarded at the time. It is a plus for the humanity of cities in the twentieth century that *some* large, powerful organizations have exercised great care and compassion in the relocation of tenants from properties they wished to redevelop. One case is the expansion of the campus of the Mother Church of Christ, Scientist, in Boston. The church advised the tenants many months in advance rather than 30 to 60 days, paid relocation expenses, and also paid a reputable rental agent to help the tenants find new quarters. Several hundred people living in 42 old buildings "found new quarters—and did so without the rancor so often associated with evictions brought on by 'urban renewal' " (Marlin 1973:39).

Local grass-roots movements are necessarily political. They require leadership, organization, and persistence. Often, if not always, they are triggered by a crisis; in the Greenpoint-Williamsburg section of Brooklyn, in 1975, the threat that the city would close the local firehouse, at a time of high arson rates, resulted in its occupation for 18 months by an activist family. An already existing network of politically active, working-class women made this effort possible (Susser 1986:112–13). In Durham, N.C., in 1978–79, a coalition of blacks and middle-class whites (with somewhat different goals) successfully prevented completion of an expressway which would have destroyed a black neighborhood (Luebke 1981:256).

Subcultural homogeneity—be it social class or ethnic—is not a prerequisite for effective local grass-roots political action. In fact, some observers might argue the reverse. Matthew Crenson, for example, in his study of politically active neighborhoods in Baltimore, found that it is frequently the relatively rich people, living in relatively poor neighborhoods, who provide the leadership (1983:301). Crenson also has some hopes that sustained local political organizations may eventually have various beneficial effects on governance of the city as a whole (pp. 296–97).

Lisa Redfield Peattie, an American city planner (and daughter of the anthropologist Robert Redfield), lived for an extended period in La Laja, a working-class neighborhood in Ciudad Guyana, Venezuela, a new city being built by American and Venezuelan engineers and bureaucrats to produce steel from nearby iron mines. Peattie had roots in La Laja, but she also had contacts with the city's power structure that people of the *barrio* did not. And so she was able to play an important role in a grass-roots movement to prevent the pollution of the *barrio's* water supply by the construction of a sewer (1968:85–89).

Besides leadership, an essential element in organizing for local livability is a well-defined locality in which some residents have pride and where people are willing to look out for one another (Young 1981:30). How its inhabitants view the neighborhood is, however, a complicated issue, as Roger Ahlbrandt (1984) has shown in connection with the great diversity of neighborhood inhabitants' attitudes, social statuses, and styles of political activism in Pittsburgh.

Diversity, between and within neighborhoods, sometimes results in conflict within the local community. Such was the case with the Manhattan Valley Development Corporation (MVDC). Manhattan Valley is a deteriorating working-class area south of Columbia University between Central Park West and Broadway. Local citizens formed the MVDC primarily to work for more low-cost housing in the area. Nevertheless, it made local enemies, one charge being that it was seeking power for its own sake (West 1981:29–32). Such conflicts may inevitably accompany social action. The research of Tridib Banerjee and William Baer among blacks, whites, and Hispanics in Los Angeles leads them to believe that the familiar model of the homogeneous neighborhood as the basic building block of urban social life may be insufficient because it is too narrow and too static. They propose the design of residential areas that consist of dwelling clusters for people of different income classes, combined with public facilities, mixed private and public facilities, and private commercial establishments. Such arrangements, recognizing the reality of social heterogeneity, would make better services available and make the area more adaptable to change (Banerjee and Baer 1984:188–89). Admittedly utopian, such areas, if realized to the extent possible, might mitigate the protractedness and bitterness of many grass-roots movements and the hopelessness of people who are not able to undertake them.

Meanwhile, there is no scarcity of ideas on how to organize grass-roots movements, particularly at the neighborhood level. Among the substantial books on this subject are Robert Cassidy's *Livable Cities* (1980), Rolf Goetze's *Building Neighborhood Confidence* (1986), and Howard Hallman's *Neighborhoods: Their Place in Urban Life* (1984). There are also surveys of neighborhood satisfaction and dissatisfaction, such as one which covered the entire city of Flint, Mich. (Charles Stewart Mott Foundation 1979).

Many of the sources cited in this section on grass roots mention interactions between individuals, and so they help to counteract the well-entrenched feeling that bureaucratic organizations are dehumanized, anonymous monoliths. Four books that further reinforce this important point are Mario Cuomo, *Forest Hills Diary* (1974); John Goering, Maynard Robison, and Knight Hoover, *The Best Eight Blocks in Harlem* (1977); Chester W. Hartman, *Yerba Buena* (1974); and Nick Wates, *The Battle for Tolmers Square* (1976).

In 1972, Cuomo (subsequently governor of New York) was an attorney in private practice in New York City. Mayor John V. Lindsay asked Cuomo, an experienced negotiator, to serve as the city's fact-finder among all the disputing parties in a prolonged confrontation between citizens' groups in Forest Hills and other parts of New York City. The city, backed by the federal government, had made plans to build three 24-story apartment buildings in Forest Hills for low-income, inner-city families. The project was part of a "scatter-site" program based on the theory that if poor people, previously heavily concentrated in inner-city slums, were relocated in smaller concentrations in different, more affluent areas of the city, they would enjoy beneficial results. The Forest Hills people, mostly middle class, Jewish, and politically liberal, opposed the project primarily on the grounds that a large influx of poor, black families would bring with it such an increase in crime that their community would be destroyed. After much bitter turmoil, a compromise was finally reached: three 12-story buildings, one of which would be for elderly people.

Cuomo's book is in diary form, and although he labels many of the actors with pseudonyms, he makes the Forest Hills affair come alive as a dispute among real individuals, not as a war between impersonal forces. His diary also includes numerous insightful observations and thoughts.

At about the same time, the Upper Park Avenue Community Association (UPACA) had been formed to build low-cost housing and rehabilitate older buildings to restore East Harlem as a residential area for poor families. UPACA was locally controlled but also supported in various ways by foundations and government agencies. It made a good start, but eventually failed because the federal government's reduction of funds for urban housing was a catalyst for the surfacing of insurmountable differences in policy between local and externally interested participants. Furthermore, the new housing was priced beyond the means of poor people who were pushed elsewhere, as typically happens with such projects (Goering et al. 1977:188). This book, like Cuomo's, takes the reader step by step, and person by person, through the career of the project and, in doing so, it is very informative about motivations, pure and mixed.

Hartman chronicles the 20-year struggle (1953–73) between Tenants and

Owners in Opposition to Redevelopment (TOOR) and the San Francisco Redevelopment Authority (SFRA) over an SFRA proposal to build a convention center on the south side of lower Market Street, necessitating complete destruction of the area:

> About 4,000 persons were living in the South of Market area slated for destruction to make way for Yerba Buena Center. Apart from about 300 families, residents of South of Market were for the most part single, elderly, male and poor, surviving on the meager proceeds of Social Security and small pensions. Some were alcoholics. Most, however, were retired or disabled working men who had come to the South of Market to spend the remaining days of their lives. The area and its 48 residential hotels provided them with inexpensive housing and eating places. It was sunny and flat, in a city where hills and fog abound. It was downtown, near Market Street, the city's transportation hub, and other facilities they needed. Most of all, it provided them with a community of other single men with common backgrounds, experience and problems. People looked out for each other and took care of one another. Men gathered to talk, watch television, and just be with other people in the hotel lobbies, streets, restaurants and bars. South of Market was their family and their home (1974:96–97).

Hartman does not refer to single-room occupancy (SRO) in discussing the 48 residential hotels, but it is very likely that SRO was frequent in them.

TOOR brought suit against SFRA to insure that relocated housing in other parts of the city be provided, but even with such provision, the social fabric of South of Market would be destroyed. Hartman is specific in delineating who all the major actors were. Knowing what kinds of people can organize movements like TOOR and what other kinds of people can disregard the humanity of South of Market in the interest of speculative profit is valuable information for those who believe in the essential humanity of cities. One of the causes of the great increase in the number of homeless people in American cities in the 1980s is the reduction in the amount of available low-cost housing, and the priorities that destroyed South of Market are major factors in the increase in homelessness.

Like Hartman, Wates provides a chronology of events (1957 to 1976) in *The Battle for Tolmers Square*. Tolmers Square is a neighborhood near the University of London campus. Already crowded by high-rise office buildings (which have become a glut on the London market), Tolmers Square residents were, beginning in the 1950s, invaded by buy-outs and evicted by speculators planning to build more office buildings. They organized and eventually succeeded in getting the government to buy back the land from the speculators and make plans for a mix of office and residential buildings, some new, some rehabilitated. Wates's account of events, in which he was a participant, is notable not only for the interplay of specific individuals, but also for the involvement of different levels of government, including shifts in power between the Conservative and Labour Parties.

All four of these books provide small-scale perspectives on large-scale events, and thus humanize them. As to the effects of grass-roots movements on the humanity of cities, we close with Cuomo's final sentences:

> I believe there is much to learn from this significant episode in the history of urban government. Forest Hills tells us a great deal about the true feelings of the people actually involved on both sides of the issues. It points

up the huge gap between abstract sociological propositions and their efficacy—or lack of it—when nailed down to the Procrustean bed of urban reality. It shows up dramatically the difficulty of attempting to sell by means of homily—and the brandishing of moral obligations—social cures that require sacrifice by some for the good of others. It shows, painfully, the need for more effective devices of communication between centralized urban government and the communities affected by governmental projects. And it reminds us that one of the serious impediments to the resolution of complex confrontations is the tendency of the parties to maintain fixed and extreme positions, the lack of subtlety in dialogue and argumentation, the loss of reasonableness. . . . In the end, any description of the Forest Hills experience will inevitably raise more questions than it answers and will necessarily be in part depressing and in part hopeful. But then, that will always be true: there will always be more problems than solutions; more to be done than has been done; more quests than conquests. The game is only lost when we stop trying (1974:150–51)

CONCLUSION

During the 1980s, the American people were bombarded by political rhetoric largely composed of mindless optimism and threats of international disaster. The optimism glossed over most of the social issues emphasized in this book, and the threats were used to justify the expenditure of more money than the federal budget could afford on military armaments. The point of view underlying this book is that there will indeed be national and international disaster (including urban disaster) unless many people apply well-informed and innovative optimism, backed by ample resources, to ameliorate the issues we have discussed.

Greed for money and power and fear of others' greed are the prime movers behind humankind's being in many ways its own worst enemy. Social science, including anthropology, provides little insight into how these powerful emotions are generated, and the religious explanation (original sin) has no pragmatic value in this world. Social science has, however, delineated the complexities of the effects of these emotions, and it has shown how those effects can be combated, as for example, in the grass-roots movements we have considered.

Throughout this book, we have referred to national, international, and worldwide problems of humankind's own making that affect life in cities but are not city specific. Effects of these megascale phenomena are felt even at the receptive microscale level of the individual city dweller. The least we can do is to face them, to accept their reality, in a spirit quite different from that of mindless optimism. Only by facing them can people combat them.

What's on humanity's agenda for the 21st century? In a series of interviews . . . leading thinkers have identified . . . the first-intensity items . . . to which humanity must devote its full attention and its unstinting resources. . . .

(1) The threat of nuclear annihilation.
(2) The danger of overpopulation.
(3) The degradation of the global environment.
(4) The gap between the developing and the industrial worlds.
(5) The need for fundamental restructuring of educational systems.
(6) The breakdown in public and private morality (Kidder 1987:D–1).

The nuclear threat affects cities in two obvious ways. One is that the arms industry diverts enormous amounts of money and brain power from constructive purposes including the needs of cities. One percent of the world's annual military expenditures amounts to about $6 billion. This sum spent each year for the next 15 years could improve world food production and health measures so that the widespread malnutrition among the world's poorest people (including millions of urban squatters) could be alleviated by the year 2000 (Grant 1983: 49–50). One percent!

Ironically, arms manufacture provides millions of jobs in many cities of the world, and there are vested interests in maintaining this situation quite apart from strategic military ones.

Military expenditures include much more than arms manufacture, of course, but nuclear arms manufacture is a major part of this entire world scene in which power seeking, greed, and fear are prime movers. Who can turn the situation toward different, more constructive goals? Clearly, powerful people who are able to persist in innovative leadership must be involved. James MacGregor Burns, the distinguished historian and political scientist, has said:

> I am trying . . . to develop a theory of leadership that embraces power but is much more subtle and realistic than crude theories of power. Leaders recognize common needs. As the leaders tap those motivational bases . . . [and] reach down to the genuine and authentic needs and wants of the people, then there is a transformation of leaders as well as . . . followers. The great distinction between the power wielder and the leader is that the power wielder is trying to achieve his own purpose, separate from that of the follower—to be a governor, to make a million, to lead a movement. . . . The leader is *leading*—arousing, recognizing, and satisfying the followers' fundamental needs. In turn, the followers are being raised up to higher levels of self-fulfillment and self-realization and self-actualization and the higher levels of moral judgment—and all this rebounds back on the leaders and affects them (1981:9).

An example of power wielders, in Burns's terms, are the real estate developers who were transforming the shape of Manhattan in the 1980s solely for their own profit. "There are the bad guys, and then there are the extraordinarily bad guys," Joe Klein quotes one of his respondents as saying, "Some of these guys think that if they can't make $100 million on a building . . . it's not worth doing" (1986:32).

Ordinary people need not remain passive in the face of such power wielding, and indeed there are growing efforts at resistance and the bending, at least, of some priorities:

> [C]ities are facing increasing pressure from community activists to redistribute the spoils of booming downtown development. . . . [C]ity planners are linking more new building permits to commitments from developers and new businesses to provide jobs, open space, child-care facilities and other amenities. San Antonio, for instance, pressured builders of a Hyatt Regency Hotel into allowing a Mexican-American group to invest $1 million in exchange for an equity stake in the project. The District of Columbia is considering requiring outside banks that want to acquire banks in the city to establish branches in poor neighborhoods, provide up to $100 million in loans to city-sponsored projects, create up to 200 jobs and sell food stamps. . . . Hartford, Conn., Chicago and Seattle . . . are waging campaigns for . . . "linkage" fees, that would be levied on downtown developers. The

taxes—already levied in San Francisco and Boston—would then be used for projects designed to ameliorate the social and economic dislocation [such as gentrification] that activists claim downtown growth causes throughout a city (Waldman 1987:1).

This discussion has led from the nuclear threat to greed and fear to urban power wielding, and at this point, we should take note of the Marxist critique of Western industrial urban dynamics, including its effects on Third World cities. This critique must be taken seriously by anyone who cares about the humanity of cities, and one need not be an ideological Marxist to do so. Simply put, the Marxist critique is that the capitalist profit motive determines the morphology, growth, and social relationships of cities, with social class exploitation as one of the results; in the form of international conglomerates, capitalism has contributed to lessening necessary, but unprofitable, food production in rural areas of the world, resulting in massive migration of poor people to cities. There is enough evidence supporting this argument that non-Marxists should accept it as a serious and legitimate challenge, rather than belligerently and thoughtlessly denying it. A very thorough presentation of the Marxist critique as applied to cities is David Harvey's *Social Justice and the City* (1975). The Marxist solution is revolutionary destruction of the capitalist system. What alternatives are there? This chapter is suggesting some that are actually being tried, but none of them is perfect. Can they be improved?

Overpopulation is discussed at many points in this book. It directly affects cities in various ways, the most conspicuous being growth rates and magnitudes unprecedented in human history. The only humane solution to the overpopulation problem is, obviously, drastic reduction in worldwide birth rates, and that depends on most of the world's child-producing couples' having no more than two children. So far, only a small proportion of those couples have realized that reduced fertility is in their own interest and that of their offspring. Many of these couples live in cities, but it is not true that city dwellers as a whole have low fertility—as we have pointed out previously. Many people in the world still believe they should have a large number of children—to achieve social status among their peers, to maximize the family work force to augment its income, to insure (they hope) support in old age, or to please a deity. Finding effective ways to counteract these values and behavioral patterns is one of the tasks of family planning agencies and institutions in almost all parts of the world. Until these efforts become noticeably successful, people must live as best they can at the same time that expanded efforts are made to control the problem. Chronic unemployment and its dire consequences, ultimately including starvation, may lead to a much more widespread realization that low fertility is in one's own self-interest, regardless of contrary considerations. For example, in Mexico, if the average number of children per couple were reduced from 4.61 to a projected 2.62, urban growth would be reduced by 14 million people by the year 2010, and there would be 200 thousand fewer job-seekers by the year 2000 (Nesmith c.1985–86:23–24). Such abstractions do not influence behavior very much, but the realities they represent can do so.

One observer contributes an encouraging note that has megascale implications:

Now, quite unpredictably and unexpectedly, and in just the last three or four years, out in most of our two million villages, we are showing a startling capacity to change. Suddenly, human fertility is falling; and agricultural productivity, rising, often spectacularly. . . . One can date the change . . . to about 1974–1975. Although I was given different local reasons in each country, the scope of what is happening is too broad to be coincidental. . . . Yearly population growth rates are plummeting, from 2.5–3 percent in the 1960s to 1–1.5 percent now, in village regions as scattered as India's Kerala and Mysore states, Sri Lanka, China and the Chinese-cultured countries from South Korea to Taiwan and the islands of Java and Bali. Scientific farming (high-yield, quick-maturing grain, multiple cropping, nitrogen-fixing crops, year-round irrigation) is spreading very fast. . . . An exodus of villagers from cities and back to the land has begun, catching most governments by surprise. India's Planning Commission has just ordered it studied. In Djakarta, it is overwhelmingly evident; more food in villages being the pull, fewer unskilled jobs in the modernizing city being the push (Critchfield 1979:18).

Richard Critchfield's demographic data come from areas where, in many cases, family planning programs have been particularly intense, unlike other areas where population trends are not so encouraging; and costs, as well as benefits, of "scientific agriculture" are a matter of serious controversy. Nevertheless, Critchfield's presentation suggests future developments that could bode well for humanity, including the humanity of cities.

In the meantime, there is the worldwide problem of environmental degradation, a problem many people, because of short-term self-interest, choose to ignore. For millions of city dwellers, however, the problem is coming closer and closer to home, and the necessity for remedial action more and more obvious. Consider, for example, garbage disposal. American cities are running out of space for landfills, and the most feasible alternative disposal method is burning. The garbage-burning business is profitable, for the process can be harnessed to generate electricity. However, garbage-burning plants threaten the environments of blue-collar neighborhoods in some cities. One of their byproducts is toxic waste of various kinds, according to some experts (Paul 1986). If harmless waste disposal were to become technically impossible, then waste disposal itself might become an agent that, like permanently diminished water supply, might stop further growth of cities.

Developers and politicians typically deny such a prospect, but despite such opposition, water planning is increasingly frequent. We have already mentioned the mandated 10 percent nationwide decrease in water consumption in Israel, and cities as different as Phoenix and Atlanta are making plans and taking steps to conserve water in the future. These actions are, or will be, extremely expensive and do not predict unlimited amounts of water in the future. The farsighted planning and the expensive and probably widely unpopular measures needed to adapt successfully to these vicissitudes will entail the kind of leadership Burns describes, and the eventual results could be an enhancement of the humanity of cities.

The gap between the industrial and developing worlds—basically a North/South gap—refers to the problems inherent in the gross disproportion between the wealth and power of industrial nations and the poverty of Third World ones whose people constitute the majority of humankind. We have seen how this situation affects Third World cities, with their dual economies. The formal economy is tied in various ways to Western industrialism, while the informal is composed of the millions of efforts of poor people to survive by means of marginal jobs. Milton Santos (1979) refers to these two economies as the upper and lower circuits of Third World urban economies. We have noted the resourcefulness and ingenuity of lower-circuit work and criticized its denigration by some development economists. However, we have also noted the concern expressed by observers like Peter Lloyd that the types of informal work by which squatters have typically supported themselves relatively well may diminish. Santos says that increases in productivity and better life conditions of the people now in the lower circuit are needed (p. 205). Virtually the same recommendation is made in a report prepared by the Urban Development Department of the World Bank (1985:3).

Santos refers to several concepts and processes whose importance for the humanity of cities we have frequently discussed: evolution, vicissitudes, and the interactions between macroscale phenomena and the microscale realities of everyday life.

Santos discusses needed changes in the "south." Erhard Eppler, minister for development cooperation of the Federal Republic of Germany, 1968–74, discusses needed changes in the "north":

> It is not our job to make countries of the South self-reliant—that is what they can only do for themselves—but it is up to us to give these nations a basis for interdependence in the future. We have not yet done so. . . . We have to change our model of development to give the Southern countries a chance to change theirs. . . . (1) We have to stop or even reverse [the arms race]. If we fail to do so . . . economic mechanisms . . . will crush all the attempts at a new model of development. Debt servitude and self-reliant development contradict each other. (2) We have to overcome the obsession with growth, even . . . with GNP. What matters is not the rate of growth but its direction and quality. . . . It is not the consumption of energy or raw materials or land that should grow, but every production or every service that can help us to save energy, to save or re-cycle raw materials, to prevent waste, to save or restore ecological cycles. . . . Changing our own pattern of development can have three positive effects on the South: (1) We are no longer forced to export destruction. (2) We liberate the elites of the South from the compulsion to imitate our traditional model and increase their chances of finding their own. (3) Once we are less occupied with the disastrous results of our development, there might be some resources left, material as well as human, to help others (pp. 62–64).

The fifth and sixth high-priority twenty-first-century issues Rushworth Kidder lists—the need for fundamental restructuring of educational systems and the breakdown in public and private morality—have clear implications for city life. To mention only a few, Starr's and Pileggi's discussions of misbehavior in distemic space include questions about improvement. New methods and content of teaching livable urban behavior, including on-the-spot law enforcement, are necessary. Fundamental changes in education, for the sake of public and private morality, were included, too, in the deliberations of a 1985 conference at which violence in American culture was perceived as a public health problem (Holden 1985:1257).

New kinds of learning—learning that directly affects behavior—are implied in our last two examples involving misbehavior in distemic space. In March 1987, *The Wall Street Journal* ran a front page article on the "rampant rudeness" in American society. The article is long on anecdotes by infuriated victims of public rudeness and rather short on analysis. Nevertheless, it cites materialistic preoccupation, high stress levels in a competitive "me first" environment, and boorishness carried over from interethnic conflicts of the past as contributing to the problem. Judith Martin (the newspaper columnist, "Miss Manners") is quoted as saying, "We're a half step above rock bottom"; the good news: "Only recently, we were *at* rock bottom." She adds: "I see some hope because the problem has been identified" (*The Wall Street Journal* 1987:22). A Roman taxi driver stated another identification of the problem (a first step in finding solutions): " 'We should do things more intelligently, less selfishly. People ought to be better mannered,' he said at the end of a nerve-wracking but spirited drive" (Eisner 1987:A–2).

Cities and their inhabitants are affected not only by worldwide phenomena such as those Kidder reviews, but also, as we have repeatedly seen, by national policies and cultural patterns. Two very different discussions of urban growth policies in the face of economic problems come from the World Bank (1987) on Third World cities and Marc Levine (1984) on United States cities. Levine's article has a Marxist, but not revolutionary, orientation.

Racism is clearly an issue involving profound moral concerns, but it is more virulent in some societies than others, and it is still a very serious issue in the United States and its cities despite all the real progress toward integration that has been made. At the end of their book on the Miami race riot of 1980, in which 18 people died, Bruce Porter and Marvin Dunn say:

> The lesson brought home most vividly by Miami seems to be the same one offered up by the earlier riots.... That keeping blacks in a position of economic and social isolation and of political disenfranchisement and where they feel deprived of basic human justice can be allowed to continue only at greater and greater peril to the health, safety and peace of mind of every member of American society (1984:178).

Here, then, is part of the challenge. What present policies should be reinforced, and what new ones should be adopted, to meet the challenge? David Schulz, in his Pruitt-Igoe housing project study, says:

> Do away with the basic economic injustice and ... the odds are that a style of life more closely resembling that of the core culture will emerge because there is no longer any need to adapt to isolation and deprivation.... [A]s Andrew Buchanan put it, "Don't ask me why I eat chittlins, I eat chittlins because I can't afford steak."
>
> Project dwellers ... want very much to be able to live like the average American. However, because they cannot and because it is painful to continue to evaluate oneself by norms that are unattainable, they have accepted an alternate set of norms that enables them to maintain some sense of self-esteem in the midst of their isolation and deprivation. Chittlins are now a significant part of what is called "soul food" in a further attempt to make desirable what is most readily attainable and to provide a concrete sacrament bestowing identity within a black brotherhood.
>
> Some form of income maintenance that goes beyond providing a minimum subsistence level of living for poor Americans seems ... the most just ... and most likely ... means of eliminating poverty and ... its culture....

[I]f the black American is to benefit equally from such reforms, racial discrimination must cease. . . . The most acceptable form of such a program . . . is one that ties income as closely as possible to a job. The majority of project dwellers would rather work than receive a dole and, in fact, the majority of the poor do work and still remain in poverty.

American cities are in crisis, the need is pressing to rebuild the American dream concretely in cities once more fit for human habitation. The economic and technological resources necessary to meet the poverty problem head-on are at hand. This problem must not be evaded any longer (1969:193–95).

During the 1970s and 1980s, the problem continued to be evaded, partly for reasons of national-level political ideology. The need continues to be as pressing as ever, if not more so. As far as the fiscal aspects of national urban policy are concerned, Richard Morris (1978) blames the Federal government and the national banking system for the fiscal crisis, and the social science journal, *Society*, devoted a whole section in one of its 1986 issues to "coping with cutbacks." The introduction to this section emphasizes the innovative responses that have evolved (MacManus and Clark 1986:49). Martin Sable (1984:42–48) lists and briefly describes a number of urban research and action programs active in the United States.

Under the heading, "Partnerships for Urban Problem Solving," Gail Schwartz sets a positive tone:

American cities present rich and varied experiences in dealing with urban problems. The belief that diversity of problems demands a diversity of solutions has been translated into a number of creative approaches. Federally funded demonstration grants have supported diverse experiments in neighborhood preservation, economic development, [and] manpower training. . . . Demonstration grant programs . . . use the community as a social laboratory; their purpose is not necessarily to replicate successful procedures but . . . to generate a variety of models. . . . Private philanthropic foundations . . . have also played a pivotal role in assisting community groups to implement programs and to leverage public funds. Banks, insurance companies, retailers, and utility companies are taking major parts in most restoration efforts. Voluntary agencies . . . often initiate community action. Many cities . . . have also taken steps to decentralize responsibility for planning, programming, budgeting, and delivering services. But aspirations toward self-help and self-management in neighborhoods and demands for more direct citizen control of local government are sometimes at odds with equally strong demands for increased efficiency in government. The potential conflict between these objectives is very great. . . . [C]onscious efforts must be made to achieve a balance in government processes between negotiating (a bargaining process) and steering (a directing process). . . .

Still a long way from evolving into primary vehicles of local government, community groups do have a recognized role as intermediary organizations. . . . [A]n inevitable tension exists between the institutionalization of such organizations and the traditional responsibilities of local government. Intermediary organizations are extremely diverse in origin, objectives, composition, organization and accomplishments. . . . Some are national in scope and have their origins in large social movements and organizations such as the Urban League, which represents the interests of black Americans. Some are limited in scope to a few blocks and focus on the welfare of the immediate residents. . . . For simplicity, intermediary organizations . . . [are] categorized as neighborhood preservation groups, public-private redevelopment organizations, human capital/human resource organizations, comprehensive community development organizations, and network organizations (1981:69–70).

Some organizations of the sort to which Schwartz alludes can, in time, become static "establishments," and so it is important to be aware of the ability of city dwellers to mobilize in response to new communal needs, often crises. For example, the earthquakes that struck Mexico City in September 1986 killed more than four thousand people, injured thousands more, and left about 300 thousand homeless.

The calamity occurred in a country . . . already in the "adjustment process" imposed by its 100 billion dollar debt, and in a city in permanent crisis— where the . . . "marginal people" account for more than half the population and where pollution, traffic congestion, housing and public services deficit . . . are growing continually (Esteva 1986:73).

And how did the citizens of this already beleaguered city respond?

On September 25, just 6 days after the first earthquake, more than 100 grass-roots organizations, encompassing both victims and support groups, decided to constitute the Self-Help Network . . . to serve as the liaison between those needing support and those who can and want to give it. It . . . has already enabled the joint implementation of various emergency actions (p. 74).

A very different kind of crisis is the growing epidemic of acquired immune deficiency syndrome (AIDS). AIDS is affecting many people in other parts of the world including heterosexual and homosexual persons, infants and children, and blood transfusion recipients of both sexes and all ages. One example of community mobilization in response to it comes from Greenwich Village in New York City. Greenwich Village is an affluent old Manhattan neighborhood with a population of about 61 thousand. It has long been famous as the residence of artists, writers, and bohemians, and in the 1980s it was assumed to have a homosexual population of 25 to 30 percent, or about 18 thousand persons. In 1987, at least seven hundred people with AIDS, out of more than nine thousand cases in the city as a whole, were concentrated in the Village. Accompanied by the unprecedented frequency of young adults' deaths and incapacitation, the epidemic has had a powerful impact on the community. Sixty AIDS support groups meet each week in the Village: healing circles, bereavement groups, and groups for parents of AIDS victims, for women with AIDS (one provides baby-sitting), for veterans with AIDS, even a group conducted in Spanish (Graham and Ricklefs 1987:1).

In conclusion, let us once again open up our perspectives in space and time: [O]bdurate factors of the economy and national policy work against cities. But there is a distinct danger in being so mesmerized by the pathology of cities that one fails to see the rich opportunities in them. . . . [C]ities have always had problems of poverty, decay, exploitation, and sometimes, actual starvation and mass death. Even in their most golden periods, appalling physical and social conditions existed within cities. None of this is surprising; cities embody the best and the worst of the human condition. Arts and advanced mercantilism often exist side by side with every evil of exploitation, from addiction to alcohol and drugs to poverty. But somehow, cities have survived through the centuries, with new social hierarchies, new economic functions and new physical profiles (Peirce and Hagstrom 1981:144).

This sense of dynamism—of the ever-presence of vicissitudes—is one of the essentials of urban life, and it is important that city dwellers maintain a positive view of it.

To assert that the humanity of cities is real is not to claim that cities ever were, are now, or ever will be, utopias. What is claimed is that the humanity of cities requires the constant striving for the best by and for all city dwellers, rich and poor, and that this striving, to be successful, must be informed by knowledge and awareness of all the options offered by life in the cities of the world.

SUGGESTED ADDITIONAL READING

Appleyard, Donald. *Livable Streets*. Berkeley: University of California Press, 1981. Advocates planning and activism in conjunction. Many photographs.

Breines, Simon, and William J. Dean. *The Pedestrian Revolution: Streets without Cars*. New York: Vintage, 1974. Acknowledging Lewis Mumford and Jane Jacobs, among others, for their inspiration, the authors write in the same spirit as William H. Whyte (1980). Excellent photographs.

Fornos, Werner. *Gaining People, Losing Ground: A Blueprint for Stabilizing World Population*. Washington, D.C.: The Population Institute; Ephrata, Pa.: Science Press, 1987. A succinct, factual, and eloquent presentation of the magnitude of the population problem; its various threats to the survival of humanity, including city dwellers; and the political obstructions that make coping with the problem more difficult than it would be otherwise.

Huth, Mary Jo. *The Urban Habitat: Past, Present, and Future*. Chicago: Nelson-Hall, 1978. Discusses British "new towns" in some detail, as well as other experiments in improving urban life. Photographs.

Perin, Constance. *Everything in Its Place: Social Order and Land Use in America*. Princeton: Princeton University Press, 1977. Perin emphasizes the effects, for good and ill, of American cultural values on housing and urban land use, consistent with a theme of this book that cities are parts of larger systems of values.

Bibliography

Abu-Lughod, Janet L. 1961. Migrant Adjustment to City Life: The Egyptian Case. *American Journal of Sociology* 67:22–32.

———. 1965. The Emergence of Differential Fertility in Urban Egypt. *The Milbank Memorial Fund Quarterly* 43:235–53.

———. 1969. Varieties of Urban Experience: Contrast, Coexistence, and Coalescence in Cairo. In *Middle Eastern Cities. A Symposium on Ancient, Islamic, and Contemporary Middle Eastern Urbanism.* Ira M. Lapidus, ed., pp. 159–87. Berkeley: University of California Press.

———. 1971. *Cairo: 1001 Years of the City Victorious.* Princeton: Princeton University Press.

———. 1981. *Rabat: Urban Apartheid in Morocco.* Princeton: Princeton University Press.

Achor, Shirley. 1978. *Mexican Americans in a Dallas Barrio.* Tucson: University of Arizona Press.

Adams, Bert N. 1968. *Kinship in an Urban Setting.* Chicago: Markham.

Adams, Robert McCormick, and Hans J. Nissen. 1972. *The Uruk Countryside:*

The Natural Setting of Urban Societies. Chicago: University of Chicago Press.

Agins, Teri. 1985a. Latin Oases. To Hispanics in U. S., a Bodega, or Grocery, Is a Vital Part of Life. *The Wall Street Journal,* 15 Mar.

———. 1985b. Urban Herbs: Why Rosemary and Basil Ride on the Subway: Because It's a Fast Way to Go from a South Bronx Farm to the Top Restaurants. *The Wall Street Journal,* 19 Mar.

Ahlbrandt, Roger S., Jr. 1984. *Neighborhoods, People, and Community.* New York: Plenum.

Ahmed, Imam. 1986. Study Stresses Gravity of Egypt's Pollution Problems. *Middle East Times* 4(19–20).

Allman, T. D. 1981. Pomp and Desperation: England's Retreat from Civility. *Harper's* 263(Nov.):14–18.

American-Arab Anti-Discrimination Committee. 1986a. First Nationwide Arab-American Consumer Protest Launched. *ADC Times. The Newsletter of the American-Arab Anti-Discrimination Committee 7(3).*

———. 1986b. *The JDL and Meir Kahane. ADC Times. The Newsletter of the American-Arab Anti-Discrimination Committee* 7(3).

Anderson, E. N., Jr. 1972. Some Chinese Methods of Dealing with Crowding. *Urban Anthropology* 1:141–50.

Anderson, Elijah. 1978. *A Place on the Corner.* Chicago: University of Chicago Press.

Arriaga, Eduardo E. 1968. Components of City Growth in Selected Latin American Countries. *The Millbank Memorial Fund Quarterly* 46 (2, Part 1):237–52.

Aschenbrenner, Joyce. 1975. *Lifelines: Black Families in Chicago.* New York: Holt, Rinehart & Winston.

Aschenbrenner, Joyce, and Lloyd R. Collins, eds. 1978. *The Processes of Urbanism: A Multidisciplinary Approach.* The Hague: Mouton.

Association of Arab-American University Graduates. 1986a. Arab-American Panel Examines Motives behind Arab "Terrorist" Image. *Newsletter* 19(1).

———. 1986b. Israeli Filmmakers Linked to Rash of Anti-Arab Films. *Newsletter* 19(1).

Aswad, Barbara C., ed. 1974. *Arabic Speaking Communities in American Cities.* Staten Island, N. Y.: Center for Migration Studies of New York City.

Bach, Rebecca, Saad Gadalla, Hind Abu Seoud Khattab, and John Gulick. 1985. Mother's Influence on Daughters' Orientations toward Education: An Egyptian Case Study. *Comparative Education Review* 29:375–84.

Bahn, Adele, and Angela Jaquez. 1984. One Style of Dominican Bridal Shower. In *The Apple Sliced: Sociological Studies of New York City.* Vernon Boggs, Gerald Handel, and Sylvia F. Fava, eds., pp. 131–46. South Hadley, Mass.: Bergin & Garvey.

Bailey, Anthony. 1978. A Singular Place Called the Creggan. *Observer Magazine* (London) (31 Dec.):22 + .

Baldassare, Mark. 1979. *Residential Crowding in Urban America.* Berkeley: University of California Press.

Baldwin, John, and A. E. Bottoms, with Monica A. Walker. 1976. *The Urban Criminal: A Study in Sheffield.* London: Tavistock.

Baltzell, E. Digby. 1979. *Puritan Boston and Quaker Philadelphia: Two Prot-*

estant Ethics and the Spirit of Class Authority and Leadership. New York: Free Press.

Banerjee, Tridib, and William C. Baer. 1984. *Beyond the Neighborhood Unit: Residential Environments and Public Policy.* New York: Plenum.

Barnes, J. A. 1969. Networks and Political Process. In *Social Networks in Urban Situations: Analyses of Personal Relationships in Central African Towns.* J. Clyde Mitchell, ed., pp. 51–76. Manchester: Manchester University Press, for the Institute for Social Research, University of Zambia.

———. 1978. Neither Peasants nor Townsmen: A Critique of a Segment of the Folk-Urban Continuum. In *Scale and Social Organization.* Fredrik Barth, ed., pp. 13–40. Oslo: Universitetsforlaget.

Barton, Josef J. 1975. *Peasants and Strangers: Italians, Rumanians, and Slovaks in an American City, 1890–1950.* Cambridge, Mass.: Harvard University Press.

Basham, Richard. 1978. *Urban Anthropology: The Cross-Cultural Study of Complex Societies.* Palo Alto, Calif.: Mayfield.

Bater, James H. 1980. *The Soviet City: Ideal and Reality.* Beverly Hills, Calif.: Sage.

Bauer, Janet. 1984. New Models and Traditional Networks: Migrant Women in Tehran. In *Women in the Cities of Asia: Migration and Urban Adaptation.* James T. Fawcett, Siew-Ean Khoo, and Peter C. Smith, eds., pp. 269–93. Boulder, Colo.: Westview.

Bayor, Ronald H. 1978. *Neighbors in Conflict: The Irish, Germans, Jews, and Italians of New York City, 1929–1941.* Baltimore: The Johns Hopkins University Press.

Becker, Howard Saul, and Irving Louis Horowitz. 1971. The Culture of Civility. In *Culture and Civility in San Francisco.* Howard Saul Becker, ed., pp. 4–19. New Brunswick, N.J.: Transaction.

Belmonte, Thomas. 1979. *The Broken Fountain.* New York: Columbia University Press.

Bensman, Joseph. 1984. Epilogue: The Apple Tree. In *The Apple Sliced: Sociological Studies of New York City.* Vernon Boggs, Gerald Handel, and Sylvia F. Fava, eds, pp. 336–46. South Hadley, Mass.: Bergin & Garvey.

Berger, Alan S. 1978. *The City: Urban Communities and Their Problems.* Dubuque, Iowa: Brown.

Berger, Peter L., ed. 1964. *The Human Shape of Work: Studies in the Sociology of Occupations.* New York: Macmillan.

Berque, Jacques, and Mustafa al-Shekaa. 1972. La Gamaliya depuis un siècle. In *Colloque international sur l'histoire du Caire.* Cairo: Ministry of Culture of the Arab Republic of Egypt. (In French.)

Black, Ellinor I., and T. S. Simey. 1954. *Neighborhood and Community: An Enquiry into Social Relationships on Housing Estates in Liverpool and Sheffield.* Liverpool: University Press of Liverpool.

Black, J. Thomas. 1980. The Changing Economic Role of Central Cities and Suburbs. In *The Prospective City: Economic, Population, Energy, and Environmental Developments.* Arthur P. Solomon, ed., pp. 80–123. Cam ridge, Mass: MIT Press.

Blair, Thomas L. V. 1974. *The International Urban Crisis.* New York: Hill & Wang.

Blake, Peter. 1977. *Form Follows Fiasco: Why Modern Architecture Hasn't Worked*. Boston: Little, Brown.

Blanc, Haim. 1964. *Communal Dialects in Baghdad*. Cambridge, Mass.: Center for Middle Eastern Studies, Harvard University.

Bleiker, Annemarie H. 1972. The Proximity Model and Urban Social Relations. *Urban Anthropology* 1:151–75.

Bloom, Justin L., and Shinsuke Asano. 1981. Tsukuba Science City: Japan Tries Planned Innovation. *Science* 212(4500):1239–47.

Blumenfeld, Ruth. 1981. Mohawks: Round Trip to High Steel. In *Anthropological Realities: Readings in the Science of Culture*. Jeanne Guillemin, ed., pp. 293–96. New Brunswick, N.J.: Transaction.

Blundell, William E. 1986. Gripe Session. New Yorkers on Panel Feel City Is Decaying, but Most Still Love It. *The Wall Street Journal*, 9 May.

Bonine, Michael E. 1979. City and Hinterland in Central Iran. In *Interdisziplinäre Iran-Forschung: Beiträge aus Kulturgeographie, Ethnologie, Soziologie, und neuerer Geschichte*. Günther Schweizer, ed., pp. 141–56. Wiesbaden: Reichert.

Boone, Margaret S. 1980. The Uses of Traditional Concepts in the Development of New Urban Roles: Cuban Women in the United States. In *A World of Women. Anthropological Studies of Women in Societies of the World*. Erika Bourguignon, ed., pp. 235–69. New York: Praeger; Brooklyn: Bergin.

Borah, Woodrow. 1980. Demographic and Physical Aspects of the Transition from the Aboriginal to the Colonial World. *Comparative Urban Research* 8:41–70.

Bott, Elizabeth. 1957. *Family and Social Network: Roles, Norms, and External Relationships of Ordinary Urban Families*. New York: Free Press.

———. 1971. *Family and Social Network: Roles, Norms, and External Relationships of Ordinary Urban Families*. 2nd ed. New York: Free Press.

Bracey, H. E. 1964. *Neighbors: Subdivision Life in England and the United States*. Baton Rouge: Louisiana State University Press.

Braidwood, Robert J., and Gordon R. Willey, eds. 1962. *Courses Toward Urban Life: Archeological Considerations of Some Cultural Alternates*. Chicago: Aldine.

Britan, Gerald M., and Ronald Cohen. 1980. Toward an Anthropology of Formal Organizations. In *Hierarchy and Society: Anthropological Perspectives on Bureaucracy*. Gerald M. Britan and Ronald Cohen, eds., pp. 9–30. Philadelphia: Institute for the Study of Human Issues.

Brown, Claude. 1965. *Manchild in the Promised Land*. New York: Macmillan.

Brown, Kenneth L. 1976. *People in Salé: Tradition and Change in a Moroccan City, 1830–1930*. Manchester: Manchester University.

Brush, John E. 1970. The Growth of the Presidency Towns. In *Urban India: Society, Space and Image*. Richard G. Fox, ed., pp. 91- 114. [Durham, N.C.]: Program in Comparative Studies on Southern Asia, Duke University.

Bunster, Ximena. 1978. Talking Pictures: A Study of Proletarian Mothers in Lima, Peru. *Studies in the Anthropology of Visual Communication* 5(1):37–55.

Bunster, Ximena, and Elsa M. Chaney. 1985. *Sellers and Servants: Working Women in Lima, Peru*. Photography by Ellan Young. New York: Praeger.

Burby, Raymond J., III, and Shirley F. Weiss. 1976. *New Communities U.S.A.* Lexington, Mass.: Lexington.

Burns, James McGregor. 1981. Power and Politics. *Society* 18(4):5–9.

Buttimer, Anne. 1980. Social Space and the Planning of Residential Areas. In *The Human Experience of Space and Place.* Anne Buttimer and David Seamon, eds., pp. 21–54. New York: St. Martin's.

Campbell, Angus, Philip E. Converse, and Willard L. Rodgers. 1976. *The Quality of American Life: Perceptions, Evaluations, and Satisfactions.* New York: Russell Sage Foundation.

Canavan, Peter. 1984. The Gay Community at Jacob Riis Park. In *The Apple Sliced: Sociological Studies of New York City.* Vernon Boggs, Gerald Handel, and Sylvia F. Fava, eds., pp. 67–82. South Hadley, Mass.: Bergin & Garvey.

Caro Baroja, Julio. 1963. The City and the Country: Reflexions on Some Ancient Commonplaces. In *Mediterranean Countrymen: Essays in the Social Anthropology of the Mediterranean.* Julian Pitt-Rivers, ed., pp. 27–40. Paris: Mouton.

Carter, Luther J. 1980. Global 2000 Report: Vision of a Gloomy World. *Science* 209 (4456):575–76.

Carter, Ronald L., and Kim Q. Hill. 1979. *The Criminal's Image of the City.* New York: Pergamon.

Cassidy, Robert. 1980. *Livable Cities: A Grass-Roots Guide to Rebuilding Urban America.* New York: Holt, Rinehart & Winston.

Castells, Manuel. 1983. *The City and the Grassroots: A Cross-Cultural Theory of Urban Social Movements.* Berkeley: University of California Press.

Celis, William, III. 1986. Crumbling Projects. Public-Housing Units Are Rapidly Decaying, Causing Many to Close. *The Wall Street Journal,* 15 Dec.

Chamie, Joseph. 1981. *Religion and Fertility: Arab Christian-Muslim Differentials.* Cambridge, England: Cambridge University Press.

Charles Stewart Mott Foundation. c. 1979. *Report to the People. The Flint* [Mich.] *Process: A Look at Our Community.*

Cherniss, Cary. 1980. *Staff Burnout: Job Stress in the Human Services.* Beverly Hills, Calif.: Sage.

Chinoy, Ely. 1964. Manning the Machines—The Assembly-Line Worker. In *The Human Shape of Work: Studies in the Sociology of Occupations.* Peter L. Berger, ed., pp. 51–82. New York: Macmillan.

Chock, Phyllis Pease. 1981. The Greek-American Small Businessman: A Cultural Analysis. *Journal of Anthropological Research* 37:46–60.

Choldin, Harvey M. 1976. Housing Standards versus Ecological Forces: Regulating Population Density in Bombay. In *The Mutual Interaction of People and Their Built Environment: A Cross-Cultural Perspective.* Amos Rapoport, ed., pp. 287–331. The Hague: Mouton.

Christaller; Walter. 1966. *Central Places in Southern Germany.* Carlisle W. Baskin, trans. Englewood Cliffs, N.J.: Prentice Hall. [1st ed., 1933.]

Cichocki, Mary K. 1980. Women's Travel Patterns in a Suburban Development. In *New Space for Women.* Gerda R. Wekerle, Rebecca Peterson, and David Morley, eds., pp. 151–63. Boulder, Colo.: Westview.

Clarke, John Innes. 1963. *The Iranian City of Shiraz.* Durham, England: Department of Geography, University of Durham.

———. 1980. Contemporary Urban Growth. In *The Changing Middle Eastern City*. G. H. Blake, and R. I. Lawless, eds., pp. 34–53. London: Croom Helm.

Clay, Grady. 1980. Close-Up. *How to Read the American City*. Chicago: University of Chicago Press.

Cohen, Abner. 1967. Stranger Communities. The Hausa. In *The City of Ibadan*. Peter Cutt Lloyd, A. L. Mabogunje, and B. Awe, eds., pp. 117–27. Cambridge, England: Cambridge University Press.

———. 1969. *Custom and Politics in Urban Africa: A Study of Hausa Migrants in Yoruba Towns*. Berkeley: University of California Press.

———. 1974. *Two-Dimensional Man: An Essay on the Anthropology of Power and Symbolism in Complex Society*. Berkeley: University of California Press.

———. 1981. *The Politics of Elite Culture: Explorations in the Dramaturgy of Power in a Modern African Society*. Berkeley: University of California Press.

Cohen, Albert K. 1955. *Delinquent Boys. The Culture of the Gang*. Glencoe, Ill.: Free Press.

Cohen, Roger. 1985. Soccer Violence Uncovers Ugly Nationalism. *The Wall Street Journal*, 5 June.

Cole, Robert E. 1971. *Japanese Blue Collar: The Changing Tradition*. Berkeley: University of California Press.

Collins, Thomas W., ed. 1980. *Cities in a Larger Context. Southern Anthropological Society Proceedings, No. 14*. Athens, Ga.: University of Georgia.

Colson, Elizabeth. 1978. A Redundancy of Actors. In *Scale and Social Organization*. Fredrik Barth, ed., pp. 150–62. Oslo: Universitetsforlaget.

Constantinides, Pamela. 1977. The Greek Cypriots: Factors in the Maintenance of Ethnic Identity. In *Between Two Cultures: Migrants and Minorities in Britain*. James L. Watson, ed, pp. 269–300. Oxford: Basil Blackwell.

Conway, Donald J., ed. 1977. *Human Response to Tall Buildings*. Stroudsburg, Pa.: Dowden, Hutchinson & Ross.

Cooper, Ashley. 1985. Doing the Charleston. *The Charleston* [S.C.] *News and Courier/The Evening Post*, 1 June.

Costello, Vincent Francis. 1977. *Urbanization in the Middle East*. Cambridge, England: Cambridge University Press.

Crenson, Matthew A. 1983. *Neighborhood Politics*. Cambridge, Mass.: Harvard University Press.

Critchfield, Richard. 1979. Revolution of the Village. *Human Behavior* 8(5):18–27.

Crookston, Peter, ed. 1978. *Village London: The Observer's Guide to the Real London*. London: Thames & Hudson.

Cross, Malcolm. 1979. *Urbanization and Urban Growth in the Caribbean: An Essay on Social Change in Dependent Societies*. Cambridge, England: Cambridge University Press.

Cuomo, Mario Matthew. 1974. *Forest Hills Diary: The Crisis of Low-Income Housing*. New York: Random House.

Dahl, Robert A. 1961. *Who Governs? Democracy and Power in an American City*. New Haven: Yale University Press.

David, Jean-Claude. 1979. Les quartiers anciens dans la croissance moderne de la ville d'Alep. In *L'Espace social de la ville Arabe*. Dominique Chevallier, ed., pp. 135–44. Paris: Maisonneuve & Larose. (In French.)

Davis, Kingsley. 1980. The First Cities: How and Why Did They Arise? In

Urban Place and Process: Readings in the Anthropology of Cities. Irwin Press and M. Estellie Smith, eds., pp. 133–43. New York: Macmillan.

Davis, Norman. 1967. *Greek Coins and Cities: Illustrated from the Seattle Art Museum.* London: Spink.

Delacoste, Frédérique, and Priscilla Alexander, eds. 1987. *Sex Work: Writings by Women in the Sex Industry.* Pittsburgh: Cleis.

De Visé, Pierre. 1979–80. The Expanding Singles Housing Market in Chicago: Implications for Reviving City Neighborhoods. *Urbanism Past and Present,* No. 9:30–39.

Dennis, Norman. 1970. *People and Planning. The Sociology of Housing in Sunderland.* London: Faber.

Deshen, Shlomo. 1982. Social Organization and Politics in Israeli Urban Quarters. *The Jerusalem Quarterly* 22:21–37.

Dike, Azuka A. 1985. Environmental Problems in Third World Cities: A Nigerian Example. *Current Anthropology* 26:501–5.

Domhoff, G. William. 1978. *Who Really Rules? New Haven and Community Power Reexamined.* New Brunswick, N.J.: Transaction.

Dore, Ronald P. 1958. *City Life in Japan: A Study of a Tokyo Ward.* Berkeley: University of California Press.

Doxiadis, Constantine Apostolou. 1975. *Anthropopolis: City for Human Development.* New York: Norton.

Du Toit, Brian M., and Helen I. Safa, eds. 1975. *Migration and Urbanization: Models and Adaptive Strategies.* The Hague: Mouton.

Dubetsky, A. R. 1977. Class and Community in Urban Turkey. In *Commoners, Climbers and Notables: A Sampler of Studies on Social Ranking in the Middle East.* C. A. O. Van Nieuwenhuijze, ed., pp. 360–71. Leiden: E. J. Brill.

Dumont, Matthew P. 1968. *The Absurd Healer: Perspectives of a Community Psychiatrist.* New York: Viking.

Duncan, James S., Jr. 1976. Landscape and the Communication of Social Identity. In *The Mutual Interaction of People and Their Built Environment: A Cross-Cultural Perspective.* Amos Rapoport, ed., pp. 391–401. The Hague: Mouton.

Dwyer, Denis John. 1975. *People and Housing in Third World Cities: Perspectives on the Problem of Spontaneous Settlements.* London: Longman.

Eames, Edwin, and Judith Granich Goode. 1973. *Urban Poverty in a Cross-Cultural Context.* New York: Free Press.

———. 1977. *Anthropology of the City: An Introduction to Urban Anthropology.* Englewood Cliffs, N.J.: Prentice-Hall.

Eddy, Elizabeth M. 1968. *Urban Anthropology. Research Perspectives and Strategies. Southern Anthropological Society Proceedings No. 2.* Athens, Ga.: Southern Anthropological Society.

Eickelman, Dale F. 1974. Is There an Islamic City? The Making of a Quarter in a Moroccan Town. *International Journal of Middle East Studies* 5:274–94.

Eisner, Jane. 1987. In Modern Times, Traffic Threatens to Conquer Rome. *The Philadelphia Inquirer,* 15 Feb.

El Mahdi, Ahmed. 1986. The Spotlight on Housing Problems. *Middle East Times,* 5 July.

el-Messiri, Sawsan. 1978. Self Images of Traditional Urban Women in Cairo.

In *Women in the Muslim World.* Lois Beck and Nikki Keddie, eds., pp. 522–40. Cambridge, Mass.: Harvard University Press.

Ellovich, Risa, and Carol Stack, eds. 1985. *The Nature of Urban Anthropology in the 1980's.* Washington, D.C.: American Anthropological Association.

English, Paul Ward. 1966. *City and Village in Iran: Settlement and Economy in the Kirman Basin.* Madison: University of Wisconsin Press.

Eppler, Erhard. 1985. Mal-Development in Industrial Countries. *IFDA Dossier* (International Foundation for Development Alternatives), No. 50 (Nov./Dec.):57–66.

Esteva, Gustavo. 1986. Mexico: Self-Help Network. *IFDA Dossier* (International Foundation for Development Alternatives), No. 51 (Jan./Feb.):73–75.

Eversley, David. 1973. *The Planner in Society: The Changing Role of a Profession.* London: Faber.

Farley, Reynolds. 1976. Components of Suburban Population Growth. In *The Changing Face of the Suburbs.* Barry Schwartz, ed., pp. 3–38. Chicago: University of Chicago Press.

Farmanfarmaian, Sattareh. 1970. *Piramun-e Ruspigari dar Shahr-e Tehran* [The Prostitution Area in the City of Tehran]. Tehran: Tehran School of Social Work. (In Persian.)

Farsoun, Samih K. 1970. Family Structure and Society in Modern Lebanon. In *Peoples and Cultures of the Middle East.* Vol. 2., *Life in the Cities, Towns, and Countryside.* Louise E. Sweet, ed., pp. 257–307. Garden City, N.Y.: Natural History Press, for the American Museum of Natural History.

Fathy, Hassan. 1973. *Architecture for the Poor: An Experiment in Rural Egypt.* Chicago: University of Chicago Press.

Fava, Sylvia F. 1980. Women's Place in the New Suburbia. In *New Space for Women.* Gerda R. Wekerle, Rebecca Peterson, and David Morley, eds., pp. 129–49. Boulder, Colo.: Westview.

Feldman, Kerry D. 1975. Demographic Indices of the Squatter Problem in Davao City, Philippines. *Urban Anthropology* 4:365–86.

Fichter, Joseph H., S. J. 1954. *Social Relations in the Urban Parish.* Chicago: University of Chicago Press.

Findlay, A. M. 1980. Migration in Space: Immobility in Society. In *The Changing Middle Eastern City.* G. H. Blake and R. I. Lawless, eds., pp. 54–76. London: Croom Helm.

Firey, Walter I. 1968. *Land Use in Central Boston.* Westport, Conn.: Greenwood. [1st ed., 1947.]

Firth, Raymond, Jane Hubert, and Anthony Forge. 1970. *Families and Their Relatives: Kinship in a Middle-Class Sector of London. An Anthropological Study.* New York: Humanities.

Fischer, Claude S. 1982. *To Dwell among Friends: Personal Networks in Town and City.* Chicago: University of Chicago Press.

Fishman, Robert. 1977. *Urban Utopias in the Twentieth Century: Ebenezer Howard, Frank Lloyd Wright, and Le Corbusier.* New York: Basic.

Flanagan, Jack. 1984. Letter to Bronx Frontier Supporters from Chairman of the Board, the Bronx Frontier Corporation, 1080 Leggett Avenue, The Bronx, N.Y. 10474.

Flandrin, Jean-Louis. 1979. *Families in Former Times: Kinship, Household, and Sexuality*. Richard Southern, trans. Cambridge, England: Cambridge University Press.

Folan, William J., Laraine A. Fletcher, and Ellen R. Kintz. 1979. Fruit, Fiber, Bark, and Resin: Social Organization of a Maya Urban Center. *Science* 204(4394):697–701.

Follett, Ken. 1981. *The Key to Rebecca*. New York: New American Library. A Signet Book.

Foner, Nancy. 1977. The Jamaicans: Cultural and Social Change among Migrants in Britain. In *Between Two Cultures: Migrants and Minorities in Britain*. James L. Watson, ed., pp. 120–50. Oxford: Basil Blackwell.

Foster, George M., and Robert V. Kemper, eds. 1974. *Anthropologists in Cities*. Boston: Little, Brown.

Fox, Richard G. 1972. Rationale and Romance in Urban Anthropology. *Urban Anthropology* 1:205–33.

———. 1977. *Urban Anthropology: Cities in Their Cultural Settings*. Englewood Cliffs, N. J.: Prentice-Hall.

Freedman, Jonathan L. 1975. *Crowding and Behavior*. New York: Viking.

Freeman, Jo. 1980. Women and Urban Policy. In *Women and the American City*. Catharine R. Stimpson et al., eds., pp. 4–22. Chicago: University of Chicago Press.

Freilich, Morris. 1977. Mohawk Heroes and Trinidadian Peasants. In *Marginal Natives at Work: Anthropologists in the Field*. Morris Freilich, ed., pp. 151–216. Cambridge, Mass.: Schenkman.

Fried, Marc, with Ellen Fitzgerald et al. 1973. *The World of the Urban Working Class*. Cambridge, Mass.: Harvard University Press.

Friedl, John, and Noel J. Chrisman, eds. 1975. *City Ways. A Selective Reader in Urban Anthropology*. New York: Crowell.

Fuguitt, Glenn V., and James J. Zuiches. 1975. Residential Preferences and Population Distribution. *Demography* 12:491–504.

Fustel de Coulanges, Numa Denis. 1956. *The Ancient City: A Study on the Religion, Laws, and Institutions of Greece and Rome*. Garden City, N. Y.: Doubleday. [1st ed., 1864.]

Galle, Omer R. 1963. Occupational Composition and the Metropolitan Hierarchy: The Inter- and Intra-Metropolitan Division of Labor. *American Journal of Sociology* 69:260–69.

Gans, Herbert J. 1962. *The Urban Villagers: Group and Class in the Life of Italian Americans*. New York: Free Press of Glencoe.

———. 1967. *The Levittowners: Ways of Life and Politics in a New Suburban Community*. New York: Pantheon.

Garson, Barbara. 1977. *All the Livelong Day: The Meaning and Demeaning of Routine Work*. New York: Penguin.

Geertz, Hildred. 1979. The Meanings of Family Ties. In *Meaning and Order in Moroccan Society. Three Essays in Cultural Analysis*. Clifford Geertz, Hildred Geertz, and Lawrence Rosen, eds., pp. 315- 91. Cambridge, England: Cambridge University Press.

Gest, Ted. 1981. Violence in Big Cities—Behind the Surge. *U. S. News and World Report* 90(23 Feb.):63–65.

Gilbert, Dennis. 1981. Cognatic Descent Groups in Upper-Class Lima (Peru). *American Ethnologist* 8:739–57.

Gillis, A. R. 1983. High-Rise Housing and Psychological Strain. In *Cities and Urban Living.* Mark Baldassare, ed., pp. 243–63. New York: Columbia University Press.

Ginsberg, Yona. 1975. *Jews in a Changing Neighborhood: The Study of Mattapan.* New York: Free Press.

Glazer, Nathan, and Daniel Patrick Moynihan. 1970. *Beyond the Melting Pot: The Negroes, Puerto Ricans, Jews, Italians, and Irish of New York City.* 2nd ed. Cambridge, Mass.: MIT Press.

Gmelch, George. 1977. *The Irish Tinkers: The Urbanization of an Itinerant People.* Menlo Park, Calif.: Cummings.

Gmelch, George, and Walter P. Zenner, eds. 1980. *Urban Life. Readings in Urban Anthropology.* New York: St. Martin's.

Godwin, John. 1978. *Murder U.S.A.: The Ways We Kill Each Other.* New York: Ballantine.

Goering, John M., Maynard Robison, and Knight Hoover. 1977. *The Best Eight Blocks in Harlem: The Last Decade of Urban Reform.* Washington, D.C.: University Press of America.

Goetze, Rolf. 1976. *Building Neighborhood Confidence: A Humanistic Strategy for Urban Housing.* Cambridge, Mass.: Ballinger.

Goffman, Erving. 1972. *Relations in Public. Microstudies of the Public Order.* New York: Harper & Row.

Goist, Park Dixon. 1977. *From Main Street to State Street: Town, City, and Community in America.* Port Washington, N.Y.: Kennikat.

Goldner, Fred H. 1984. The Daily Apple: Medicine and Media. In *The Apple Sliced: Sociological Studies of New York City.* Vernon Boggs, Gerald Handel, and Sylvia F. Fava, eds., pp. 214–33. South Hadley, Mass.: Bergin & Garvey.

Goodall, Alan. 1986. Squeezed Residents Grow Weary of Bulging Tokyo. *USA Today,* 9 May.

Gordon, Margaret T., Stephanie Riger, Robert K. LeBaily, and Linda Heath. 1981. Crime, Women, and the Quality of Urban Life. In *Women and the American City.* Catharine B. Stimpson et al., eds., pp. 141–57. Chicago: University of Chicago Press.

Gordon, Milton M. 1978. *Human Nature, Class, and Ethnicity.* New York: Oxford University Press.

Gould, Peter, and Rodney White. 1980. Mental Maps. In *Urban Place and Process: Readings in the Anthropology of Cities.* Irwin Press and M. Estellie Smith, eds., pp. 96–104. New York: Macmillan.

Graham, Ellen, and Roger Ricklefs. 1987. Plague Years. AIDS Has Been Cruel to Greenwich Village and Its Homosexuals. *The Wall Street Journal,* 13 Mar.

Grant, James P. 1983. A Children's Revolution for 6 Billion Dollars a Year (or 1% of World Military Expenditure). *IFDA Dossier* (International Foundation for Development Alternatives), No. 37 (Sept./Oct.):37–51.

Graves, Theodore D. 1971. Drinking and Drunkenness among Urban Indians. In *The American Indian in Urban Society.* Jack O. Waddell and O. Michael Watson, eds., pp. 274–311. Boston: Little, Brown.

Gregory, David D. 1982. The Meaning of Urban Life: Pluralization of Life Worlds in Seville. In *Urban Life in Mediterranean Europe: Anthropological*

Perspectives. Michael Kenny and David I. Kertzer, eds., pp. 253–72. Urbana: University of Illinois Press.

Greenberg, Stephanie W., William M. Rohe, and Jay R. Williams. 1981. *Safe and Secure Neighborhoods: Physical Characteristics and Informal Territorial Control in High and Low Crime Neighborhoods.* RTI/1888/00–02F. Research Triangle Park, N. C.: Research Triangle Institute.

Greenbie, Barrie B. 1976. *Design for Diversity: Planning for Natural Man in the Neo-Technic Environment: An Ethological Approach.* Amsterdam: Elsevier.

Gugler, Josef, and William G. Flanagan. 1978. *Urbanization and Social Change in West Africa.* Cambridge, England: Cambridge University Press.

Guldin, Gregory. 1980. Whose Neighborhood Is This? Ethnicity and Community in Hong Kong. *Urban Anthropology* 9:243–63.

Gulick, John. 1963. Images of an Arab City. *Journal of the American Institute of Planners* 29:179–98.

———. 1967a. Baghdad: Portrait of a City in Physical and Cultural Change. *Journal of the American Institute of Planners* 33:246–55.

———. 1967b. *Tripoli: A Modern Arab City.* Cambridge, Mass.: Harvard University Press.

———. 1969. Village and City: Cultural Continuities in Twentieth Century Middle Eastern Cultures. In *Middle Eastern Cities: A Symposium on Ancient, Islamic, and Contemporary Middle Eastern Urbanism.* Ira M. Lapidus, ed., pp. 122–58. Berkeley: University of California Press.

———. 1974a. Private Life and Public Face: Cultural Continuities in the Domestic Architecture of Isfahan. *Iranian Studies* 7:629–51.

———. 1974b. Urban Anthropology. In *Handbook of Social and Cultural Anthropology.* John J. Honigmann, ed., pp. 979–1029. Chicago: Rand McNally.

———. 1986. The Essence of Urban Anthropology: Integration of Micro and Macro Research Perspectives. *Urban Anthropology* 13:2–3.

Gulick, John, and Margaret E. Gulick. 1974. Varieties of Domestic Social Organization in the Iranian City of Isfahan. In *City and Peasant: A Study in Sociocultural Dynamics. Annals of the New York Academy of Sciences,* Vol. 220, Art. 6. A. L. LaRuffa, Ruth S. Freed, Lucie Wood Saunders, Edward C. Hansen, and Sula Benet, eds., pp. 441–69. New York: New York Academy of Sciences.

———. 1975. Kinship, Contraception and Family Planning in the Iranian City of Isfahan. In *Population and Social Organization.* Moni Nag, ed., pp. 241–93. The Hague: Mouton.

Gullestad, Marianne. 1984. *Kitchen-Table Society: A Case Study of the Family Life and Friendships of Young Working-Class Mothers in Urban Norway.* Oslo: Universitetsforlaget.

Gurock, Jeffry S. 1979. *When Harlem Was Jewish, 1870–1930.* New York: Columbia University Press.

Gutkind, Peter C. W. 1974. *Urban Anthropology: Perspectives on Third World Urbanization and Urbanism.* New York: Barnes & Noble.

Hackenberg, Robert A. 1980. New Patterns of Urbanization in Southeast Asia: An Assessment. *Population and Development Review* 6:391–419.

Hall, Peter G. 1979. *The World Cities.* 2nd ed. New York: McGraw-Hill.

Hallman, Howard W. 1984. *Neighborhoods: Their Place in Urban Life.* Beverly Hills, Calif.: Sage.

Halpenny, Philip. 1975. Three Styles of Ethnic Migration in Kisenyi, Kampala. In *Town and Country in Central and Eastern Africa.* David Parkin, ed., pp. 276–87. London: Oxford University Press, for the International African Institute.

Hammam, Mona. 1981. Woman and Industrial Work in Egypt. *Al-Raida* (Beirut University College) 4(17):6–7.

Hampton, William A. 1970. *Democracy and Community: A Study of Politics in Sheffield.* London: Oxford University Press.

Handelman, Howard. 1979. *High-Rises and Shantytowns: Housing the Poor in Bogotá and Caracas.* American Universities Field Staff Reports. 1979/No. 9, South America. Hanover, N.H.: American Universities Field Staff.

Hannerz, Ulf. 1969. Soulside. *Inquiries into Ghetto Culture and Community.* New York: Columbia University Press.

———. 1980. *Exploring the City: Inquiries Toward an Urban Anthropology.* New York: Columbia University Press.

Haqqi, Yahya. 1973. The Saint's Lamp. In *The Saint's Lamp and Other Stories.* M. M. Badawi, trans., pp. 1–38. Leiden: E. J. Brill.

Hardoy, Jorge E. 1975. Two Thousand Years of Latin American Urbanization. In *Urbanization in Latin America: Approaches and Issues.* Jorge E. Hardoy, ed., pp. 3–55. Garden City, N.Y.: Anchor/Doubleday.

Harlow, Nora. 1975. *Sharing the Children: Village Child Rearing within the City.* New York: Harper & Row.

Harris, Walter D., Jr. 1971. *The Growth of Latin American Cities.* Athens: Ohio University Press.

Hart, Kathy. 1977. Carolina's Campus-Oriented Students Living in Psychological Ghetto. *The Daily Tar Heel* (University of North Carolina at Chapel Hill), 30 Aug.

Hartman, Chester W. 1974. *Yerba Buena: Land Grab and Community Resistance in San Francisco.* San Francisco: Glide.

Harvey, David. 1975. *Social Justice and the City.* Baltimore: The Johns Hopkins University Press.

Haugh, James Bertram. 1980. *Power and Influence in a Southern City: Compared with the Classic Community Power Studies of the Lynds, Hunter, Vidich and Bensman, and Dahl.* Washington, D.C.: University Press of America.

Hazlehurst, Leighton W. 1970. Urban Space and Activities. In *Urban India: Society, Space and Image.* Richard G. Fox, ed., pp. 186–95. [Durham, N.C.]: Program in Comparative Studies on Southern Asia, Duke University.

Helyar, John, and Robert Hanson. 1986. Tale of Two Cities. Chicago's Busy Center Masks a Loss of Jobs in Its Outlying Areas. *The Wall Street Journal,* 16 Apr.

Henslin, James M. 1968. Trust and the Cab Driver. In *Sociology and Everyday Life.* Marcello Truzzi, ed., pp. 138–58. Englewood Cliffs, N.J.: Prentice-Hall.

Herbert, David T. 1973. *Urban Geography: A Social Perspective.* New York: Praeger.

Hess, Karl. 1979. *Community Technology.* New York: Harper & Row.

Hilali, Abdul-Razzak. 1958. *Migration of Rural Folk to Towns in Iraq*. Baghdad: al-Najah. (In Arabic.)

Hill, Carole E. 1975. Adaptation in Public and Private Behavior of Ethnic Groups in an American Urban Setting. *Urban Anthropology* 4:333–47.

Hochschild, Arlie Russell. 1973. *The Unexpected Community: Portrait of an Old Age Subculture*. Berkeley: University of California Press.

Hodder, B. W. 1967. The Markets of Ibadan. In *The City of Ibadan*. Peter Cutt Lloyd, A. L. Mabogunje, and B. Awe, eds., pp. 173–90. Cambridge, England: Cambridge University Press.

Holden, Constance. 1985. Violence Seen as Public Health Issue. *Science* 230(4731):1257.

Hollingshead, August B., and Frederick C. Redlich. 1958. *Social Class and Mental Illness: A Community Study*. New York: Wiley.

Hollnsteiner, Mary. 1976. The Urbanization of Metropolitan Manila. In *Changing South-East Asian Cities: Readings on Urbanization*. Yue-Man Yeung and C. P. Lo, eds., pp. 174–84. Singapore: Oxford University Press.

Hummon, David M. 1986. Urban Views: Popular Perspectives on City Life. *Urban Life* 15(1):3–36.

Hunter, Albert. 1974. *Symbolic Communities: The Persistence and Change of Chicago's Local Communities*. Chicago: University of Chicago Press.

Hunter, Floyd. 1963. *Community Power Structure: A Study of Decision Makers*. Garden City, N.Y.: Anchor/Doubleday.

Ianni, Francis A. J. 1974. *Black Mafia: Ethnic Succession in Organized Crime*. New York: Simon & Schuster.

Idris, Yusuf. 1967. Farahat's Republic. In *Modern Arabic Short Stories*. Denys Johnson-Davies, comp. and trans., pp. 1–18. London: Heinemann.

Ikemma, William N. 1977. Revitalizing Inner-City Minority Communities. The Black Neighborhood-Based Environment in Houston. *Urbanism Past and Present*, No. 4:11–18.

Jackson, Kenneth T., and Stanley K. Schultz, eds. 1972. *Cities in American History*. New York: Knopf.

Jacobs, Jane. 1961. *The Death and Life of Great American Cities*. New York: Random House.

———. 1972. *The Economy of Cities*. Harmondsworth, England: Penguin.

Jacobs, Jerry. 1983. *Fun City: An Enthnographic Study of a Retirement Community*. Prospect Heights, Ill.: Waveland. [1st ed., 1974.]

Jefferson, Mark. 1939. The Law of the Primate City. *Geographical Review* 29:226–32.

Jeffries, Richard. 1978. *Class, Power and Ideology in Ghana: The Railwaymen of Sekondi*. Cambridge, England: Cambridge University Press.

Johnson, Sheila K. 1971. *Idle Haven: Community Building among the Working Class Retired*. Berkeley: University of California Press.

Jones, Steven H. 1978. The Necessity for a Macro-Cosmic Model in Urban Anthropological Studies. In *The Processes of Urbanism: A Multidisciplinary Approach*. Joyce Aschenbrenner and Lloyd R. Collins, eds., pp. 19–43. The Hague: Mouton.

Joseph, Suad. 1978. Women and the Neighborhood Street in Borj Hammond, Lebanon. In *Women in the Muslim World*. Lois Beck and Nikki Keddie, eds., pp. 541–57. Cambridge, Mass.: Harvard University Press.

Kandell, Jonathan. 1985. Nation in Jeopardy: Mexico City's Growth, Once Fostered, Turns into Economic Burden. *The Wall Street Journal*, 4 Oct.

Kang, Gay E., and Tai S. Kang. 1978. The Korean Urban Shoeshine Gang: A Minority Community. *Urban Anthropology* 7:171–83.

Kanter, Rosabeth Moss. 1979. Communes in Cities. In *Co-ops, Communes and Collectives: Experiments in Social Change in the 1960s and 1970s*. John Case and Rosemary C. R. Taylor, eds., pp. 112–35. New York: Pantheon.

Kaplan, Fredric, Julian Sobin, and Arne de Keijzer. 1985. *The China Guidebook*. Boston: Houghton Mifflin; New York: Eurasia.

Kaplan, Samuel. 1977. *The Dream Deferred: People, Politics, and Planning in Suburbia*. New York: Vintage.

Kark, Ruth, and Shimon Landman. 1980. The Establishment of Muslim Neighbourhoods in Jerusalem, Outside the Old City, During the Late Ottoman Period. *Palestine Exploration Quarterly* (July-Dec.):113–35.

Karpat, Kemal H. 1976. *The Gecekondu: Rural Migration and Urbanization*. Cambridge, England: Cambridge University Press.

Kasarda, John D., and Morris Janowitz. 1974. Community Attachment in Mass Society. *American Sociological Review* 39:328–39.

Katznelson, Ira. 1981. *City Trenches: Urban Politics and the Patterning of Class in the United States*. Chicago: University of Chicago Press.

Kaye, Barrington. 1960. *Upper Nankin Street Singapore: A Sociological Study of Chinese Households Living in a Densely Populated Area*. Singapore: University of Malaya Press.

Kazemi, Farhad. 1980. *Poverty and Revolution in Iran: The Migrant Poor, Urban Marginality, and Politics*. New York: New York University Press.

Kearns, Kevin C. 1981. Urban Squatter Strategies: Social Adaptation to Housing Stress in London. *Urban Life* 10:123–53.

Keefe, Susan Emley. 1979. Urbanization, Acculturation, and Extended Family Ties: Mexican Americans in Cities. *American Ethnologist* 6:349–65.

———. 1980. Personal Communities in the City: Support Networks among Mexican-Americans and Anglo-Americans. *Urban Anthropology* 9:51–74.

Keegan, Anne. 1987. Neighbors in Uptown Fight Crime on Its Turf. *Chicago Tribune* (17 Aug.).

Keiser, R. Lincoln. 1969. *The Vice Lords: Warriors of the Streets*. New York: Holt, Rinehart & Winston.

Keller, Suzanne Infeld. 1968. *The Urban Neighborhood: A Sociological Perspective*. New York: Random House.

Kemper, Robert V. 1977. *Migration and Adaptation: Tzintzuntzan Peasants in Mexico City*. Beverly Hills, Calif.: Sage.

Kenny, Mary. 1978. Bloomsbury. In *Village London: The Observer's Guide to the Real London*. Peter Crookston, ed., pp. 23–31. London: Thames & Hudson.

Kenny, Michael. 1966. *A Spanish Tapestry: Town and Country in Castile*. New York: Harper Colophon.

Kerr, Madeline. 1958. *The People of Ship Street*. London: Routledge & Kegan Paul.

Khalaf, Samir. 1965. *Prostitution in a Changing Society: A Sociological Survey of Legal Prostitution in Beirut*. Beirut: Khayats.

———. 1968. Primordial Ties and Politics in Lebanon. *Middle Eastern Studies* 4:243–69.

Khalaf, Samir, and Per Kongstad. 1973. *Hamra of Beirut: A Case of Rapid Urbanization.* Leiden: E. J. Brill.

Khalaf, Samir, and Emilie Shwayri. 1966. Family Firms and Industrial Development: The Lebanese Case. *Economic Development and Cultural Change* 15:59–69.

Khan, Verity Saifullah. 1977. The Pakistanis: Mirpuri Villagers at Home and in Bradford. In *Between Two Cultures: Migrants and Minorities in Britain.* James L. Watson, ed., pp. 57–89. Oxford: Basil Blackwell.

Khuri, Fuad Ishaq. 1975. *From Village to Suburb: Order and Change in Greater Beirut.* Chicago: University of Chicago Press.

Kidder, Rushworth M. 1987. Peace, Overpopulation Top Agenda for 21st Century. *The Raleigh* [N.C.] *News and Observer,* 8 Mar.

Kilson, Marion. 1974. *African Urban Kinsmen: The Ga of Central Accra.* New York: St. Martin's.

Kimmelman, Michael. 1987. Urban Planning: What Went Wrong? *U.S. News and World Report* 102(30 Mar.):76–77.

King, A. D. 1976. Cultural Pluralism and Urban Form: The Colonial City as Laboratory for Cross-Cultural Research in Man-Environment Interaction. In *The Mutual Interaction of People and Their Built Environment: A Cross-Cultural Perspective.* Amos Rapoport, ed., pp. 51–76. The Hague: Mouton.

Kirkup, James. 1966. *Tokyo.* South Brunswick, N.J.: A. S. Barnes.

Klein, Joe. 1986. They'll Take Manhattan: The Brash New Builders. *New York* 19 (24 Feb.):30–38.

Klieman, Carol. 1980. *Women's Networks: The Complete Guide to Getting a Better Job, Advancing Your Career, and Feeling Great as a Woman Through Networking.* New York: Lippincott & Crowell.

Koepp, Stephen. 1987. Pul-eeze Will Somebody Help Me? *Time* 129 (2 Feb.): 48–53+.

Kohl, James, and John Litt. 1974. *Urban Guerrilla Warfare in Latin America.* Cambridge, Mass.: MIT Press.

Koran, The Glorious. 1976. A Bi-Lingual Edition with English Translation, Introduction and Notes by Marmaduke Pickthall. London: Allen & Unwin.

Kornblum, William. 1974. *Blue Collar Community.* Chicago: University of Chicago Press.

Kornhauser, David. 1976. *Urban Japan: Its Foundations and Growth.* London: Longman.

Krase, Jerome. 1979. Stigmatized Places, Stigmatized People: Crown Heights and Prospect-Lefferts Gardens. In *Brooklyn USA: The Fourth Largest City in America.* Rita Seiden Miller, ed., pp. 251–62. New York: Brooklyn College Press.

Lambert, Jack, as told to Jenny Pearson. 1974. *Adventure Playgrounds: A Personal Account of a Play-Leader's Work.* Harmondsworth, England: Penguin.

Lapierre, Dominique. 1985. *The City of Joy.* Kathryn Spink, trans. Garden City, N.Y.: Doubleday.

Lawless, R. I. 1980. The Future of Historic Centres: Conservation or Redevelopment? In *The Changing Middle Eastern City.* G. H. Blake and R. I. Lawless, eds., pp. 178–208. London: Croom Helm.

Lawson, Ronald, with the assistance of Mark Naison. 1986. *The Tenant Move-*

ment in New York City, 1904–1984. New Brunswick, N.J.: Rutgers University Press.

Leeds, Anthony. 1971. The Concept of the "Culture of Poverty": Conceptual, Logical, and Empirical Problems, with Perspectives from Brazil and Peru. In *The Culture of Poverty: A Critique.* Eleanor Burke Leacock, ed., pp. 226–84. New York: Simon & Schuster.

———. 1980. Towns and Villages in Society: Hierarchies of Order and Cause. In *Cities in a Larger Context.* Thomas W. Collins, ed., pp. 6- 33. Athens: University of Georgia Press.

Leeds, Anthony, and Elizabeth Leeds. 1976. Accounting for Behavioral Differences: Three Political Systems and the Responses of Squatters in Brazil, Peru, and Chile. In *The City in Comparative Perspective: Cross-National Research and New Directions in Theory.* John Walton and Louis H. Masotti, eds., pp. 193–248. Beverly Hills, Calif.: Sage.

Leichter, Hope J., and William E. Mitchell. 1980. Family-Kin Businesses among New York Jews. In *Urban Life: Readings in Urban Anthropology.* George Gmelch and Walter P. Zenner, eds., pp. 167–75. New York: St. Martin's. [1st ed. 1967.]

LeMasters, E. E. 1975. *Blue-Collar Aristocrats: Life-Styles at a Working-Class Tavern.* Madison: University of Wisconsin Press.

Leonetti, Donna Lockwood, and Laura Newell-Morris. 1982. Exogamy and Change in the Biosocial Structure of a Modern Urban Population. *American Anthropologist* 84:19–36.

Levine, Hal B., and Marlene Wolfzahn Levine. 1979. *Urbanization in Papua New Guinea: A Study of Ambivalent Townsmen.* Cambridge, England: Cambridge University Press.

Levine, Marc V. 1984. Review Essay: The Political Economy of Urban Development. *Urbanism Past and Present* 9(2):34–41.

Lewis, Anthony. 1986. Giant Office Towers Spoil Boston's Charm. *The Raleigh* [N.C.] *News and Observer,* 19 July.

Lewis, Michael. 1979. *The Culture of Inequality.* New York: Meridian/ New American Library.

Lewis, Oscar. 1952. Urbanization without Breakdown: A Case Study. *The Scientific Monthly* 75(1):31–41.

———. 1959. *Five Families: Mexican Case Studies in the Culture of Poverty.* New York: Basic.

———. 1961. *The Children of Sánchez: Autobiography of a Mexican Family.* New York: Random House.

———. 1968. *A Study of Slum Culture: Backgrounds for La Vida.* New York: Random House.

Liebow, Elliot. 1967. *Tally's Corner: A Study of Negro Streetcorner Men.* Boston: Little, Brown.

Little, Kenneth Lindsay. 1974. *Urbanization as a Social Process: An Essay on Movement and Change in Contemporary Africa.* London: Routledge & Kegan Paul.

———. 1978. Countervailing Influences in African Ethnicity: A Less Apparent Factor. In *Ethnicity in Modern Africa.* Brian M. Du Toit, ed., pp. 175–89. Boulder, Colo.: Westview.

The Livelier Baltimore Committee of the Citizens Planning and Housing As-

sociation. 1978. *Bawlamer: An Informal Guide to a Livelier Baltimore.* Baltimore: Citizens Planning and Housing Association.
Lloyd, Barbara B. 1967. Indigenous Ibadan. In *The City of Ibadan.* Peter Cutt Lloyd, A. L. Mabogunje, and B. Awe, eds., pp. 59–83. Cambridge, England: Cambridge University Press.
Lloyd, Peter Cutt. 1967. The Elite. In *The City of Ibadan.* Peter Cutt Lloyd, A. L. Mabogunje, and B. Awe, eds., pp. 129–50. Cambridge, England: Cambridge University Press.
———. 1979. *Slums of Hope? Shanty Towns of the Third World.* Harmondsworth, England: Penguin.
Lloyd, Peter Cutt, A. L. Mabogunje, and B. Awe, eds. 1967. *The City of Ibadan.* Cambridge, England: Cambridge University Press.
Lobo, Susan. 1982. *A House of My Own: Social Organization in the Squatter Settlements of Lima, Peru.* Tucson: University of Arizona Press.
Lofland, Lyn H. 1973. *A World of Strangers: Order and Action in Urban Public Space.* New York: Basic.
Lomnitz, Larissa Adler. 1977. *Networks and Marginality: Life in a Mexican Shantytown.* Cinna Lomnitz, trans. New York: Academic.
Loomis, Terrence M. 1980. Tinkers Gully: Perspectives on Social Change in an Auckland Renovation Neighborhood. *Urban Anthropology* 9:163–97.
Lottman, Herbert R. 1976. *How Cities Are Saved.* New York: Universe.
Lublin, Joann S. 1986. Reaching Out. Some Shelters Strive to Give the Homeless More Than Shelter. *The Wall Street Journal,* 7 Feb.
Luebke, Paul. 1981. Activities and Asphalt. A Successful Anti-Expressway Movement in a "New South City." *Human Organization* 40:256–63.
Lundsgaarde, Henry P. 1977. *Murder in Space City: A Cultural Analysis of Houston Homicide Patterns.* New York: Oxford University Press.
Lynch, Kevin. 1960. *The Image of the City.* Cambridge, Mass.: The Technology Press and Harvard University Press.
———, ed. 1977. *Growing Up in Cities: Studies of the Spatial Environment of Adolescence in Cracow, Melbourne, Mexico City, Salta, Toluca, and Warszawa.* Cambridge, Mass.: MIT Press.
Lynch, Owen M. 1969. *The Politics of Untouchability: Social Mobility and Social Change in a City of India.* New York: Columbia Unviersity Press.
———. 1979. Potters, Plotters, Prodders in a Bombay Slum: Marx and Meaning or Meaning versus Marx. *Urban Anthropology* 8:1–27.
Lynd, Robert Staughton, and Helen Merrill Lynd. 1937. *Middletown in Transition: A Study in Cultural Conflicts.* New York: Harcourt Brace.
———. 1956. *Middletown: A Study in American Culture.* New York: Harcourt, Brace. [1st ed., 1929.]
Maasdorp, Gavin, and P. A. Ellison. 1975. Beyond Cato Manor. In *From Shantytown to Township: An Economic Study of African Poverty and Rehousing in a South African City.* Gavin Maasdorp and A. S. B. Humphreys, eds., pp. 59–146. Cape Town: Juta.
Mabogunje, A. L. 1967a. The Morphology of Ibadan. In *The City of Ibadan.* Peter Cutt Lloyd, A. L. Mabogunje, and B. Awe, eds., pp. 35–56. Cambridge, England: Cambridge University Press.
———. 1967b. Stranger Communities. A. The Ijebu. In *The City of Ibadan.*

Peter Cutt Lloyd, A. L. Mabogunje, and B. Awe, eds., pp. 85–95. Cambridge, England: Cambridge University Press.

Macdonald, Michael C. D. 1984. *America's Cities: A Report on the Myth of Urban Renaissance.* New York: Simon & Schuster.

McGee, T. G. 1967. *The Southeast Asian City: A Social Geography of the Primate Cities of Southeast Asia.* New York: Praeger.

McKean, Charles. 1977. *Fight Blight: A Practical Guide to the Causes of Urban Dereliction and What People Can Do About It.* London: Kaye & Ward.

MacManus, Susan A., and Terry Nichols Clark. 1986. Learning to Cope. *Society* 23(6):48–49.

Mahfouz, Najib. 1981. *Midaq Alley.* Trevor Le Gassick, trans. Washington, D.C.: Three Continents.

Makhlouf, Carla. 1979. *Changing Veils: Women and Modernization in North Yemen.* Austin: University of Texas Press.

Makofsky, David. 1977. In the Factories: The Development of Class Consciousness among Manual Workers in Istanbul. *Urban Life* 6:69–96.

Mancini, Janet K. 1980. *Strategic Styles: Coping in the Inner City.* Hanover, N.H.: University Press of New England.

Mangin, William. 1970. *Peasants in Cities: Readings in the Anthropology of Urbanization.* Boston: Houghton Mifflin.

Mangum, Garth L., and Stephen F. Seninger. 1978. *Coming of Age in the Ghetto: A Dilemma of Youth Employment.* A Report of the Ford Foundation. Baltimore: The Johns Hopkins University Press.

Mariotti, Amelia, and Bernard Magubane. 1978. Urban Ethnology in Africa: Some Theoretical Issues. In *The Processes of Urbanism: A Multidisciplinary Approach.* Joyce Aschenbrenner and Lloyd R. Collins, eds., pp. 45–68. The Hague: Mouton.

Marlin, William. 1973. Formed Up in Faith: The Christian Science Center in Boston's Back Bay Embodies a Regenerative Attitude toward Our Society and Cities. *Architectural Forum* 139(2):24–39.

Marx, Emanuel. 1982. Rehabilitation of Slums? The Case of Hatikva Quarter. *The Jerusalem Quarterly* 22:38–44.

Mayer, Egon. 1979. *From Suburb to Shtetl: The Jews of Boro Park.* Philadelphia: Temple University Press.

Mellaart, James. 1975. *The Neolithic of the Near East.* London: Thames & Hudson.

Merry, Sally Engle. 1981. *Urban Danger: Life in a Neighborhood of Strangers.* Philadelphia: Temple University Press.

Meyer, Karl E. 1979. Love Thy City: Marketing the American Metropolis. *Saturday Review* 6(28 Apr.):16–18 + .

Michelson, William M. 1976. *Man and His Urban Environment: A Sociological Approach, with Revisions.* Reading, Mass.: Addison-Wesley.

———. 1977. *Environmental Choice, Human Behavior, and Residential Satisfaction.* New York: Oxford University Press.

Milgram, Morris. 1977. *Good Neighborhood: The Challenge of Open Housing.* New York: Norton.

Milgram, Stanley. 1970. The Experience of Living in Cities. *Science* 167(3924):1461–68.

Miller, Peggy J. 1982. *Amy, Wendy, and Beth: Learning Language in South Baltimore*. Austin: University of Texas Press.

Miller, Zane L. 1981. *Suburb: Neighborhood and Community in Forest Park, Ohio, 1935–1976*. Knoxville: University of Tennessee Press.

Millon, René. 1973. *Urbanization at Teotihuacán, Mexico*. Vol. 1. *The Teotihuacán Map*. Part 1. *Text*. Austin: University of Texas Press.

Mills, Herb. 1977. The San Francisco Waterfront: The Social Consequences of Industrial Modernization. Part Two: The Modern Longshore Operations. *Urban Life* 6:3–32.

Miner, Horace Mitchell. 1953. *The Primitive City of Timbuctoo*. Princeton: Princeton University Press, for the American Philosophical Society.

Mitchell, J. Clyde, ed. 1969. *Social Networks in Urban Situations: Analyses of Personal Relationships in Central African Towns*. Manchester: University of Manchester Press, for the Institute for Social Research, University of Zambia.

Mitchell, Robert Edward. 1971. Some Social Implications of High Density Housing. *American Sociological Review* 36:18–29.

Mitchell, William E. 1978. *Mishpokhe: A Study of New York City Jewish Family Clubs*. The Hague: Mouton.

Miyamoto, S. Frank. 1984. *Social Solidarity among the Japanese in Seattle*. Seattle: University of Washington Press. [1st ed. 1939.]

Molina, José M. 1978. Cultural Barriers and Interethnic Communication in a Multiethnic Neighborhood. In *Interethnic Communication. Southern Anthropological Society Proceedings*, No. 12. E. Lamar Ross, ed., pp. 78–86. Athens: University of Georgia Press.

Moore, Joan W., with Robert Garcia, Carlos Garcia, Luis Cerda, and Frank Valencìa. 1978. *Homeboys: Gangs, Drugs, and Prison in the Barrios of Los Angeles*. Philadelphia: Temple University Press.

Moorhouse, Geoffrey. 1983. *Calcutta: The City Revealed, with a New Introduction*. New York: Penguin.

Morgan, Ron. 1986. Pollution Threat in Mexico City. *USA Today*, 9 May.

Morris, Richard S. 1978. *Bum Rap on America's Cities. The Real Causes of Urban Decay*. Englewood Cliffs, N.J.: Prentice-Hall.

Mumford, Lewis. 1938. *The Culture of Cities*. New York: Harcourt, Brace.

———. 1961. *The City in History: Its Origins, Its Transformations, and Its Prospects*. New York: Harcourt, Brace & World.

———. 1964. *The Highway and the City*. New York: Mentor/New American Library.

Munro, John. 1987. Looking Back at Beirut. *Middle East Times* 5(30):1 +.

Murphey, Rhoads. 1980. *The Fading of the Maoist Vision: City and Country in China's Development*. New York: Methuen.

Murphy, Thomas P. 1977. Ethical Dilemmas for Urban Administrators. *Urbanism Past and Present*, No. 4:33–39.

Nader, Laura. 1980. The Vertical Slice: Hierarchies and Children. In *Hierarchy and Society: Anthropological Perspectives on Bureaucracy*. Gerald M. Britan and Ronald Cohen, eds., pp. 31–43. Philadelphia: Institute for the Study of Human Issues.

Nadim, Nawal el-Messiri. 1975. The Relationships between the Sexes in a Harah of Cairo. Ph.D. diss., Indiana University.

Nathan, Richard P. 1986. Liberals and Conservatives = Workfare. *Wall Street Journal*, 16 Oct.

Nelson, Joan M. 1969. *Migrants, Urban Poverty, and Instability in Developing Nations*. Cambridge, Mass.: Center for International Affairs, Harvard University.

Nesmith, Jeff. c. 1985–86. Mexico, Central America Robbing the Future. In *Natural Disasters: The Human Connection*. A Cox Newspapers Special Report. [Atlanta.]

Newfield, Jack, and Paul Du Brul. 1978. *The Abuse of Power. The Permanent Government and the Fall of New York*. Harmondsworth, England: Penguin.

Newman, Katherine S. 1985. Urban Anthropology and the Deindustrialization Paradigm. *Urban Anthropology* 14:5–19.

Newman, Oscar. 1972. *Defensible Space: Crime Prevention through Urban Design*. New York: Macmillan.

———. 1980. *Community of Interest*. Garden City, N.Y.: Anchor/ Doubleday.

Niezing, Johan, ed. 1974. *Urban Guerilla: Studies on the Theory, Strategy and Practice of Political Violence in Modern Societies*. Rotterdam: Rotterdam University Press.

Noe, Samuel V. 1984. Shahjahanabad: Geometrical Bases for the Plan of Mughal Delhi. *Urbanism Past and Present* 9(2):15–25.

Norbeck, Edward. 1978. *Country to City: The Urbanization of a Japanese Hamlet*. Salt Lake City: University of Utah Press.

Obbo, Christine. 1975. Women's Careers in Low Income Areas as Indicators of Country and Town Dynamics. In *Town and Country in Central and Eastern Africa*. David Parkin, ed., pp. 288–93. London: Oxford University Press, for the International African Institute.

Okonjo, C. 1967. Stranger Communities. B. The Western Ibo. In *The City of Ibadan*. Peter Cutt Lloyd, A. L. Mabogunje, and B. Awe, eds., pp. 97–116. Cambridge, England: Cambridge University Press.

Ottensmann, John R. 1978. Social Behavior in Urban Space: A Preliminary Investigation Using Ethnographic Data. *Urban Life* 7:3–22.

Palmer, Robin. 1977. The Italians: Patterns of Migration to London. In *Between Two Cultures: Migrants and Minorities in Britain*. James L. Watson, ed., pp. 242–68. Oxford: Basil Blackwell.

Parkin, David J. 1969. *Neighbours and Nationals in an African City Ward*. Berkeley: University of California Press.

Partridge, William L. 1973. *The Hippie Ghetto: The Natural History of a Subculture*. New York: Holt, Rinehart & Winston.

Paul, Bill. 1986. Burning Garbage Becoming Big Business. *The Wall Street Journal*, 13 Oct.

Peattie, Lisa Redfield. 1968. *The View from the Barrio*. Ann Arbor: University of Michigan Press.

Peirce, Neal R., and Jerry Hagstrom. 1981. Inner City in Three Countries. In *Advanced Industrialization and the Inner Cities*. Gale Garfield Schwartz, ed., pp. 141–55. Lexington, Mass.: Lexington.

Pellow, Deborah. 1977. *Women in Accra: Options for Autonomy*. Algonac, Mich.: Reference Publications.

———. 1981. The New Urban Community: Mutual Relevance of the Social and Physical Environments. *Human Organization* 40:15–26.

Perlman, Janice E. 1976. *The Myth of Marginality: Urban Poverty and Politics in Rio de Janeiro.* Berkeley: University of California Press.

Perry, Elizabeth J. 1980. Report on the Mayors Delegation to the People's Republic of China. *Urbanism Past and Present* 5(2):21–28.

Perry, Stewart E. 1978. *San Francisco Scavengers: Dirty Work and the Pride of Ownership.* Berkeley: University of California Press.

Pettigrew, Thomas F. 1980. Racial Change and the Intrametropolitan Distribution of Black Americans. In *The Prospective City: Economic, Population, Energy, and Environmental Developments.* Arthur P. Solomon, ed., pp. 52–79. Cambridge, Mass.: MIT Press.

Pilcher, William W. 1972. *The Portland Longshoremen: A Dispersed Urban Community.* New York: Holt, Rinehart & Winston.

Pileggi, Nicholas. 1981. Wounded City: What's Happened to Our Life Here? *New York* 14(2 Nov.):27–32.

Pirenne, Henri. 1925. *Medieval Cities: Their Origins and the Revival of Trade.* Frank D. Halsey, trans. Garden City, N.Y.: Doubleday.

Plotnicov, Leonard. 1967. *Strangers to the City: Urban Man in Jos, Nigeria.* Pittsburgh: University of Pittsburgh Press.

Polenberg, Richard. 1986. Suburbia: Great Escape. Review of *Crabgrass Frontier: The Suburbanization of the United States,* by Kenneth Jackson. *Washington Post* 10 Mar.

Pons, Valdo. 1969. *Stanleyville: An African Urban Community under Belgian Administration.* London: Oxford University Press, for the International African Institute.

Popenoe, David. 1977. *The Suburban Environment: Sweden and the United States.* Chicago: University of Chicago Press.

The Population Institute. 1986a. Mega-cities: New 3rd World Phenomenon. *Popline* 8(4):4.

———. 1986b. Problems Abound in Karachi. *Popline* 8(6):3.

Porteous, J. Douglas. 1977. *Environment and Behavior: Planning and Everyday Life.* Reading, Mass: Addison-Wesley.

Porter, Bruce D., and Marvin Dunn. 1984. *The Miami Riot of 1980: Crossing the Bounds.* Lexington, Mass.: Heath.

Portes, Alejandro. 1976. The Economy and Ecology of Urban Poverty. In *Urban Latin America: The Political Condition from Above and Below.* Alejandro Portes, and John Walton, eds., pp. 7–69. Austin: University of Texas Press.

Press, Irwin. 1979. *The City as Context: Urbanism and Behavioral Constraints in Seville.* Urbana: University of Illinois Press.

Press, Irwin, and M. Estellie Smith, eds. 1980. *Urban Place and Process: Readings in the Anthropology of Cities.* New York: Macmillan.

Price, Barbara J. 1978. Secondary State Formation: An Explanatory Model. In *Origins of the State: The Anthropology of Political Evolution.* Ronald Cohen and Elman R. Service, eds., pp. 161–86. Philadelphia: Institute for the Study of Human Issues.

Prothro, Edwin Terry. 1961. *Child Rearing in Lebanon.* Cambridge, Mass.: Harvard University Press.

Prothro, Edwin Terry, and Lutfy Najib Diab. 1974. *Changing Family Patterns in the Arab East.* Beirut: American University of Beirut.

Punch, Maurice. 1979. *Policing the Inner City: A Study of Amsterdam's War-moesstraat.* Hamden, Conn.: Archon.

Pynoos, Jon. 1986. *Breaking the Rules: Bureaucracy and Reform in Public Housing.* New York: Plenum.

Quinones, Sam. 1986. San Francisco: Quadri-Lingual Paper Serves Changing Community. *IFDA Dossier* (International Foundation for Development Alternatives), No. 52:15–16.

Raban, Jonathan. 1975. *Soft City.* London: Fontana/Collins.

Raimy, Eric. 1979. *Shared Houses, Shared Lives: The New Extended Families and How They Work.* Los Angeles: Tarcher.

Rainwater, Lee. 1966. Fear and the House-as-Haven in the Lower Class. *Journal of the American Institute of Planners* 32:23–31.

———. 1970. *Behind Ghetto Walls: Black Families in a Federal Slum.* Chicago: Aldine.

Ramati, Raquel. 1981. *How to Save Your Own Street.* Garden City, N.Y.: Dolphin & Doubleday.

Rapoport, Amos. 1977. *Human Aspects of Urban Form: Toward a Man-Environment Approach to Urban Form and Design.* Oxford: Pergamon.

———. 1982. *The Meaning of the Built Environment: A Nonverbal Communication Approach.* Beverly Hills, Calif: Sage.

Ray, Talton F. 1969. *The Politics of the Barrios of Venezuela.* Berkeley: University of California Press.

Read, Kenneth E. 1980. *Other Voices: The Style of a Male Homosexual Tavern.* Novato, Calif.: Chandler & Sharp.

Redfield, Robert. 1941. *The Folk Culture of Yucatan.* Chicago: University of Chicago Press.

Redfield, Robert, and Milton B. Singer. 1954. The Cultural Role of Cities. *Economic Development and Culture Change* 3:53–73.

Reed, Wallace. 1970. Administrative Links and India's Urban System. In *Urban India: Society, Space and Image.* Richard G. Fox, ed., pp. 115–66. [Durham, N.C.]: Program in Comparative Studies on Southern Asia, Duke University.

Reina, Ruben E. 1973. *Paraná: Social Boundaries in an Argentine City.* Austin: University of Texas Press.

Rieder, Jonathan. 1985. *Canarsie: The Jews and Italians of Brooklyn against Liberalism.* Cambridge, Mass.: Harvard University Press.

Roberts, Bryan R. 1973. *Organizing Strangers: Poor Families in Guatemala City.* Austin: University of Texas Press.

———. 1978. *Cities of Peasants: The Political Economy of Urbanization in the Third World.* Beverly Hills, Calif.: Sage.

Roberts, M. Hugh P. 1979. *An Urban Profile of the Middle East.* New York: St. Martin's.

Ross, Marc Howard. 1973. *The Political Integration of Urban Squatters.* Evanston: Northwestern University Press.

———. 1975. *Grass Roots in an African City: Political Behavior in Nairobi.* Cambridge, Mass: MIT Press.

Roszak, Theodore. 1978. *Person/Planet: The Creative Disintegration of Industrial Society.* Garden City, N.Y.: Anchor/Doubleday.

Roth, Henry. 1964. *Call It Sleep.* New York: Avon. [1st ed., 1934.]

Rowland, Jon. 1973. *Community Decay*. Harmondsworth, England: Penguin.

Rubin, Lillian Breslow. 1976. *Worlds of Pain: Life in the Working-Class Family*. New York: Basic.

Rugh, Andrea B. 1979. *Coping with Poverty in a Cairo Community*. Cairo Papers in Social Science. Vol. 2, monograph 1. Cairo: The American University in Cairo.

Rykwert, Joseph. 1976. *The Idea of a Town: The Anthropology of Urban Form in Rome, Italy and the Ancient World*. Princeton: Princeton University Press.

Sable, Martin H. 1984. Professional Associations and Action Programs in Urban Studies. *Urbanism Past and Present* 9(2):42–48.

Safa, Helen Icken. 1974. *The Urban Poor of Puerto Rico: A Study in Development and Inequality*. New York: Holt, Rinehart & Winston.

Safdie, Moshe. 1979. Jerusalem by Design. *Moment* 4(May):15–26.

Salutin, Marilyn. 1973. Stripper Morality. In *The Sexual Scene*. John H. Gagnon and William Simon, eds., pp. 167–92. 2nd ed. New Brunswick, N.J.: Transaction.

Santos, Milton. 1979. *The Shared Space: The Two Circuits of the Urban Economy in Underdeveloped Countries*. Chris Gerry, trans. London: Methuen.

São Paulo Justice and Peace Commission. 1978. *São Paulo: Growth and Poverty*. London: Bowerdean, in association with the Catholic Institute for International Relations.

Sapir, Edward. 1949. Culture, Genuine and Spurious. In *Selected Writings of Edward Sapir in Language, Culture, and Personality*. David G. Mandelbaum, ed., pp. 308–31. Berkeley: University of California Press.

Scheper-Hughes, Nancy. 1981. Dilemmas in Deinstitutionalization: A View From Inner-City Boston. *Journal of Operational Psychiatry* 12:90–99.

Schulz, David A. 1969. *Coming Up Black: Patterns of Ghetto Socialization*. Englewood Cliffs, N.J.: Prentice-Hall.

Schwab, William B. 1954. An Experiment in Methodology in a West African Urban Community. *Human Organization* 13:13–19.

———. 1965. Oshogbo—An Urban Community? In *Urbanization and Migration in West Africa*. Hilda Kuper, ed., pp. 85–109. Berkeley: University of California Press.

Schwartz, Gail Garfield. 1981. Urban Policy and the Inner Cities in the United States. In *Advanced Industrialization and the Inner Cities*. Gail Garfield Schwartz, ed., pp. 37–98. Lexington, Mass.: Lexington.

Schwartzman, Helen B. 1980. The Bureaucratic Context of a Community Mental Health Center: The View from "Up." In *Hierarchy and Society: Anthropological Perspectives on Bureaucracy*. Gerald M. Britan and Ronald Cohen, eds., pp. 45–59. Philadelphia: Institute for the Study of Human Issues.

Scrimshaw, Susan C. 1975. Families to the City: A Study of Changing Values, Fertility, and Socioeconomic Status among Urban In-Migrants. In *Population and Social Organization*. Moni Nag, ed., pp. 309–30. The Hague: Mouton.

Selby, Henry A., and Arthur D. Murphy. 1982. *The Mexican Urban Household and the Decision to Migrate to the United States*. Philadelphia: Institute for the Study of Human Issues.

Selby, Hubert, Jr. 1965. *Last Exit to Brooklyn*. New York: Grove.

Sennett, Richard. 1974a. Afterword. In Mario Matthew Cuomo, *Forest Hills*

Diary: The Crisis of Low-Income Housing, pp. 152–76. New York: Random House.

———. 1974b. *Families against the City: Middle-Class Homes of Industrial Chicago, 1872–1890.* New York: Vintage.

Shanabruch, Charles. 1981. *Chicago's Catholics: The Evolution of an American Identity.* Notre Dame, Ind.: University of Notre Dame Press.

Shankland, Graeme, Peter Willmott, and David Jordan. 1977. *Inner London: Policies for Dispersal and Balance.* Final Report of the Lambeth Inner Area Study. London: Her Majesty's Stationery Office.

Shannon, Lyle W. 1979. The Changing World View of Minority Migrants in an Urban Setting. *Human Organization* 38:52–62.

Shapiro, Joan Hatch. 1971. *Communities of the Alone: Working with Single Room Occupants in the City.* New York: Association.

Sharff, Jagna Wojcicka. 1986. Free Enterprise and the Ghetto Family. In *Annual Editions: Anthropology.* Elvio Angeloni, ed., pp. 139–43. Guilford, Conn.: Dushkin.

Sharon, Arieh. 1973. *Planning Jerusalem: The Old City and Its Environs.* Jerusalem: Weidenfeld & Nicolson.

Shepard, Jon M. 1971. *Automation and Alienation: A Study of Office and Factory Workers.* Cambridge, Mass.: MIT Press.

Shomon, Joseph James. 1971. *Open Land for Urban America: Acquisition, Safe-Keeping, and Use.* Baltimore: Johns Hopkins Press, in cooperation with the National Audubon Society.

Short, James F., Jr. 1969. Introduction to the Revised Edition. In *Juvenile Delinquency and Urban Areas: A Study of Rates of Delinquency in Relation to Differential Characteristics of Local Communities in American Cities.* Clifford R. Shaw and Henry D. McKay, eds., pp. xxv–liv. Chicago: University of Chicago Press.

Sidel, Ruth. 1974. *Families of Fengsheng: Urban Life in China.* Harmondsworth, England: Penguin.

———. 1978. *Urban Survival: The World of Working-Class Women.* Boston: Beacon.

Siegal, Harvey A. 1978. *Outposts of the Forgotten: Socially Terminal People in Slum Hotels and Single Room Occupancy Tenements.* New Brunswick, N.J.: Transaction.

Sills, David L., ed. 1968. *International Encyclopedia of the Social Sciences.* [New York]: Macmillan & The Free Press.

Silverman, Sydel. 1975. *Three Bells of Civilization: The Life of an Italian Hill Town.* New York: Columbia University Press.

Simmel, Georg. 1950. *The Sociology of Georg Simmel.* Kurt H. Wolff, ed. and trans. Glencoe, Ill.: Free Press.

———. 1971. *On Individuality and Social Forms.* Donald N. Levine, ed. Chicago: University of Chicago Press.

Singh, Atiya. 1986. We Had No Time for Weeping. *Popline* (The Population Institute) 8(5):2.

Sjoberg, Gideon. 1960. *The Preindustrial City: Past and Present.* New York: Free Press of Glencoe.

Skogan, Wesley G., and Michael G. Maxfield. 1981. *Coping with Crime: Individual and Neighborhood Reactions.* Beverly Hills, Calif.: Sage.

Smith, M. Estellie. 1975. A Tale of Two Cities: The Reality of Historical Differences. *Urban Anthropology* 4:61–72.

Snow, David A., Susan G. Baker, Leon Anderson, and Michael Martin. 1986. The Myth of Pervasive Mental Illness among the Homeless. *Social Problems* 33:407–23.

Snyder, Peter Z. 1976. Neighborhood Gatekeepers in the Process of Urban Adaptation: Cross-Ethnic Commonalities. *Urban Anthropology* 5:35–52.

Sorkin, Alan L. 1978. *The Urban American Indian*. Lexington, Mass.: Lexington.

Southall, Aidan. 1975. Forms of Ethnic Linkage between Town and Country. In *Town and Country in Central and Eastern Africa*. David Parkin, ed., pp. 265–75. London: Oxford University Press, for the International African Institute.

————, ed. 1973. *Urban Anthropology. Cross-Cultural Studies of Urbanization*. New York: Oxford University Press.

Sovani, N. V. 1969. The Analysis of "Over-Urbanization." In *The City in Newly Developing Countries: Readings on Urbanism and Urbanization*. Gerald Breese, ed., pp. 322–30. Englewood Cliffs, N.J.: Prentice-Hall.

Spicer, Chester W. 1982. Nitrogen Oxide Reactions in the Urban Plume of Boston. *Science* 215 (4536):1095–96.

Spradley, James P. 1970. *You Owe Yourself a Drunk: An Ethnography of Urban Nomads*. Boston: Little, Brown.

Spradley, James P., and Brenda J. Mann. 1975. *The Cocktail Waitress: Woman's Work in a Man's World*. New York: Wiley.

Stack, Carol B. 1974. *All Our Kin: Strategies for Survival in a Black Community*. New York: Harper & Row.

Starr, Joyce R., and Donald E. Carns. 1973. Singles in the City. In *The Sexual Scene*. John H. Gagnon, and William Simon, eds., pp. 81–97. 2nd ed. New Brunswick, N.J.: Transaction.

Starr, Roger. 1985. Crime: How It Destroys, What Can Be Done. *New York Times Magazine*, 27 Jan.

Stein, Howard F., and Robert F. Hill. 1977. *The Ethnic Imperative: Examining the New White Ethnic Movement*. University Park: Pennsylvania State University Press.

Stephens, Joyce. 1976. *Loners, Losers, and Lovers: Elderly Tenants in a Slum Hotel*. Seattle: University of Washington Press.

Stren, Richard E. 1978. *Housing the Urban Poor in Africa: Policy, Politics, and Bureaucracy in Mombasa*. Berkeley: Institute of International Studies, University of California.

Susser, Ida. 1986. Political Activity among Working-Class Women in a U.S. City. *American Ethnologist* 13:108–17.

Suttles, Gerald D. 1968. *The Social Order of the Slum: Ethnicity and Territory in the Inner City*. Chicago: University of Chicago Press.

————. 1972. *The Social Construction of Communities*. Chicago: University of Chicago Press.

————. 1984. The Cumulative Texture of Local Urban Culture. *American Journal of Sociology* 90:283–304.

Swetnam, John J. 1978. Interaction between Urban and Rural Residents in a Guatemalan Marketplace. *Urban Anthropology* 7:137–53.

Taeuber, Conrad, and Irene B. Taeuber. 1975. *The Changing Population of the United States*. New York: Russell & Russell.

Taylor, Nicholas. 1973. *The Village in the City*. London: Temple Smith.

Terkel, Studs. 1974. *Working: People Talk about What They Do All Day and How They Feel about What They Do*. New York: Pantheon.

Thomas, Piri. 1967. *Down These Mean Streets*. New York: New American Library.

Thorns, David C. 1973. *Suburbia*. London: Paladin.

Thrasher, Frederic M. 1927. *The Gang: A Study of 1,313 Gangs in Chicago*. Chicago: University of Chicago Press.

Tönnies, Ferdinand. 1957. *Community and Society*. Charles P. Loomis, trans. New York: Harper & Row. [1st ed. 1887.]

Touba, Jacquiline Rudolph. 1985. Effects of the Islamic Revolution on Women and the Family in Iran. Some Preliminary Observations. In *Women and the Family in Iran*. Asghar Fathi, ed., pp. 131–47. Leiden: E. J. Brill.

Trigger, Bruce G. 1980. Determinants of Urban Growth in Pre-Industrial Societies. In *Urban Place and Process: Readings in the Anthropology of Cities*. Irwin Press, and M. Estellie Smith, eds., pp. 143–67. New York: Macmillan.

True, William R., and Joan H. True. 1977. Network Analysis as a Methodological Approach to the Study of Drug Use in a Latin City. In *Street Ethnography: Selected Studies of Crime and Drug Use in Natural Settings*. Robert S. Weppner, ed., pp. 125–41. Beverly Hills, Calif.: Sage.

Trufanov, Ivan. 1977. *Problems of Soviet Urban Life*. James Riordan, trans. Newtonville, Mass.: Oriental Research Partners.

Tschirhart, Don, and Mary Kaull. 1986. Study: Whites Continued Flight to the Suburbs. *USA Today*, 8 Apr.

Turner, John F. C. 1977. *Housing by People: Towards Autonomy in Building Environments*. New York: Pantheon.

Turner, John F. C., and Robert Fichter, eds. 1972. *Freedom to Build: Dweller Control of the Housing Process*. New York: Macmillan.

United Nations. Department of International Economic and Social Affairs. 1980. *Patterns of Urban and Rural Population Growth. Population Studies No. 68*. ST/ESA/SER.A/68. New York: United Nations.

———. 1985. *Estimates and Projections of Urban, Rural, and City Populations, 1950–2025: The 1982 Assessment*. ST/ESA/SER.R/58. New York: United Nations.

United Press International. 1981. Chicago Mayor Plans to Move into Tenement. *The Raleigh* [N.C.] *News and Observer*, 23 Mar.

United States Bureau of the Census. 1981. *Statistical Abstract of the United States, 1981*. 102nd ed. Washington, D.C.

Uzzell, J. Douglas, and Ronald Provencher. 1976. *Urban Anthropology*. Dubuque, Iowa: Brown.

Valentine, Charles A. 1968. *Culture and Poverty: Critique and Counter-Proposals*. Chicago: University of Chicago Press.

van den Berghe, Pierre L., and George P. Primov. 1977. *Inequality in the Peruvian Andes: Class and Ethnicity in Cuzco*. Columbia: University of Missouri Press.

Vance, Rupert, and Nicholas Demerath, eds., with Sara Smith and Elizabeth

M. Fink. 1971. *The Urban South.* Freeport, N.Y.: Books for Libraries [1st ed., 1954].

Vidich, Arthur J., and Joseph Bensman. 1960. *Small Town in Mass Society: Class, Power and Religion in a Rural Community.* Garden City, N.Y.: Doubleday.

Vogel, Ezra F. 1971. *Japan's New Middle Class: The Salary Man and His Family in a Tokyo Suburb.* 2nd ed. Berkeley: University of California Press.

Waldman, Peter. 1987. Cities Are Pressured to Make Developers Share Their Wealth. *The Wall Street Journal,* 10 Mar.

The Wall Street Journal. 1987. Rampant Rudeness. In the U.S. Today, "Common Courtesy" Is Contradictory Phrase, 12 Mar.

Ward, Colin. 1978. *The Child in the City.* New York: Pantheon.

Warner, Sam Bass, Jr. 1971. *The Private City: Philadelphia in Three Periods of Its Growth.* Philadelphia: University of Pennsylvania Press.

Warner, W. Lloyd, ed. 1963. *Yankee City.* Abr. ed. New Haven: Yale University Press. [1st ed. in 5 vols., 1941, 1945, 1947, 1959.]

Warner, W. Lloyd, and Paul S. Lunt. 1941. *The Social Life of a Modern Community. Yankee City Series.* vol. 1. New Haven: Yale University Press.

Warren, Donald I. 1981. *Helping Networks: How People Cope with Problems in the Urban Community.* Notre Dame, Ind.: University of Notre Dame Press.

Wates, Nick. 1976. *The Battle for Tolmers Square.* London: Routledge & Kegan Paul.

Watson, James L. 1977a. The Chinese: Hong Kong Villagers in the British Catering Trade. In *Between Two Cultures: Migrants and Minorities in Britain.* James L. Watson, ed., pp. 181–213. Oxford: Basil Blackwell.

———. 1977b. Introduction: Immigration, Ethnicity, and Class in Britain. In *Between Two Cultures: Migrants and Minorities in Britain.* James L. Watson, ed., pp. 1–20. Oxford: Basil Blackwell.

———. 1977c. *Between Two Cultures: Migrants and Minorities in Britain.* Oxford: Basil Blackwell.

Watson, Lawrence C. 1981. "Etic" and "Emic" Perspectives on Guajiro Urbanization. *Urban Life* 9:441–68.

Weaver, Thomas, and Douglas White. 1972. *The Anthropology of Urban Environments.* Monograph No. 11. Boulder, Colo.: Society for Applied Anthropology.

Weber, Max. 1962. *The City.* Don Martindale and Gertrud Neuwirth, eds. and trans. New York: Collier. [1st ed., 1921.]

Wekerle, Gerda R. 1980. Women in the Urban Environment. In *Women and the American City.* Catharine R. Stimpson, Elsa Dixler, Martha J. Nelson, and Kathryn B. Yatrakis, eds., pp. 185–211. Chicago: University of Chicago Press.

West, Richard. 1981. Fighting to Save a Neighborhood. *New York* 14 (20 July):24–30.

White, Edmund. 1980. *States of Desire: Travels in Gay America.* New York: Bantam.

White, James. 1982. *Migration in Metropolitan Japan: Social Change and Political Behavior.* Berkeley: Center for Japanese Studies, Institute of East Asian Study, University of California.

White, Lynn T., III. 1978. *Careers in Shanghai: The Social Guidance of Per-*

sonal Energies in a Developing Chinese City, 1949–1966. Berkeley: University of California Press.

Whiteford, Andrew H. 1964. *Two Cities of Latin America: A Comparative Description of Social Classes.* Garden City, N.Y.: Doubleday.

Whyte, Martin King, and William L. Parish. 1984. *Urban Life in Contemporary China.* Chicago: University of Chicago Press.

Whyte, William Foote. 1981. *Street Corner Society: The Social Structure of an Italian Slum.* 3rd ed. Chicago: University of Chicago Press. [1st ed. 1943.]

Whyte, William H., Jr. 1956. *The Organization Man.* New York: Simon & Schuster.

———. 1980. *The Social Life of Small Urban Spaces.* Washington, D.C.: The Conservation Foundation.

Wikan, Unni. 1980. *Life among the Poor in Cairo.* London: Tavistock; New York: Methuen.

Williams, Brett. 1985. Owning Places and Buying Time. Class, Culture, and Stalled Gentrification. *Urban Life* 14:251–73.

Williams, Melvin D. 1981. *On the Street Where I Lived.* New York: Holt, Rinehart & Winston.

Willmott, Peter. 1963. *The Evolution of a Community: A Study of Dagenham after Forty Years.* London: Routledge, Kegan Paul.

———. 1969. *Adolescent Boys of East London.* Rev. ed. Harmondsworth, England: Pelican.

Wilsher, Peter, and Rosemary Righter. 1977. *The Exploding Cities.* New York: Quadrangle.

Wilson, Godfrey, and Monica Wilson. 1945. *The Analysis of Social Change, Based on Observations in Central Africa.* Cambridge, England: Cambridge University Press.

Wirt, Frederick M. 1974. *Power in the City: Decision Making in San Francisco.* Berkeley: University of California Press, for the Institute of Governmental Studies.

Wirth, Louis. 1938. Urbanism as a Way of Life. *American Journal of Sociology* 44:1–24.

Wirth, Louis, and Eleanor H. Bernert, eds. 1949. *Local Community Fact Book of Chicago.* Chicago: University of Chicago Press.

Wisan, Gail. 1979. The Other Fort Greene: The Urban Renewal Movement. In *Brooklyn USA: The Fourth Largest City in America.* Rita Seiden Miller, ed., pp. 265–77. New York: Brooklyn College Press.

Wolf, Deborah Goleman. 1979. *The Lesbian Community.* Berkeley: University of California Press.

Wolfgang, Marvin E., and Franco Ferracuti. 1982. *The Subculture of Violence: Towards an Integrated Theory in Criminology.* Beverly Hills, Calif.: Sage. [1st ed., 1967.]

Wong, Bernard P. 1982. *Chinatown: Economic Adaptation and Ethnic Identity of the Chinese.* New York: Holt, Rinehart & Winston.

The World Bank. 1985. A Fresh Look at Urban Development. *The Urban Edge. Issues and Innovations* 9(8):1–3+.

———. 1986. Tackling the Problem of "Lost" Water. *The Urban Edge. Issues and Innovations* 10(6):1–3.

280 THE HUMANITY OF CITIES

―――. 1987. Urban Strategies and National Development. The Urban Edge. *Issues and Innovations* 11(1):1–3.

Yablonsky, Lewis. 1970. *The Violent Gang.* Rev. ed. Baltimore: Penguin.

Yaukey, David. 1961. *Fertility Differences in a Modernizing Country: A Survey of Lebanese Couples.* Princeton: Princeton University Press.

Young, Michael Dunlap, and Peter Willmott. 1957. *Family and Kinship in East London.* Glencoe, Ill.: Free Press.

―――. 1975. *The Symmetrical Family: A Study of Work and Leisure in the London Region.* Harmondsworth, England: Penguin.

Young, Randy. 1981. The City's Safest Neighborhoods. *New York* 14(19 Oct.): 30–35.

Zonis, Marvin. 1971. *The Political Elite of Iran.* Princeton: Princeton University Press.

Index

Abadan, Iran, 88
Accommodation: spirit of, 221–22
Accra, Ghana, 177; women in Adabraka, 130
Active scale, 35; in Agra, 41–42; in Chicago, 40–41; class differences, 39; as distemic space, 56; of Hispanics in New York, 138–39; for Jatavs and Hausa, 152; versus large receptive scale, 36; in Levittown, 196; limited, 36, 39, 205; of London teen-agers, 39; and magnitudes, 44, 54–55; neglected, 35; often small, 35, 36, 37, 39, 40, 83; as proxemic space, 56; in São Paulo, 48–49; restricted, 37; of social movers, 40
Actors' scales, 35–42; defined, 35; necessity of small, 36; range, 37–39
Adaptability: and built environments, 164; and community, 152; among marginals in Latin America, 122–23; among squatters, 124, 126
Adaptation, 78, 246; African, 82, 146; in *barrio*, 189–90; black, 185, 189; British, 95; of children to city life, 229; Chinese, 84, 85; cross-cultural, 106; to distemic space, 232; failure, 108; and gatekeeper, 225; Hispanic, 185; in housing project, 248; immigrant, 122, 191–92; of Irish tinkers, 142; in Japanese corporations, 136; Jatav, 145; *madina* as form, 87–88; Mohawk, 190; occupational, 142, 143; of retirees, 207–8; residential, 240; rewarding, 108; squatting as form, 92; in Toronto, 126, 127; of underclass, 198–99; and urban support systems, 152–53
Addicts, 119, 154, 158, 187, 227. *See also* Alcoholism; Drug traffic
Africa: active scale, 36; city evolution, 75, 81–82; colonial urbanization, 24; Hausa, 145; migration patterns, 108; natural increase, 89; occupational patterns, 133; regal-ritual cities, 14; Rhodes-Livingston Institute, 13, 16; segregation, 82; social ties, 223–24; urban anthropological studies, 11, 12, 13, 24; urban social organization, 177; urban tribalism, 16, 223–24; violence, 132; women, 133, 135
Agra, India, 86; Jatavs in Bhim Nagar, 41–42, 145, 152, 165, 171
Agriculture: in China, 99, 102; and earliest cities, 68, 68–69, 69, 74, 75; scientific, 246; urban, 235; systems, 12, 19. *See also* Farmers
AIDS, 250
Air pollution, 48, 52, 105, 108, 250

Alcoholism, 120, 250; in Chicago, 158; and culture of poverty, 197; in *barrio*, 190; of Navajos, 190; of Latino marginals, 123; of SROs, 37; in San Francisco, 242; on Skid Road, Seattle, 14, 26, 27. *See also* Addicts
Alexandria, Egypt, 88
Algiers, 88, 111
Alienation, 116–21, 122, 148, 151, 157, 158; and bipolar model, 37; in Britain, 95; and bureaucracy, 216; in Dallas *barrio*, 189, 190; of homosexuals, 209; and large-scale phenomena, 40; in modern society, 6; and social distance, 16; in suburbs, 195; of treaty port Chinese, 99
Ambience: in Cairo, 59; in Montecastello and Salé, 19; in New York, 46, 220
Amenities, urban, 41, 82, 124, 244. *See also* Parks
America, 6, 7; culture, 15; density, 59; high-density life, 39–40; idealized small towns, 5; middle-class family, 37
American cities, 2, 3–4, 44; alienation, 117; classic growth models, 55; community newspapers, 222; compared, 79, 101; in crisis, 249; decentralization, 83; downtown renaissance, 96; evolution, 90; fertility, 80; garbage, 246; homelessness, 199, 200, 242; and melting pot theory, 191–92; minorities, 10, 104; multicultural society, 26; neighborhood density, 164; neighborhood organizations, 65; networks, 166; 1980 populations, 44–45; office vacancies, 95; organized crime, 141; personal service, 214; population trends, 130–31; problems, 17, 74, 249; public housing, 104, 199–200, 222–23, 248; racial integration, 131; rank-size rule, 107; residence-job mismatch, 128; residential stability, 153; rudeness, 247–48; scale, 22; skyscrapers, 46; southwest cities, 53; suburban growth, 10; values of manual workers, 36; violence, 211, 247; well-being, 54; women's protective networks, 135; work environment, 144
Americans: Arab, 191; and automobile, 111; business executives, 120; and dead-end jobs, 123; elderly, 157, 158, 207–8; ethnic groups, 184; fertility, 170; "old-line," 144; opinions on city living, 53–54; personal relationships, 178; personality traits, 201, 212; the poor, 248–49; and race, 184; social class, 192–93; social policy, 197; values, 186, 209; views of city growth, 73–74;

Fear *(continued)*
106; of undesirables, 233; of unknown "others," 223; of violence, 92, 188, 210; of voluntary organizations, 238
Feedback: corrective, 228, 230, 234; negative, 228; positive, 228
Fertility: American versus Egyptian, 170; in Beirut, 88–89; falling, 246; low, 245; rural versus urban, 80, 88, 89
Flint, Mich., 241
Food, 124, 126, 138; catering, 142; ethnic, 190; large-scale aspects, 22, 24, 25; major Third World concern, 53; and migration, 246; and the poor, 7, 32, 84–85, 102, 123, 238, 244, 245; rationing, 125; sharing and household concept, 170, 175; vending, 61, 62, 128, 129
Forest Park, Ohio, 111, 155–56
Freetown, Sierra Leone, 194
Friendship, 2, 18, 178–79; advantages in city, 48; aided by automobile, 63; in Bergen, 203; and community, 41, 221; of Cubans in Washington, D.C., 180; and ethnic variety, 223; and high density, 164; and home range, 162; in Levittown, 195, 196; of marginals, 122–23; of Native Americans, 130; in New York, 154; "old-boy network," 39; as personal communities, 179–80; in Salta, 56; in Sekondi-Takoradi, 147; *shilla*, 179; as small-scale contact, 22, 53; and social status, 224; in suburbs, 120; ties in Japan, 83; work-related, 3, 135–37, 149, 177, 223. *See also* Visiting
Frost Belt, 3, 74
Fun: as neighborhood activity, 209–10

Gang bang, 165, 202, 211
Gangs: Bethnal Green, 178, 211; Boston, 11, 184, 202; boys', 201–2; Chicago, 156, 211; delinquent, 202; Los Angeles *barrio*, 119; as neighborhood defenders, 166; social, 202; violent, 119, 156, 201–2
Gans, Herbert, 12, 36, 195–96, 202–3, 204, 210, 222–23
Gap: between abstract propositions and urban reality, 242–43; bridging, between small and large community living, 54; North-South, 246, 247
Garbage disposal/collection: 123, 143–44, 144, 246
Gatekeepers, 224, 225
Gender, 220; and alienation, 120; and job accessibility, 26, 125, 133; and residential patterns in Bombay, 236; subculture, 184, 202, 204
Gentrification, 95, 154, 208, 209, 215, 221, 245

Ghetto: children, 200; creation, 94; and gypsy cabs, 141; isolation, 197; as proxemic space, 55; residents, 158, 185–87, 201; stability, 154; and suburban jobs, 134; in United States, 7–8, 14. *See also* Culture of poverty; Slums; Squatter settlements
Girls: in Cairo, 193; differences in language acquisition, 200–1; liberation of, 230; restrictions on, 57. *See also* Children
Grass-roots activities, 40, 100, 122, 124, 189, 209, 214, 219, 236–43, 249, 250; neighborhood organizations, 99–100, 101–2, 156, 160, 237
Great Britain, 153; adventure playground, 234–35; children, 229; kin connections, 167; occupations, 142–43; overpopulation, 132; planning, 236; public housing, 104; suburban friendships, 170; suburbs, 109, 110, 195; unemployment, 119, 128, 220, 235; violence, 132, 210
Greater Khartoum, Sudan, 88
Greed, 219, 220, 243, 244, 245; among the Mafia, 215
Greek-Americans, 137, 140, 192
Greensboro, N.C., 44, 167
Guangzhou, China, 99, 99–100
Guatemala City, 237
Guayaquil, Ecuador, 51, 80

Haifa, Israel, 30
Heterogeneity: in Chicago, 148, 235; cultural, 18; and deviant activities, 139–40; fear of, 210; Gans's recommendations, 222; in Istanbul, 147; in Kisangani, 27; in Montecastello, 19; proximity of, 222–23; and residential design, 240; in Tokyo, 29; urban, 2, 9, 12, 160, 166, 180, 183; and work accessibility for women, 133. *See also* Subcultures
Heterogenetic cities, 69
Heterogenetic functions, 81
High-rise buildings: in Britain, 92, 104, 242; Caracas, 124; in China, 101, 103; and density, 94; Hong Kong, 15, 46, 104; impacts, 236; Indian, 46, 47, 86; in Middle East, 58, 87, 95, 170, 174; and multiproblem families, 156, 164; Toronto, 164, 178–79; in United States, 46, 47, 64, 104, 215
Hindus, 46, 47, 84, 86, 165
Hinterlands, 19, 31–32, 33, 62, 129; British, 132; Chinese, 102; and cities, 20, 68; and social bridges, 31; Spanish American, 79
Hispanics: American, 10, 104, 138–39, 184, 185, 188, 189, 190, 209, 222, 225, 240; and civil rights, 197; urban, 26. *See also* Mexican-Americans